Music and Musicians at the Collegiate Church of St Omer

Music played a key role in late medieval devotional life – articulating people's social, psychological and eschatological needs. The process began with the training of choirboys whose skill was key to institutional identity. That skill was closely cultivated and directly sought by kings and emperors, who intervened directly in the recruitment of choirboys and older singers in order to build and articulate their self-image and perceived status. Using the documentation of an exceptionally well-preserved archive, this book focuses on music's functioning in an important church in late medieval northern France. It explores a period when musicians from this region set the agenda across Europe, developing what is still some of the most sophisticated music in the Western musical tradition. The book allows a close focus not on the great compositional achievements of those who cultivated this music, but on the personal motivations that shaped their life and work.

ANDREW KIRKMAN is the Peyton and Barber Professor of Music at the University of Birmingham. He has published widely on English and Continental music of the fifteenth century, with Cambridge and Oxford University Presses and in the top journals in the field. He is also conductor of the award-winning Binchois Consort, with which he has recorded twelve CDs on the Hyperion label.

Music and Musicians at the Collegiate Church of St Omer

Crucible of Song, 1350–1550

ANDREW KIRKMAN

University of Birmingham

CAMBRIDGE
UNIVERSITY PRESS

CAMBRIDGE
UNIVERSITY PRESS

Shaftesbury Road, Cambridge CB2 8EA, United Kingdom

One Liberty Plaza, 20th Floor, New York, NY 10006, USA

477 Williamstown Road, Port Melbourne, VIC 3207, Australia

314–321, 3rd Floor, Plot 3, Splendor Forum, Jasola District Centre, New Delhi – 110025, India

103 Penang Road, #05–06/07, Visioncrest Commercial, Singapore 238467

Cambridge University Press is part of Cambridge University Press & Assessment, a department of the University of Cambridge.

We share the University's mission to contribute to society through the pursuit of education, learning and research at the highest international levels of excellence.

www.cambridge.org
Information on this title: www.cambridge.org/9781108813655

DOI: 10.1017/9781108884990

First published 2020
First paperback edition 2022

A catalogue record for this publication is available from the British Library

Library of Congress Cataloging-in-Publication data
Names: Kirkman, Andrew, 1961– author.
Title: Music and musicians at the collegiate church of St-Omer : crucible of song, 1350–1550 / Andrew Kirkman.
Description: [1.] | New York : Cambridge University Press, 2020. | Includes bibliographical references and index.
Identifiers: LCCN 2020014105 (print) | LCCN 2020014106 (ebook) | ISBN 9781108839723 (hardback) | ISBN 9781108813655 (paperback) | ISBN 9781108884990 (epub)
Subjects: LCSH: Church music–France–Saint-Omer (Pas-de-Calais)–History–To 1400. | Church music–France–Saint-Omer (Pas-de-Calais)–History–15th century. | Church music–France–Saint-Omer (Pas-de-Calais)–History–16th century. | Church music–Catholic Church–History–To 1400. | Church music–Catholic Church–History–15th century. | Church music–Catholic Church–History–16th century.
Classification: LCC ML3027.8.S26 K57 2020 (print) | LCC ML3027.8.S26 (ebook) | DDC 781.71/200944272–dc23
LC record available at https://lccn.loc.gov/2020014105
LC ebook record available at https://lccn.loc.gov/2020014106

ISBN   978-1-108-83972-3   Hardback
ISBN   978-1-108-81365-5   Paperback

Philippe, qui ducit me,
ducit et discipulos suos.
In piam memoriam Philippi Welleri
12.2.58.–1.12.18.

Contents

Figures and Map

(Photos by the author unless otherwise indicated)

Cover   Triptych of Jean Thorion, Cathedral of St Omer, chapel of
             Antoine de Wissoq, detail: right wing © Carl Peterolff

Frontispiece Atelier of Simon Bening, figure of St Omer, Missal of Oudart de
             Bersacques, Saint-Omer, Bibliothèque de l'Agglomération du
             Pays de Saint-Omer, ms. 60, f. 45r © BAPSO

Figures

Map

Acknowledgements

This book has been a long time in the making. Its origins date back to the early 1990s, when I was toying with the idea of an archival project and Rob Wegman, recalling a footnote in an article by Jeremy Noble, suggested Saint-Omer.[1] I set off to this town, then unknown to me, almost on a whim, the extent of my planning such that I spent the first night there sleeping in my car. But my lack of general preparation was as nothing compared with my unpreparedness for the task I had set myself. Installing myself in the Bibliothèque de l'Agglomération de Saint-Omer and experiencing for the first time the sense of fear (which has never entirely left me) when confronted by strange, unfamiliar handwriting, I persevered anyway. Patient and kind early assistance with reading my first haul of photocopies came from Rob himself, from Bonnie Blackburn and Barbara Haggh-Huglo.

Since that halting start and over an intermittent and long-term 'holiday project' I have come to know this lovely town and its surroundings well, and to forge many friendships and contacts there. The library itself quickly introduced me to a cast of characters almost as colourful as those whose lives were unfolding before me in the documents. My fellow 'archive rats' Ludovic Nys and Sarah Staats (their own volumes now long-since completed)[2] offered companionship, 'street smarts' and humour. Françoise Patschkowski, for many years the archive's guardian angel and now a dear friend, gave invaluable support in negotiating a collection that, in the early days, was a good deal less organised and accessible than it is today. The

---

[1] Noble's article discusses a St-Omer canonry listed in papal documents as having been conferred on Josquin, but that was clearly not taken up. See 'New Light on Josquin's Benefices', in Edward E. Lowinsky and Bonnie J. Blackburn (eds.), *Proceedings of the International Josquin Festival-Conference* (London: Oxford University Press, 1976), 76–102, at 80–4 and 90. Noble notes 'The remaining archives of Notre Dame [St Omer] are preserved … in the Bibliothèque Municipale [now the Bibliothèque de l'Agglomération de Saint-Omer]. The chapter acts for the relevant period … might well repay detailed examination' (p. 84).

[2] Marc Gil and Ludovic Nys, *Saint-Omer gothique* (Valenciennes: Presses Universitaires de Valenciennes, 2004); Sarah Staats, with the collaboration of Caroline Heid, Donatella Nebbiai and Patricia Stirnemann, *Le catalogue médiéval de l'abbaye cistercienne de Clairmarais et les manuscrits conservés* (Paris: CNRS Editions, 2016).

unique sparkle and kindness of Olivier Ferlin has added a brightness and sense of joy that, on his impending retirement, will be sadly missed. The late Jacques Engrand and the indefatigable local historian Dr Philippe Derieux provided insights and details that I would have been unlikely to trace on my own.

In more recent times I have benefited greatly from the encyclopedic knowledge and invaluable assistance of the library's *responsable des fonds anciens* Rémy Cordonnier. Mme Rose-Marie Pasquier of the Bibliothèque des antiquaires de la Morinie has been unfailingly thoughtful and helpful, even photographing and sending me many images of rare materials from that remarkable collection. Carl Peterolff's generosity and promptness in sharing his exquisite photographs has greatly enriched not just the appearance of the book but also the vividness of the history it recounts. Another recent pleasure has been the infectious passion for the former collegiate church and (now) *cathédrale*[3] of its wonderful sacristan Benoît Meens: through Benoît I have had access to dark corners of the building whose treasures I could never have suspected, much less seen. Mutual love of the *cathédrale* has also led recently to burgeoning friendships with Jean Luc Montois and Anne Piérard, who have also provided useful historical detail. Claude and Marie-Laure Galamez have given my stays in the region (and in particular in their lovely smallholding) a warm glow that I reconnect with every time I return.

This book would have been frankly impossible in the absence of two people. Without the microfilms made in connection with Ludovic Nys's own book project and which he made available to me, the necessarily intensive study of the deliberations of the St Omer chapter (henceforth 'chapter acts') would have been effectively impossible. The brilliance and sheer tenaciousness of Henry Howard's engagement with my Latin documents has gone far beyond what could possibly be encompassed by the word 'translator'.

The broad frame of reference of a book of this nature carries with it many pitfalls, from many of which I have undoubtedly been saved by the generosity of colleagues to whom I shall be forever grateful. Barbara Haggh-Huglo and Robert Nosow kindly read the entire script in an earlier iteration; their continuing expertise and enthusiasm has been a gift that I can only hope, over time, to be able to repay. John Harper's input in all

---

[3] Although known as *la cathédrale*, the building was only actually an episcopal seat between 1561, following the destruction of Thérouanne, and 1801, when Saint-Omer was incorporated into the diocese of Arras.

things ritual and liturgical has gone far beyond what the word 'colleague' could possibly encompass: his acuity, fund of knowledge and the remarkable speed of his responses have added immeasurably to the finished product; truly a friend-colleague in a million.

Having no expertise myself as an organist, I have drawn, for Chapter 4, on the feedback of a wide range of authorities. I must first express my deep thanks to Robert Bates, who has with unfailing generosity placed at my disposal his extraordinary range of knowledge of organ-building and organ practice in this period and region. Other friends and colleagues who have commented in detail on this chapter have been John Caldwell, Dominic Gwynne, Barbara Haggh-Huglo, John Harper, Franz Körndle, Kimberly Marshall, Robert Nosow, Jonathan Wainwright and Magnus Williamson. Alison Adams has given wonderful and prompt expert feedback on my French translations, while Douglas Brine's insights have provided valuable enrichment in the area of funerary monuments. Darwin Smith has shared with me his writings and insights concerning Jean Thorion and Florence, while David Fiala has supplied prosopographical data as well as responding to sundry questions concerning obscure (at least to me) expressions in French.

Heartfelt thanks are due to Kate Brett and Eilidh Burrett of Cambridge University Press for their kindness and efficiency in the whole process of shepherding this book through to publication.

My wife Amy and children, William and Dave, have put up with long periods of distraction from me as this book has come into being, especially and perhaps inevitably in the later stages.

Finally I cannot end this litany of thanks without acknowledging the input, over decades, of my dear friend Philip Weller. As I think back over many wonderful times in Saint-Omer across what is at this point a large chunk of my life, Philip is a presence in many of the very best, sharing the joy of discovery not just in the archive and in the great building around which this story revolves, but over wonderful meals, wine (of course), views, walks and almost everything else that makes life worth living. I know I share feelings of gratitude with many whose lives he so richly touched; I can only hope that what I, and they, do in our turn can be in some way worthy of the enrichment he so selflessly gave to those he left behind.

Note on Editorial Policy, Currency and Dates

It is in the nature of a narrative about life as lived in a particular time and location to draw in a wide range of quotations from original documents. In citing these I have aimed to preserve the tenor of the original 'voices' to as great an extent as seems consistent with coherence and clear comprehension. Hence I have avoided wholesale rationalisation to modern orthography and punctuation, maintaining, for example, local dialectical practices in French ('le' in certain circumstances where the modern norm would be 'la', for example) and avoiding the accents and punctuation of modern French. Rationalisation has been applied, however, to capitalisation and to certain orthographic variants ('ii' for 'ij' for example), and editorial expansion of standard abbreviations has not been indicated, square brackets being reserved for instances of ambiguity. Non-consecutive quotation and the beginning or ending of quotations in the midst of sentences have been signalled by use of '. . .'.

New-style dating has been tacitly applied unless otherwise stated.

All monetary sums are quoted in livres, solidi and sous (expressed as £ s. d., or pounds, shillings and pence), the pound in every currency encountered comprising twenty shillings, with each shilling in turn divisible into twelve pence. The local money ('monnaie courant') is the livre d'Artois, equal to forty groats of the livre de Flandres. Accounts are often expressed in royal livres parisis, then converted into monnaie courant. To illustrate the prevailing exchange rates I shall enlist the authority of Nicole de Le Salle, receiver of the fabric account at St Omer for the year 1453/4: Nicole announces that his ledger will be entered in royal livres parisis, with each livre, or 'pound', worth 22s. 6d. in current money (the livre d'Artois). At the same time, the royal livre parisis equals forty-five groats in money of Flanders, while two groats of Flanders equates to 12d. (= a shilling) in current money, a ratio of 1 : 6.[1] To determine the relationship between the livre d'Artois ('monnaie courant') and the royal livre parisis it suffices to

---

[1] Toute le quele recepte sera mise et avaluee a monnoye parisis, a compter chascune lb. monnoye parisis dessusdit pour xxii sc vi d monnoye courans, qui valent xlv gros monnoye de flandres, [et] deux gros de flandre comptes pour xii d. monnoye courant. (1453/4, f. 1r)

reduce Nicole's comparative sums to their smallest component, the denier or penny. Hence the equation between the 20s. of the pound parisis and 22s 6d. of the pound of Artois boils down to a relationship of 240d. parisis to 270d. Artois, a ratio of 8 : 9, the pound parisis therefore equating to 1.125 (or 11/8) livres d'Artois. This relationship pertains across the documents that will concern us, as can easily be ascertained by comparing any pair of figures expressed in 'money parisis' and 'current money'. In sum:

16 royal livres parisis = 18 livres d'Artois
16 royal livres parisis = 3 livres de Flandres
3 livres de Flandres = 18 livres d'Artois[2]

Of course the breakdown and relationship of currencies carries little meaning in the abstract: what matters is their relation to income and, by extension, purchasing power. One tangible yardstick is offered by the income of the individuals at the top of the St Omer food chain: the church's canons. While, as will be detailed in the Prologue, the taxable income for a major canonry at St Omer according to the survey of 1362 was £80, the total emoluments were in reality (as Alain Derville observes) closer to £200, and this just for one canonry: a number of St Omer's canons enjoyed multiple benefices. By comparison, Derville notes, a master craftsman, commanding daily remuneration of 4s., would work hard to achieve an annual income of £50.[3] Closer to home, the annual salary of the church's organist at least until 1475 was £4, augmented by a further 24s. for playing for the weekly *Salve* devotion at the chapel of Notre-Dame sur le marchiet, home of the icon of Notre Dame des Miracles. Salaried clerics and other employees of the church had access to other piecemeal sources of income and, then as now, in-kind benefits such as accommodation. But the gulf in income between the beneficed canons and the rest of the church's personnel speaks clearly enough.

Documents quoted and referred to belong, unless otherwise stated, to the series II. G. (chapitre de Saint-Omer) of the Bibliothèque de l'agglomération de Saint-Omer. To avoid unnecessarily cumbersome referencing, the annual fabric accounts are here referred to only by year covered (beginning in all cases on All Saints' Day (1 November)). The earliest

---

[2] See Peter Spufford, *Monetary Problems and Policies in the Burgundian Netherlands, 1433–1496* (Leiden: Brill, 1970), 20–3. My thanks to Robert Nosow for his clarifications on these matters.

[3] 'Les chanoines de Saint-Omer aux XIVᵉ et XVᵉ siècles', in Nicolette Delanne-Logié and Yves-Marie Hilaire (eds.), *La cathédrale de Saint-Omer: 800 ans de mémoire vive* (Paris: CNRS, 2000), 92–3.

accounts (1378–1410, with gaps), entered on rolls, each receive a separate call number in the archives (II. G. 2797–2814); the pamphlet accounts of subsequent years under consideration (1412–1550) are preserved in bundles of between two and six years per call number (II. G. 2815–40). Specific years' accounts are easily locatable on site via reference to the series catalogue.

Prologue

Saint-Omer and the Growth of Urban Power

To open a fabric account from a late medieval church is to open a window onto the workings of a distant culture. These are accounts concerned not with the lofty achievements of a society but with the raw materials of its day-to-day functioning, the details of the payments and purchases through which its needs were shaped. This is clear straight away in the lists of payments for the commodities which underpinned and articulated those needs: the petrol and supermarket receipts of today yield to costings for vast quantities of torches and candles, the perishable materials of the constant round of divine services which shaped the daily life of an institution and – through the income it generated from members of church and community fearful for their souls – filled its coffers. More details of those needs emerge in the costings for the upkeep of the church and its contents: heavy emphasis, for example, on the maintenance of the clock reminds us of the vital role of timekeeping in ensuring the smooth running of what must have been an elaborate choreography of choirboys, chaplains, vicars and canons crossing and recrossing the nave to perform the plethora of Masses – for church and individuals – being celebrated at altars around the building.

Such accounts allow us also to piece together a vivid image of the sight which would have greeted the visitor to a great religious institution in the late Middle Ages. Even to approach such a church, its walls gleaming with immaculate white stone, and pass under its great tympanum with its brightly painted Last Judgement must have been awe-inspiring. But to enter the building itself, especially from a landscape that – as in fifteenth-century Artois – was frequently wracked by pestilence and warfare, must have been an experience of almost frightening intensity. To view the hive of ordered clerical activity and intricately painted and gilded figures of angels and saints via the light only of hundreds of candles and the sun streaming through stained glass windows must truly have evoked a vision of the new Jerusalem.

Compared with this heavenly picture, the image presented by the acts (or minutes) of a church's chapter often appears distinctly, and much more recognisably, prosaic. Here we see a picture of humanity which feels immediately closer to home: human nature, warts and all, reveals itself in an all-too-familiar round of squabbles, backbiting and jockeying for position, often elevated into long and bitter legal proceedings. The objects of such disagreement – usually ecclesiastical benefices and privileges – may belong to a bygone age, but the enmities and petty jealousies they generate are universal enough. Striking about such disputes is the contrast between their vehemence and the refined legal formulas in which they are garbed, a contrast that seems to mirror the incongruity which, on the political stage, pits the extreme violence and chaos of the warfare so frequently being waged against the language of politesse and legalese used in tidying up its effects.[1] Such conflicts – which often, as we shall see, involved the church's musicians – provide invaluable insights into the infrastructures of ecclesiastical institutions: snapshots of the society in question, they are at the same time reflections of the professional and social structures which generated them.

For all too many religious houses, though, such vignettes, evocative and suggestive as they may be, are almost all that remains. Five centuries in one of the most volatile regions of Europe, to say nothing of the effects of the French Revolution, have left their mark in the destruction of innumerable documents and records. For some institutions nothing survives, and for most what is left is incomplete. For records of an important medieval religious house to have remained – over a period of some four hundred years – more or less continuous is therefore remarkable; even more so when the archive in question has, from a musical viewpoint, received little attention. Such is the case with the great collegiate church of St Omer.[2]

Continuity of this nature offers the signal advantage to be able to trace the developments of an institution as they unfold through history. Threading its way through that history, and enmeshed with the other aspects of its functioning, is its musical establishment. We thus have a rare chance to follow in detail such shifts as the steady growth in musical income and provisions, the turnover of its functionaries and – although, as more or less everywhere else, the music itself has been lost – its provision of notated polyphony. The archives of Saint-Omer, then, present an unusual opportunity: while perhaps not so opulent as that of such musical

---

[1] In the case of Saint-Omer this is most starkly revealed in the mid-sixteenth century in the delicacy of requests made to the dean and canons of Saint-Omer by Mary of Hungary on behalf of the canons of Thérouanne in the aftermath of the destruction of their cathedral, and indeed their entire city, by her brother, Charles V (letters preserved in II. G. 193).

[2] Throughout this study 'St Omer' will refer to the church, 'Saint-Omer' to the city that houses it.

pinnacles of the region as Cambrai Cathedral and St Donatian in Bruges, the musical life of St Omer reflects its high status as a wealthy collegiate church which, since the thirteenth century, had answered for its authority directly to Rome. Still more importantly, in allowing such an extended, largely unbroken view, it affords valuable insights into northern European musical culture more generally.

Of course the documentary richness of the kinds of material that form the substance of this study has long been recognised. The work of local antiquarian societies – of which few are more venerable than Saint-Omer's own Société des antiquaires de la Morinie – continues to feed the curiosity of modern citizens concerning the lives of their forebears; and the now classic studies of music at St Donatian in Bruges, Cambrai Cathedral and Notre-Dame of Paris built on traditions of musical antiquarianism extending back to Haberl and beyond.[3] Each generation, each specialist body has sought answers to its own questions, ways of understanding past societies that can offer enrichment to its own; and each has sought them in the same corpus of source material. Given all that has already been written, and given the level of destruction alluded to above, it is sobering to observe the scale of documentation that remains to be mined; yet even if, in some future time, the process of initial 'discovery' were to come to an end, it seems hard to conceive that representatives of changing societies would not continue to seek, in historical documents, insights into a continually reimagined past.

Various kinds of musical story, from different stages in the church's history, could unfurl from its voluminous archives, still preserved in the town library. Still, I feel that what I am offering here has a particular significance, and one not addressed in the same way elsewhere. In examining one closely circumscribed musical environment and its key players with particular scrutiny this book allows us to approach our musical forebears more closely than is typically possible. This is not a story of great men, though a few of them arguably achieved greatness; it is a story of

---

[3] On St Donatian and Bruges see Reinhard Strohm, *Music in Late Medieval Bruges* (2nd, rev. ed., Oxford: Clarendon Press, 1990). On Cambrai Cathedral see Craig Wright, 'Performance Practices at the Cathedral of Cambrai, 1475–1550', *Musical Quarterly* 64/3 (1978), 275–328; 'Musiciens à la cathédrale de Cambrai, 1475–1550', *Revue de musicologie* 62/2 (1976), 204–28. On Paris see Craig Wright, *Music and Ceremony at Notre Dame of Paris, 500–1550* (Cambridge: Cambridge University Press, 1989). Franz Xaver Haberl, *Bausteine für Musikgeschichte* I: Wilhelm Du Fay; II: Katalog der Musikwerke welche sich im … Archiv der päpstlichen Kapelle im Vatikan zu Rom vorfinden; III: Die römische "schola cantorum" und die päpstlichen Kapellsänger bis zur Mitte des 16. Jahrhunderts (Leipzig: Druck und Verlag von Breitkopf und Härtel, 1885–8; repr. Hildesheim and New York: Georg Olms, 1971).

day-to-day life, albeit lived in a society very different from anything familiar in today's world. That society was one that fostered high achievement – the source, ultimately, of its interest to modern music historians – but it did so amidst patterns of interaction that are essentially timeless and (I would argue) timelessly absorbing.

My historical focus here though is on a particular time: the fifteenth and early sixteenth centuries, the 'golden age' of music in the Low Countries and, perhaps not coincidentally, that for which the archives offer the richest yield. St Omer during this period had the prestige to attract an impressive roster of singers and composers, many of them familiar from service in some of the great musical establishments of Europe. Although the active singers, including the master of the boys, seem at least largely to have been restricted to the rank of vicar, a number of the twenty-nine canons (resident and otherwise) were known musicians. In fact interconnections of personnel between the chapter of St Omer and the chapels of the Burgundian court, St Donatian and the Papal Chapel are such as to suggest close relationships between the musical establishments of these great institutions. As for other wealthy northern religious houses, though, the key to its musical importance, in its own region and far beyond, was its choir school, or maîtrise.[4]

Every student of late medieval music knows that the maîtrise was the crucible of contemporary sacred music. Without it the shape of music from the time as it has survived would be unimaginable. Most of the composers whose names resonate with us today began as choirboys in the choir schools of the cathedrals and collegiate churches of northern France and the Burgundian Netherlands, and the quality of their training flowered in music that held sway across the great courts and ecclesiastical establishments of western Europe for more than a century. At the same time, the development of the maîtrise is inextricable from that of polyphony, in which boys' voices played a signal part and whose developments came so closely to reflect shifting patterns in the ritual and social needs of institutions and individuals.

Our story begins, therefore, as it must, with the choirboys themselves. From their arrival, aged eight or younger, at the maîtrise, it will trace the surviving material threads of their young lives, gathering what can be gleaned of their duties and other activities, the priorities and structures that

---

[4] For a useful introduction to the term and the growth of the phenomenon see Laurenz Lütteken, 'Maîtrise', in *Die Musik in Geschichte und Gegenwart* (Kassel: Bärenreiter, 2002), 2, *Sachteil 5*, cols. 1597–1602.

sustained them, and the rapidly augmenting status that accrued to them in the course of the fifteenth and early sixteenth centuries. Teasing out individual identities, we will follow post-pubescent careers through the ranks of 'escotier', vicar and chaplain, and on to the university training sponsored for so many by their host institution.[5] Even before their physical change, though, the best young singers, their voices prized by even the greatest of magnates, could become embroiled in priorities of much larger dimensions, their gifts conducting them as far as the chapels of the ruling dynasties.

If political forces could guide musical careers from their outset, they became all-embracing as, talent and connections permitting, former boys progressed up the ladder of ecclesiastical preferment. Local institutional patronage could lead only so far; major careers depended on the structures of the larger European stage: the ducal House of Burgundy, the chapels of the Habsburgs, even Medici Florence, and – ultimately for the very best – the papal curia. Such power structures could build careers of truly international currency. But the soundscape to which they contributed was generated not only by voices: enveloping, augmenting and announcing the messages articulated by human tones to the greater church building and beyond were the grander voices of organs and bells, the subjects, respectively, of Chapters 4 and 5.

Only a few former choirboys achieved elevation to the major church benefices of canon, cantor, dean or provost; such a post – which brought with it a 'prebend' (comprising property and revenue), a vicar assigned to perform the canon's ostensible ritual duties, a house and considerable status – tended to be the province of wealthy families and even (at the upper stratum) of the nobility. Talent and industry, even of the highest levels, were seldom sufficient on their own to make the leap to the security of tenure that such posts would bring. But connections forged by talent, as for major figures such as Du Fay and Josquin, could lead, via patronage at the highest level, to eventual attainment of high ecclesiastical office on home *terroir*. Chapter 6 will enter the St Omer chapter to trace the careers of three senior figures who, via success in the chapels of the Burgundian and papal courts, established themselves as major players on the St Omer stage. Looming largest at the turn of the fifteenth century is the figure of Nicolas Rembert, canon and, from 1494 until his death in 1504, dean of the

---

[5] 'Escotier', a term seemingly particular to St Omer, refers to a category of poor clerics, aged eighteen or over, verbally and musically literate, who were fed and maintained, in their own 'escoterie' situated in the cloister, at the expense of the chapter. For more detail see below, pp. 48, 67.

collegiate church (henceforth the collégiale). Sewing together an international tissue of professional musical traffic by means of connections
and diplomacy, Rembert's career provides a vivid demonstration that
musical influence in the late Middle Ages need not necessarily involve
the direct practice of musical skill. Exercising – typically at considerable
expense to its beneficiaries – his influence and political adroitness in Rome
in the offices of papal preferment, Rembert offers a striking case of a
musical 'fixer' of a kind without whose aid most international musical
careers at this time would have been scarcely feasible.[6]

Besides its intrinsic interest, then, the story of late medieval music at the
church of St Omer has a far broader reach: it affords insights into the
musical (and hence broader political) life at great religious institutions
more generally, and across the musical melting pot of the north and
beyond. With this observation we can begin to see how the main series
of documents with which this discussion began, evocative as they are on a
local level, also beckon us out again into the larger world, into the social,
economic and political landscape which enabled and sustained the opulent,
if sometimes myopic, society of church and cloister. Before entering more
fully into institutional musical machinations, then, it will be valuable to
offer a brief sketch of the origins of the larger civic polity which enveloped
and (to at least some degree) sustained them.

Saint-Omer in the Late Middle Ages

However one might characterise the political landscape of fifteenth-century
Saint-Omer, it was not, at least in a political sense, French.[7] Rooted
historically in the larger region of Flanders, and subsequently on the
eastern edge of the County of Artois, it became in 1384 part of the northern
territories of the dukes of Burgundy when the first Valois Duke, Philip the
Bold, married Margaret, daughter of Louis de Male, Count of Flanders.[8]

---

[6] A rare and important earlier discussion of this function (focusing on the career of Johannes
Puyllois (or Pullois)), can be found in Pamela Starr, 'Music and Music Patronage at the Papal
Court, 1447–1464', unpublished PhD dissertation, Yale University (1987), 38–62.

[7] For a survey of the history of the city see Alain Derville (ed.), *Histoire de Saint-Omer* (Lille:
Presses Universitaires de Lille, 1981), especially chs. 1–3, 11–105 (all by Alain Derville). For a
more detailed account up to *c*.1300 see his *Saint-Omer: Des origines au début du 14ᵉ siècle* (Lille:
Presses universitaires de Lille, 1995).

[8] On the emerging political, economic and cultural identity of Artois see Carola Small, 'Artois in
the Thirteenth Century: A Region Discovering Its Identity?', *Historical Reflections* 19 (1993),
189–207.

Via this brilliant nuptial strategy Philip acquired (among other territories) the counties of Flanders and Artois, the latter already inherited by Count Louis on the death, two years earlier, of his mother. Artois, from the tenth century a southern part of the territory of Flanders, had in 1180 been cleaved away as part of the dowry of Isabella of Hainault in her marriage to King Philip Augustus of France. While Saint-Omer, Aire and Guines were briefly regained for Flanders in 1198 they were soon firmly back under royal control, where they remained for almost two centuries.[9] Embroiled in the penury and destruction of the Hundred Years War, the city's identity in the fourteenth century became strongly wedded – especially through its role as a frontier town with Flanders – to the French crown, and a sense of loyalty to the king lingered long after its joining of the territory of his (at least technical) vassal the duke of Burgundy. But from 1384 Saint-Omer, nudging the eastern border of Artois defined by the river Aa, returned to political union with the Flanders that, economically and culturally, it had never completely left. In terms of its growth and rising prosperity it was closely bound up, as I shall outline below, with the (particularly water-borne) commerce of the nearby trading centres of Ypres, Bruges and Ghent.

With its inheritance of the regions of Flanders and Artois the Duchy of Burgundy assumed control of the most populous and urbanised region in Europe north of the Alps,[10] and also, at least periodically, one of its richest. For the city of Saint-Omer, though, the best was yet to come: the Burgundian takeover ushered in a period of prosperity rooted in a peace that reigned for almost a century; and if parallels between wealth and cultural efflorescence can perhaps too easily be drawn,[11] there is no doubt that conditions in the city were exceptionally propitious for urban and ecclesiastical display. Not least of these was the example of the dukes themselves:

---

[9] David Nicholas, *Medieval Flanders* (London and New York: Longman, 1992), 73, 75. Nicholas offers a synoptic view of the history of the region, including Saint-Omer, until the division of Flanders and Artois in the twelfth century. See also Derville, *Histoire*, 48.

[10] For detailed (and vivid) analysis of the remarkable relative population density from Artois to Liège, see Norman J. G. Pounds and Charles C. Roome, 'Population Density in Fifteenth Century France and the Low Countries', *Annals of the Association of American Geographers* 61/1 (1971), 116–30, and Norman J. G. Pounds, 'Population and Settlement in the Low Countries and Northern France in the Later Middle Ages', *Revue belge de philologie et d'histoire* 49/2 (1971), 369–402.

[11] See John H. Monro, 'Economic Depression and the Arts in the Fifteenth-Century Low Countries', *Renaissance and Reformation* 7/4 (1983), 235–50, which points out the frequent disjunction between artistic flowering in the Burgundian Netherlands and economic depressions associated with fluctuations in (especially cloth) trade and population depletion.

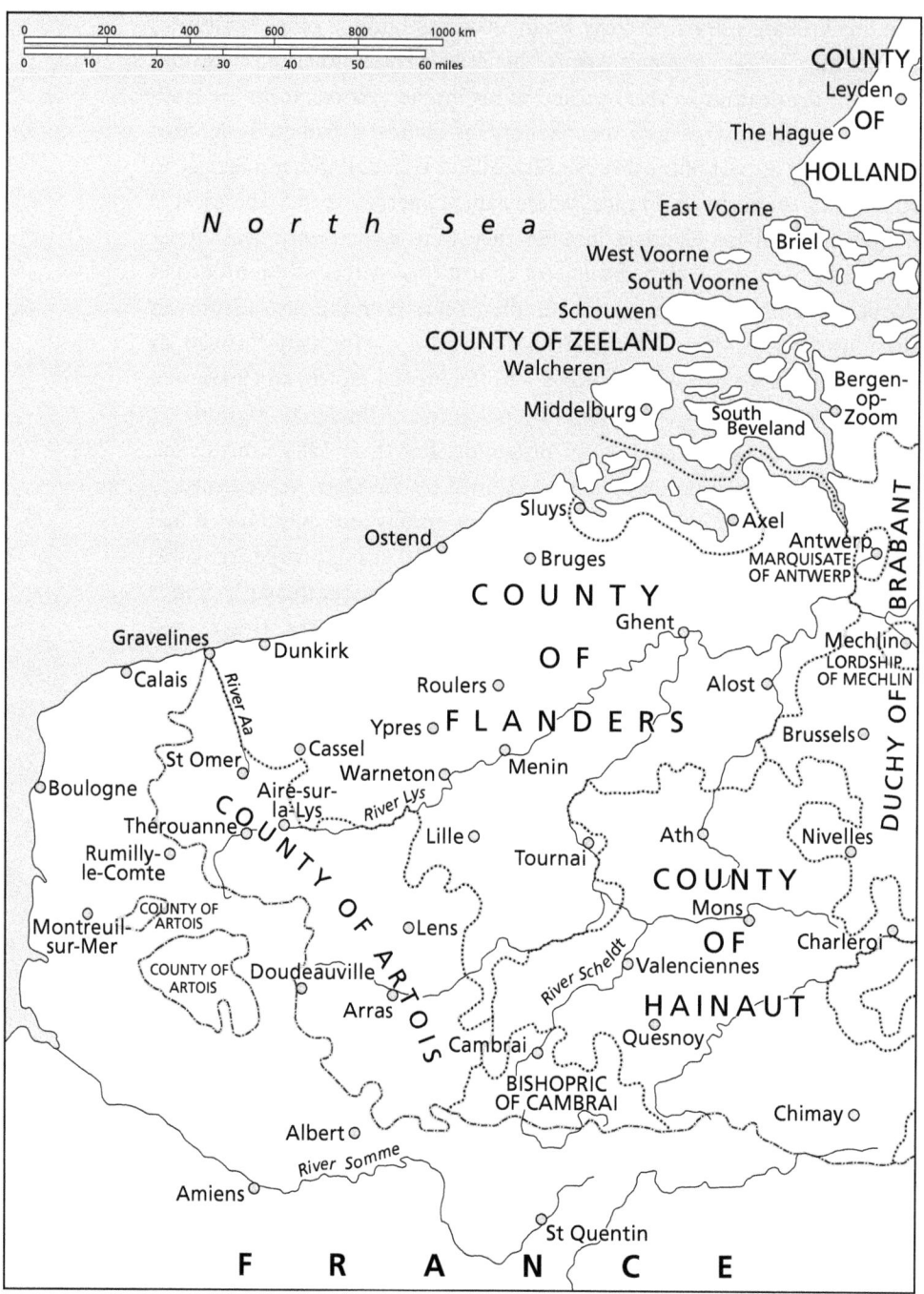

Map P.1 Artois, Flanders and environs, late Middle Ages

Philip's *joyeuse entrée* into Saint-Omer on 22 November 1389 was the first of an effusion of grandiose entries, festivals, aristocratic weddings and tournaments that included two meetings (in 1440 and 1461) of the Order of the Golden Fleece and the 1449 tournament of the Belle Pèlerine to name but a few. There can be little doubt that the Burgundian taste for pomp and ceremony rubbed off on the elite individuals and institutions of the city, including the collegiate church of St Omer, whose personnel – singers included – were enmeshed in deep and continuous patterns of Burgundian clientelism.

In a region studded with proud and prosperous cities, then, Saint-Omer was one of the jewels in the Burgundian crown; this in spite of the fact that, to quote David Nicholas, it 'developed in the least promising physical location of any Flemish city'.[12] Hence it is worth considering the source of the prosperity that enabled such wealth and high status and as a consequence that, in turn, of its collegiate church.

The origins of the city's status rest in its great antiquity as a place of learning and devotion. Its story begins in the seventh century with the arrival of its founding, and eponymous, saint and his disciple Bertin in the proselytysing wake of the Frankish King Dagobert. In this marshy, unworkable and scarcely habitable terrain they founded what was to become the great Benedictine abbey of St Bertin, situated in what was then known as Sithiu in the lower part of today's town. By the ninth century, when the region was ravaged by Norse invaders, the abbey and its dependencies stood alone. But around 820, the Abbot Frigudise dispatched thirty observants up to the butte, the one point of elevation and the centre of the present town, where they were to serve God, albeit under the rule of the single abbot, not as monks but as canons according to the rule of the 817 Council of Aix.[13] With this cleavage the foundations were laid of the division, often uneasy, between abbey and collegiate church which were to persist until the dissolution and despoiling of St Bertin at the Revolution.

The surrounding marshland and dense forest being unsuitable for agriculture, the future Saint-Omer owed its development to trade, marketing produce from the rich soils of Artois to its west to the heavily populated cities of the Flemish marshes to its east. Even with increased drainage and cultivation this was a role that was to expand hugely over the centuries, with a relatively low, agriculturally based population and fertile soil to the

---

[12] Nicholas, *Flanders*, 36.   [13] Derville, *Histoire*, 17.

west supplying a relatively high urban population to the east.[14] Its catalyst was probably the sale of tithed grain that was surplus to the sustenance of the abbey, which already by the mid-ninth century held sway over some fifty villages and fifty thousand hectares. Around the year 1000 the first walls were built around the butte, the location, from 874,[15] of the grain market and the site of the collegiate church of St Omer.

With the ascendancy, in the late ninth century, of the counts of Flanders, their co-opting of the estates of the abbey, and the establishment – the first in the region – of the market came a shift in the power structure and an economic tilt away from ecclesiastical service to trade; the development, in other words, of a town, as opposed to a large composite monastic institution. This is not to imply that the prior history of Sithiu was one only of disinterested service to the *opus dei*: foreshadowing the similar power structures of the future collegiate church, the abbots had already long been scions of great temporal dynasties including, in the ninth century, a bastard son of Charlemagne and the uncle of the king of France. In the later part of that century, however, the abbey was given over by the king to the counts who for the following century functioned – either directly or via an intermediary – as abbots.[16]

From this point on, control of the surrounding populace, its housing and its produce came directly under comital aegis, as did the upper church, now for the first time under the separate leadership of a provost. Even at this early stage, relations between the temporal powers and the canons of the upper town were symbiotic, with the provost typically an appointment of the count, while the canons, being literate, managed the comital accounts. Thus the first citizenry of Saint-Omer came together within the ramparts of the upper town, generated by the market and the needs of the adjacent comital château, in the environs of the early collegiate church. Urbanisation, once started, accelerated rapidly: from a population of a few hundred around 900, Derville estimates a rise to *c.*35,000 by 1300, with a similar shift over the same period in relative numbers between town and locality from *c.*6 per cent to *c.*60 per cent.[17]

If grain was always fuel to the city's economic engine, its wealth in the high Middle Ages was built on the Flemish cloth trade. Like neighbouring

[14] See Pounds and Roome, 'Population Density', 127 and *passim*, and Pounds, 'Population and Settlement', 392–3.

[15] Derville, *Histoire*, 18–19, 21.   [16] Ibid., 18, 25.

[17] Ibid., 29; Derville, 'Le nombre d'habitants des villes de l'Artois et de la Flandre Wallonne (1300–1450)', *Revue du Nord* 65/257 (1983), 277–99.

cities heavily dependent on English wool, Saint-Omer was in the twelfth century the pre-eminent city in the English trade, with perhaps half its workforce engaged in the production both of moderately priced and luxury cloth, much of the latter destined to be sold back to its country of origin. If by 1215 it had lost its primacy in English wool importation to Ypres and Douai, its international marketing of cloth of various grades – including a strong presence in Iberia, Italy and southern France – continued its momentum into the late thirteenth century. In fact it now seems clear that the decline in the trade once thought to have swept the urban north in the early fourteenth century has been overstated. In reality, the Saint-Omer business, although necessarily flexible in terms of the quality of its produce, continued to be buoyant into the fifteenth century, when it benefited particularly, if intermittently, from sales to Hanseatic German traders.[18]

Expansion and commerce on this scale was only possible via the draining and cultivation of marshland and the opening of major transport thoroughfares. With ever-improving methods of cultivation, by 1409 the grain trade was the most important source of revenue, with Saint-Omer and Douai emerging as the principal markets exporting French grain to the north.[19] Such was the power wielded by the city's grain market in the fifteenth century that in the 1430s Philip the Good made it exempt from the ban otherwise preventing the export of grain from the duchy's French territories to Flanders, Zeeland and Holland; reciprocally, when famine in Flanders led to a ban on its food exports, the duke made an exception for Saint-Omer, allowing delivery of livestock and dairy produce in return for grain.[20] What really set Saint-Omer apart, however, driving the fortunes of its merchants, and in turn of its institutions – including the collegiate church – was its waterborne trade.

---

[18] Nicholas, *Flanders*, 55, 112–18, 167–8, 173–5, 203–4; Derville, *Histoire*, 42–4, 85. The literature on this topic is considerable and has seen substantial interpretative shifts. Among useful (comparatively) recent contributions see Marci Sortor, 'Saint-Omer and Its Textile Trades in the Late Middle Ages: A Contribution to the Proto-industrialization Debate', *American Historical Review* 98 (1993), 1475–99, and Derville, 'Les draperies flamandes et artésiennes vers 1250–1350', *Revue du Nord* 54/215 (1972), 353–70.

[19] Marci Sortor, 'The Ieperleet Affair, the Struggle for Market Position in Late-Medieval Flanders', *Speculum* 734 (1998), 1091; Derville, *Histoire*, 85–6. For a sense of the sheer scale of this market see Derville, 'Le grenier des Pays-Bas médiévaux', *Revue du Nord* 69/273 (1987), 267–80.

[20] Sortor, 'Ieperleet', 1093. The same practice could work in reverse, however. When, in 1456, the merchants of Saint-Omer placed a ban on grain exports this was reciprocated by a similar ban on dairy, beer and agricultural provisions going in the opposite direction, with the net result that Saint-Omer farmers were driven into bankruptcy.

The major turning point came in the twelfth century with the digging of a network of waterways culminating in the deep-water canal following the route of the old river Aa along the Artois–Flanders border to the coast at Gravelines. The initiative of the enterprising Count of Flanders Philip of Alsace, via his chancellor, Robert d'Aire, provost of the collégiale, the 'Great River' allowed access to large seagoing vessels such as even the contemporary Oudezwin canal to Bruges could not accommodate. Besides revolutionising direct trading capability the canal amassed huge tax revenues from the surrounding region, since the town, enforcing a wholesale 'staple' on the waterway, forbade the discharging of any cargo between Saint-Omer and the coast.[21] All cargos had to pass through the city's Haut Pont, making Saint-Omer the main marketplace in the region for everything from grain to fish to cloth and wine. The 'bons vins de Saint-Omer' were renowned across the north throughout the later Middle Ages,[22] with a number of fifteenth-century canons of the collégiale – which was itself a prodigious wine consumer – directly involved in the trade.[23] Still more strikingly, the city's production and marketing of fine-quality Flemish textiles inflicted, at least in the twelfth century, major damage on the indigenous trade of England.

Saint-Omer's access to a network of waterways continued also to broaden its inland market reach to an extent with which, by the late fourteenth century, only Bruges and Ghent could compete. Like Ghent and Ypres, it also had a lucrative grain staple that, around the turn of the fifteenth century, extended its wholesale control far beyond the radius of twenty-five or so kilometres which had circumscribed its earlier operations. By 1485 its range had pushed from two leagues to three, with staples on wine and general wholesale goods further augmenting its income and restricting those of potential competitors, while attracting merchants from as far away as Holland, Zeeland and Brabant to join the city's bourgeoisie.[24]

This same shift in fortune fed the fabulous wealth of merchant families whose scions would in turn raise the fortunes – and assume the canonries – of the collégiale. Certain key factors guaranteed the financial and political domination of a handful of families. One was the sheer financial muscle needed to cope with fluctuations of cash flow, spread risk and pay the kinds

---

[21] Derville, *Histoire*, 36–8; Nicholas, *Flanders*, 118.

[22] On the huge significance of the wine trade to the city see Derville, *Histoire*, 38–40 and *passim*, and particularly his 'Le marché du vin a Saint-Omer: ses fluctuations au XVe siècle', *Revue belge de philologie et d'histoire* 40/2 (1962), 348–70, a study that draws heavily on the detailed cellar accounts of the collégiale.

[23] Derville, 'Le marché', 350–1.   [24] Sortor, 'Ieperleet', 1094–6.

of advances necessary to exercise control over the markets; another was membership of the Hanse, which restricted access to distant markets to members, and which the high cost entailed kept in the hands of the few.[25] Financial control was paralleled by civic control: aldermen, initially appointed from among the wealthy oligarchs by the count to maintain order on his behalf, steadily acquired their own independent power, solidifying the grip of the merchant class. Appointed theoretically for only a year, aldermen in fact conventionally chose their successors who in turn reinstated their predecessors, resulting in alternations, year on year, between the same pairs of appointees.[26] By the late thirteenth century their power was effectively absolute, controlling commerce, levying tithes, taxes and fines, determining all rights of citizens and imposing all levels of discipline.

If the thirteenth century, like the fifteenth, was one at least mostly of stability, the intervening years witnessed death and destruction on an unprecedented scale. As ever the nexus point between Artois and Flanders, Saint-Omer was caught up from 1297 in war between the crown and the County of Flanders; and if the well-defended city itself held firm in 1303 even against the overwhelming force of the Flemish army, it was at the cost, as so often, of the burning of its suburbs. But behind the military success lay civil disquiet, and resentment at the oppressive power of the oligarchs erupted in 1305–6 in communal insurrection. In the end this proved of sufficient force to elicit concessions on representation, wages, commerce, punishments and taxes, many of them lasting, from the redoubtable Mahaut, Countess of Artois; in the following years, though, the dominant families, some of whom would continue to provide the city's dramatis personae into the fifteenth century, re-assumed more or less gradually their customary positions of power.[27]

But the disruptions caused by the communal revolution were relatively minor compared to the cataclysms of the mid-fourteenth century. From its first outbreak in 1349 and with devastating recurrences thereafter, it has been estimated that roughly two-thirds of the populace succumbed to the Black Death, reducing the population from *c.*35,000 to between 10,000 and 15,000, a level at which it was to remain until the later seventeenth century.[28] Added to this was the re-eruption, in 1337, of the Hundred

---

[25] Derville, *Histoire*, 57.

[26] On this practice see Claude Petillon, 'Les élites politiques de Saint-Omer dans la première moitié du XVe siècle d'après l'enquête de 1446', *Revue du Nord* 91 (1999), 86.

[27] Derville, *Histoire*, 64–71.   [28] Derville, 'Le nombre', 278–9; *Histoire*, 29, 74.

Years War and some fifty years of intermittent predation by English and Flemish troops. While, as at the beginning of the century, the defensibility of the high ground of the butte meant that enemies could usually be repelled from the city itself, this was at the repeated expense of flooding the marais and of burning any buildings outside the ramparts that could provide aid for invaders. The city was in more or less constant fear of attack and/or infiltration by hostile forces and, neither for the first nor the last time, deprived regularly of the sustenance of its – necessarily external – food production, commerce and rental revenues. In inverse proportion to the squeeze on its resources were the rising demands of royal levies for the costs of the ongoing war for which Saint-Omer, as one of the two major cities of Artois, was hit particularly hard. Rampant inflation and the ability, shamelessly exploited, of the oligarchs to avoid the payments collected universally from the less fortunate rump of society combined to exacerbate still further the prevailing state of misery.[29]

After decades of strife and pestilence, Burgundian rule brought a flowering of renewed prosperity. The Hundred Years War as well as the internal conflicts of the Kingdom of France mostly stayed at a safe distance. No amount of ducal splendour could spare the city – including the collégiale – from plague, however, nor indeed from famine, which particularly in 1437–9 tore into a populace still struggling to recover from waves of epidemic. At around ten thousand in the early fifteenth century, the city's population was still struggling to reach a third of what it had been at its high point some two centuries earlier. At the same time, though, records show an unprecedented rise in enrolment of new members of the bourgeoisie, across all the city's many lucrative trades. In times of peace, Saint-Omer's location between the fertile soils of Artois and highly populated and urbanised Flanders would always bring market dividends; and while maintenance of waterborne commerce via the dock at Gravelines would require civil engineering on a vast scale, it continued, via the 'Great River', to guarantee a powerful seafaring presence, as well as, beginning in the fifteenth century, bringing in tax revenue at the point of maritime access.[30]

In all this the most enterprising of the city's oligarchs were always key players, with its aldermanic public servants, like today's politicians, never far from the centre of economic transaction. In tandem with commercial advancement they almost invariably sought to burnish their financial status, developed in the marketplace, with noble preferment, acquiring

---

[29] Derville, *Histoire*, 73–80.   [30] Ibid., 87.

positions in the ducal administration and seeking for their scions advantageous marriages and university training, the latter often culminating in lucrative canonries.[31] Preferment by the dukes also brought with it still greater aldermanic control, as when, in 1467, an uprising in protest at their imposition of increased duty on barley culminated in an appeal to ducal power that resulted in brutal suppression. A small coterie of families was in almost untrammelled control of all the city's dealings, including its finances, a situation that led, unsurprisingly, to rampant abuses. While an inquiry instigated by the duke in 1446 into this wildly unbalanced state of affairs seems, at least in the short term, to have had little effect,[32] by the end of the century the situation had shifted radically, with aldermen no longer drawn from the mercantile class. More typically wealthy property owners or members of the legal and medical professions, aldermen had by this time essentially risen beyond the marketplace to the status of individuals 'living nobly'.[33] Perhaps the most significant result of the inquiry of 1446, however, was to tighten still further the grip of the duchy on the reins of the city's control, and to entrench still more deeply the clientelism through which it was exercised.[34]

Whatever the inequalities of life under Burgundian rule, the city remained steadfastly loyal to the duchy when, following the untimely demise in 1477 of Charles the Bold at the Siege of Nancy, the French crown reasserted direct control of Artois. As in the past, the city held firm against French siege, but again as in the past, at the cost of burning down the suburbs. Even at the Peace of Arras in 1482, marking the betrothal to the dauphin of France of Margaret of Austria, granddaughter of Charles the Bold and daughter of the Emperor Maximilian I, Saint-Omer was able to stay neutral, and it officially returned to the rule of Maximilian in 1487. Only four months later, however, the city fell victim to a coup, supported by the aldermen, that saw the French army breach the city wall on the side of the Marais and take the town. But its triumph was short-lived: on 11 February 1489, counter-plots supported by the peasantry and bourgeoisie restored the inheritors of the Valois dukes, and although conflicts that persisted until 1493 saw much of the city reduced to ruin, it was to remain from this point under control of the now Habsburg-Burgundian dynasty until 1678. While warfare returned

---

[31] Derville, *Histoire*, 88–90; Petillon, 'Les élites'.

[32] On this enquiry and the insight it provides into the functioning and, particularly, abuses of the city's ruling body see Petillon, 'Les élites'.

[33] Derville, *Histoire*, 104.   [34] Petillon, 'Les élites', 115–16.

in 1521 and again, with intervening respites, until 1559, Saint-Omer itself was at least spared the miserable destruction of the surrounding countryside and of many of its neighbours. This culminated, in 1553, in the complete demolition by the Habsburg army of the fiercely French episcopal city and great cathedral of Thérouanne, its demise leading to the foundation of the new see of Saint-Omer and the raising of the collégiale to the status of cathedral.

Saint-Omer Then and Now

Internal rumblings notwithstanding, to an outside observer Saint-Omer in the greater part of the fifteenth century must have appeared the epitome of civic stability and prosperity. Peace and commerce brought with them an elegant cityscape of broad streets and elegant houses, crowned by the towers and steeples of its many fine churches and convents. Those towers afforded a sonic stratum for a plethora of bells whose timbres, each of them distinct to the well-attuned ears of a late medieval citizenry, combined with a ground-level soundscape of commerce, criers, processions, mystery plays, entertainments, tournaments and music to mark out the daily round and the events, cyclic as well as occasional, of the city's life.

That prosperity is reflected in an opulence that emerges vividly from the accounts of the collégiale in the later fifteenth century and on into the sixteenth, resonances of a pride and sense of status beyond what is detectable hitherto and that, arguably, would not be replicated. For us today they are tantalising witnesses to the vanished world of a wealthy church in one of the great cities of the urban north; and for Saint-Omer, they are essentially all we have: the accounts of Saint-Bertin, lost to the carnage of 1915, plus any that once existed for the parish churches and other religious houses, are long gone, their affairs refracted only through mentions in the documents of the city and collégiale.

Saint-Omer in the late Middle Ages boasted six parish churches, houses of the Franciscans, Dominicans, Carthusians, Poor Clares, and sundry religious hospitals and Beguinages, not to mention the great Benedictine abbey of St Bertin and the grand Marian 'chapelle sur le marchiet', built for the veneration of its thirteenth-century figure of Notre Dame des Miracles. Richest by far was the abbey of St Bertin, its abbot taxed, according to the 1362 records, on an estimated income of £8,300. A famous seat of learning for centuries, St Bertin was home to an important scriptorium and library, of which a large proportion is now housed in the town library. Two of its fifteenth-century abbots, Guillaume Fillastre and Jean de Lannoy, were chancellors of the Order of the Golden Fleece, meetings of which were held at St Bertin in 1440 and 1461. The taxable income of the abbot clearly dwarfed the already substantial income of the provost of St Omer, taxed at £800. By way of comparison, the assumed income in the same accounts of the dean and twenty-six major prebends of St Omer was £80 each, with the church's three minor prebends estimated at £40 and its chaplaincies ranging from £12 to £25. Curacies at the parish churches, some of them, as we shall see, held by canons of St Omer, varied in estimated income from a relatively paltry £26 at St Martin in Insula to a combined income of two curates at St Denis, the substantial church of the mayor and aldermen of the town, of £120.[35] For most of these buildings, documentary mention and old cityscapes are their only surviving mode of existence. Victims of an anti-clericalism of particular virulence even by broader national standards, most of them succumbed in the late eighteenth century to revolutionary zeal.

The reduction in 1791 to four parishes – the cathedral (former collégiale), St Bertin, St Denis and St Sepulchre – signalled the neglect of the former parish churches of St John, St Aldegonde and St Margaret, culminating only two years later in their demolition. All those in holy orders were expelled from their convents, now decreed to be state property. First to go from the buildings themselves, perhaps unsurprisingly, were their bells, transforming at a stroke the centuries-long soundscape of the city along, it was surely hoped, with all their associations, fraternal, hierarchical, ritual, disciplinary. Along with the sale of the buildings came the emptying of their contents. Everything in precious metal – including the entire treasury of the cathedral – was sold or melted down, while buildings were stripped of their furniture and no fewer than 5,563,686 books. But more was to follow: 1793's renunciation of the Catholic faith saw the repudiation of the

---

[35] For these details see August Longnon, *Pouillés de la province de Reims*, vol. 6, part 2 (Paris: Klincksieck, 1907), 608–9. Alain Derville points out the elevated value of the St Omer prebends compared to those of other nearby institutions, comparing them with, for example, those of Arras (£62), Thérouanne and Tournai (£60), and Lille (£45). Yet the real sum, he notes, was considerably higher, including numerous pre-tax deductions and reliefs. He cites the example of Canon Jean Pigouche, who died in 1443, and whose annual income could amount to £550, including £200 gross, £99 from daily distributions for attendance at Mass and office, and more then £44 for attendance at obits. This, compared with a maximum income of around £50 per annum for a master craftsman, gives some indication of the relative wealth of St Omer canons, many of whom, of course, held a number of canonries with associated prebends (Derville, 'Les chanoines de Saint-Omer', 92–3).

priesthood. All devotional images were targeted: metal ones melted down, wooden ones burned, those in stone defaced.[36]

One signal act of destruction did not even need to wait for the Revolution: in 1785, after many years' deliberation and in the face of strenuous objection from the cathedral and confraternity of Notre-Dame-des-Miracles, the chapel on the marketplace succumbed to anti-clericalism in the secular administration and was pulled down.[37] On 23 June the icon that it had housed for five hundred years, so long the symbol and patron of the city, was ceremoniously carried by canons of the cathedral, followed by all the city's clergy and most of its populace, to the cathedral and installed in the south transept. In this space formerly occupied by the chapel of St Nicholas, almost exactly coextensive with her former home and with its surrounding walls and pillars covered by accounts of her miracles, she stands to this day.[38]

For St Bertin the reprieve of 1791 was brief: sold off as state property in 1799, its first indignity was the stripping of its roof. Decades of insouciance culminated, in 1830, in the city's giving it up to quarrying, under the pretext of providing work for the unemployed. Through all this, the elegant fourteenth-century west tower clung on; a landmark from which, on a good day, even the coast of England was visible until, as recently as 1947, it finally succumbed to neglect and collapsed.[39]

To stand today before the rump of that tower and its meagre associated ruins is to confront a sorry sight indeed. It can easily come as a relief to turn one's back and tread gently uphill to the butte and the centre of modern-day Saint-Omer. As one follows the sleepy streets, their quietness disturbed by little beyond the rumble of tyres on cobbles, one can at least trace the outlines of the medieval city. Yet what rises above them is almost exclusively of a later time: Saint-Omer today is every inch a French provincial town, its white stone and yellow brick evocative of earlier days, yes, but now put to the service of tall houses of the seventeenth and eighteenth centuries. A detour off to the right quickly affords access to the fifteenth-century tower of St-Denis, lacking the steeple that in 1705 collapsed into its nave, the latter rebuilt in the succeeding years in contemporary style. A further detour opens

[36] Martine Le Maner, 'De l'ordre ancien à l'ordre nouveau', in Derville (ed.), *Histoire*, 158–64.
[37] For a three-dimensional reconstruction of the building see www.patrimoines-saint-omer.fr/Les-monuments-historiques/Les-monuments-disparus-en-3D/Chapelle-Notre-Dame-des-Miracles, accessed 30 October 2018.
[38] The story of the building, history and demise of the chapel is told in detail in Oscar Bled, 'La Vieille Chapelle du Grand Marché à Saint-Omer, 1270–1785', *Bulletin de la Société des antiquaires de la Morinie* 12 (1907–12), 767–802.
[39] Jacques Thiébaut, 'L'art monumentale', in Derville (ed.), *Histoire*, 242–4.

up visual access to the single steeple that still graces the city's skyline, that of St-Sepulchre; yet even this is a nineteenth-century reconstruction, while the greenery on the medieval building beneath is slowly clawing it back to nature.

Reaching the summit of the butte, passing by, in the vieux marché (now Place Victor Hugo), the elaborate fountain marking the spot once occupied by the parish church of St Aldegonde, the view of the great cathedral, sheltered to the last seconds by tall townhouses, looms finally into view (Figure P.1). The massive Gothic building is even more striking given the

Figure P.1 St Omer: view of the west tower from the north

Figure P.2 St Omer from the air © Carl Peterolff

Figure P.3 St Omer: interior looking east © Carl Peterolff

Figure P.4 Notre Dame des Miracles

almost total destruction of the medieval city over which it once presided (Figure P.2). In the interior, though, the student of the archives of the collégiale feels quickly on familiar ground (Figure P.3). Entering from the south under the recently restored tympanum of the Last Judgement, one finds oneself face to face with the thirteenth-century figure of Notre Dame des Miracles (Figure P.4), standing watch here since the fateful day, more than two hundred years earlier, when she was carried from her former home. Turning from her chapel into the building proper, one is quickly among friends: fifteenth-century epitaphs, surviving in profusion, invite us to pray for the souls of the canons and vicars who will people our story. The names are instantly evocative: Wissoc, Breion, Toussains de Le Ruelle, Rembert. We have come home.

1 | The Maîtrise

chantez, anges: c'est le miex Que je cy vois . . .[1]

The first approach of a choirboy to the church which was to occupy his entire pre-adult life must have been a bleak experience. Aged eight or younger, he would be constrained by parental agreement to serve the chapter typically for as long as it wished to retain him; infringements could be punishable by a fine. Whatever fulfilment awaited him, the young recruit would be saying farewell to the familiarities of home life, exchanging the succour of parents for the – often harsh – discipline of an unknown master. Even before admission the would-be young servant of the church typically faced daunting musical tests in front of the full gathering of the chapter whose agreement of sufficiency would normally be a precondition of his admission.[2]

While the archives lack a set of regulations for the choir school, stipulations surviving from elsewhere give a general impression of the life on which the incipient choirboy could expect to embark.[3] These indicate that,

---

[1] From an anonymous fourteenth-century play, *Un Miracle de nostre-dame*, in Louis-Jean-Nicolas Desrochais Monmerqué and Francisque Michel (eds.), *Théâtre français au moyen âge* (Paris: Firmin Didot, 1842), 363. Parts of this and the next chapter were published in Andrew Kirkman, 'The Seeds of Medieval Music: Choirboys and Musical Training in a Late-Medieval Maîtrise', in Susan Boynton and Eric Rice (eds.), *Young Singers, 650–1700* (Woodbridge: Boydell, 2008), 104–22.

[2] For general details concerning choirboy admission see Otto Frederick Becker, 'The Maîtrise in Northern France and Burgundy during the Fifteenth Century', unpublished PhD dissertation, George Peabody College for Teachers, Nashville, TN (1967), 138–44.

[3] The oldest, dating from around 1350, is that of the Sainte-Chapelle of Paris; see the edition in Michel Brenet, *Les musiciens de la Sainte-Chapelle du Palais* (Paris: Picard, 1910), 15–20. Jean Gerson's famous *Doctrina pro pueris et iuventibus chori ecclesiae Parisiensis* for the boys of Notre-Dame of Paris dates from 1411; see the translation in Craig Wright, *Music and Ceremony at Notre Dame of Paris, 500–1500* (Cambridge: Cambridge University Press, 1989), 166–9. The regulations of Reims dating from 1533 still show an indebtedness to the widely promulgated rules of Gerson. The complete text is transcribed in Patrick Demouy, Michel Dricot and Janine Grassin, *La maîtrise de la cathédrale de Reims, des origines à nos jours* (Reims: Cathédrale de Reims, 1996), 21–6. See also the discussion in Patrick Demouy, 'Les *pueri chori* de Notre-Dame de Reims: Contribution à l'histoire des clergeons au Moyen Age', in *Actes des congrès de la Société des historiens médiévistes de l'enseignement supérieur public. 22ᵉ congrès, Amiens, 1991: Clercs*

as at St Omer, such schools typically had two masters: one in music and the other in grammar (the latter taken in the larger sense of the teaching of reading and writing). Following standard practice, the singing duties of the boys at St Omer would have been focused particularly on Mass and vespers, and on matins on feasts of double or higher rank, hence on those observances with the most diverse and sophisticated sung items. The boys were also expected to fulfil other functions, especially censing, bearing candles and carrying the cross or ritual books in processions. Beyond the circulating responsibility of duty boy for the week, though, their presence would not have been required at the other offices.[4]

Outside their ritual duties their time was mostly occupied by rehearsal and lessons, in music (chant and polyphonic singing, both written and 'discanted' on the book) and grammar, but with the emphasis on the former.[5] Relaxation would be permitted during a period or two of time-tabled recreation. While the specifics of choirboy education at St Omer remain unknown they surely, as elsewhere, involved wholesale memorisation of the church's liturgy, including the psalms and Hours of the Virgin, along with a thorough grounding in musical literacy based on the hexachordal system that afforded negotiation of chant and written polyphony.[6]

Like most of the city's career paths, that of choirboy was paved by patronage and, quite literally, nepotism – while, as elsewhere, access surely extended from the poor to the bourgeoisie and even the nobility, the only demonstrable family links lead to nephews of canons.[7] Besides a strong voice and good ear, morality also figured almost invariably in a chapter's

---

séculiers au Moyen Age (Paris, 1993), 135–49. For a general discussion of such sets of rules see Etienne Anheim and David Fiala, 'Les maîtrises capitulaires et l'art du contrepoint du XIVe au XVIe siècle', *Analyse Musicale* 69 (2012), 13–20. It would appear that such a document did once exist for the St Omer maîtrise: an item in the (rotulus) fabric account for 1397–8 reads 'Item for fastening together a certain book of vigils that the choirboys have torn apart and a certain book containing the duties of the choirboys' ('Item pro ligatione cuiusdem libri vigiliarum quem pueri chori dilaceraverant et cuiusdem libri continentis officia puerorum chori'). 'Vigils' in this case likely refers to matins responsories and lessons sung by the boys. My thanks to John Harper for this detail.

[4] For the range of practices typically conducted by boys see the late medieval texts transcribed and translated in *The Sarum Customary Online*, part of The Experience of Worship in Late Medieval Cathedral and Parish Church, www.sarumcustomary.org.uk/, accessed 21 June 2019.

[5] A record in the fabric account for 1475/6 (f. 23r) clarifies that the boys were taught to sing directly from chant books: 'A Jehan du Quesnel escripvent pour avoir reloye et recolle en plusieurs lieux et escript / ung petit grel ou les enfans de coeur aprendent a canter paie xvi s.'

[6] For the example of Notre-Dame of Paris see Wright, *Music and Ceremony*, 174–80.

[7] On the social backgrounds of choirboys see Becker, 'The Maîtrise', 136–8.

stipulations, and parents were typically required to provide proof of legitimate birth. As elsewhere, though, rules were made to be broken, and illegitimacy could doubtless be overlooked in cases, like the famous examples elsewhere of Guillaume de Malbecque and Guillaume Du Fay,[8] of exceptional ability.

Such leeway with otherwise standard preconditions reflects the remarkable cachet of exceptional choirboy voices. Examples from St Omer that will be addressed later demonstrate the pinnacle of eminence from which such talent could be sought. Impressment into royal chapels was widespread, with even kidnapping far from unknown. However hazardous it may have been for the particular mother church in whose bosom such a talent had been nurtured, though, for the boy himself such attention could be hugely advantageous. As examples in the next chapter will illustrate, the untrammelled power of royal preferment that had permitted his abduction in the first place would often, following the breaking of his voice, function reciprocally in securing a chaplaincy for him back in his mother church.

Of course such lofty attentions were driven by more than disinterested musical patronage: scriptural underpinnings to the special value adhering to boys' voices and the burnish they gave to the disciplined choirs of the great noble households were clearly seen to provide an appropriately grand sonic reflection of their patrons' self-image. More generally, the exponential growth in the importance of the maîtrise, attested by corresponding documentary expansion in the course of the fifteenth century and beyond, reflects the growing number and elaboration of the public and – particularly – private devotions to which it made such a powerful contribution. All that, though, is for the next two chapters. For now my attention shall remain focused on the boys themselves, and on the material circumstances of the maîtrise which nurtured them; this will provide a platform from which to consider the circumstances that led to their increasing cultivation and importance.

Material Investment

While expansion of the St Omer maîtrise reflects that of its counterparts in other contemporary major ecclesiastical institutions, the virtual completeness of the most important accounts allows us to trace that growth with

---

[8] On these two cases see for example Alejandro Enrique Planchart, *Guillaume Du Fay*, 2 vols. (Cambridge: Cambridge University Press, 2017), vol. 1, respectively 211, 28–33.

unusual precision. Key here are the church's chapter acts, the executors' accounts of deceased canons and, especially, the church fabric accounts.

The fabric accounts provide a running commentary on the maintenance of the boys and of the house in the cloister that they shared with their master. Prosaic in themselves, they allow us to piece together a detailed, and sometimes poignant, picture of their daily lives. Payments relate the making and provision of their clothes, beds and other necessities, while records of the purchase and repair of their books shed light on their education and liturgical duties, considerably sharpening the focus provided by other contemporary sources of information including iconography.

While documentation concerning the founding of the choir school is apparently lacking, six boys were already stipulated by 1378, the presumed date of the first surviving fabric account, and that number seems to have remained more or less stable over the succeeding two centuries.[9] If the number of boys was largely fixed, though, their provisions were anything but. Increasingly elaborate institutional and privately founded observance was accompanied by a significant growth in the boys' prestige, matched by similar enhancement in their presentation and material conditions.

As with inhabitants of today's world, the clearest indication of rising prestige for the master and boys is the growing size and scope of their house. The fabric account of 1433/4 witnesses payments for masonry and carpentry for the 'maison des enfans', while from August to October 1440 there was major new building work on their accommodation. In addition to five thousand bricks used on the house of the boys, which included a kitchen, payments indicate substantial roof-tiling and carpentry work.[10] It may well be that the lavish sums spent on cloth and vestments

[9] This document (II. G. 2797) is in a poor state of repair and lacks the opening material which conventionally carries the date. The latter, drawn from the library's inventory of the chapter archives, presumably derives from a cover that has since been lost. Multiples of six still characterise the listing of choirboy vestments in the church inventory of 1557 (II. G. 2787, f. 29r; see the transcription in Louis Deschamps de Pas: 'Inventaire des ornemens, reliquaires, etc., de l'église collégiale de Saint-Omer en 1557', *Bulletin archéologique du Comité des travaux historiques et scientifiques* 1 (1886), 96).

[10] 1439/40 (II. G. CF 31), f. 5r: Item a Tassard Mauffait et laultre couvreur de tieulle avoeques i varlet pour avoir couvert empres le revestiaire et en lostel des enffans et de le carpenterie . . .; . . . pour les aisemens widier des enffans . . .; . . . au machons [sic] qui firent le vaulte desdits aisemens . . .; . . . pour iii milliers de briques pour lesdits aisemens et aultres choses pourfitables pour lostel desdits enffans . . .; . . . a Jaques de Boulogne drapier pour encore ii.^{m} de briques pour ledit ostel des enffans de coeur . . . ; . . . aux machons qui paverent le cuisine dudit ostel et machonnerent une petite paroit [interior wall] de briques contre le despense etc . . .; f. 6r: . . . pour xxx belnees de savelon [= sable] xxx s tant pour lostel des enffans que pour leglise // pour

the same year (amounting to £404 19s. 3d.) were part of the same upturn in provision for the boys.

Whatever the state of the house after this construction work, 1443/4 saw further building involving wooden flooring and another 1,500 bricks.[11] More expenses in 1447/8 on carpentry for the attic of the 'basses chambres' of the choirboys and for retiling the roof is difficult to interpret, since 'lower rooms' would seem to imply multiple storeys;[12] perhaps the future addition of an upper floor was already anticipated. In 1455/6 Jehan de Le Stegle was paid 'pour avoir fait trois fenestres de toille pour le maison des enfans de coeur', likely a reference to a contemporary form of canvas window, insulated with turpentine and stretched over a wooden frame.[13] Two pages of construction accounts for their house in the account for 1463/4 demonstrate that, along with the expected masonry, carpentry and roof work, the boys' hygienic needs were not neglected,[14] while the roof of the 'maison du maistre de chant' received a retiling in 1464/5. Further expansion of the house is marked out by payments for materials and for workmen who, in 1468/9, 'extended the said house by height; on the carpentry there [they] made a floor, a wall and two windows in the loft ('ont Ralongie ledit maison par [le] hault sur le carpenterie y fait ung plancquier une paroit et deux fenestres ens ou comble'). This clearly comprised the addition of a new floor, planned to function – as can be inferred from further records quoted below – as a dormitory.[15] The account of 1469/70 reveals that the master of the boys had his own chamber, distinct from that of the boys, and that the carpenters were paid for adding a separate outbuilding to this to provide access from the

---

lamenage de v.^m de briques pour ledit ostel des enffans ... pour ramener le terre qui fust ostee dudit ostel a cause des aisemens ...

[11] 1443/4, second copy, f. 2r: ... aisselles pour faire le plancquiet desdis enfans...; pour milier et demi de bricques pour ledit ostel ... aux machons pour journees ... commenchans le vi^e jour de novembre iiii^c xliii et finant le xxiii^e jour dudit mois pour ouvrages fais a lostel des enfans ... A Tassart Mauffait et son varlet pour avoir couvert sur le maison des enfans par lespace dun jour ...

[12] F. 14v: under 'Carpentiers, etc.': ... pour le fachon du comble des basses chambres des enfans de coeur; f. 15v: under 'Aultrez mises pour couvreux de tieulez' ... tant pour couvrir le librarie / basses chambres des enfans de coeur / comme aultres pluiseurs [sic] lieux ...

[13] My thanks to Ludovic Nys for this information.

[14] 1463/4, 48v: Pour ung bac [vessel] de dure pierre assis empres les aisemens a pissier ... viii sc; ... pour ung bac de dure pierre assis en le maison pour laver les mains ... viii sc

[15] 1468/9, f. 50r. The concomitant question concerns what arrangements had pertained hitherto, and the reasons for their change. It seems reasonable to surmise that before this time the boys were accommodated with the canons, but that a need was felt for a collective living arrangement, presumably to ensure a common regimen of work, study and pastoral care.

hallway.[16] Renewal work on the same outbuilding in 1494/5 indicates that it extended to the 'court de le fabrique', the presumed location, therefore, of the master's lodgings.[17]

The accounts afford a clear sense of the boys' sleeping arrangements: numerous entries that speak of their three beds and regular costs for fashioning three pairs of sheets reveal that, as elsewhere, they were billeted two to a bed. From time to time, as in the account of 1495/6, new beds had to be made, and the production that year of an extra bed besides the usual three reveals that provision was in place for the extra boy or two who from time to time (as we shall see) joined the regular cohort of six.[18]

The same cluster of records offers some rare insight into the layout of the boys' sleeping quarters, and hence a little more potential detail on their pattern of life. Besides the making of new beds, the carpenters were that year paid for 'remaking the chests of the said children, placed in front of their beds', for fashioning a construction of some kind 'to store their vestments and clothes' and 'for making an enclosure [perhaps a space separated off in case one of them fell sick] for the bed beneath the stairs to the attic'. Most intriguingly, they were instructed to provide 'two planks a foot wide and eight–nine feet long on which to place the boys' books above their beds'.[19] Occupied as they frequently were from darkness to

---

[16] 1469/70, f. 14a, r: 'Aux carpentiers pour avoir aisselle et planquie le chambre du maistre / et aussi fait ung petit hangart pour aler de le sallette en bas au retrait ou ils ont vacque par certains jours dont ils ont eu comme il appert par cedule xliii s ii d.' Materials listed for the job include a cart of bricks, along with tiles and materials in oak and 'white wood'.

[17] 1494/5, 32: 'Item a ung homme qui a placquie le hangart fait de nouvel entre le maison des enffans et le court de le fabrique / latte et fait son mortier ou il a vacquie vii jours chaqun jour iii sont xxi s.' Alison Adams points out to me that 'court de le fabrique' likely refers to a yard, or workspace, for stonemasons and possibly also carpenters.
32': Item a Jehan de Le Venne pour avoir solle [pavé?] le hangart fait entre le fabricque et le maison des enffans du cant xii s

[18] See 1495/6, f. 29r: Item A Gilles du Lunechon pour xx crouttes [rough planks of wood drawn from a tree trunk] de quesne employes a faire les iii lits des enffans de coeur le lit du maistre et ung aultre en le chambre desdits enffans lesquelz sont mobilles et cordes par dessouls chacune croutte achettee xv d sont xxv s

[19] Item pour iii aisselles de ii pies de large et secques pour refaire les coffres desdits enffans estans devant leurs lits a ii s chacune aisselle valent vi s
Item deux autres aisselles dung piet de large et de viii a ix pies de long pour mettre leurs livres desseure leurs lits et deux aisselles tennenes pour tout iii s vi d
Item iii quartiers de quesne soye a quarrure de viii pies de long pour faire les montans des cornes [bedposts] de leurs lits et vi lambourdes [long pieces of wood] de quesne pour les travers [crosspieces] pour tout x s
Item audit pour vi aisselles de blancq boys pour faire une taile [presumably an (unspecified) wooden structure of some kind] pour mettre leurs robes et habits[.] Et aussy pour faire une clotture au lit dessoubs le montee du grenier a xii d pieche sont vi s

dusk by worship and collective study, one might imagine the boys had little time (or daylight) for private reading; yet the payments in some years' accounts for the making and binding of 'six petis livres' clearly suggest provision of individual volumes, perhaps of works for private devotion or study.[20]

Greater clarity on the layout of the boys' lodgings comes from the series of mid-sixteenth-century inventories of the contents of houses in the cloister.[21] At least part of the function of the lower floor by that date is revealed by the subheading 'in the lower room, otherwise known as the chapel' ('En la chambre bas alias la chapelle'). A kitchen stocked with a typical range of kitchenware and utensils, often in the telltale number of six, also housed a bed for 'the servant girl' ('la meschine'), clearly a live-in matron.[22] An adjoining space for baking bread included the necessary equipment. The accoutrements of the master's room – a little table and two stalls, plus a large slate – suggest use for teaching as well as sleeping.[23] The presence in the boys' bedroom of eight beds and couches not only reveals provision for two more young singers than had hitherto been the norm, but the greater luxury of separate sleeping arrangements. The presence of 'an iron trolley to heat the children' (presumably some kind of brazier on wheels) shows similar concern for their comfort.[24] On the other hand, the 'little bell to wake the boys' serves to remind us that their slumbers, however comfortable, may not always have concluded voluntarily.[25] The presence, in the room for baking, of 'a bedframe of planks in case of any illness' would seem to support the above supposition concerning the purpose of the bed beneath the stairs to the attic.[26]

While the fundamentals of shelter came from wood, bricks and mortar, the rising status of the boys is most vividly revealed in the extent and expense of their annual provisions. The early ledgers from the late fourteenth and early fifteenth centuries, where expenses for the boys are buried among the 'despenses extraordinaires', suggest an ad hoc approach to their

---

[20] E.g. 1512/13, f. 27r. It must be acknowledged that since the number is not invariably six there may be some other explanation for such records; see 1509/10, 25v: Primes a Micquelot Le Cras pour avoir relyet les petis livres que sont en nombre ix payet pour chacun iiii sc sont xxxvi s

[21] I shall refer to the account of 1559, II. G. 599, ff. 9r–10r; the available accounts are strikingly consistent across available years.

[22] Une couche lict traversain et couvertoir rouge pour la meschine (f. 9v)

[23] Une petite table et deux hetaulx ... Une grande ardoyse (f. 9v)

[24] Ung chariot de fer pour chauffer les enffans (f. 9r)

[25] En le chambre des enfans / Huict petites couches / huict licts / huict traversains ... Une clochette pour renveillier les enffans (f. 9v)

[26] Ung calict faict daisselles pour quelques mallade (f. 9v)

maintenance. In ?1378, for example, they each received a new tunic and linen girdle, while cloth was purchased in 1407/8 to make six amices and six albs. The absence of noted provision for the boys in the intervening records suggests a hand-me-down approach or, perhaps, provision by their families. Maybe, as at Rouen,[27] parents were obliged, on first delivering their child to the maîtrise, to supply a required list of clothing, and conceivably to replenish it as and when it wore out. Certainly parental cash injection was not unknown, as when, from 1458 to 1461, limited revenue to the church fabric account led to parents being obliged to support the maintenance of their children to the tune of half its cost. Scattered comments in the chapter acts likewise suggest at least a periodic expectation of parental contribution, seemingly a yearly payment of a livre to the master of the boys. When in 1494 the father of a certain 'little Judocus', choirboy, was accidentally burned ('accidentaliter combustus'), rendering him unable to pay his dues for three years, the chapter waived them provided that the father could pay for his son's other necessaries.[28] Similarly, when the premature death in 1495 of the mother of the choirboy Clay Lamps left him with meagre means, the chapter agreed to pay his yearly dues of a livre to the master, provided the boy's father and legal representative would not reduce the twenty livres due to be paid to the chapter on the death of the said mother.[29]

It is at least possible that there was some fluctuation in numbers during the early period: the provision of 'le lit des enfans du choer' in 1409/10 may suggest that the two boys who, with two chaplains, guarded the relic of the head of St Omer on the day of 'Saint Omer en fleurs' that year were the only ones enrolled at the time. More likely, though, the boys were at this early stage accommodated in more piecemeal fashion in the houses of

---

[27] See Becker, 'The Maîtrise', 161, quoting Adolphe Bourdon and Armand Collette, *Histoire de la maîtrise de Rouen* (Rouen, 1892; repr. Geneva, 1972), 89–90.

[28] ... domini concesserunt parvo Judoco puero chori ad supplicationem sui patris qui nuper fuit accidentaliter combustus veritus quod non solvet librum grossorum suo magistro spacio trium annorum proviso quod aliis necessariis ipsum Judocum pater intertenebit (II. G. 355, f. 104r, entry of 20 August, 1494)

[29] Ledit jour Jehan Lamps et Marc Choquel pere et advoez de Clay Lamps enffant de coeur de leglise de cheens[.] A cause de la formorture [succession falling on someone by death of another] de sa mere et quil a peu de biens messieurs ont accorde de supporter lesdits Jehan et Marc dune livre de quel quils paioyent au maistre de chant pour ses despens pourveu quils ne diminuront point ce qui luy appartient montant a xx libz de la formorture de sadit mere[.] Ce quils ont proumis faire et riens diminuer de ladite somme en bonne foy en la main de monseigneur le doyen et de moy Marant Danvet notaire presens Maistre Philippe de Mussen et Baudin des Gruselliers tesmoing / Sur paine de payer a sondit maistre le livre dessusdit[.] (II. G. 355, f. 109r, entry of 16 February 1495)

members of the adult clergy. But by 1431 there were clearly sufficient bodies to justify six new albs for the boys, and demand enough also to repair the old ones, while in subsequent years payments for vestments for the boys and the rest of the clergy accelerate substantially.

The most tangible shift came when, in the late 1450s, the expense and bulk of annual provision for the boys had expanded to the point of meriting a separate section of the accounts. Yet the first truly dedicated account, that of 1462/3, covering half a page and with expenditure totalling £8 9s. 3d., pales beside that for, say, 1516/17, whose three and a half densely packed pages outline costs weighing in at no less than £72 11s. 6d., mostly for material and clothing.[30] To follow the accounts from the second half of the fifteenth century and into the sixteenth is to trace a remarkable upward trajectory in money spent on ever-plusher garments and other provisions as the boys' ritual and singing duties became increasingly varied and, as a consequence, more remunerative. A vivid illustration can be made by juxtaposing two accounts, a little more than forty years apart, for the making of garments. In the account of 1472/3 the maîtrise's long-standing seamstress Kateline (or 'Katerine') Jullers is paid eighteen sous 'for the making of six albs and six amices for the children made from the old linen (presumably curtains) of the said organs'. Set against this hand-me-down approach, payments in the accounts of 1515/16 look like the height of extravagance: here expenses on materials and garments in lambs' wool alone total almost five livres.[31]

Occasional entries in the chapter acts suggest that such developments may have been responses to official policy. For example, on 24 February 1486, the chapter decreed that, from that point on, each year on the Feast of St Bavo advantage should be taken of the markets being held to buy cloth in order that the master and boys could be provided with vestments the following Easter.[32] Certainly the purchase of cloth rose to prodigious levels, as, in consequence, did bills for tailoring. By the early sixteenth century, provision of new hose and shoes (double-soled) was a thrice-yearly occurrence, at Christmas, Easter and the Assumption (15 August); purchase of twenty or more lamb fleeces for lining garments (presumably to shield

---

[30] The total sum of £180 12s. 6d. for the latter account includes salaries of the two (successive) masters of the boys; in earlier documents such salaries appear elsewhere in the ledger.

[31] 1472/3, f. 9v and 1515/16, f. 30v.

[32] Eadem die concluserunt domini quod deinceps de anno in annum in festo Bavonis propter concursum mercatorum ad molendinas venientium emerentur panni de quibus vestiri debebunt pueri chori cum eorum magistro in pasca subsequente ut commodosius eisdem provideatur[.] (II. G. 355, f. 59v)

against cold weather) occurred yearly; and supplies of vestments including cassocks, surplices/albs and amices, and regular 'livery' including shirts, hoods and more generic 'robes', were replenished annually and old ones repaired. Such provision mirrors that at other institutions, revealing that St Omer was very much in line with prevailing developments in major religious houses.[33]

Payments for bedding suggest steadily increasing comfort there also. The arrival in 1456/7 of feathers for the boys' beds in addition to the traditional straw would seem to bespeak growing concerns for physical well-being;[34] but this was easily trumped in 1498/9 (f. 33v) by the purchase of three quilts where there had hitherto only been sheets. By 1508/9 the boys had their live-in matron,[35] presumably ameliorating the maintenance of 'bouche et soing' which, from masters at this time, could sometimes struggle to reach the standard even of tough love.

None of this, of course, could cushion the boys from the (frequent) vicissitudes of war and plague, as when, in 1513/14, pestilence claimed the life of the choirboy Jennet Deubry. To guard against the contagion, the remaining boys were packed off for a month to the nearby town of Esques, where they were to be cared for by the 'widow Collart le Pappre'.[36] Their sojourn seems to have been one far from privation: the accounts tell us that they were provided with six individual 'couches' for sleeping, six dishes, and even 'a rod and six stone fish'. No such sabbatical safeguarded the carpenter Jan Daspere, who, as we shall learn in Chapter 4, spent the period working on the organ case and, for his pains, succumbed to the disease. Sadly plague was far from a rarity: only four years later a payment is made for a lock and key to secure the gate by the chapter that affords access, above the school, to lodgings, 'to avoid danger of infection by plague'.[37]

---

[33] See Becker, 'The Maîtrise', 146–7.

[34] See the account of that year, f. 13r–v: '... pour xxxvi. livres de plume pour les lis des enfans de coeur ...'. Prior to this, one finds mention in this connection only of straw ('pesach').

[35] 1508/9, f. 28r: Item a este achete ung lit noef pour le cambre de le mesquinne [servant girl] a une femme nommee Marioie Rose payet l. sc

[36] 1513/14, f. 29v: Mais pour cest an a cause de la peste et que lung desdit enfans en morut / assavoir Jennet Deubry a este seullement paiet pour xi^e mois chacun mois lesdits ix libs sont iiii^{xx} xix libs et quant a lautre mois lesdits enfans furent a Esque et en fust paie a le vesve Collart Le Pappre par accord fait avec messires la somme de xv libs courant. dont fault rebattre pour le verdellet l s ... Ainsy reste pour les cincq enfans xii lb x s somme totale pour lan c xi libs x s. F. 30v: Item audit tamps leur fu achete une canne et six poichonnes de gres ii s iii d Et pour vi escuelles et vi couches de bois ii s sont iiii s iii d

[37] 1517/18, f. 34v: A [blank] securier en le cleutrye pour ung bngt [?bugnoir = 'partie d'une porte' (Godeffroy)] et le clef y servant pour fermer lhuys pres le capitle pour passer deseure lescolle a aller aux retrets pour eviter dangier des infectes de peste iiii s

In general, though, the boys' circumstances only improved. If fear of purgatory and desire for its speedy transition provided the economic engine for the spread of increasingly elaborate devotions, a principal component in the 'fuel' for that engine was supplied by the boys. Further, the perceived value of their performances seems increasingly to have been viewed, like the polyphony they crowned, as an emblem of prestige: as we shall see in addressing private devotions established by the church's wealthier luminaries, they were swept up in a spiral of extravagance that saw the expense and visibility of devotions assume ever-greater emphasis.

The rising sums spent in the course of the fifteenth century on the upkeep of the boys give abundant testimony to their growing importance. Substantial though the income generated via their involvement may have been, though, it was still subject to fluctuations that could not be anticipated, the reason why, for example, the church felt compelled for a brief period in the late 1450s to renege on half of the upkeep costs and levy the balance on the boys' families. As in other institutions, therefore, the chapter needed the income required for the choir school's upkeep to be placed on a firmer footing. Since each canon received a stable income generated from property assigned to his particular canonry or 'prebend', a common method for achieving such stability derived from the 'suppression' of a prebend (or more minor office) and redirection of its income to the maintenance of the maîtrise. Pamela Starr lists twenty-five other institutions which used such suppressions to support choirboy maintenance, a trend she sees as linked to the contemporary growth in currency of, and demand for, polyphony, in which choirboys were integrally involved.[38] The later fifteenth and early sixteenth centuries at St Omer saw three such initiatives, of which by far the most significant was the suppression, in 1490, of the prebend attached to one of the high offices of the church, that of cantor.

The 'Bulle Conservatoire'

The suppression of this canonry and its associated prebend was an event of major significance in the history of the maîtrise: unlike other offices and entitlements suppressed for its maintenance during the same period, this was a 'grande prebende', carrying considerable financial weight. This much is clear from subsequent fabric accounts, where the distributions and other

---

[38] On this tradition see Pamela Starr, 'Rome as the Centre of the Universe: Papal Grace and Music Patronage', *Early Music History* 11 (1992), 241–4.

incomes arising from the prebend, now directed to the maîtrise, are annually recorded. Clearly the importance of this provision was not lost on the dean and chapter, whose discussion, in which it is frequently referred to as the 'bulle conservatoire', reveals a certain self-consciousness about the status and significance of the suppression and the redirection of its associated income.[39]

Convenient though such a suppression may have been, though, its accomplishment was no straightforward matter, requiring significant investment of time and money in Rome to acquire the papal bull necessary to secure its passage. The church's chapter acts allow us to trace this process through its various stages, and particularly its final phases in 1490. It is in this connection that we encounter for the first time two of the central players of our dramatis personae: the cantor of the day, Johannes de Hemont, and Nicolas Rembert, former *contratenorista* of St Peter's, Rome, lawyer and notary in the papal curia, canon of St Omer from 1484 and, from 1494 until his death ten years later, dean.

Clearly the idea of a 'conservatoire' had been in the air for a long time: an entry in the fabric accounts for 1454/5 records the dispatching of an emissary to enquire after the 'conservatoire de cheux de Saint Pierre de Cassel'.[40] The implication here is that this collégiale in the next large town (known to musicologists as the seat of a canonry held until 1459 by Binchois) had the jump on St Omer in terms of provision for its maîtrise. Apparently things at St Omer got off to a slow start: the next record comes only in 1484, when on 12 September the canon Ludovicus Touret was instructed to go to the Roman curia to expedite 'the new conservatory according to the form which seems to him most convenient for the church and personnel'.[41] Following debate in the chapter more than a year later, on 24 October 1485, the distinguished and long-standing vicar-singer Hugues Lucian was sent to investigate the cost of other conservatories in order to consider both how, in his estimation, such an establishment at St Omer could be paid for, and how it might most conveniently be set up.[42]

---

[39] Starr (ibid., 242) notes the use of the analogous term *psalleta* for similar foundations elsewhere.

[40] Item audit Jehan Fin pour avoir ale a Cassel querir le copie de le conservatore de cheux de Saint Pierre de Cassel avoec le copie dune moniton viii sc et pour lesdits copies viii sc sont comme appert par cedule xvi sc (1454/5, f. 13v of one copy; f. 14r of the other.)

[41] Ipso die quo superius dicti prefati domini dederunt in commissionem ipsi Ludovico Touret ad expediendum in curia Romana novam conservatoriam sub forma / qua sibi convenientius ecclesie et personis videbitur / et signatura habita pecuniam transmittent in b[e]n[fi]c[i]o sibi dirigendam s[ecundu]m quod ipse dictis dominis mandabit / iii l aliud parisien[ses] (II. G. 355, f. 55v)

[42] ... ad expediendum novam conservatoriam domini inter se disputantes / deliberarunt quod expetendum esset a Magistro Hugone Luciaen et in suis comp[uti]s inspiciendum / quantum

The key figure in bringing the whole process to fruition, though, was clearly Rembert, whose connections in and knowledge of the curial system had a significant impact on the church's musical provision generally. As the process reached its climax, Rembert was permitted frequent absences for the negotiations in Rome, where he also had the assistance of the chapter's scribe – and (as we shall see in Chapter 6) his eventual nemesis – Johannes Derviller.[43] The fabric accounts attest to considerable traffic of correspondence between the church – including its canons Robert Peppin, Osto Machecler and Philippe de Le Bricque – and its agent at the curia.[44] An entry on folio 26r of the fabric account for 1490/1 records how Rembert has

procured, obtained and dispatched, in the said court of Rome, the bulls of suppression of the prebend of the same church … and perpetual union of the same prebend with the said [fund of the] fabric for the sustenance of the master and choirboys of the said church, and otherwise to transform the augmentation of the divine service, at the discretion of my lords of the chapter. And for the bulls of the reservation of the value of the said prebend to the said Hemont for the rest of his life. Pay in total £103 9s.[45]

---

expeditio / alterius conservatorie costetit et a quibus solvi decretum fuit et postea avisare sub qua forma et ad que suppo[si]ta valeret commodosius expediri (II. G. 355, f. 62r[a])

[43] Die xxiiiᵃ aprilis / Magister Johannes de Cruiller [sic] in capitolo supplicavit quod possit se absentare per spacium unius mensis pro suis negociis et Magistri Nicolai Rembert lucrando / quique domini in contemplacione prefati Magistri Nicolai annuerunt quod possit negociando dicto mense durante se absentare lucrando (II. G. 355, f. 77v)

[44] 1490/1, f. 25v: Audit [Robert] Peppin pour avoir minute et grosse les instructions envoyes a Maistre Nicole Rembert pour la suppression de la prebende monsieur le chantre et ichelle vnyr a ladite fabricque pour la sustentacion des maistre de chant et enffans de coeur / et a ceste fin escript plusieurs lettres audit Rembert xlviii s
F. 25v: Audit Peppin pour avoir fait les instructions envoyes audit Rembert / pour obtenir reformacion tant de la bulle de l union de ladicte prebende comme de la bulle conservatoire des privileges de ladite eglise et a ceste fin fait plusieurs dilligences xxxii s
F. 25v: A Maistre Ph[ilipp]e de Le Bricque chanoine de ladite eglise pour plusieurs dilligences par luy faicte touchant lesdites suppression unyon et reformacion desdites bulles
F. 26r: Audit Sire Oste Macheclier et Sire Robert de Monte pour pareillement avoir entendu a la reformacion de ladite bulle conservatoire[.] Et aussy ledit Sire Oste a limpetracion [obtaining/getting] de ladite suppression et en escript plusieurs lettres audit Rembert a chacun diceulx xl s sont iiii lbs

[45] A Maistre Nicole Rembert chanoine de ladite eglise demourant en court de Rome pour avoir impetre obtenu et despechie en ladite court de Rome les bulles de la suppression de la prebende dichelle eglise … et unyon dichelle prebende perpetuelement a ladite fabrique pour la sustentacion des maistre et enfans de coeur de ladite eglise et aultremens convertir laugmentacion du service divin a la discrecion de messeigneurs de chapitle. Et pour les bulles de la reservation de la valleur de ladite prebende audit Hemont sa vie durant, paye en tout C. iii lbs ix s

The chapter act for 5 August 1490 provides the memorandum document-ing the renunciation of Hemont's prebend and agreement that all its emoluments be used 'for the support of a master of scholars of song or music, and of six choirboys who will be instructed in music and song by the same master of song and who in the same church shall devote themselves to the divine office'.[46] The document affirms that papal permission for this is being pursued in Rome by Rembert; but it adds other signal details that will have a role to play in the workings of the maîtrise and particularly in Hemont's functioning within it. Key to the position of cantor, in which post Hemont is to remain, is to oversee the music and to present his recommendation for master of the boys, a choice that, however, is subject to approval by the chapter. The bull itself expands on these conditions, noting that the chosen master 'may be removed by the said dean and chapter [and] of whom the presentation pertains to the cantor, while admission pertains to the dean and chapter'. As we shall see in Chapter 3, the perceived irreconcilability, in a particular instance, of these two condi-tions will in fairly short order set the two sides on a collision course.

Of more immediate concern to Hemont, though, was his own future welfare, and pains are taken in the process of his renunciation to establish that he is to be allowed, in recompense for giving up his prebend, to continue to enjoy its emoluments as long as he remains in position as cantor. He is permitted to sell the rents of his house or live in it as he wishes until his death, provided he ultimately reimburses the full amount of the rent to be used for the founding of his annual posthumous obit service. Hemont's privilege is the subject of another bull, likewise pushed through by Rembert, as confirmed by the document already quoted from the fabric account of the same year: here Rembert is credited for expediting 'the bulls of the reservation of the value of the said prebend to the said Hemont for the rest of his life'.[47]

The scale of the payment to Rembert for expediting the two bulls – £103 9s – gives some sense of how lucrative, and hence presumably desirable, such work could be; but it also indicates the perceived difficulty, and hence expertise involved, in steering the negotiations to successful conclusion. Perhaps, notwithstanding all his efforts, the protocols extracted by Rembert were not as watertight as they might have been, at least as far as the transac-tions involving Hemont's welfare and pension were concerned: still in 1495/6

---

[46] Provided in full in the Appendix at the end of this volume, which also includes transcriptions of the three bulls of suppression under discussion here.

[47] See above, and note 45.

the cantor was embroiled in complicated exchanges over his income and was only that year recorded as paying for the expediting of the bulls concerning the assignment of his future payment.[48] While it is impossible with any certainty to impute moods and intentionality in a case this distant and ramified, it could well be that such difficulties and delays contributed to what was clearly a strained relationship between Hemont and the chapter.

At any rate the 'conservatory' was founded, and its importance to the church's self-image and finances is clear from the fabric accounts which annually, from this time forth, commence with transactions concerning the suppressed prebend, headed in each case by words closely echoing those of the founding bull. The formulation as found on the first page of the account for 1501/2 serves as well as any:

And of one of the large prebends that Master Jehan de Hemont formerly obtained and possessed, suppressed and annulled by the said authority for the maintenance of six choirboys and a master to instruct and teach them in music for the augmentation of the divine service in the said church, applied and instituted by the said [fund of the] fabric according to the tenor of the apostolic bulls and letters dispatched for this purpose and housed in the treasury of the said church.[49]

A watershed though it clearly was in the life of the maîtrise, however, the plan to suppress Hemont's prebend for this purpose was not unprecedented. An entry in the chapter acts for 30 September 1476 reveals the intention of the chapter to suppress the first vicariate becoming vacant through death, subject to agreement by the pope, and to use its income for the feeding and maintenance of the boys. Provision is also made for a small vicariate to fulfil the appropriate workload for the canon who, as a result of the suppression, would lose his assigned vicar.[50] That papal approval for

---

[48] 1495/6, 34r: Item de Maistre Jehan de Hemont chantre pour ses gaiges de vicariat quil promist sur les biens de feu Monsieur le Prevost de Luxembourg appartenant a ladite fabricque ce que nont accoustume les vicaires lx libs
Item dudit pour lexpedicion de ses bulles touchant lassignacion de pension quil a chacun an et mise sur les tailles de cap[it]le par prest a luy fait xl duc[ats] dor valent lxxii libs

[49] Et de lune des grandes prebendes que obtint et possessa ja pieca Maistre Jehan de Hemont supprime et extainte par ledit auctorite pour lentretenement de six enffans de coeur et dung maistre pour les instruire et aprendre en musicque a laugmentation du saint service divin en ladite eglise applicquies et mises es comptes et estans de ladite fabricque selonc le teneur des bulles et lettres apostolicques sur ce expedies et estans en la thesaurarie de ladite eglise . . .

[50] Hac die ultima mensis septembris anno lxxvi domini mei Symon Godefroy decanus P. Pauchet Jo. Bonniele T. de Vitry Hugo de Monchi Egidius Pepin Jo. de Hemont Judocus Dausque Osto Machecler M. Wastable Matheus Advisse Jacobus du Val canonici in suo loco capitulari capitulariter congregati se fortes facien[tes] de Domino Nicolao Sauvage Walrando Pepin et Roberto Pepin etiam de Magistro Radulpho de Donqueurre Jacobo de Houchin et Philippo de

the suppression of a vicariate, and indeed of its associated canonry, was forthcoming is evident from a bull issued by Sixtus IV in December of the same year. Its terms provide for the suppression of the minor prebend currently held by Mattheus Advisse plus the one of the twenty-eight perpetual *sine cura* (i.e. without 'cure of souls', hence unordained) vicariates serving the associated canonry. Designed to ease the burden on the funds of the fabric, an income is stipulated of not more than 24 livres tournois from the minor prebend plus 10 livres tournois from the vicariate, topped up by 50 livres tournois coming from the fabric itself.[51] Clearly the plan gained headway: arrival of the required papal documentation was announced on 30 July the following year, permitting the lords to suppress, as soon as it should become available, Advisse's prebend for provision for the boys. The nub of the problem was in the latter point, however, for which the 1477 document offers important clarification: Advisse himself was to be permitted to enjoy his canonry, or indeed to permute it for another, for as long as he liked or was able to. A codicil underscores the point: the chapter pledges to issue documents assuring his security.[52] Since Advisse held onto his benefice, and did not die until late in 1494, events clearly overtook this early plan. Realising as they must have done the pitfalls of their earlier largesse, the chapter in 1490 suppressed Hemont's canonry directly, providing separately to compensate its erstwhile occupant. Living long enough to see the difficulties that pursued Hemont in safeguarding his post-prebendary income, Advisse must have considered himself fortunate to have secured his own future in the way that he had.

The above developments notwithstanding, it is clear that by the early sixteenth century existing income was proving insufficient to cover the

---

Mailli canonicis resident[ariis] concluserunt et consenserunt primam vicariam ecclesie sue Sancti Audomari per decessum vaccaturam de consensu domini nostri pape fore extinctam et suppressam ad opus ~~alimentationis et mantenementi puerorum chori~~ fabrice dicte ecclesie / pro alimentandis et mantenendis pueris chori / Et ne dominus canonicus cuius erit vicaria defraudetur vicario / dominus decanus et canonici predicti decreverunt quod parva vicaria dicte ecclesie serviat domino canonico in omnibus cuius vicaria erit suppressa[.] In omnibus et per omnia prout vicarius suus faciebat Magistro Anthonio de Tramecourt canonico in omnibus premissa se opponenti et nullo modo consens[cienti] [the page is ripped off at this point] (II. G. 354, 205v-6r)

[51] The text of this bull (for which see the Appendix to this volume) is preserved in an eighteenth-century copy in II. G. 393.

[52] ... voluerunt domini mei prefati quod dictus Matheus possit uti vita sua comite de suis prebende et canonicatu pro suo libito eosdem permutando quando voluit non obstantibus dictis litteris apostolicis aut clausa earundem de hoc faciente mentionem accordante eidem Magistro Matheo exinde sibi fieri per capitulum litteras pro securitate predictorum ad laudum seu consilium totiens quotiens voluerit idem Magister Matheus[.] (II. G. 354, 209v)

costs of the church's ever-expanding raft of devotions, public and private.[53] A further bull from 1506 details the similar redirection of the income from the vicariate formerly associated with Hemont's suppressed prebend. As the bull makes clear, this was an exceptional move for *sine cura* vicariates, typically positions assigned to each canonry to cover the singing and other statutory duties nominally assigned to the canons themselves.[54]

At Saint-Omer as elsewhere, such suppressions provide a barometer of the growth in prestige and wealth of the maîtrise and, in turn, of the perceived value of music, and polyphony in particular, to the church and to the private founders whose rituals it housed. But the fact remains that use of boys is in and of itself a *sine qua non* neither of ritual extravagance nor indeed of polyphony itself; rather their significance rests on their perceived status as rooted in scripture.

Heavenly Innocence

Underpinned by such biblical commonplaces as 'Out of the mouth of babes and sucklings thou hast perfected praise,' and 'Suffer the little children, and forbid them not to come to me, for theirs in the kingdom of heaven,' the image fostered by the singing of boys was one of heavenly innocence on earth and its attendant promise of future salvation.[55] In this their role had something in common with that of the poor as participants in private Masses, likewise individuals whose advocacy for the souls of departed founders was untainted by the wealth and political manoeuvring of earthly power. The foundational stipulations of Philip the Good's Burgundian court maîtrise for 'four little children, innocent and of good behaviour, for the service of the chapel ' are replicated in countless descriptions of the period.[56] Selection was based not only on the quality of the boys' voices but also on their (at least notionally) unblemished morals.

To this emphasis on innocence, however, may be added a further dimension of their role: since at least Augustine they had been perceived

---

[53] Inflation or reduction in the value of endowments could lead to similar developments (see for example Becker, 'The Maîtrise', 187–8).

[54] II. G. 53., Bull of 1506 (for full text see the Appendix to this volume).

[55] 'Ex ore infantium et lactantium perfecisti laudem' (Psalms 8:3), and quoted by Christ in Matthew 21:16; 'Jesus vero ait eis sinite parvulos et nolite eos prohibere ad me venire talium est enim regnum caelorum' (Matthew 19:14). For these latter points and the biblical references see Wright, *Music and Ceremony*, 165, and Becker, 'The Maîtrise', 64.

[56] '... quatre petis enfans innocens, de bonnes moeurs, pour le service de la chappelle', Jeanne Marix, *Histoire de la musique et des musiciens de la cour de Bourgogne sous le règne de Philippe le Bon* (Strasbourg: Heitz, 1939; repr. Geneva: Minkoff, 1972), 162.

as earthly metaphors for the choirs of cherubim whose singing they fore-echoed and whose hearing the endowers of foundations involving them aimed to expedite.[57] All the more reason, then, for their training to be sufficiently regulated and strict as to produce the maximum polish, thereby adumbrating to the closest degree possible the sounds of their heavenly counterparts. Here also we see the reason why boys, once installed by their parents, were confined to the house and activities of the maîtrise and forbidden from mixing with their families and with the outside world more generally.[58] The *règlements* for the maîtrise of Reims describe how the boys were to be 'like little angels in the service of God', and were to 'excite all to devotion ... with an appearance of modesty such that one could see them rather as angels than children'.[59] From this perspective, furthermore, we begin to perceive the degree to which, via foundations with polyphony, the prestige of the contribution of choirboys was itself instrumental in driving the contemporary expansion of sacred polyphony.

Even the regulation of the number of boys in the St Omer maîtrise, as in sundry other establishments, at six may have been related to their angelic status: Ezekiel 9:2 notes that six angels were appointed to guard Jerusalem in Ezekiel's day.[60] A payment recorded in the fabric account for 1412/13 'to repoint and re-gild the six angels before the high altar' suggests that their identity and number were further emblematised by statuary in the

---

[57] See Becker, 'The Maîtrise', 64; Demouy, 'Les *pueri chori*', 138.

[58] See Becker, 'The Maîtrise', 143.

[59] '"comme petits anges au service de Dieu" ils doivent "exciter chacun à dévotion"; qu'ils se déplacent "avec telle contenance et modestie qu'on les puisse plutôt estimer anges qu'enfants"', Demouy, 'Les *pueri chori*', 138.

[60] There were six choirboys also, for example, at the Sainte-Chapelle (already in 1305, see Brenet, *Les musiciens de la Sainte-Chapelle*, 15); at Cambrai Cathedral (see Craig Wright, 'Performance Practices at the Cathedral of Cambrai, 1475–1550', *Musical Quarterly* 64 (1978), 310; at St Martin of Tours (see Yossy Maurey, *Medieval Music, Legend, and the Cult of St. Martin* (Cambridge: Cambridge University Press, 2014), 39; at the collegiate church of St Quentin (see Becker, 'The Maîtrise', 33); at Seville Cathedral (see Juan Ruiz Jiménez, *From Mozos de Coro towards* Seises: *Boys in the Musical Life of Seville Cathedral in the Fifteenth and Sixteenth Centuries*, in Boynton and Rice (eds.), *Young Singers*, 95); at Tournai Cathedral (see Barbara Haggh, 'Music, Liturgy and Ceremony in Brussels, 1350–1500', 2 vols., unpublished PhD dissertation, University of Illinois at Urbana-Champaign (1988), 160; at St Goedele, Brussels (ibid., 222); and in the Hofburg choir of Maximilian I in Vienna (see Martin Picker, 'The Habsburg Courts in the Netherlands and Austria, 1477–1530', in Iain Fenlon (ed.), *The Renaissance: From the 1470s to the End of the 16th Century* (Basingstoke and London: Macmillan, 1989), 234). Widespread maintenance of precisely this number of choirboys suggests that it possessed some symbolic and/or practical significance. John Harper points out to me that at Salisbury Cathedral four boys were needed in the presbytery at Mass and at least two in choir to sing the gradual verse; similar practicalities may have dictated numbers elsewhere.

precise location where, at Mass, they would attend on their redeemer's transubstantiated presence.[61]

Duties of the Choirboys

Beyond their perceived status, though, the radical advance in the boys' fortune raises questions concerning the extent, as well as importance, of their duties. How could such sums have been afforded, and what could the boys have been doing to merit their outlay?

It seems clear from the provision of and repairs to their books that their specifically assigned singing duties, following general practice, included many of the more elaborate items in the yearly round. A representative early example is the following record entered on folio 7r of the account for 1428/9:

Item: Paid for a song booklet for the choirboys containing the incipits and verses of the responsories for the entire year, 32s.[62]

Since boys, as the lowest in the ecclesiastical hierarchy, were typically responsible for the first responsory at matins on feasts of double or higher rank, the high copying cost for this book may be down to sheer bulk, there being, by the early sixteenth century, some sixty feasts annually of this standing.[63] The periodic recurrence of similar records could suggest a relatively high turnover of such books resulting from what was surely heavy usage, though the variety of sums involved may also indicate a number of discrete volumes addressed, perhaps, to different divisions of the church year or distinct parts of the repertory. At any rate, these later records add further specifics to the one already quoted.

---

[61] '... pour rapointier et redorer les vi. angeles devant le grant autel' (1412/13, f. 4r). It is clear from related records that these figures of angels were positioned on a series of columns around the choir: 'A Pierrequin du Molin pour avoir fait une ele nouvelle a ung des angeles est[ans] au tour du grant autel et pour le avoir paint et dore comme il appert en le kalends davril xxi s' (1460/1, f. 8v).

[62] Item paiet pour ung livret de cant pour les enfans de coeur contenant les komenchemens et verses des respons de toute lannee xxxii s. See the similar record quoted by Wright (*Music and Ceremony*, 181).

[63] See the comparative table of feasts compiled from surviving liturgical books in Jean-François Goudesenne and Marc Gil (eds.), *L'antiphonaire de la Paix de Princes chrétiens* (facsimile edition of a St Omer manuscript antiphonal of *c.*1550–1561), Publications of Medieval Music Manuscripts, 30 (Ottawa: Institute of Medieval Music, 2003), xliiii–v.

The first entry following is one of many recording the work on books undertaken over a long period by Vincent Breion, vicar, whose epitaph survives in the church and with whom we shall cross paths again. It is also informative both concerning the trouble taken over such books and its performance detail, to the effect that the responsories were clearly, following standard practice, delivered from the middle of the choir:

1443/4, f. 9r: Item: to the said Sire Vincent for several further parchment skins to make a book, written and with music, with the responsories serving at double [feasts] for the duration of the year, to place in the middle of the choir, 43s.

Item to the said Sire Vincent for having painted [presumably the initials of] the said book and for having been several times to Aire[-sur-la-Lys] to consult the individual who must notate and neatly write the said book by the decree of the chapter, 60s.[64]

1444/5, f. 4v: Item: for writing the new book of responsories and for entering the music, as is paid to Master Ghuy Le Maistre, priest, as appears in the bill, 8 l. 8s.[65]

Like Breion, Thomas Boucoud ('Le Becourt' or 'de Bouchout') was a priest employed over a long period as a scribe and bookbinder.[66] 'Legendes' refers to a lectionary including extracts from the lives of saints, appropriate entries of which were assigned, here as elsewhere, to be read aloud by the boys during the office of matins:

1451/2, f. 14v: To Master Thomas Le Becourt for having written a book in which are the 'legendes' and responsories for the choirboys, 5 l. 12s.[67]

Later records attest also to the likewise widespread tradition of the boys reading, in the chapter room at the office of prime, the daily lists of martyrs from the martyrology:

1507/8, f. 30r: To Valletin de Le Clitte for having rebound the choirboys' martyrology, paid as appears in the receipt, 11s. 9d.

---

[64] Item audit Sire Vincent pour pluseurs aultres peaulx de parchemin pour faire ung livre escript et notte des respons servans a doubles au long delan pour mettre au moillon [centre] du coeur xliii s
     Item audit Sire Vincent pour avoir minie ledit livre et avoir este par pluseurs fois a Aere [Aire-sur-la-Lys] pour soliciter cellui qui doit notter et escripre au net ledit livre par lordonnance de capital paie lx s

[65] Item pour escripre le nouvel livre de respons et le avoir note ainsi quil est payet a Sire Ghuy Le Maistre prestre comme apparoit par cedule viii l viii s

[66] For a complete survey of Boucoud's work in copying and rebinding the books of St Omer see Marc Gil and Ludovic Nys, *Saint-Omer gothique* (Valenciennes: Presses Universitaires de Valenciennes, 2004), 378–9.

[67] A Sire Thomas de Becourt pour avoit escript ung livre ou quel sont les legendes et respons pour les enfans de coeur v lb xii s

1515/16, f. 29v: To Sire Andrieu Boulengier for having rebound and repaired the boys' martyrology.

1520/1, f. 28v: To Jan Alixandre for having rebound the boys' book of collects and martyrology, paid by Sire Georges Thibault in total 60s.[68]

The boys would have been required, as was standard, to intone lessons ('lichons/ lychons', see below) at matins on feasts of nine lessons or of higher rank. Since lessons, like responsories, were typically delivered by clerics in ascending order of dignity this usually meant the first lesson:

1456/7, f. 13v: Item, to Sire Thomas de Bouchout for having ... rebound and glued the book of responsories and lessons of the choirboys, and a book containing the vigils, and several others, the same thing, in total 60s.[69]

Subsequent records include one referring to the melismatic verses for graduals and alleluias at Mass on the many feast days of semi-double or higher rank that, as elsewhere, were to be sung by the boys from the choir screen (pulpitum):[70]

1471/2, f. 15r: To Messires Eustache Maistresse and Gille Guerard, for having corrected and put in columns the new book containing the graduals and alleluia[s] that are sung at double and semi-double [feasts] on the screen, 6s.

1493/4, f. 37v: Item, to Sire Andrieu Boullenguier for those quires of the book that he made for lessons and responsories for the choirboys 10s.

1494/5, f. 31v: Item, for a quire of paper provided to the older Tingry for writing the lessons of the boys and the responsories, because they did not have a book and a new one was being made, for this 18d.

Fol. 32v: Item, pay to Sire Andrieu Boullenguier for the advance for a book in parchment for the choirboys, in which are contained all the responsories, antiphons and readings for the year, which Master Walran Peppin had had made, 36s.

1503/4, f. 32r: Item, to [blank] for having bound the book of responsories, and for the clasps to put on the book here present, Sire Jehan Scacthre, 17s. 6d.[71]

---

[68] Item a Vallentin de Le Clitte pour avoir reloyet le matrologe pour les enffans de coeur payet comme appert par quittance xi s ix d

A Sire Andrieu Boulengier pour avoir reliet et repointiet le matroloige des enfans ...

A Jan Alixandre pour avoir reliet le collectaire et mathrologe des enfans paiet par Sire Georges Thibault pour tout lx s

[69] Item a Sire Thomas de Bouchout pour avoir ... reliiet et cole le livre as respons et lichons des enfans de coeur et ung livre contenant les vegilles / et pluiseurs aultres mesmes choses pour tout lx s

[70] For the same practice as conducted, for instance, at Notre-Dame of Paris see Wright, *Music and Ceremony*, 181.

[71] A Messires Extasse [Eustache] Maistresse et Gille Guerard / pour avoir corrigie et collonne le nouvel livre contenant les graduales et alleluia que len chante aux doubles et demi doubles sur le dossal vi s

Polyphony in Public and Private Devotions

The role of boys in the solo sections of chants was clearly of long tradition by the time of the documents quoted above. Wright quotes Johannes Beleth writing of the boys of Notre-Dame of Paris singing such items already in the twelfth century, and the practice is widely attested.[72] But as far as the fifteenth and early sixteenth centuries are concerned, there can be little doubt that, as more generally, the increasing importance of the choirboys was closely linked with concurrent enhancement in the importance and scope of polyphony. The accounts reveal the instigation of ever-increasing outlets for their polyphonic skills, both in public and, especially, in privately founded observances.

As elsewhere, knowledge of polyphonic specifics at Mass and office is obscured by the nature of the records, which detail only items calling for specific payment. Even so, the nature of both personnel and copying records give, as we shall see, some indication of their likely nature and extent. Direct detail on devotions (institutional and private) additional to the yearly round also suggests inferences concerning more regular provision.

As might be expected, prominent among these are the regular Marian observances, which in St Omer meant most obviously the singing of the *Salve regina* before Notre Dame des Miracles in the chapel of Notre-Dame on the marketplace (Notre-Dame sur le marchiet), on Saturdays and on the vigils of all the six Marian feasts of Conception, Nativity, Annunciation, Visitation, Purification and Assumption. Precisely when this began is

---

Item, a Sire Andrieu Boullenguier en tant mains du livre quil fait a lischons et respons pour les enffans de coeur x s

Item pour une main de pappier baillie au grant Tingry pour escripre les lychons des enffans et les respons[.] A cause quils navoient point de livre et que lon en faisoit ung nouvel pour ce xviii d

Item paye a Sire Andrieu Boullenguier pour le prepaye dung livre en parchemin pour les enffans de coeur / ou quel sont contenus tous les respons ant[iphons] et lectures durant lan lequel Maistre Walran Peppin avoit fait faire xxxvi s

Item a [blank] pour avoir relyet le livre aux respons et pour les cleux a mettre sur ledit livre present Sire Jehan Scacthre xvii s vi d

[72] Beleth names the versicle concluding each grouping of psalms/antiphons at matins, the *Benedicamus domino* at lauds, vespers and compline, and the gradual at Mass on particular feast days (see *Music and Ceremony*, 166). For such choirboy duties at Cambrai in the fifteenth and early sixteenth centuries, including singing of the gradual, see Wright, 'Performance Practices', 301 and *passim*. For the similar patterns of practice according to the Use of Salisbury see *Sarum Customary Online*, www.sarumcustomary.org.uk/, accessed 21 June 2019.

unknown, but the tradition emerges clearly with the advent of regular payment sections in the fabric accounts:

To the master of singing and the choirboys, by whom my lords have arranged to have recited, each year at the expense of the said fabric, every Saturday of the year and at every vigil of Our Lady, the *Salve* at the chapelle sur le marchiet, 50s. current; here for this year by receipt, 50s.

To Sire Jehan Caignart for playing the organ at the said *Salve*, 24s.[73]

Performance of the antiphon itself in polyphony is strongly suggested by the annual payments concerning the ritual, and is likely to have been the purpose of 'the book from which the choirboys sing the *Salve*' ('le livre ou les enfans de coeur chantent le Salve') for the rebinding of which Thomas de Boucoud was paid in 1463/4.[74] The icon itself was a major revenue source for the chapter: annual accounts of its 'oblations' show that donations it stimulated regularly dwarfed all other such income strands, whether from offerings to the cross on Good Friday, or to the patron's relics on his feast days of 'Saint Omer en fleurs' (celebrating the return to the church of the saint's relics, on 8 June) and his *depositio* (the anniversary of his death, on 9 September).[75]

The incentive to enhance the ritual surrounding the *Salve* was therefore considerable, something clearly not lost on those canons who endowed it with specific augmentations. Thus in the late 1450s Johannes Dessinges donated three sous per year towards the upkeep of the *Salve* from the rental of a house, while from 1462 Loys Prerlamps assigned rent from land amounting to sixteen sous per annum for six years to the same service.[76] It seems reasonable to surmise that donations to the *Salve* were especially attractive to clergy who lacked the financial wherewithal for a personally

---

[73] Au maistre de chant et aux enfans de cuer / ausquels messeigneurs ont ordonne avoir chaqun an sur ledit fabricque pour dire chaqun samedi de lan et chaqune veille de nostre dame le Salve a le chappelle sur le marchiet l s courant / yci pour ceste annee par quittances l s; A Sire Jeh[an] Caignart pour jouer des orgues audit Salve xxiiii s (1459/60 f. 8r)

[74] A Sire Thomas de Boucoud pour avoir reloyet le livre la [sic] les enfans de coeur chantent le Salve et avoir mis nouvelles aisselles iiii s (1463/4, f. 49v)

[75] For the patronal feast days see Monique Ducrocq, *La Cathédrale de Saint-Omer: son symbolisme, ses grands dignitaires* (Saint-Omer: Association Cathédrale de Saint-Omer, 1997), 21.

[76] 1459/60, f. 2r: 'Des anniversaires de ladicte eglise par la main du receveur diceulx pour iii s parisis de rente heritable chaqun an apaier au jour St Michiel que Johannes Dessinges canoine de ladite eglise a nouvellement donnes pour lentretenement du Salve que len dist chaqun samedi a le cappelle sur le marchiet . . .' For Prerlamps's donation see for example the record for the fifth annual payment in 1466/7, f. 3r, which notes that it was assigned: 'pour lentretenement dudit Salve baillie a louaige par lespace de vi ans . . .'

founded devotion or chantry. An entry in the chapter acts for 8 December 1481 gives an insight into the strategy whereby a private individual could in one fell swoop impose his proxy presence on a public space such as this in forms both permanent and recurring. On that day we are told how Pierre de Le Nesse has endowed a 'tabula' (presumably some kind of reredos) for the high altar of Notre-Dame sur le marchiet

... very beautiful and precious, in return for which gift he asked the lords that for his lifetime on every Saturday after the salutation of the Blessed Mary [i.e. *Salve*] there should be sung by the master and boys of the choir and the chaplain of the aforesaid chapel one antiphon verse and collect of the Holy Spirit. And after his death there should be read *De profundis* with short prayers and the collect for the faithful.[77]

The account goes on to record the canons' response:

In consideration of the same Pierre's zeal and pious devotion which he has visibly demonstrated to the same chapel, on account of the good deeds which he has previously done and will do in the future, the lords graciously accorded him this and instructed me, Jean Derviller his scribe, to make out a document for him concerning this matter.[78]

The major change in the late fifteenth and early sixteenth centuries was the foundation of devotions on behalf of the souls of canons, with or without polyphony, that sometimes, as in the above case, stipulate the boys. The scale of these frequently elaborate and expensive rituals at St Omer is clear enough from the complexity and sheer bulk of its fabric accounts, in which, for every fiscal year, outgoings on the more involved foundations each receive a dedicated section.

At the more modest end of the spectrum stand such foundations as the following, according to which a certain Simon Acthe requested the performance by the choirboys, in a chapel of his choice (which in practice would usually be the burial chapel), of an annual requiem Mass for his soul. As was typical in such directives, the service was to be paid for by rents from property:

[77] ... multam venustam et preciosam pro quo dono requisivit dominos ut sua vita comite singulis diebus sabbati post salutationem Beate Marie canetur per magistrum et pueros chori et capellanum capelle predicte una anth[iphona] versa et collecta de sancto spiritu et post mortem eius legatur de profundis cum parvis precibus et collecta fidelium[.]

[78] Domini considerante zelum et piam devotionem ipsius Petri quam gerere visus est eidem capelle propter bona huiusmodi quas antea fecit et facturus est eidem benigne accordarunt et iusserunt michi Johanni Derviler suo scribe eidem suas litteras super hoc conficere. (II. G. 355, f. 25v)

1458/9, f. 1r: From Simon Acthe for two measures of land lying in the said place of Lannoy of which the borders are declared as above, each year at the said term of St Michael, four sous and eleven deniers in money of Paris / which the said deceased gave to the choirboys in order than they be obliged each year to say and sing the day after Trinity in the chapel of St Mary of Egypt a requiem mass for his soul. And for this here the said four sous and eleven deniers in money of Paris which are worth 5s. 6d.[79]

Determining whether such payments for singing 'à note' were for chant or polyphony is typically down to interpretation of the forces and costs involved. No such doubt, for example, pertains to the foundations of the canon and later dean Nicolas Rembert, whose grandiose ritual edifices will be addressed in Chapter 6. Striking in their lavishness, Rembert's foundations were, however, far from alone in kind.

Starting in the mid-1450s, rents assembled from a wide range of lands by the deceased former cantor of St Omer Pierre de Le Tour began to be applied to candles to burn in various chapels, and 'aux enfans de coeur adfin que cascun an le maistre desdits enfans defist ou fist dire une messe de requiem lendemain du jour de le Trinite en le capelle Sainte Marie dEgipte'. As frequently in such cases, the terminology from year to year is fluid, adding to the difficulty of determining whether the observance involved improvised or composed polyphony in addition to chant. But the analogous stipulation for 1501/2, for example, instructing 'chanter une messe de requiem a notte par les enffans de coeur par chacun an le lendemain de la Trinite', would seem clearly to imply composed polyphony. Presumably that had been the case from the beginning; or perhaps the nature of the fulfilment of such an observance could mutate over time in response to changing conventions.[80]

A codicil to the testament of Guillaume Fasselin (defined as 'bourgois de la ville de Saintomer') endows rents to maintain:

... on the day of St Sebastian in the month of January a Mass with music and discant by the choirboys, with deacon and sub-deacon and organ, the which should be sung directly after matins in the chapel of St Sebastian. And the large bells should be sounded. And the next day during the lives of myself and my wife, a

---

[79] De Simon Acthe pour deux mesures de terre gisant audit lieu de Lannoy dont les abouts sont declairies comme dessus chaqun an audit terme St Michiel iiii s xi d parisis / que ledit feu donna aux enfans de cuer moyennant quils sont tenus chaqun an de faire dire et chanter a note lendemain de le Trinite en le cappelle Ste Marie // dEgypte une messe de Requien [sic] pour lame de lui[.] Et pour ce cy lesdits iiii s xi d par[isis] qui valent v s vi d

[80] Accounts of 1454/5, f. 3r and 1501/2, f. 1v.

Mass of the Holy Spirit. And after the death of one of us, in place of the said Mass the requiem, with deacon and sub-deacon, sung by the choirboys.[81]

Entries in the fabric accounts confirm that the Mass for the Holy Spirit was likewise to be performed 'a notte', and involved a deacon, subdeacon and choirboys alongside the officiating priest.[82] Whether this latter Mass, like its companion, involved 'descant' as well as chant must ultimately remain an open question, but given the paired nature of the foundation the likelihood must be that it did.

Boys are specified also for Masses founded by Thierry de Vitry, donor in 1475/6 (as we shall see in Chapter 5) of the bell 'of the tone of la' in the church's new peal of bells, besides being secretary to Maximilian and Mary of Burgundy, cantor and canon of St Pierre, Aire-sur-La-Lys and, from 1460, canon of St Omer. Although interred, following his demise in 1478, at St Bertin, where he also founded Masses,[83] de Vitry also founded three sung Masses per week at St Omer to be performed by 'priest, deacon, subdeacon and choirboys'.[84]

Elsewhere, the boys received regular distributions for patronal feast days and for the inductions of new canons, paid for by the arriving canons themselves. Entries of important individuals also offered regular showcases for the boys' skills, as when, on the morning of 5 November 1493, Anthonius de Croy, Bishop of Thérouanne, made his first procession into the church. This culminated, during his prayer on bended knee at the high altar, with a sung responsory, followed by a versicle performed by two of the boys, after which the bishop himself sang the collect.[85]

---

[81] ... le jour Saint Sebastien ou mois de janvier une messe a notte et descant par les enffans de coeur a diacre a soubs diacre et a orghes laquelle doit chanter incontinent apres matines en le cappelle de mondit seigneur Saint Sebastien[.] Et se doit estre sonne des grosses clocques[.] Et le lendemain durant les vyes de my et de me femme une messe de Saint Esprit[.] Et apres le trespas de lun de nous deux ou lieu de ladite messe de Requien [sic] a diacre et soubs diacre cantee par les enffans de coeur ... (Dainville (Arras), Archives Départementales du Pas-de-Calais, Justice échevinale de Saint-Omer, MS 15 B1, f. 107r–v)

[82] See for example 1475/6, f. 3v; 1478/9, f. 20v.

[83] On de Vitry's posts, and his burial and four weekly Masses (augmented just before his death to seven) at St Bertin, see Daniel Haigneré and Oscar Bled, *Les Chartes de Saint-Bertin, d'après le grand cartulaire de Dom Charles-Joseph Dewitte*, 4 vols., vol. 4 (Saint-Omer: Société des antiquaires de la Morinie, 1899), 22 and 316.

[84] ... pour trois messes celebrees pour Maistre Therry [sic] de Vitry chanoine pour chacune messe avoir prebstre ii s parisis / aux dyacre et soubsdyacre chacun xxi d parisis / aux enffans de coeur pour avoir cante lesdits messes pour chacune viii sc courant aux clocqueman et aydes viii sc p / au par[?] coustre pour avoir ayde a dire lesdits messes xii d par jour xlvi s (1478/9, f. 19v)

[85] II. G. 355, f. 99r: '... et Ibidem flexis genibus oravit resp[onsoriam] cantato / et finito versiculo per duos pueros chori cantato / prelibatus dominus episcopus collectam perfecit cantando /'

Choirboys and Ritual Drama

The great festivals of Christmas and Easter gave vent to what was surely in the late Middle Ages, as today, the natural propensity of young minds for dramatic fantasy. A partially surviving St Omer ordinal from the late thirteenth century provides vivid details concerning the various roles taken by boys in unfurling the Easter Day drama of the Resurrection.[86] Following the recitation of psalms and prayers around midnight, a procession, headed by crosses, censers and candles, led to the tomb of St Omer, where three or four of the 'older scholars', kitted out as soldiers and lying as if asleep, were stationed in the roles of the soldiers posted around Christ's tomb.[87] Clearly the tomb itself was adorned for the occasion: successive entries in the church inventory of 1557 describe narratively appropriate hangings:

A hanging of red velvet with the image of the Resurrection, which is used to place before the altar table and at the tomb at Easter.

Item, another similar hanging and of the same size as the one above with a depiction of the three Marys coming to the sepulchre, used at the said tomb on the said days of Easter.[88]

Three or four of the older priests picked up the cross that had been 'buried' on Good Friday beneath a cloth on the tomb and, beginning with the responsory 'Christus resurgens', carried it in procession to the altar of St John, and thence on to the choir where the clergy sang matins. Only after the third responsory were the 'sleeping' soldiers finally disturbed, when two further boys, dressed as angels, positioned themselves at each end of the tomb and three others, wearing amices over their heads to signify veils and carrying little bowls or jars in reference to their roles as the three Marys come

---

[86] Bibliothèque de l'Agglomération de Saint-Omer MS 909. Discussed in detail and cited *in extenso* in Louis Deschamps de Pas, 'Les cérémonies religieuses dans la collégiale de Saint-Omer au XIIIᵉ siècle: Examen d'un rituel manuscrit de cette église', *Mémoires de la Société des antiquaires de la Morinie* 20 (1886–7), 99–213.

[87] '. . . tres vel quatuor pueri de majoribus scolarum armati ad modum militum qui jacentes ibi fingunt se dormire' (quoted in Deschamps de Pas, 'Les cérémonies', 176). It is possible that these soldiers were drawn from the ranks of the escotiers, a body of poor clerks usually fixed in number at fourteen, and housed, nourished and taught by the chapter. Admission required a minimum age of eighteen and the ability to read and write (for further detail see pp. 66–7). See M. Vallet de Viriville, 'Essai sur les archives historiques du chapitre de l'église cathédrale de Notre-Dame à St-Omer: Catalogue des archives de Notre-Dame: première série- Liaisses', in *Mémoires de la Société des antiquaires de la Morinie* 6 (1841–1843), XXXII.

[88] Ung drap de velours rouge, avec l'imaige de la Résurrection, lequel sert à mettre devant la table d'aultel et au tombeau es festes de Pasques.
Item, ung aultre drap pareil et de mesme grandeur comme cesluy dessus à portraicture des trois Maries venant au sépulchre, servant audict tombeau esdits jours de Pasques. (II. G. 2787; édition by Deschamps de Pas: 'Inventaire', 87.)

to anoint Christ's body, arrived to enact the little drama of the *Quem queritis*. Standing at a distance from the tomb, they began the proceedings by singing 'Who [will] remove the stone for us?' ('Quis removet nobis lapidem'), to which the angels responded 'Whom do you seek in the sepulchre, Christian?' ('Quem queritis in sepulcro, o Xristicole'). Following the realisation that Christ has risen, the episode concluded with the approach of the Marys to the altar to announce 'Alleluia. He speaks the truth: the Lord is risen' ('Alleluia, verum dicit, resurrexit Dominus'). The singing by one of the angels of the verset 'Verum dicit Maria' cued the dean or cantor to intone the *Te Deum*, whereupon the procession (accompanied by the 'Marys' and 'angels') re-entered the choir to the joyful pealing of the full complement of bells.[89]

Sadly the opening gatherings of the ordinal which supplies knowledge of these events are lost, depriving us of any detail of dramatic representations in the Advent and Christmas period. But it is clear from sundry payments in the fabric accounts that, as more general practice would in any case lead us to expect, the boys were required to don their angel wings to mark the key events also of that season:

1407/8 (rotulus): Item, to remake and repaint the wings and the caskets which serve for the choirboys on Easter Day at matins for the resurrection, etc. 7s.[90]

1425/6, f. 6v: Item, to Wauter Pinque, painter, for completely remaking and repainting the four wings serving for the choirboys at matins on Christmas and Easter days and for remaking and regilding the three caskets of the three Marys which are used on Easter Day at matins, for everything, 36s.[91]

1442/3, f. 6r: Item, to Colard de Sauty, painter, for having properly repaired the wings of the angels belonging to the boys, etc. And also for cleaning the angels and the crucifix of the high altar ...[92]

1456/7, 13r: Item, to Gamot, painter, for having bonded and re-gilded the three boxes that the three Marys carry on Easter Day at the Resurrection, 3s.[93]

1469/70, 14v: To [Pierre Pol, painter] for having re-gilded the three goblets/vases that the three Marys carry on Easter Day, 12s.[94]

---

[89] Deschamps de Pas, 'Les cérémonies', 120–4; document transcription on 175–80.

[90] Item pour refaire et repaindre les eles et les boystes qui servent a[u]s enfans de cheur le jour de Pasques a matines pour le resurexion etc. vii s

[91] Item a Wauter Pinque paintre pour refaire et repaindre tout de nouvel les iiii elles que servent aux enfans du coeur aux matines du jour de Noel et Pasques et pour refaire et redorer les iii boistes des trois maryes qui servent au jour de Pasques aux matines pour tout xxxvi s

[92] 'Item A Colard de Sauty paintre pour avoir remis apoint les eles des angles appartenant aux enfans etc. Et aussy pour nettoyer les angles et le crucefix du grant autel ...'. The latter part of this record refers to cleaning the figures of angels (already mentioned) surrounding the choir.

[93] Item a Gamot paintre pour avoir recole et redore les trois boistes que portent les trois maries le jour de Pasques a la resurection 3s

[94] A lui [Pierre Pol paintre] pour avoir redore les iii couppes que portent les iii maries le jour de Pasques 12s

The angel wings and caskets for the Marys appear also in the church inventory of 1557:

Four wooden wings for the choirboys acting as the angels on the days of Easter and Christmas

Three painted wooden boxes for the three Marys[95]

Wearing of wings, with the same angelic associations, was stipulated when the boys sang the first responsory at Christmas Day matins, as this record from 1494/5 attests:

Item: for having remade the leather straps that secure the wings of the choirboys on Christmas Day when they sing the responsory at matins, 8s.[96]

Lack of the Advent and Christmas sections of the ordinal is at least partially compensated by a record surviving elsewhere concerning a particular dramatic function fulfilled by the boys in Advent. A widespread tradition involved performance of the 'Missus', a celebration of Mass so-called due to the commencement of the day's gospel reading with the words 'The angel Gabriel was sent' ('Missus est Gabriel angelus'). At St Omer such a per-formance was (apparently) instigated in 1535 by the terms of the will of the cantor and former choirboy Robert le Fevre (or Fabri).[97] Fabri's provision is dubbed (following common parlance) an *Aurea missa*, and involves the dramatic representation of the Annunciation staged, as elsewhere, as part of Mass on the Ember Wednesday after the third Sunday in Advent.[98] The

---

[95] Quatre aisles de bois pour les enfans de coeur faisans les anges, es jours de Pasques et de Noël; Trois boittes de bois painct pour les trois Maries (See Deschamps de Pas: 'Inventaire', 86)

[96] Fol. 32v: Item pour avoir refait les cuirs qui portent les helles des enffans de coeur au jour de nowel quant ils chantent le re[spond] a matines viii s

[97] Fabri's executors' account survives as II. G. 482. Deschamps de Pas (Les cérémonies', 208) notes that Fabri's executors presented their request to the chapter for the fulfilment of these terms on 12 October 1543. No explanation is given for the long delay following Fabri's death in 1535; nor does Deschamps de Pas specify his source for this request, which does not appear in the relevant volume of the chapter acts.

[98] Edition in Karl Young, *The Drama of the Medieval Church*, 2 vols. (Oxford: Clarendon Press, 1933), vol. 2, 482–3, after Deschamps de Pas, 'Les cérémonies', 209–10. Young also reprints, drawing on Deschamps de Pas, a list of accoutrements that were used in the performance and that are itemised in the earliest surviving complete inventory of the church's ornaments and reliquaries of 1557. A number of these, originally stored in a leather coffer, are described as having been 'armoiez des armes dudit Sr Fabri'. The church inventory survives in the archives as MS II. G. 2787. See the complete edition published by Deschamps de Pas, 'Inventaire', 78–98. On the *Aurea missa* more generally see Young, *The Drama*, vol. 2, 246, and Anne Walters Robertson, 'Remembering the Annunciation in Medieval Polyphony', *Speculum* 70 (1995), 284–6. See also the discussion of the *Aurea Missa* and its performance in various churches of Bruges in Reinhard Strohm, *Music in Medieval Bruges* (2nd, rev. ed., Oxford: Clarendon Press, 1990), 46, 52–3 and 158.

foundation by Fabri, with whom we shall become better acquainted in the next chapter, comes rather late in the history of this popular Mass-cum-drama: Karl Young notes its existence in nearby Tournai already in 1231. Deschamps de Pas points out the close resemblance of the St Omer drama to what would appear to be its direct precursor in Tournai, right down to the presence of a 'dove' bathed in light which, at the moment the 'Virgin' utters her 'Behold the handmaid of the Lord' ('Ecce ancilla Domini'), descends to the oratory surrounding the figure of the Virgin. While mention of this symbol of the descending Holy Spirit is lacking in Fabri's stipulations, its appearance in the church inventory of 1557 strongly suggests its involvement also in the enactments at St Omer.[99] As in other manifestations of the tradition, and surely in pointed reminiscence of Fabri's own childhood experience in the church, two boys, singing from opposite sides of the altar, are specified in the roles of the archangel Gabriel ('dressed as an angel as one does on the day of the Resurrection'; 'acoustré en angele comme on faict le jour de la resurrection') and the Virgin ('dressed as a maiden'; 'accoustré [sic] comme une pucelle'). The pertinent section of the inventory lists further accoutrements aimed at enhancing verisimilitude. Its first entry reveals that, like its probable model in Tournai, the St Omer drama positioned its protagonists beneath two tabernacles on opposing sides of the altar, in this case each adorned with Fabri's arms.[100] Costumes added further to the scene's visual eloquence:

Two short sleeves ending in a double point and worked also with gold thread that are the accessories for the Virgin Mary.

An outfit made of hair, a gilded wooden crown with a little cross at the front, a sceptre of the same kind, for the angel.[101]

Fabri's foundation specifies the passage of the drama as follows:

As far as the mystery of the Mass directly after matins is concerned, it will be done, if it pleases my lords, in the following manner:

First, the introit of the Mass, that is to say *Rorate. Gloria in excelsis Deo.* The epistle at the large candelabra in the choir; the gradual by two vicars; and the

---

[99] Deschamps de Pas, 'Les cérémonies', 209–10. See also the listing in Deschamps de Pas, 'Inventaire', 96: 'Ung colomb de bois revestu de damas blancq'.

[100] Huict pendans de cortines et deux voies de toille blanche servans aux deux tabernacles, armoiez des armes dudit Sr Fabri; Huict coupettes de bois doré pour mettre aux pilliers des deux tabernacles (Deschamps de Pas, 'Inventaire', 96; Young, *The Drama*, vol. 2, 483).

[101] Deux mancherons frinchez et ouvrez aussy de fil d'or qui sont les accoustrementz de la Vierge Marie. Ung trousseau de cheveulx, une couronne de bois doré avec une petite croix par devant, ung sceptre de mesme pour l'ange. (Ibid.)

Alleluia, Angelus Domini [gospel] shall be sung by three canons before the eagle [from which the gospel is always read]. The prosa *Hec clara die*, with *Ave Maria* repeating, at the sound of the organ.[102]

For the organist for playing the organ, 11s.; for his assistant 12d.

As far as the gospel of the Mass is concerned, the deacon assisting at the said Mass will commence the gospel *Missus est* as is sung daily, that is before the candelabrum in the choir where one sings the gospel, up to the point of the angelic salutation *Ave gratia*. At that point a little choirboy vested in an alb and dressed as an angel as one does on the day of the resurrection, instructed by the master of song to do this, is to sing with fine tone and at the same time in a natural manner (?) all that follows in the said gospel by the said angel, and this at the left-hand side of the high altar and below. Likewise also to the right side, one of the said children representing the Virgin Mary, dressed as a maiden, as virtuously as can be done, instructed as said above, will sing thoroughly devoutly as the gospel requires.

After the gospel, the Credo. The remainder in accordance with the day.[103]

Embedded in the standard progress of Mass for the day after matins, the dramatic proceedings commenced in the gospel reading at the point of the angelic salutation 'Ave gratia'. With these words the boy to the left of the altar took up the story in the voice of the archangel Gabriel, his counterpart to the right articulating Mary's compliant rejoinder. The two boy actors playing the angel and Virgin were (respectively) instructed by the master 'to sing with fine tone and in a natural manner[?]' ('chanter a

---

[102] John Harper points out to me that the line 'Ave Maria gratia dei plena per secula' is sung threefold during this item on the Feast of the Purification; a similar practice is clearly indicated here, albeit in this instance performed on the organ.

[103] Quant au faict du mystere de la messe justaument après matines se fera, si plaist a MM. [messeigneurs] en la manière que sensieult.

Primes. Lintroite de la messe ass' *Rorate. Gloria in excelsis Deo.* Lepistre au grand candelabre du coeur; le gradual par deux vicaires, et le *Alleluia, Angelus Domini* par trois chanoines, se chanteront au coeur devant laigle. Prosa *Hec clara dies*, repetendo *Ave Maria*, au son des orgues.

A lorganiste pour jouer des orgues 11^s; a son assistant xii^d.

Quant au faict de lévangille de la messe, le dyacre assistant de la dicte messe commencera lévangille *Missus est* en la manière que lon chante journelement estant devant le chandelabre ou on chante les evangilles au coeur, jusques au point de la salutation angelique *Ave gratia*. Lors ung petit enffant de coeur revestu dune aulbe, acoustré en angele comme on faict le jour de la resurrection, instruict du maistre de chant a ce faire et chanter a bon ton et a loisir parellement a tout ce que sensuit en ladite evangille par ledict angele, et ce au costé senestre du grand autel en bas. Pareillement aussi au costé dextre, ung desdictz enffans representant la vierge Marie, estant accoustré comme une pucelle, le plus honestement que faire se porra, instruict comme dessus est dict chantera bien dévotement comme levangille requiert.

Après levangille, *Credo.* Le reste selon le jour. (See Deschamps de Pas, 'Les cérémonies', 209–10 and Young, *The Drama*, vol. 2, 482–3.)

bon ton et a loisir') and 'with proper devotion' ('bien dévotement'), and were required, in a poignant turn of the wheel, to 'pray to God for the soul of the said founder' ('prier Dieu pour lame dudict fondateur'), their eminent choirboy predecessor.[104] Following the end of the gospel, the Mass proceeded according to the standard liturgy of the day.

The widespread currency of stipulations for boys to sing from high places was surely also motivated by desire to draw on their metaphorical status as angels, as when, in the Use of Salisbury, the boys, clad in white, on Christmas Day sang the words of the angels to the shepherds in the first verse of the first responsory from the triforium above the high altar.[105] In further angelic personifications, at St Omer the gospel 'Angelus Domini apparuit' on the Feast of Holy Innocents was instructed to be read by the deacon 'or by a boy if preferred' ('vel si placet a puero'), while the responsory 'Angeli eorum, Allelluia, Alleluia' was to be sung by two boys.[106] On the return procession in Saint-Omer to the collégiale on Palm Sunday the boys, heading the procession, were to climb to the top of the town gate, which was closed to those following them, to sing 'at the top of their voices' the hymn *Gloria laus*, with the choir replying in normal vocal delivery following each verse. On inclement days, which resulted in the procession being confined to the town, other lofty settings served the same purpose: on rainy days the boys sang the hymn instead from the house above the gate of the canons, while weather severe enough to keep the observance within the limits of the church saw them positioned on the 'old tower or granary' above the cloister.[107]

A further instance of boys assuming female roles occurred on the Feast of All Saints (1 November). On this one day, in contrast to the usual hierarchy on feasts of nine lessons according to which a boy, representing the lowest rank, would perform the first antiphon, lesson and responsory, boys were instead assigned the eighth grouping. The reason for this reversal can be found in the procession of saintly cohorts addressed in the

---

[104] See Young, ibid.

[105] *Sarum Customary Online* (www.sarumcustomary.org.uk/), accessed 21 June, 2019; see *The New Customary, from Oxford Corpus Christi College, MS 44 in Frere's Order*, 30.

[106] Deschamps de Pas, 'Les cérémonies', 145–6.

[107] See the description in Deschamps de Pas, 'Les cérémonies', 111–12; original texts on 158–9. The first (good weather) stipulation reads: ' the gate of the town is shut against the procession. Then the boys who are above the said gate sing at the top of their voices [in volume and/or pitch] *Gloria laus* with its verses and after each verse the choir takes up, in a moderate voice [in volume and/or pitch], *Gloria laus*.' ('portam ville ... clauditur contra processionem. Tunc pueri qui sunt supra predictam portam cantant quanto altius possunt "Gloria laus" cum suis versibus et post quemlibet versum, resumit chorus mediocri voce "Gloria laus".')

successive matins lessons, with the eighth, in honour of virgins, finding its appropriate expression by boys with unbroken voices. While the lesson was intoned by a single boy, the antiphon and responsory were sung by his five confrères representing the five wise virgins, attired as girls and carrying lighted lamps.[108] That this particular case of role-playing may not always have elicited the most serious response from lively young boys is suggested by the note in the ordinal to the effect that 'if one [of them], Heaven forfend, should wittingly break one, as sometimes happens, he will be summarily reprimanded by the cantor or the master of the boys and removed from the choir'.[109]

Details scattered across the accounts provide evidence of sundry other assignments to the boys of one kind or another. While some of these, like that on All Saints' Day, were of wide currency, others expanded on more local venerations and traditions. Very much in the latter category was the celebration on 8 June of the translation of St Omer, or 'Saint Omer en fleurs'. The feast marks the translation back to the church by St Folquin, Bishop of Thérouanne, of the patron's relics, stolen – so the story goes – in 843 by Hugues, Abbot of both St Bertin and St Quentin. Reaching no further than the nearby village of Lisbourg and finding the relics – in true saintly fashion – to be immovable, the thieves had hidden them under a pile of manure, where their presence was miraculously revealed to St Folquin and his followers by a spread of flowers.[110]

The response to this was clearly some kind of annual representation of the saint lying in his tomb. Perhaps, as Deschamps de Pas surmises, this entailed a mannequin with sculpted and painted head and hands, covered with a painted fabric; alternatively, though, the records he cites from the fabric accounts might refer to an actual depiction in flowers. While the

---

[108] The same pattern obtained generally, as for example in the Use of Salisbury, in which a single boy was likewise to read the eighth lesson, with five boys singing the corresponding responsory (see *The Sarum Customary* online (www.sarumcustomary.org.uk/).

[109] The meaning of the first part of this instruction is worth emphasising in English: 'And note that the eighth antiphon at nocturns, the eighth lesson and eighth responsory are sung by the schoolboys whose voices have not broken, and while the eighth responsory is sung, they should appear as girls and hold lighted lamps.' ('Et nota quod octava A, ad nocturnos, octava lectio et octavum R:, dicuntur a scolaribus qui non mutaverunt vocem, et dum cantant viii R:, parentur ad modum puellarum et teneant lampades accensas et si quod absit quis quam scienter fregerit sicut aliquando contigit, a domino cantore vel magistro statim corrigatur et a choro expellatur.') See Deschamps de Pas, 'Les cérémonies', 142 (discussion) and 203 (transcription). Deschamps de Pas quotes a payment from the fabric account of 1529/30 (an account now apparently lost) for the repair of precisely these lamps: 'Pour avoir reffait les lampes que les enffans portent au respons des vierges le jour de Toussaint iii s.'

[110] See Deschamps de Pas, 'Les cérémonies', 136–8.

payment (from 1386/7) 'pro pictura capitis et manuum Beati Audomari jacentis in floribus' might indeed be read as 'for a painting of the head and hands of St Omer lying in flowers', it might also refer to 'a depiction in flowers of the head and hands of a recumbent St Omer'. Similarly the 1452/3 payment to 'David [(de) Sautil/Saulty/Sauti] the painter for having repainted the sheet on which one makes Saint Aumer in flowers', the 1467/8 payment 'to Pierre Pol for the fabric and for the painting of the template on which to make the St Omer in flowers', and the 1510/11 commission 'to Salmon Basin, painter, for having painted a new cloth to make the St Omer in flowers' could simply refer to a pattern over which depictive flowers were to be arranged. More directly suggestive is the payment, assigned to 1477/8, 'for six women for three days who were picking the flowers to make the image of our Lord St Aumer'.[111]

Whatever their eventual configuration, collecting of flowers for this joyful day in the calendar was clearly a task also of the boys, as is evident from the payment in the fabric account for 1456/7 for a 'banner' that they were to carry 'when they go to gather the flowers for Monsieur Saint Aumer'.[112] A further payment on the same page to 'Madame Vars for hats of roses for the day of Monsieur Saint Aumer en fleurs' reveals in this instance both the nature of the flowers being picked and their purpose in being fashioned into headgear.[113] Clearly the tradition was a long and continuous one, as revealed by a payment from 1504/5 for making 'a new banner for the boys to go to the flowers'.[114]

Collecting of flowers and foliage was a feature of various feasts throughout the church year, and was clearly a characteristic duty of the boys. It emerges again in the following record of the 1456/7 account, but this time, ironically,

---

[111] A David [not 'Daine' as in Deschamps de Pas] le paintre pour avoir repaint le drap sur lequel on fait Saint Aumer en fleure xii^s [1452/3, f. 16v]; A Pierre Pol pour le toile et pour le paincture du patron fait pour sur ce faire le Saint Aumer en fleurs xx^s [1467/8, f. 31v]; A Salmon Basin paintre pour avoir paint ung nouveau drap pour faire le Sainct Aumer en fleurs xxiiii^s [1510/11, f. 25r]; Pour trois journées de six femmes qui furent coeuller les fleurs pour faire lymaige mons^r Saint Aumer à vi^s pour jour sont xviii^s. All the above are quoted in Deschamps de Pas, 'Les cérémonies', 137–8. It would appear that the last of these records is assigned to the wrong year: I have not been able to trace it, though the following closely analogous record appears on f. 29r of the same year's account: 'A vi femmes qui allerent coeullier les fleurs pour faire lymaige St Aumer ou ils vacuerent iiii jours xxiiiis.'

[112] 1456/7: f. 13v: a Colart Beliquet pour avoir fait deux banieres est assavoir lune que les enfans portent quant ils vont cuellier les fleurs pour Monseigneur Saint Aumer

[113] Item a la dame Vars pour six chapeaux de roses pour le jour Monseigneur Saint Aumer en fleurs xiiii s

[114] 1504/5, f. 34v: Item pour avoir fait faire une nouvelle baniere pour les enffans aller aux fleurs pour toille bougran et faicon xiii s

to the effect that they had failed to fulfil their assigned task. We learn that on the night of Pentecost (which in 1457 fell on 5 June) a visit by boat was paid to the (now ruined) abbey of Clairmarais in the marshland to the north-east of the city to collect holly and beech, the abbot having reported that 'he is not content that the children of the school had been there, as they have customarily been'.[115] The tradition on Pentecost was to hang such branches from the vaults of the choir amid painted depictions of clouds as part of a representation of the mystery of the descent of the Holy Spirit to the Apostles.[116]

It seems likely that the country air of Clairmarais filled the boys' lungs at regular points through the year, or at any rate whenever there was foraging to be done. Another regular such fixture was Palm Sunday, for which the forest provided the required 'palms', as we learn, for example, from the fabric account for 1498/9:

Item, for the palms that one goes to fetch from Clairmarais as is the custom, to bless on Palm Sunday, 8s.[117]

In a similar vein, the accounts provide annually for apples and pears for the Feast of St James, likely following the widespread custom of blessing this crop on St James's Day.[118] At any rate this was one of many occasions for a miracle play in the town, as we learn from an entry in the chapter acts for 27 July 1497, clearly pertaining to the saint's feast two days previously. Several burghers had requested that the chapter might permit boys to perform interludes with other singers in intervals of the play, but received short shrift:

Several burghers, wanting to perform a certain miracle of Saint James with characters, requested that during the interval, for the interlude, the lords might permit choirboys with several singers to sing the said interlude. The lords,

---

[115] Item pour avoir ale le nuit de le penthecouste querir du may a Clermares [Clairmarais] pour cause que monsieur labbe navoit point este contens que les enfans de lescole y alassent / comme ils avoient a coustume / et depuis manda que se on en envoioit querir que leur en fust delivre pour quoy fu paie pour le batel iii s (1456/7, f. 13v)

[116] Albert Legrand, 'Réjouissances des écoliers de Notre-Dame de St-Omer, le jour de St-Nicolas, leur glorieux patron (6 décembre 1417)', *Mémoires de la Société des antiquaires de la Morinie* 7 (1844–6), 188–9. The tradition is affirmed in Deschamps de Pas, 'Les cérémonies', 128, in the form of a payment quoted from the 1395 fabric account 'pro cordis quibus rami cum nebulis appensi fuerunt in vigilia pentecostes'. (This account has been lost since Deschamps de Pas published his study.) The role of branches is further corroborated by his quotation of the related payment of 1483 'pour herbe estramee au coeur es festes de Penthecouste en may quant les seigneurs et dames revenoyent de convoyer la dophine' (ibid.).

[117] Item pour les palmes que lon est alle querir a Clermares ainssy quil est a coustume pour benir in dominica palmarum viii s (1498/9, f. 33r)

[118] Item pour pommes et poyres le jour Sainct Jacques viii s (1498/9, f. 33r). The blessing at least of apples on St James's Day (25 July) is of long and widespread currency.

considering that, as in many other places they do this with some instrument or other, so they can do it in the same way, without them.[119]

The likely implication of instrumental involvement is that this performance was enacted outdoors, a situation that was avowedly the case in the following instance, a mystery held outside the chapelle sur le marchiet following the return of a procession with holy relics:

To Jehan de Le Steghele for having made several tables to place the torches around the said holy body at the return of the said procession, as also for having made a machine for a mystery performed on the said day before the chapelle sur le marchiet, as appears in the bill, 18s.[120]

Al fresco representations of various kinds must have been a familiar feature in the boys' lives. Outdoor miracle plays were a commonplace, including the 'Miroir de l'homme', and the mystery of the 'Trois mors et trois vifs', mounted, as in the above case, on the old marketplace before the great mass of the populace, clerical and lay, rich and poor.[121] And whatever the outcome of the above request for their involvement in the representation of the miracle of St James, it is hard to imagine that they were not from time to time co-opted into such 'interludes', and indeed into the bodies of the plays themselves, in which singing and angels, often coincidentally, were such a ubiquitous feature.[122] One obvious focus for such performance was their patron, St Nicholas.[123] Legrand discusses the mounting of a St Nicholas play in 1416 before Jehan Sacquespée, receiver general of the duke of Burgundy and mayor of Arras and involving dramatic roles for 'lawyers and other notables from the town of Thérouanne', plus experienced actors from the suburb of the Haut-Pont.[124]

---

[119] … aliqui burgenses volentes per personas demonstrare aliqua miracula de Sancto Jacobo supplicarunt ut durante intervallo pro sylete domini vellent permittere pueros chorales cum aliquibus cantoribus pro cantando dictum sylete. Domini considerantes quod ut in pluribus faciunt aliis in locis de aliquo instrumento et sic faciant sine eisdem[.] (II. G. 355, f. 127v)

[120] A Jehan de Le Steghele tant pour avoir fait pluiseurs banques pour mettre les torsses entour lesdits corps sains au retour de ladite procession comme pour avoir fait ung engien servant a une mistere juee audit jour devant le capelle sur le marchie comme appert par cedule xviii s (1464/5, f. 17v)

[121] For details of the mounting of mystery plays and their documentation (beginning in 1403) see Legrand, 'Réjouissances', 169–71, 197–201.

[122] *Le Théâtre français au moyen âge, passim.*

[123] See the details in Legrand, 'Réjouissances', 169–71; discussed also in Max Harris, *Sacred Folly: A New History of the Feast of Fools* (Ithaca, NY: Cornell University Press, 2011), 202. See also Deschamps de Pas, 'Les cérémonies', 133.

[124] '*Ceux de la loi et autres notables de la ville de Terrouanne, s'étaient déjà offerts … de venir … représenter, en cette ville, avec leur prince des peu profitants, tel mystère qu'il conviendrait à*

It could well be that the spirituality inherent in these productions, not to mention the income from building their sets, was sufficient to have encouraged Rasse de Holst ('Houls'/'Hoest'), the 'maistre carpentier et maistre des engiens de le ville' who was charged in 1417/18 with erecting the stage for the mystery of the 'Trois mors et trois vifs', to found Masses for his posthumous soul. Indeed Rasse is one of the few deceased with foundations entered in the chapter acts who was not a cleric.[125]

In a rather different kind of street theatre, we know for example that – as elsewhere – on the three rogation days leading up to Ascension and on Ascension Day itself the clergy, led by a bell-ringer, paraded annually through the streets preceded by four banners and followed by the effigy of a dragon, a stark reminder to earthly sinners of the Devil's former dominion over earth.[126] Deadly serious in intent, this long-tailed, brightly coloured figure must surely, nonetheless, have made a vivid impact on impressionable young minds.[127]

---

nos Seigneurs. Dans leur offre de services, figurait le mystère de St-Nicolas … Il fut convenu que l'on mettrait à leur disposition, *Jehan Neudin, Willeaume Jaquemin et consors, artistes dramatiques du faubourg du Haut-Pont,* déjà en possession de représenter le *mistère de l'Arbre de Jessé, devant le Saint Sacrement,* le jour de la procession solennelle de la Fête-Dieu' (Legrand, 'Réjouissances', 170–1; italics as in source). While Legrand is nothing if not opaque, it seems clear from his description and references that the year in question was 1416, not 1417 as stated by Harris (*Sacred Folly*, 202).

[125] 1459/60, 2r: 'De Jacque [sic] Le Clerc sur ung manoir gisant a Combronne les Esque contenans iii quartiers et demi de terre gisant daval a le terre de le Holande ou chief Jehan de Le Wige chaqun an au terme de Noel vii s parisis / dont en appartient a le cappelle St Estenne fondee en leglise de St Aumer pour ii messes lan que a fonde Maistre Rasse de Houls carpentier iiii s parisis / Reste iii sc parisis qui valent iii s iiii d ob.' Clearly funds were sufficient to maintain this devotion for a long period: the same foundation, 'fondee par Rasse de Hoest jadis carpentier', appears for example in 1497/8, f. 3v.

[126] '… feruntur IIII vexilla et draco a laicis quos ad hoc conducet pulsator campanarum …' See Deschamps de Pas, 'Les cérémonies', 183 (from the St Omer ordinal MS Bibliothèque de l'Agglomération de Saint-Omer MS 909). See the discussion in Anne Walters Robertson, 'The Savior, the Woman, and the Head of the Dragon in the *Caput* Masses and Motet', *Journal of the American Musicological Society* 59 (2006), 574–80. See also the brief discussion in Deschamps de Pas, 'Les cérémonies', 126. Clearly the dragon received another outing on the procession to mark the Feast of the Ascension, when '… feruntur vexilla ante processionem et draco post …' (Ibid., 184).

[127] See the following entries in fabric accounts: 1388/89 (rotulus): 'Item pro reparacione vexillarum que consueverunt portari in rogatione v s. vi d.'; 1516/17, f. 26v: 'Item deux bastons pour les bannieres des processions en rogations ii sc vi d et pour vi boytes mises ausdits batons et banieres xviii d et pour paindre lesdits bastons et boytes ii sc sont vi sc'. Deschamps de Pas gives the following record, which appears to have been lost: ?1389: 'Pro ferro posito in summitate baculi quo portatur draco vi d'; and that for 1407/8, which survives: 'Pour .I. baston a porter le dragon as processions etc. ix d' ('Les cérémonies', 126).

Certainly not everything about the choirboys' lives was concentrated seriousness and heavenly innocence. Records suggest that some care was expended on their comfort: for example, a document recounts how – at a meeting on 4 May 1474 – the chapter ordered that a garden formerly used by a mason be given over to the boys, and that a door be provided for their access.[128] And information, gleaned from the fabric account for 1446/7, concerning some windows they had recently broken reveals that not all their waking hours were devoted to the pursuits of study, liturgy, singing and worship.[129]

As with maîtrises everywhere, the high point of the boys' year was surely that marked by the election by his confrères, on the vigil of St Nicholas (5 December), patron saint of choirboys, of a 'boy bishop', or 'bishop of innocents'. In this reversal of the usual hierarchy the new 'bishop' would announce to the chapter that on the following evening, the night of St Nicholas, patron saint of children, there would be a banquet followed by disguisings, games and the performance of a mystery play in the saint's honour.[130] He would ask for the agreement of the chapter, which would provide funds and wine for the meal. Whatever the potential for horseplay surrounding the festival as a whole, the 'liturgy' enacted on the Feast of Innocents seems to have been underpinned by a serious purpose: Max Harris characterises actions of the boy bishop and his underlings for the day as an entirely sanctioned replica of standard ritual, and indeed a practice for future clerical service.[131] Such high jinks as occurred do not, at least typically, seem to have encroached on the interior of the collégiale itelf. Certainly this observation is supported, as Deschamps de Pas notes, by the partially surviving thirteenth-century St Omer ordinal, though, as we shall see, by the fifteenth century behaviour seems to have sunk far below the exemplary.[132]

See also the account for 1424/5, f. 6v: 'Item a Colin le paintre pour avoir repaint le dragon viii s'; 'Item au fil [sic] Ph[ilipp]e de Fernacles pour avoir fait le queuue dudit dragon et pour lestoffe xvi s'.

[128] II. G. 354, f. 177v: Messeigneurs ... ont ordonne que le gardinet de le carpenterie que soloit obtenir le machon Deloyle soit attribue a le maison des enffans de coeur et que on fache au mur de le maison desdits enffans ung huis pour entrer audit gardin[.]

[129] Fol. 10r: Item paiet a Jehan Lapenser pour avoir revisite les verrieres desrannement [= dernièrement] brisies par les enfans de ceur comme appert par cedule xxii s

[130] See Deschamps de Pas, 'Les cérémonies', 133. It is tempting to surmise as to whether the 'teraches dessus le cappelle St Nicolay' on which masonry work was carried out in 1475/6 (f. 25v) had something to do with liturgical drama, a speculation that may be supported by the fact that the very next work detailed was on 'le cuisine des enfans de coeur'.

[131] *Sacred Folly*, 145.   [132] 'Les cérémonies', 105–6.

It would appear that at St Omer the lower (and hence younger) ranks of clerics elected their own 'bishop of fools' on the same day: on 5 December 1431, 'Seraphin Cotinet, vicar of the church of St Omer and succentor, for this year bishop of fools', successfully canvassed the chapter for 24s. and a jug of wine per head towards the episcopal meal on St Nicholas' Night, and agreement that anyone from the chapter who chose to attend (they were free to do so or to abstain) should present something to the bishop, as for example a further jug (or several) of wine 'as is the convention'.[133] This coincidence of the election of the bishops of innocents and fools was clearly not unique to St Omer, and in some churches the two functions were combined: Harris notes that at the cathedral of St Stephen, Toul, '"All the boys and the subdeacons celebrating the holiday [*subdiaconi feriati*], who are reckoned in the number of innocents," elected one of the boys as "bishop".'[134] The fact that, as Harris observes, 'children' and 'innocents' referred at the time to both boys and unmarried young men likely explains more generally how, although in general the bishop of fools was typically drawn from the ranks of subdeacons,[135] his seat could also be occupied by a choirboy. The latter is clearly attested by the instructions, in the thirteenth-century ordinal, for the Feast of the Circumcision and subsequent days up

---

[133] Die quinta mensis decembris, anno proxime dicto, Seraphin Cotinet vicarius ecclesie Sancti Audomari et succentor pro hoc anno episcopus fatuorum, comparuit in capitulo ipsius ecclesie asserendo quod erat nox Beati Nicolay, in qua nocte interdum solitum est fieri gaude in cena ob reverentiam ipsius sancti, et quesivit ab ipsis dominis utrum placeret eis utrum gaude fieri et interesse, tandem deliberatione habita super et causa ipsos ad hoc movente, pro hac vice deliberaverunt non interesse capitulariter; si qui vellet interesse hoc facere possit solvens ut moris aliquam curialitatem, ut puta canam vini vel prout eis placet, nichilhominus [sic] ipsi domini decanus et capitulum ad subventionem expensarum fiendarum in ipsa cena, generose dederunt dicto Seraphin episcopo, pro se et suis, sommam xxiiii solidorum currentium, eidem dicendo quod ab officiariis et bursariis ipsius ecclesie exigeret, videlicet a quolibet eorum canam vini, ut moris est. (Deschamps de Pas, 'Les cérémonies', 134; the same account is summarised in French in Legrand, 'Réjouissances', 189–90.) While it was allegedly taken from the chapter acts, in fact the source for this record remains a mystery: the relevant volume (II. G. 351) contains only records for the September general chapter meetings in 1431 and 1432, with nothing in between. While loss of folios would be a plausible explanation, the surviving folios are numbered consecutively in a contemporary hand.

[134] Harris, *Sacred Folly*, 246, quoting Marcel Jerôme Rigollot, *Monnaies inconnues des évêques des innocens, des fous, et de quelques autres associations singulières du même temps* (Paris: Merlin, 1837), 42. The celebrations of Innocents and Fools were combined into a single feast also at Besançon (see *Sacred Folly*, 227).

[135] This tradition was a long one: Fassler quotes Beleth, who in the 1160s referred to 'The feast of the subdeacons, which we call *of fools*' (Margot Fassler, 'The Feast of Fools and *Danielis ludus*: A Popular Tradition in a Medieval Cathedral Play', in Thomas Forrest Kelly (ed.), *Plainsong in the Age of Polyphony* (Cambridge: Cambridge University Press, 1992), 74. On this see also Harris, *Sacred Folly*, 66).

to Epiphany where, as Deschamps de Pas points out, 'bishop of fools' and 'bishop of boys' ('episcopus puerorum') are used interchangeably.[136] Conversely, as Oscar Bled notes, the 'bishop of innocents' could apparently be a junior cleric. He alludes in this connection to a record, quoted by Deschamps de Pas, concerning provision of bread and wine for a meal 'if a choirboy who has become holder of a benefice is made bishop of innocents or bishop of fools, or celebrates his first Mass'.[137] The perceived connection between the two roles and the ranks of their occupants is surely also related to the expected progression, to be discussed in Chapter 2, of choirboy to lower orders and priesthood.

It is clear, though, that the 'bishop of innocents' and 'bishop of fools' at St Omer were, as more generally, distinct entities. Bled, who asserts this directly, cites in corroboration the parallel appointment in Christmas week of a 'bishop of deacons', on St Stephen's Day (26 December), and a 'bishop of priests', on St John's Day (27 December).[138] By the fifteenth century at least, the chapter had recognised that the boys and junior clerics were not the only groups that needed to let off steam. Fassler notes the general prudence of this system of role reversal, whereby 'a tightly organized and carefully governed community won the psychological release that allowed the rest of the year to turn smoothly'.[139] The record, in 1494/5, of a dinner at St Omer for the 'bishop of the priests' gives a glimpse of the annual licence given to this particular subordinate group to taste the good life more normally reserved for its ecclesiastical superiors.[140] An entry in the chapter acts for 1 December 1495 again differentiates between the 'bishop

---

[136] 'Les cérémonies', 106. See also the discussion of the Feast of St Nicholas, 133.

[137] '... si un enfant de choeur devenu bénéficier est fait évêque des Innocents ou évêque des fous, ou fait sa première messe, et qu'il veuille donner un repas dans l'enclos, on lui donnera six bouteilles de vin et une demi-rasière de blé' ('Les cérémonies', 104). Deschamps de Pas ascribes this quotation to a chapter act of 17 April 1433, which, like the one noted in footnote 133, is absent from the relevant volume as it survives.

[138] Bled, 'La fête des innocents dans l'église de Saint-Omer', *Bulletin de la Société des antiquaires de la Morinie* 8 (1887–91), 59, 62. Deschamps de Pas likewise, if less emphatically, surmises the existence of bishops both of fools and innocents ('Les cérémonies', 103–4). For a general consideration of the revels of deacons, priests and their more junior confrères see Fassler, 'Feast of Fools', 68–80. For similar goings-on elsewhere see Wright, *Music and Ceremony*, 237–43 and Reinhard Strohm, *Music in Late Medieval Bruges* (2nd, rev. ed., Oxford: Clarendon Press, 1990), 33–4.

[139] 'Feast of Fools', 70. Harris notes also the theological significance of the inversion of power, summed up in the words of the Magnificat, whereby God 'has put down the mighty from their seat and exalted the humble' (*Sacred Folly*, 49, 284).

[140] 1494/5, 31v: Prime pour ung disner a cause de le custodie fait en la maison dudit receveur pour ce que ledit custodie estoit en son tour destre evesque des prebtres et le fist le grant custre en son lieu auquel disner furent aucuns de messeigneurs et xii vicaires parmy les visiteurs et petit

of boys' and 'bishop of fools', noting that 'the lords ordered 24 s. etc. to be given to the bishop of the boys in charity, and that it should be done and given to the bishop of fools according to ancient and approved custom as is customary also for other bishops'. In this case, the plural form of the latter presumably alludes not just to the 'bishop' of innocents but to his fellow bishops of deacons and priests.[141]

Individual vicars and even canons were at liberty to – and frequently did – attend the meal of the bishop of fools, provided they offered its host a gift, commonly a jug (or more) of wine. More funds would be donated by individual chapels of the mother church,[142] and the mayor and burghers of the town would contribute to the revels held on the vigil and Feast of Holy Innocents (28 December). On this occasion the bishop of innocents, bedecked in pontifical robes, would 'officiate' at Mass, where he would be waited on by his fellow choirboys, carrying candles and dressed as angels. He would bless his 'flock' from the bishop's chair, and the boys would perform their own special offices, singing from the upper choir stalls normally assigned to the canons.[143]

A few apparent performance details have survived in the thirteenth-century ordinal. One of these concerns the epistle for Holy Innocents, 'Vidi supra montem Syon', which, 'if preferred, should be sung *cum sua farsina* ["with its 'farse', or 'trope"] by two or four boys'.[144] Deschamps de Pas's

---

coustre / ou fu despendu tant en vyande vin cervoise comme aultres despens en tout la somme de v libs i s

[141] '... domini ordinaverunt episcopo puerorum dari in elemosina xxiiii s etc. et episcopo fatuorum secundum antiquam et approbatam consuetudinem ut ceterisque episcopis solitum est fieri et dari' (II. G. 355, f. 114v). A record for the following 16 December likewise notes that 'The lords ordered a moderate gift to the bishop of the innocents to support him in his duties, and likewise to the bishop of fools.' ('... domini ordinaverunt episcopo innocentium per supportandum oneribus medium donum et similiter episcopo fatuorum') (II. G. 355, f. 122v). Notwithstanding some apparent conflation of the two roles, it would seem therefore that Harris is mistaken in assuming, from two similarly separate payments to the 'évesque des ygnocens' and 'évesque des sos' from 1417 cited by Legrand ('Réjouissances', 191) that the scribe concerned was guilty of 'confusion of the clerical feast and the secular celebrations' (*Sacred Folly*, 202).

[142] Legrand (Réjouissances', 190) cites examples from 1399 and 1407.

[143] For commentary on this ceremony based on the records of various churches see Becker, 'The Maîtrise', 149–50. For the festivities at Notre-Dame of Paris and St Donatian, Bruges, see respectively Wright, *Music and Ceremony*, 191–2 and Strohm, *Bruges*, 33–4. A special medal struck for a boy bishop possibly named (doubtless with humorous intent, the surname being a slang term for 'penis') 'Etienne Vit', discovered in Belgium though of uncertain origin, is described in Louis Deschamps de Pas, 'Un plomb des évêques des innocents', *Bulletin trimestriel de la Société des antiquaires de la Morinie* (1852–6), 129–30.

[144] See Deschamps de Pas, 'Les cérémonies', 105; text on 145: 'Epistola apocal: "vidi supra montem syon"; vel si placet cantatur cum sua farsina a duobus pueris vel quatuor.' Drawing on Du

interpretation, from the rubric for the Feast of the Circumcision, that the liturgy for the day should be performed by the lower ranks of the choir 'as was done for the Feast of Holy Innocents, except … as loud as possible, raising their voices and even shouting', may however be the result of a misreading.[145] Harris suggests that, far from indicating a burlesque delivery, the word 'ullulando', which gives rise to this interpretation, probably has a far more serious connotation. Coming as it does from the 'Vox in Rama' antiphon performed at the feasts both of Holy Innocents and the Circumcision, it should more plausibly, he proposes, be read as a reference to Rachel weeping for her children (Matthew 2:18). Read in this way, the rubric would have been an admonition not to 'shout' or 'howl' but to produce a heightened delivery in imitation of Rachel's mourning.[146]

The period of inverted authority clearly extended through the Feast of the Circumcision (1 January) and as far as Epiphany (5 January), whereafter its absence of reference in the ordinal clearly signals reversion to business as usual.[147] Town and church authorities agreed not to interfere with the revels and masquerades of the bishop of fools who, in his turn, had to promise, on pain of a fine, not to enter into churches with his rabble while (genuine) holy offices were in progress.[148] The repeated incidence of such admonitions suggests, all the same, that they were not always

Cange, Deschamps de Pas (145) defines 'farsina' as a synonym or diminutive of 'farsa'. Notably the 'farsing' of this epistle echoes the similar insertion of amplifying additions to the epistle for the Feast of the Circumcision, as documented for Paris, Sens and Beauvais (see Harris, *Sacred Folly*, 90–1, 104, 107).

[145] 'La rubrique du commencement de cette fête fait connaître que les vicaires et les autres clercs habitués du choeur, avec leur évêque, chanteront et officieront ce jour-là, comme il a été dit pour la fête des SS. Innocents, excepté, est-il ajouté, que tout ce qui se fait le jour de la fête des fous, doit être aussi fait complètement autant que possible, et même en criant, en élevant la voix.' '… vicarii ceterique clerici chorum frequentantes et eorum episcopus se habeant in cantando et officiando sicut superius dictum est in festo sanctorum Innocentium, hoc tamen excepto quod omnia que ista die fiunt officiando quando est festum fatuorum, pro posse fiunt et etiam ullulando.' (Deschamps de Pas, 'Les cérémonies', 106 (description) and 147 (transcription).)

[146] Harris offers the following translation: '…the vicars and other clerics crowding the choir, together with their [boy] bishop, occupy themselves in singing and observing the office just as has been described above for the feast of the Holy Innocents – with the exception, however, that everything from that day becomes what is designated for the office of the Feast of Fools – as far as possible and even *ullulando*.' *Sacred Folly*, 146–7. 'Pro posse', here given as 'as far as possible', may perhaps better be translated as 'to the best of one's power or ability' (see R. K. Ashdowne, D. R. Howlett and R. E. Latham (eds.), *Dictionary of Medieval Latin from British Sources* (Oxford: British Academy, 2018) s.v. posse. Online version: http://clt.brepolis.net/dmlbs/Default.aspx).

[147] Deschamps de Pas, 'Les cérémonies', 106–7.

[148] Legrand, 'Réjouissances', 191, referring to a ruling of 1421.

observed. Already in 1407 the provost, Pierre Trousseau, apparently forbade abuses surrounding the feast, following which, allegedly, no one dared (at least for some time) assume the title of bishop or of any other dignitary of the Feast of Fools.[149] By 1438 the downward spiral seems to have acquired some momentum, however: that year the bishop and his mob were reminded of their obligation to restraint as instructed by the ordinal:

Also because in past times many offences and numerous scandals, breaches of the peace and bad behaviour have occurred, occasioned by the *Episcopus fatuorum* and his band, we decree and ordain that in future on the Feast of the Circumcision of the Lord, the vicars and other members of the choir and their *bishop* should behave themselves properly in singing and officiating as is described in full in the ordinal of the church, and those doing otherwise should be punished by judgement of the provost or his representative.[150]

No such unruliness impeded the annual celebration, however, until, in 1516, the Feast of Fools was finally suppressed by order of the then provost François de Melun. In response, the amateur players of the 'most illustrious and pleasurable art of rhetoric' asked that the forty sous traditionally granted for the revels be converted into an annual prize for whoever could perform the most beautiful morality play, a likely more edifying, if also more sober, undertaking. The money was converted into a double cross (the emblem from the arms of the city of Saint-Omer), to be awarded 'for this time only'.[151]

If the St Omer Feast of Fools did indeed become the victim of its own hubris, however, a celebration – inside and outside the church – of the Feast of Innocents persisted, according to François Quenson, until the Revolution:

[149] Bled, 'La fête des innocents', 62, quoting François Quenson, *Notre-Dame de St-Omer* (Douai: Wagrez, 1830), 91, who in turn refers, as his source, to Charles-François Deneuville, *Annales de la ville de Saint-Omer*, volume 3, 65.

[150] 'Item et quia retroactis temporibus multi defectus et pluria scandala deordinationes et mala, occasione *episcopi fatuorum* et suorum, evenerunt, statuimus et ordinamus quod de cetero in festo Circumcisionis Domini, vicarii, ceterique chorum frequentantes et eorum *episcopus* se habeant honeste cantando et officiando sicut continetur plenius in ordinario ecclesie, et contrarium facientes ad arbitrium prepositi seu ejus vicarii puniantur.' Pièce 8, 'Texte des status de N.-D. renouvelés et réformés, arrêté en chapitre général le 11 décembre 1432', in M. Vallet de Viriville, 'Essai', XXXII. The same record, without citation or date, is cited by Charles Du Cange, *Glossarium mediae et infimae latinitatis*, 'episcopus fatuorum' (vol. 3, 278). See http://ducange.enc.sorbonne.fr/EPISCOPUS#EPISCOPUS-17. Harris, *Sacred Folly*, 201–2, quotes it from Du Cange.

[151] For these details see Legrand, 'Réjouissances', 189–92. By contrast Deschamps de Pas ('Les cérémonies', 107) dates the suppression to 1515.

Each year on 27 December young boys strolled through the town dressed in various religious costumes, and at the church the sacristans or choirboys sat solemnly in the place of the singers, and these latter, in an exchange of functions, comically squeezed their bulky statures onto the sacristan's bench, trying, with their falsetto, to imitate children's voices, while the latter, for their part, tried to mimic the low voice, and the grimaces, of the cantor.[152]

Colourful and, penned within living memory of the Revolution, probably hyperbolic, Quenson's description probably merits circumspection, at least as it pertains to activities in the chancel. Indeed an anonymous mid-eighteenth-century letter quoted by Bled paints an altogether more dignified picture of choirboys articulating their liturgy with the greatest reverence and ritual and musical skill.[153]

Much will inevitably remain obscure; as should by now be clear, though, the ample surviving accounts offer numerous and varied insights into the lives of the boys and the financial and societal structures that sustained them. Channelled, though they may be, through well-defined conventions, they nonetheless offer glimpses of real lives lived under conditions that, however fraught with misfortune, could nonetheless be socially and music-ally propitious. Yet to be addressed, though, is the question of who – socially – the church's choirboys were and what – professionally – they could become. These will be the topics of the next chapter.

---

[152] 'Chaque année ... le 27 décembre, on promenait par la ville de jeunes enfants revêtus de divers costumes religieux, et à l'église les coûtres ou enfants de choeur s'asseyaient gravement à la place des chantres, et ceux-ci, en échange de fonctions, accroupissaient burlesquement leurs épaisses et larges carrures sur le scabelle du petit coûtre, cherchant de leur fausset à imiter la voix de l'enfant, et celui-ci, de son côté, à contrefaire la basse taille, et les grimaces du chantre.' *Notre-Dame de St-Omer*, 91; quoted in Bled, 'La fête des innocents', 63.

[153] Ibid., 64–6.

2 | Identities and Career Patterns

Up to now, our concern with the boys has been addressed very much in the abstract: to the general patterns of their lives and the structures that sustained them. But who were these juvenile workers, and why were they considered worthy of such high – and hard-won – levels of support? The question is of more than local curiosity: choirboys grew into men with the skills and knowledge necessary to serve as the adult male voices – not to mention the composers – of the future, and in fortunate cases to become candidates for higher clerical office.[1] The focus in this chapter, therefore, will be on the boys as individuals: their identities, motivations and careers.

Named Boys: Backgrounds and Beginnings

Though typically unnamed in the records, boys do from time to time emerge from collective anonymity. When they do, we may begin to get a sense of the burgeoning talents that can occasionally, through the church's wealth of documentation, be followed through to their future careers. Whatever advantages in life lay ahead of them, it is hard not to feel sympathy for the little souls of six to eight years of age who were deposited in maîtrises across the region by the parents who over the next decade would become strangers to them. A detail such as the payment in the fabric account of 1508/9 'for having cleaned out the ordure from the beds' ('pour avoir fait widier lordure es lits') of the boys seems poignant in light of their age and familial isolation.[2]

It would be tempting, as noted in Chapter 1, to surmise that the sung prayers of poor innocents, like the prayers of the poor more generally, would have been seen to carry special efficacy, and it may indeed be the

---

[1] See Craig Wright, *Music and Ceremony, at Notre Dame of Paris, 500–1550* (Cambridge: Cambridge University Press, 1989), 165 and Otto Frederick Becker, 'The Maîtrise in Northern France and Burgundy during the Fifteenth Century', unpublished PhD dissertation, George Peabody College for Teachers, Nashville, TN (1967), 65.

[2] F. 28r.

case that the poor clerical 'escotiers' comprised just such a body of former choirboys of limited means. The rank of 'escotier' or 'scotterius', peculiar to St Omer, requires some explanation. The 'escotiers' were a body of poor clerics, aged eighteen or over, verbally and musically literate, who were fed and maintained, in their own 'escoterie' situated in the cloister, at the expense of the chapter. Their statutory number, at least by 1438, was fourteen, although, funds permitting, that figure could be augmented. Detailed already in the statutes of 1227, the responsibilities of the escotiers are reaffirmed in the regulations of Eugenius IV, ratified by the chapter on 11 December 1432.[3] Another manifestation of late medieval alms-giving that, the chapter surely presumed, would be reflected in the prayers of the poor recipients on their donors' behalf, the escoterie was also a site of further education leading at least to the rank of subdeacon and, it would have been hoped, maintenance of moral rectitude. Progress further up the ranks of preferment either in the home church or elsewhere was an expectation of membership of the body, which persisted until the French Revolution.

As noted earlier, though, the only directly available demographic detail, analogously to the situation in other institutions, links choirboys of St Omer to the families of its canons. Repeated notices in the chapter acts make it clear that Rembert was particularly prone to tactics of familial favouritism, a practice that dates to the beginning of his tenure at St Omer. On 2 January 1483 a Johannes Rembert (surely a nephew) assumed the chaplaincy of St Maurice in the parish church of St Aldegonde. In keeping with the nature of this appointment, it passed, on his resignation from it on 7 January 1485, to a Johannes de Hemont, likely a nephew of the cantor. We learn more of this Rembert's history when, on 2 October 1493, Johannes Rembert 'uno de sex pueris chori' receives a one-year temporary vicariate, filling in for Marco le Tueur, who has been given a year's leave as an assistant to the likewise absent older Rembert.[4] On 4 June 1501 the lords endowed an escoterie, rendered vacant by death, onto 'the worthy youth

---

[3] A. Vallet de Viriville, 'Essai sur les archives historiques du chapitre de l'église cathédrale à St-Omer', II–LXXXVII, comprising a 'Catalogue des Archives de Notre-Dame' and 'Rapport à M. le Ministre de l'Instruction Publique sur les archives de Notre-Dame de Saint-Omer', *Mémoires de la Société des antiquaires de la Morinie* 6 (1841–3); see pp. XXXII and LXXIV–LXXV. De Viriville's study gives an invaluable indication of the state of the archive in 1843, following years of post-Revolutionary neglect and depredation. The substantial later decline also makes it a rich resource concerning material lost in subsequent years.

[4] II G. 355, f. 98r. For the same tendency at Lyon see Becker, 'The Maîtrise in Northern France and Burgundy', 137 (quoting Jean Marie H. Forest, *L'école cathédrale de Lyon* (Lyon: Briday, 1885), 58).

Johannes Rembert, formerly a choirboy, in favour of and at the request of the lord dean [his uncle], and they made provision for the same although he is absent'.[5] The apple did not fall far from the tree when, following Johannes's death, on 22 August 1502 'at the request of the lord dean the lords endowed the same escoterie on Mattheus Rembert, and made provision for the same although he is absent'.[6] Unsurprisingly, the tentacles of Rembert's family clearly extended much further, since when, on 16 June 1503, Mattheus resigned this post he was named as a 'cleric of the diocese of Amiens'. Advancement of canons' family members further up the ecclesiastical ladder suggests choirboy origins in such instances too, though the absence in most cases of the boys' names means this cannot usually be demonstrated with certainty.

If named at all while prepubescent, boys are typically referred to by first names only, usually in diminutive forms. Thus in 1506/7 we learn of hose being supplied to 'Charlot', 'Marquel', 'Jacquet' and 'Jennes'.[7] Since such names seem often to have stuck after the boys matured out of the maîtrise they sometimes permit us to track them up the early steps of the church hierarchy. Thus the aforementioned 'Charlot' is likely to have been the 'Charlot Gautran' who three years later, through the death of Loys de Renty, picked up the junior position of escotier.[8]

A cluster of references to 'Jennes' between 1506 and 1510 seems likely, since this is not a widespread name, to point to the same boy/man. Thus, also in 1506/7, a payment is made to Jean Thorion – along with Guillaume Massier one of the two masters of the boys for that year – 'for the expense of "petit Jennes" since he was received until Easter, which marked his departure' (presumably from the choir).[9] It seems reasonable to surmise that this is the 'Jennes (le) grave' who is paid as organist in 1506/7 (along with Alleanus/Alleannie Gerin) and 1507/8 (alone).[10] If so, this would be an unusual instance of a choirboy progressing from the stalls to performance on the organ, though why this was in fact a rarity at this time is unclear. The resignation, via the procuracy of the cantor, on 26 June 1510 from the chaplaincy of the chapel of 'petit St Andrieu' of 'Jennes

---

[5] ... *honesto juveni Johanni Rembert nuper choriolo in favorem domini decani et ad sui requestam et de eadem providerunt licet absenti* (II. G. 356, f. 46v).

[6] *Ad requestam domini decani domini contulerunt eadem scotteriam Matheo Rembert licet absen[ti] et de eadem providerunt* (II. G. 356, f. 57v).

[7] 1506/7, f. 30v.   [8] 1509/10, f. 9r.

[9] *A Sire Jehan Thorion pour le despense du petit Jennes depuys quil fut receu jusques a Pasques que marquet se partir par ordonnance de mesditseigneurs vi l* (1506/7, 35v).

[10] 1506/7, f. 23v and 1507/8, f. 25r respectively.

Maneque' is probably, notwithstanding the difference of name, another reference to the same individual; perhaps 'grave' referred to a character trait.[11] The very next page of the same document sees 'Jacquet Maneque' receiving, in September of the same year, an escoterie 'from the hands of Christofle Journy', the shift from 'Jennes' to 'Jacquet' perhaps marking a perceived graduation in stage of life. Finally, before disappearing from the records, the same named individual finds himself (as detailed further down the same page) embroiled in legal proceedings with 'ung nomme Guillaume Le Coustre escolier demourant a Paris'. The point of contention is a chaplaincy of St Pierre that had been granted to him by the chapter on 23 December 1509, but had been bestowed on his rival by the papal legate. For the period during which the proceedings – which had progressed from the local court at Montreuil to the Chatelet in Paris, where they are now being deliberated upon by the provost of Paris – have been occupying the opposing parties, the fruits of the chaplaincy under dispute have reverted to the chapter. Both densely packed and ramified, this concentration of records perhaps provides a cautionary tale, even in the context of a richly surviving archive, in attempts to isolate and track individuals; but it also gives some indication of the highways and (unfortunate) byways that could await a young cleric fresh out of a maîtrise.

Supplies of clothing to individuals or to numbers smaller than the full cohort often provide the context for the emergence of named boys. In 1506/7 Nicolas Petit was paid for material for making capes for boys including 'le petit Nannet' and 'le petit Robin'.[12] In 1520/1 cloth was purchased and fashioned into a cassock for a boy named 'Baudechon'.[13] Along with his six confrères, a later 'Jennes', Jennes Hanon, became the recipient in 1516/17 of a gown and hood, 'at his departure from the choir', fashioned by the long-standing city tailor Pierre du Broeuc, whose name we shall revisit in a more directly musical context at the end of this chapter.[14] A little later in the same document, again along with the six continuing boys, a bonnet is given to 'Jennes Hanon leaving the choir this year', while a certain George de Buz is paid for providing the same boy with a pair of black hose.[15] There are scattered suggestions that one of the six boys may have occupied a senior position vis-à-vis the other five, and it may be that black hose denoted seniority over boys wearing white: the fabric account for 1502/3 stipulates that 'les cauches dedits enffans sont blacquet excepte les dernieres cauches de Robin qui furent de noir'.[16]

---

[11] 1509/10, f. 9r.   [12] 1509/10, ff. 9r and 31r respectively.   [13] 1520/21, f. 30r and v.
[14] 1516/17, f. 27r.   [15] 1516/17, f. 28r.   [16] 1502/3, f. 25v.

Illness and misfortune might also occasion emergence from anonymity, as in the case of the unfortunate Jennet Deubry who, as noted in the previous chapter, succumbed in 1513/14 to plague. Payments to the barber-surgeon, charged with tonsuring the boys and curing their ailments, pull other boys out of collective obscurity. Thus on 30 April 1512, 'iiii enfants de coer [sic] a scavoir Sebastien Doudeville Jo[.] Baledent Jo[.] Hanon [clearly the 'Jennes Hanon' already encountered] Thonin de Saisy … furent tonsure par monsieur de Gilbelde'.[17] Recorded cures for (unspecified) head ailments provide similar details. In 1509/10 a payment was made on behalf of Jacquet de Hesdin 'le petit' 'pour luy avoir fait medicinier [sic] se teste par ung barbier'. Similarly, in 1510/11 'ung barbier' received 20 sols 'et ung lot de vin' 'pour avoir gari le teste Picquet', while in 1512/13 'Jan Storme barbier' was paid 'pour avoir gary a Bastien le mal des yeulx' ('for having healed the eye ailment of Bastien').[18]

Upward Mobility: First Steps

Choirboys emerge much more strongly from obscurity once their voices have broken and their tenure has reached its natural conclusion. While the experience of departing choirboys was not invariably positive, at its best the church could provide a powerful support network for its incipient clerics, with considerable advantages for their future education and career development. It is at this point that they would ideally make the natural progression onto the lower rungs of the church hierarchy, moving into chaplaincies or joining the ranks of 'escotiers' and vicars.

The rank of vicar, which carried more favourable financial returns than that of escotier, was clearly preferable, as patterns of progress usually demonstrate. As elsewhere, each of these perpetual positions was 'without cure of souls' (*sine cura*), meaning that the (unordained) holder lacked the right to administer the sacraments. As noted earlier, there were twenty-eight such positions at St Omer, each shadowing a canonry and literally providing a 'substitute' for a superior opposite number in the choir in Mass and office. As a consequence all had to be capable of singing chant and polyphony and, while the former skill was supposed to be maintained

---

[17] 1511/12, f. 29r. Sebastien Doudeville was presumably a relative of the Robert Doudeville who, as recorded in the fabric account for 1507/8 (f. 37r), had recently been paid for copying two new polyphonic Masses.

[18] 1509/10, f. 27v, 1510/11, f. 27v and 1512/12, f. 28r respectively.

by the canons themselves, this was sometimes more of an aspiration than an actuality. Other posts, some of them apparently more ad hoc, including chaplaincies operating for private foundations at side chapels, offered extra opportunities for employment, and further potential bolstering of the choir. All such positions had in common, however, the fact that they were held at the pleasure of the chapter or whomever paid for them, and could be terminated without notice or recourse. Since most seem also to have been presented according to a rota of the canons,[19] they were also, perhaps needless to say, subject to favouritism and nepotism. The income involved, which came chiefly from 'distributions', typically of six deniers per day, for attendance at the daily round (two deniers for each of matins, Mass and vespers), plus small payments for occasional services, was also paltry by comparison with the substantial, and guaranteed, incomes of the canons.[20]

The documents frequently allow us to trace patterns of musical chairs as choirboys advance and others take their places. A record of 21 November 1458 offers a snapshot of the chain of promotion that a diligent choirboy might expect to enter: on that day a vicariate vacant through the death of Johannes Robert was given to Johannes Caignart; in turn, Caignart's escoterie passed to Petrus Marcel, while a *parva vicaria* that Petrus had held went to Psalmonus de Caille, who had been a choirboy.[21] While the specific duties of a 'small' or 'half' vicar are not clear, usage suggests that, like the position of 'cappella clericus' that we shall encounter shortly, such jobs represented a kind of halfway house between the status of choirboy and escotier or vicar.

If fortunate, a choirboy might advance directly to an escoterie, as when, on 29 October 1495, the death of Jacobus Vincent opened up a position for 'the worthy youth and lately choirboy Johannes Tingry'.[22] As the record reminds us, Tingry's position meant only that he was 'remaining in the chapel until he swears his oath [presumably once a vacancy arises for him], at the lords' pleasure'.[23] Within little more than a year, Tingry, by then assigned (though in what capacity is not made clear) to the chapelle sur le

---

[19] As when, on 28 May 1490, Petrus de Wailly, 'qui de novo puerorum choristarum fuit' requested 'quod fiet sibi provisio in turno suo si repertus fuerit habilis et ydoneus' (II. G. 355, f. 77v).

[20] For example, on 13 September 1492 Pierre Basin and 'Balduinus laprentis' ('the apprentice'; later named as Balduinus des Grousilliers) are each specified to receive six deniers daily, with the latter's total accumulating to twenty sous per month, amounting to twelve livres per annum (II. G. 355, f. 92v).

[21] II. G. 353, f. 45r. [22] ... honesto iuveni et de novo puero chori Johanni Tingry

[23] ... remanente in Capella usque ad beneplacitum dominorum iuravit, etc. iuramentum[.] (II. G. 355, f. 114r)

marchiet, was also presented with the keys of minor churchwarden (parvus custos), a post until then held by a cleric named only as Jacobus, Tingry's own position in the chapel going to a certain Bredenardo.[24] It would appear that the post of minor churchwarden also entailed skill in singing, since on 27 January 1497 Tingry's position was passed on to Johannes Flahault, 'provided he can sing well at the lords' pleasure'.[25]

Since a certain Natal/Noel Tingry crops up at exactly the same time, also as an advancing choirboy, it seems likely that this was the same individual with two forenames or, conceivably, with a moniker, perhaps relating to performance in nativity plays.[26] A twin brother is not out of the question, though the continuing presence, well into maturity, of 'Johannes', a lack of simultaneous mentions of both 'Noel' and 'Johannes', plus the absence of the usual posting of the death of 'Noel' and consequent dispersal of his clerical posts suggests otherwise. If this was indeed the same individual, the work of Johannes/Noel had clearly been considered valuable at the chapelle sur le marchiet since, on 8 February following, the chapter unanimously appointed 'Natalem Tingry' to a position there.[27]

It would appear that it was customary to give the choir time off in August, opening up the possibility of extra work for cash-strapped young clerics. On 8 August 1496 'the lords ordered Magister Johannes Clerici, director of the boys, that he might enquire after two or three young boys to serve in choir; and the lords brought in Natal de Tingry and the nephew of the lord dean [presumably the already encountered Johannes Rembert], staying behind for the whole month of August'.[28]

Whether the same person or not, Johannes Tingry was likewise no stranger to financial need: on 13 January 1497 he appealed to the chapter, in a document describing him as an escotier, for a grant of two sous per week for a month.[29] The chapter granted the request up until Easter,

[24] II. G. 355, f. 122v.

[25] II. G. 355, f. 123r: Eadem die domini ordinaverunt parvam custodiam loco Joh[anne] Tingri in ecclesia Sancti Audomari proviso quod dabit bonam cantionem ad voluntatem dominorum Johannem Flahault[.]

[26] My thanks to Robert Nosow for this suggestion.

[27] II. G. 355, f. 123v: ... domini concluserunt unanimiter instituere et collocare Natalem Tingri ad capellam super forum ...

[28] ... domini ordinaverunt Magistro Johanni Clerici rectori puerorum quod inquirat pro duobus vel tribus pueris iuvenibus ad serviendi in choro / et domini deportaverunt Natalem de Tingry et nepotem domini decani remanentibus [sic] per totum mensem Augusti / (II. G. 355 f. 119r)

[29] ... supplicavit Johannes Tingry clericus scotterie ut domini de gracia vellent habere compatientiam de eodem prout succurren[tes] sibi velleri[n]t de ii sc ebdomadatim pro mense super qua requesta domini concluserunt sibi dare qualibet ebdomada ii s. usque ad pascha super lucro vicariatus Domini Michaelis Le Gay. (II. G. 355, f. 123r)

supplied from the money normally accruing to the vicar Michael le Gay who, as we learn from an entry further up the page, had been given four months' leave, 'allowing for all delay', starting on 4 January, to complete an already begun course of hours of the Virgin 'through the diocese' (whatever, in practice, this may have meant).[30] On 6 May, 'Johannes Tingry parvus custos' is before the chapter again, returning the keys of his office and thanking the lords for their generosity towards him.[31]

Whatever his early vicissitudes, Johannes Tingry (for the name 'Noel/ Natal' disappears from the records after 1497) was clearly able to build a continuing livelihood in the church as a vicar/singer: from 1509/10 and on into the 1520s he is listed annually as one of the four singers paid, along with the master and boys, to perform the daily polyphonic *Salve regina* founded by Nicolas Rembert, a foundation that will be addressed in detail in Chapter 6.[32]

With untimely death a frequent pitfall and given the slimness of the pickings, the turnover could be quite rapid. In an early reference to (Noel) Tingry, his path crosses that of a choirboy of a slightly earlier vintage whose career was curtailed long before its time. Both this latter individual, Philippe du Hecq, and Tingry were beneficiaries of the division of spoils on the death in 1496 of the tenorist Grigoire Bourgois, a significant figure in the history of the church whose story will be picked up in the next chapter. Du Hecq, who had lodged in Bourgois's house as a graduating choirboy, inherited his patron's vicariate, his own 'demie vicarie' going to 'Clay Lemps, lung des vi enffans party du coeur' ('one of the six boys [who has] left the choir') while the chaplaincy of the chapel of St Laurence passed in turn, through du Hecq's resignation, to Noel/Natal Tingry. Finally the chapel of St Louis, also presided over while living by Bourgois, was conferred on a certain Jehan Vendame.[33] In the same connection, this latter cleric is referred to in the chapter acts as 'Mimim', a name

---

30 ... domini ad requestam dominorum decani et capituli ecclesie Morinensis concesserunt Domino Michaeli Le Gay vicario licentiam quod possit complere cursum Beate Marie inceptum per diocesim usque ad quatuor menses a datis presentibus diei pro omni dilatione / et in casu quo non venerit ad residenciam ex nunc prout ex tunc et econtra domini procedent contra eum secundum statuta et ut iuris fuerit et rationis[.] (II. G. 355, f. 123r)

31 Eadem die Johannes Tingry parvus custos reportavit claves custodie regraciando dominos de bonos [sic] sibi per dominos collatis[.] (II. G. 355, f. 125r)

32 Interestingly, in the account for 1520/ 1 he is referred to as 'Sire Jan de Raulers dit Tingri', suggesting that the former was his family name, and the latter a toponymic referring to the village of Tingry, to the south of Boulogne.

33 1495/6, f. 14v. The same transfer of du Hec's 'parva vicaria' to Clay Lemps (here 'Nicolas Lamps') is recorded in the chapter act for 12 August 1496 (II. G. 355, f. 119r).

intriguingly applied ('le petit Mimim') in 1505/6 to a choirboy;[34] perhaps this was a sobriquet for the smallest ('minimus') choirboy at any given time.[35] At any rate Vendame's tenure as a vicar in the institution seems to have persisted at least until 1506/7, when 'Jehan de Voeullame' is named as one of the singers of Rembert's daily *Salve*. The fact that all Bourgois's positions seem to have passed to practising singers suggests that each of his posts, as one might expect in the case of this distinguished tenorist, carried a strongly musical component.

Occasional comments on the quality of voices leave a clear impression that perceived high achievement involved more than simple efficiency in fulfilling assigned tasks. A chapter act of 22 July 1484 introduces us to the 'worthy youth Martin' who, 'having a sonorous and trumpet-like voice, at his humble petition, so that he may study and progress in singing and letters, prevailed to be given by the said lords two livres of groats, for which grant he humbly thanked the lords, promising to continue to serve the church and to continue until such point as it might be pleasing to the lords that he may approach another church'.[36]

Du Hecq's first appearances in the records give an indication of the support an able choirboy could expect to receive. A chapter act of 2 September 1492 records that 'the lords conceded to Philippus du Hec, choirboy, who on account of the change of his voice may no longer serve in the choir, that until next Easter he will continue to have his victuals with the master of song, paying the same master his expenses as is customary'.[37] Come the following 12 April, presumably following the end of this arrangement (Easter falling on 7 April in 1493), 'Philippe du Hec, cleric departing

[34] II. G. 355, f. 119v (19 August 1496); 1505/6, 34r.

[35] Mention is often made of the smallest boy, as when, in 1509/10 (f. 28r), payment was made for the material and making of a silk cloak for 'le plus petit enffant de coeur'.

[36] *Eadem die honestus iuvenis Martinus habens vocem sonoram ac tubalem ad sui humilem petitionem ut discere et proficere possit in cantu et littera optinuit a dictis dominis sibi dari duas libras grossorum super quo dono regratiatus est dominis humilissime / promittens se ecclesie serviturum et permansurum donec dominis placeret quod aliam ecclesiam adiret[.]* (II. G. 355, f. 54r)

[37] '... *domini concesserunt Philippo du Hec puero qui propter vocem mutatam amplius non valet servire choro quam usque ad pascha proximum / habebit victum cum magistro cantu solvendo pro rata eidem magistro expensis ut consuetum est*[.]' (II. G. 355, f. 91v). A similar circumstance occurred four years later, when 'Augustinus puer choralis' found himself in what were presumably similar circumstances. Again 'the lords ordained on a majority vote that he could continue his services until Easter but on condition that he will pay and provide payment as is customary, and only Master Judocus Dausque opposed this happening.' ('*Item domini ordinaverunt pro maiori parte quod Augustinus puer choralis adhuc continuabit suum exercium usque ad pascha sub tamen conditione quod solvet et procurabit solucionem ut moris est et tantum quo hoc non fecerit Magister Ju. Dausque se opposuit.*') (f. 118r, 18 June 1496)

the choir' is given 'six denarii daily, every day lodging with the tenorist Gregorius Bourgois and attending the school and choir, and being present daily at matins and the other daily hours, especially on Sundays and feast days'.[38]

He advanced another increment later that year when, on 2 August, 'an escoterie, vacant through the death of Petrus Godin' was endowed on 'Julien de Berghes, since he was for a long time one of the six choristers, provided that in his place as cleric in the capella will be Philippe du Hecq, one of the choirboys'.[39] It is possible that this latter position might correspond to the 'cerofferarii' ('taper bearers') at Tournai Cathedral or the two 'virgiferi chori' ('rod bearers' or 'virgers') at St Donatian, Bruges, the latter being positions normally reserved for former choirboys and similarly functioning as halfway houses en route to more substantial posts.[40] But whatever the relative responsibilities of 'cleric in the capella' and 'small' or 'half' vicar it seems clear that, in du Hecq's case at least, a 'parva vicaria' was seen as a step up, since it was such a post, along with a chaplaincy at the altar of St Laurence, that, some three months later, through the resignation of Allerinus (or 'Alleannie') Gerin, passed to 'Philippe du Hec formerly one of the six choirboys'.[41] Given his elevation to the deceased Bourgois's full vicariate in 1496, it seems curious that du Hecq did not celebrate his statutory first Mass at the high altar until 1499, specifically on Misericordia Sunday, the third Sunday in Easter, which that year fell on 14 April.[42] With this position his career apparently plateaued since, apart from permission granted to him in 1497 to make a 'pilgrimage to St Job', he is otherwise absent from the records until, in 1505/6, his demise led to the windfall of his vicariate to Ansel le Maire.[43]

This progress, from choirboy via escotier to vicar, with or without intervening layovers as a 'cleric in the capella' or as a small/half vicar, seems to represent the typical aspiration, provided they were 'found to be

---

[38] ... Philippo du Hec clerico exeunti chorum sex denarios dietim et omni die manendo cum Gregorio Bourgois et frequentando scolas et chorum / et existenti cothidie in matutinis et aliis diurnis horis presertim d[omini]cis et festivis diebus / etc. (f. 94v)

[39] ... vaccante scotteria per obitum Domini Petri Godin domini in Dei nomine et quare fuit de sex choristis longo tempore providerunt et contulerunt Juliano de Berghes proviso quod sui loco in capella clericus erit Philippus du Hecq etc. unus de sex pueris chori. (f. 95v)

[40] My thanks to Robert Nosow for this suggestion.

[41] ... domini habita super hac matura deliberatione parvam vicariam et capellaniam ad altarem Beati Laurencii sitam in ecclesia Sancti Audomari quam obtinebat dictus Allerinus Gerin contulerunt Philippo du Hec quondam uno de sex pueris chori[.] (11 November 1493, II. G. 355, f. 99r)

[42] II. G. 356, f. 20r.   [43] 1505/6, f. 11v.

apt and suitable' ('repertus habilis et ydoneus') for boys entering the maîtrise, though some, as we shall see, did manage to rise above the status of hired hand and into the more secure and comfortable stratum of beneficed cleric. Progression out of the maîtrise, and particularly the celebration of one's first Mass, was clearly perceived as a kind of coming of age. We see this, for example, in the case of the aforementioned Julien de Berghes, who on 31 July 1495 was given licence to celebrate his first Mass, 'and since in his youth he was one of the six boys, the lords permitted to be given to him bread and wine as is customarily given to others in such cases'.[44]

Nepotism could definitely help, as in the case of one Johannes Brahier. Records of 11 September 1494 inform us of two chaplaincies granted to him. The first of these, that of St Nicasius, was bestowed on him 'with all its rights and appurtenances' ('cum suis iuribus et pertinentiis') following the resignation of its prior incumbent, Jacobus de Resin. Having just received this benefice, however, we find him on the very same day requesting absence from another, which he is permitted, while still enjoying its fruits, provided he pursues his schooling:

Johannes Brahier, cleric and chaplain of the chaplaincy at the altar of St Peter, requested of the lords that they may deign to concede him licence to be absent. To which request the lords generously assented, provided that he will attend school, and by this means may receive the fruits of his chaplaincy . . .[45]

A notice of only four days later, however, suggests that the chapter's generosity to Brahier was not limitless. From this it would appear that an attempt to be granted a similar grace with regard to his newly acquired chaplaincy of St Nicasius has, following judgement passed down by one Guillaume de Walde, been rebuffed. Even in this case all was not lost, however: the chaplaincy carried with it the expectation of attendance in choir and the extra advantage of collection of the associated distributions. Advocating on Brahier's behalf, his uncle, the canon Johannes Caroulle (or 'Carouwe'), managed to retain for him these distributions even in his absence, on the grounds that he was formerly in the choir (presumably as a choirboy) and will in future attend:

---

[44] Et quia in iuventute fuit de sex pueris domini concesserunt sibi dare panem et vinum ut consuetum est dari aliis in casu simili. (II. G. 355, f. 111r)

[45] Eadem die Johannes Brahier clericus capellanus capellanie ad altare Sancti Petri requisivit dominis ut sibi licen[tiam] concedere dignarentur. Cuiquidem requisitioni domini generose annuerunt proviso quod frequentabit scolas et hoc medio recipiet fructus sue cappellanie . . . (II. G. 355, f. 105v)

On the same day [appeared] Lord Johannes Caroulle, canon and tutor of Johannes Brahier, cleric for seven years and chaplain of the chaplaincy of Saint Nicasius, who due to the aforesaid chaplaincy has the right to secure distributions in the choir after the manner of a vicar. But as he is unable (since his young age was not taken into account) to serve the same chaplaincy by singing or reading, or to receive the emoluments (as was found in the judgement of Magister Guillaume de Walde), nonetheless it was conceded to the same Johannes Brahier, at the request of the aforementioned Lord Johannes [Caroulle], his uncle, that he may be permitted grace to receive the said distributions on account of his study, since he was formerly in the choir and will [in future] attend.[46]

While evidence of clerics pushing their luck is widespread, such progress through the ranks was desirable not only for the recipients but also, in maintaining the smooth running of its particular customs and requirements, for the chapter itself. Thus the canons took great pains, whenever outside interests sought to intervene, to assert their rights and privileges of appointment. On 17 August 1481 Johannes Rogier approached the chapter with papal letters of appointment to a 'parva vicaria of this church vacated in the curia through the death of Antonius de Le Forge'.[47] He later emphasised that 'the vicariate was vacated in the [papal] curia, as a result of which it is by law fully reserved to the apostolic see, and it had been arranged for him [to be installed] in it, and therefore he had no need to present his document to judges or have his suit judged'.[48] The chapter took a contrary view:

The lords having seen these letters replied that there was in them no derogation of their privilege that benefices that are 'under their roof' [i.e. theirs to appoint] do not come in any way to be demanded by apostolic letters that make no mention of this exemption, and that such provisions are reserved for choirboys and others involved in the church's choir who are instructed in the ceremonies of [this particular]

---

[46] Johannes Caroulle canonicus tutor Johannis Brahier clericus vii annorum capellanus capellanie ad altare Sancti Nicasii qui ad causam capellanie prefate habet ius percipiendi distributiones in choro ad instar vicarii / sed quia eidem capellanie cantando vel legendo minime attenta etate iuvenili deservire nequeat nec emolumenta recipere / ut per oppinionem Magistri Guille. de Walde compertum est / Nichilominus eidem Johanni Brahier ad supplicationem prefati Domini Johannis sui avunculi causa studii concessum est sibi de gratia ut dictas distributiones recipere possit quoniam prius in choro erat et se presentabit[.] (II. G. 355, f. 106r)

[47] Johannes Rogier venit ad dominos ... cum certis litteris provisionis sanctissimi domini nostri pape qui sibi providerat de parva vicaria huius ecclesie vacante in curia per obitum Anthonii de Le Forge petens ab eis ut eum recipere et admittere vellent ad possessionem eiusdem parve vicarie. (II. G. 355, f. 21v)

[48] Dictus Johannes Rogier replicavit quod vicaria predicta vacavit in curia quopacto est sedi apostolice pleno iure reservata. et de eadem sibi est provisum in eadem quare non fuit opus presentare litteras iudicibus aut facere processus decerni. (II. G. 355, f. 21v)

church. Item, also that vicariates are held by personal residency, which is a benefice of service.[49]

In the event, Rogier withdrew his claim, 'because vicariates of this kind are held via personal residency, neither is he steeped in the ceremonies of the church, and neither will he intend presently to be resident'. He did not, however, back down from his claim concerning 'the right providing for [the post] to belong to him', and – presumably with that to back him up – agreed to withdraw only if the chapter would strip Balduin Le Sage, its actual appointee, of the position and confer it instead on Johannes Dergny.[50] Given the manipulation and general skullduggery that regularly accompanied attempts to acquire ecclesiastical preferment it is quite possible that Rogier knew he was on a hiding to nothing, but was rather attempting to scratch the back of a colleague who would reciprocally also be expected to scratch his.[51] Whatever the case in this particular instance, whose full ramifications will never be known, the key point for the present purpose is the vigour with which the chapter sought to maintain the consistency of its local observances and, concomitantly, its minor appointments.

But if the progress of the above-mentioned Balduin Le Sage had encountered roadblocks to this point, they were trivial compared to the next obstacle thrown in his way. On 10 December the same year the chapter

---

[49] 'Domini visis suis litteris responderunt quod in eisdem non erat derogatum suo privilegio quod beneficia sub tecto existentia non veniunt ullo pacto impetranda per litteras apostolicas non faciendas de indulto huiusmodi mentionem et quod hee provisiones reservate sunt pro pueris chori ac aliis chorum ecclesie frequentare et qui sunt instructi in ceremoniis ecclesie. Item et quod vicarie tenentur ad personalem residentiam quia est officium servile.' Appealing also to more legalistic argumentation, the chapter cited the fact that Rogier 'did not present his bulls within the legal year, and his suits had not been judged, all of which things being hindrances, the lords obstructed his reception'. ('Similiter aliud oberat quia ipse Johannes Rogier non presentavit suas bullas infra annum iudicibus nec decreti sunt sui processus. Quibus omnibus obstan[tibus] domini fecerunt difficultatem ipsum recipiendi[.]') (II. G. 355, f. 21v)

[50] Sed tamen quia vicarie huiusmodi tenentur ad personalem residentiam nec est imbutus in cerimoniis ecclesie / neque intendebat de presenti residere ipse contentus est dimittere ius quod sibi competere providebat et cedere in manibus dominorum proviso quod conferrent eandem Domino Johanni Dergny et Balduinus Le Sage eiusdem possessor omni iuri quod sibi providebat in eadem virtute litterarum collocationis ipsorum dominorum renuntiaret prout et quemadmodum renunciavit dictusque Jo. Rogier cessit et dimisit dicti quod domini providerunt eidem Domino Johanni Dergny de eadem et tam ex cessione dimissioneque renuntiatione aut alias quovis modorum predictorum contulerunt eandem et mandarunt michi notario litteras expediri habuit litteras et solvit iura. (II. G. 355, f. 21v)

[51] For a particularly egregious case of this kind see my article 'Johannes Sohier *dit* Fede and St Omer: A Story of Pragmatic Sanctions', in Fabrice Fitch and Jacobijn Kiel (eds.), *Essays on Music and Musicians in Honour of David Fallows: Bon jour, bon an, et bonne estraine* (Woodbridge: Boydell and Brewer, 2011), 68–79.

reported a letter received from the dowager Duchess of Burgundy (Margaret of York), requesting, on behalf of the 'lord of St Albans' (presumably William of Wallingford, then Abbot of St Albans), the vicariate of a certain deceased Johannes de Le Court for the abbot's chaplain, Johannes Fabri alias Macque.[52] The chapter, 'considering the poverty of some of those who were choristers of this church, refused at first sight, and deputed certain of its agents, who approached the same lady duchess in order that they might persuade her'.

The duchess, however, was having none of it, and the next day the chapter gave way to her insistence and installed her candidate on the right side of the choir. At this point, however, Balduin, 'who in his childhood was one of the choirboys', entered the picture, asserting himself, since it was his turn to receive preferment, to be 'very much aggrieved and cheated'. Following debate, the canons duly decided to appoint him instead:

... the more sensible and greater party of the lords was for telling the same lady duchess that with God and a clean conscience they could not and should not confer [it] on anyone except their own choirboys or, if there were no boys of an age and good morals, on other men practised in the ceremonies of the church and suitable, otherwise they would be abusing their privilege. But if she would not be satisfied they should go back to her and place the whole thing entirely as a burden on her conscience; and if she did not want the burden of appointing the aforesaid Johannes Macque they would confer the vicariate on the aforesaid Balduinus Le Sage. On the same day all the lords approached the same lady and Lord Simon, the dean, related these words.[53]

---

[52] That de Le Court (or 'de Curia') – who was after all only a vicar – had friends in high places is strongly suggested by the fact that, as we read in the previous note in the chapter acts, he had been able to command a burial place 'in ambitu chori' (II. G. 355, f. 25v).

[53] ... ad exhortationes domini du Wrolant [St Albans] illustrissima Domina Margarita ducissa dotaria fecit requestam eisdem dominis de capitolo ut recommissum habuerunt Dominum Johannem Macque capellanum domini du Wrolant predicti in collatione vicarie vacantis per obitum Johannis de Le Court. Domini considerantes paupertatem aliquorum qui fuerunt chorales huius ecclesie renuerunt prima facie et deputarunt certos ex ipsis commissarios qui adirent eandem dominam ducissam ut eam contentam facerent qua assidue instante et requirente pro dicto Johanne Macque.

Die xi sequenti domini contulerunt vicariam predictam per obitum ipsius Johannis de Le Court ut prefertur vacantem eidem Johanni Fabri alias Macque presbitero. Et habuit litteras et fuit installatus in latere dextro chori.

Dominus Balduinus Le Sage presbiter qui fuit in etate puerile de pueris chori huius ecclesie sentiens et asserens se per maxime gravatum et frustratum huiusmodi vicaria qua sibi tam ex permisso quam ex turno anthiquitate et prioritate ut dixit debebatur protestatus fuit de gravamine et petiit sibi exinde fieri actum et notum.

A record of less than two years later suggests, however, that the chapter had been unable to make their decision stick in the face of such powerful opposition: thus, finally, on 16 April 1483, a death allowed them, 'taking account of the poverty of the Lord Balduin Le Sage, who was for a long period a choirboy of this church and has no provision', to provide him with a vicariate.[54]

Such hardship as afflicted Le Sage was not exceptional for former choirboys. When, as periodically happened, warfare raging on lands owned by the church restricted its income supply,[55] the lower ranks of the clergy bore the brunt of the resulting penury. Thus on 18 January 1482 the chapter 'gave licence to "Honzelet" that, during this time of wars he may seek promotion anywhere at all, since the possibility of sustaining him is not propitious'. They do however allow that 'if the chance of a vicariate or escotier should arise, it will be given to him in his turn, just as was considered for all other choirboys'.[56]

Discipline

Whatever the fears or insecurities of life after choir school, they did not, however, necessarily lead to application and diligence. On 18 September 1486 Ludovicus Calligarius, who had 'been a chorister for far longer than the other choristers', was granted six livres d'Artois 'to be distributed at the pleasure of the lords', but only 'on the condition that he will turn more agreeably and more attentively to those things repeatedly demanded of

In deliberatione tamen inter ipsos dominos habita super collatione vicarie huiusmodi sanior et maior pars dominorum fuit dicere eidem domine ducisse quod cum deo et sana consciencia non poterant nec debebant conferre nisi suis pueris chori aut aliis si in etate et moribus pueri non forent constituti in serimoniis ecclesie imbutis et ydoneis alias suo privilegio abuterentur tamen si contentari non posset se referrent et rem huiusmodi omnino imponerent oneri sue consciencie quae si nollet ad onus huiusmodi predictum Johannem Macque nominare conferebant vicariam predicto Balduino Le Sage. Ipso die omnes domini adierunt eandem dominam et Dominus Simon Decanus verba pertulit[.] (II. G. 355, f. 25v)

[54] ... attendentes paupertatem Domini Balduini Le Sage qui fuit longo tempore puer choralis huius ecclesie et nullum habebat provisionem ... dictam vicariam per obitum ipsius Domini Mathei Probi vacante contulerunt dicto Domino Balduino habuit litteras et prestitit iuramentum. (II. G. 355, f. 41r)

[55] Warfare in Flanders presented a particular liability since, as noted in the chapter act of 6 July 1487, II. G. 355, f. 70r, most of the church's lands were in Flanders.

[56] ... domini dederunt licentiam [blank] Honzelet quod pendente hoc tempore guerrarum posset hinc inde suam promotionem querere quia occasione predicta ipsum sustentare non valebatur. Si vero casus alicuius vicarie vel scoterie acciderit servabitur eidem suus turnus prout et omnibus aliis pueris chori fieri deliberaverunt[.] (II. G. 355, f. 26v)

him, whether within the choir or outside of it, or otherwise he will receive nothing'.[57]

Unauthorised absences meant that a potential hazard of maintaining such an extensive clerical workforce was the need to round up missing vicars. On 31 July 1497 the chapter ordered a missive to be despatched to a certain 'Judocus vicarius' in Bruges, ordering him to return to residency or face legal proceedings. They gave notice, furthermore, that – at the request of the magister cantus – he would be deprived of the fruits of his vicariate for the period of his absence even though he had had permission to be away.[58] Along similar lines, on 3 June 1483 the vicars Guillaume Didier and Gerardus de Vledrezelle were admonished to be present by the day of the next patronal feast or be sacked, because, without permission, they had each been absent for more than four months.[59]

While such warnings may seem to suggest excessive leniency on the part of the chapter, they might rather be a sign of desperation. There are some indications that retaining vicars up to the desired number may have proved a challenge. When, on 13 September 1492, Balduino 'laprentiz' (des Grousilliers) was assigned six deniers per day in distributions for attending matins, Mass and vespers (see note 20) this was stated to be due to lack (or absence) of vicars ('defectibus vicariorum'). Perhaps the rewards were sufficiently paltry that some clerics felt unconstrained by strictures of attendance, or – as far as risk of dismissal is concerned – that they might as well try their luck elsewhere as attempt to curry what little favour was available at St Omer.

That much is certainly suggested by an entry in the fabric account for 1466/7, according to which a certain Michiel Le Blocq presented to the fabric rent from land that had been bought by the chapter to pay money distributed, for their services, to the vicars and escotiers. The workforce

---

[57] ... provisum est de gracia speciali Ludovico Calligarii qui longo tempore et longe ampliori omnibus aliis coralibus fuit coralis / de sex libri arthesii sibi distribuendi ad placitum dominorum / ea tamen conditione stante quod melius et attentius in hiis que sibi repetuntur tam in choro quam extra serviat / aut alias gracia nulla. (II. G. 355, f. 67v)

[58] ... domini ordinaverunt quod scribatur Judoco vicario existenti Brugis quod veniat ad residentiam alias domini intendunt procedere contra eum / et etc. quia magister cantus in capitulo petiit licentiam a fructibus sue vicarie tempore sue absentie licet licentiam habeat lucrando privaverunt. (II. G. 355, f. 127v)

[59] ... domini iusserunt michi suo scribe scribere Dominis Guillelmo Didier et Gerardo de Wledrezelle quod una monitione pro omnibus habea[n]tur reverti et personaliter residendo deservire suis vicariis infra proxime instantia festum Inventionis Sancti Audomari alias procedi facietur ad eorem privationem quia absque licentia quilibet ipsorum iam per quadrimestre et ultra se absentav[erunt]. (II. G. 355, f. 42v)

had objected that the proposed annual remuneration of forty sous each was insufficient, and the fabric was forced rather to pay each of them the annual sum of sixty-three sous and nine deniers that – they asserted – they had actually earned.[60]

Study and Patronage

To overemphasise such issues would, however, be to present an unrealistically bleak picture of what could in many instances prove a highly propitious career path. This is perhaps nowhere more obvious than in the advantages offered in terms of education. That benefit did not cease on the breaking of the voice: on the contrary, the St Omer archives, like those of other large ecclesiastical institutions, bear repeated and diverse witness to the provision of funds for university study.

University privileges were assigned to both canons and vicars, who typically received the fruits of their benefices while absent; such absence in turn provided work, and hence income, for other clerics fulfilling their colleagues' normal duties. Payment in advance was another generous privilege that could be assigned to servants of the church while engaged in study. We learn, from a notice of 16 October 1495, that the nephews of the canons Robert de Monte and Eugenius Labitte, both away studying, have been permitted the year's payment for their chaplaincies up front, provided the duties of their posts continue to be served.[61] The assignment of escoteries to Rembert's two nephews while absent, mentioned above, is probably likewise explicable by their being away from Saint-Omer studying. Indeed likely corroboration in one case may be found in Rembert's

---

[60] De Michiel Le Blocq a Hellefault sur v. mesures et demie de terre gisants /estassavoir dela le mont sur le quemin de Therouanne iiii mesures aux termes de Noel et St Jehan xl s parisis et vi gisants(?) sur le chemin que Marie de Helfaut a[d]joyne(?) comme il appert ou compte iiiic liii qui furent achates de largent de le fabricque pour bailler aux vicaires et escotiers tantmoins de ce que ledit fabricque leur doit chacun an pour furnir les distributions des ficefaches lesquels vicaires et escotiers nont volu [sic] accepter lesdits xl s disans que lassennement nest point souffissans et par ce est demoure a ledit fabricque ladite rente et en Icelluy ce lieu elle est chargie de paier chacun an a iceulx vicaires et escotiers pour lesdits ficefaiches le somme de lxiii s ix d courant comme appara cy apres en la despence de ce present compte jusques ad ce que ledit fabricque leur ara assigne autant de rente[.] Et pour ce icy xl s parisis qui valent ... xlv s (1466/7, f. 3r)

[61] ... domini considerantes studium in quo vacant et intendunt nepotes Magistrorum Roberti de Monte cap[ellanus] Sancti Petri Eugenii Labitte cap[ellanus] Beate Marie super dossale et cap[ellanus] Sancti Johannis Ewangelisti concesserunt eisdem fructibus suarum capellanarum per hoc anno dumtaxat proviso quod eisdem capellaniis secundam fundationem deservatur[.] (II. G. 355, f. 113v)

executors' account, which includes payments to 'Jo. de Molendino, principal of Cardinal Le Moisne in Paris for Mahieu Rembert, kinsman of the testator whom he looked after at the schools in Paris'.[62]

Residence elsewhere for study could last three years or even six when, as in the case of the canon Jacques Plurion, an individual progressed from one course of study to another. Plurion's case offers a good example of the proceedings and rationale involved. On 2 June 1487 he received permission from the chapter to study at the University of Louvain or elsewhere, while continuing to receive the fruits of his prebend as if resident. Almost exactly three years later, and back from Louvain, he asked for a further three years to study for a 'higher level' at the University of Paris or elsewhere 'in order that in the same study [he may become] more fit for the praise of God and the glorification of the church'. The chapter agreed so long as he would provide an annual testimonial, and with the caveat that the funding would stop were he to take up a resident benefice elsewhere. These conditions having been fulfilled and his studies completed, on 20 September 1493 he requested resumption of his residence.[63] In a similar instance, in November 1492 a letter of testimony from the University of Louvain is presented for the canon Anthonius de Lannoy, affirming that he has spent six years there as a student.[64]

Entries on this topic sometimes give details of the faculty where study will take place, and even the name of the master under whom it will be conducted. Thus, in July 1490, privilege is granted to Balduin de Roteleur, 'cleric studying in the University of Paris', where he is to study in the faculty of arts under Master Johannes Gaultier.[65] Similarly, in June 1494 Johannes de Marthen presents a testimonial to the effect that Johannes Bailly, chaplain of the chapel of St Mary Magdalene, is resident in Paris, studying in the faculty of theology under master Johannes Roullin. The fact that Bailly was under the tutelage of the same master two years later suggests that such student–teacher ties typically lasted for the duration of the period of study.[66] Another testimonial, presented some three months later, concerns Johannes de Poilly, studying in Paris under Johannes Renerius, professor of theology.

But while Paris and Louvain were the most usual destinations for clerics wanting to make themselves 'more fit for the glorification of the church' they were far from the only ones, with cities much further afield also

---

[62] . . . a Jo. de Molendino principal du Cardinal Le Moisne a Paris pour Mahieu Rembert cousin dicelluy testateur quil entretenoit aux escolles a Paris (II. G. 484, f. 29v)

[63] II. G. 355, ff. 70v, 78r, 96r.   [64] II. G. 355, f. 93v.   [65] II. G. 355, f. 78r.

[66] II. G. 355, ff. 102v, 121v.

figuring in the purview of St Omer clerics. On 26 April 1493, for example, Petrus de Rabodengues and Johannes de Le Valee request, and receive, nominations for vacant bursaries in the Collegio della Sapienza Vecchia in the city of Perugia that have been historically in the gift of the church. The dean's extended pro forma recommendation for the two clerics follows.[67]

High Achievers

The status of vicar represented, for most former choirboys, the pinnacle of their careers. For those who managed to make the leap to the rank of canon, however, much richer possibilities awaited. Such was undoubtedly the case for Robert Fabri (or Le Fevre), whose life provides a textbook case of a successful ecclesiastical career beginning in the maîtrise. On 17 January 1463 a vicariate vacated by the death of its prior incumbent was given to 'Roberto Fabri puero chori'.[68] The fact that Fabri made the move directly from choirboy to vicar, omitting the usual steps (or half-steps) of 'small' or 'half' vicar and escotier, already speaks strongly of his perceived ability, or at least of the weight of patronage behind him. That his musical capabilities were highly regarded is clear from a record in the executors' account of Toussains de Le Ruelle, former papal singer and long-time member of the Burgundian court chapel, who held a canonry at Saint-Omer from 1425 until his death in 1470.[69] Among the items given by Toussains according to the terms of his will are two music books, lent to Fabri while the testator was alive and now bequeathed to him.[70]

By 28 February 1474 he had made the logical progression for a gifted former choirboy when the cantor presented 'Robert Le Fevre, priest, vicar' ('Robertum Le Fevre presbiterum vicarium') 'for the governance of the singing school' ('ad regimen scolarum cantus').[71] And in more than one

---

[67] II. G. 355, f. 95r.   [68] II. G. 353, f. 57r.

[69] For a detailed discussion of Toussains's career see below, pp. 248–56.

[70] 'Item une cedulle en date du xix[e.] jour de may lan lxix par laquelle Sire Robert Le Fevre vicaire confesse avoir deux livres de musicque appartenant audit feu.' A marginal note adds 'dati sunt libri gratis' (MS II. G. 476, f. 13r). It is possible that Toussains and Fabri were linked by familial or at least pseudo-familial ties: one of the other gifts bequeathed in Toussaint's will was the sum of six pounds, 'a Clay Le Fevre pour Toussains Le Fevre son fils et filleul dudit feu' (II. G. 476, no. 11, f. 24v). While Fabri/Le Fevre ('Smith') was of course one of the commonest French surnames, the combination of its presence here and the frequency of references to Robert Le Fevre in the same account is suggestive.

[71] 353, f. 174r. Since it is to be expected that choirmasters began their careers as boys in a maîtrise, it is unsurprising to find analogous examples elsewhere. For a comparative case see the career of

case in the same year Fabri was named as one of the sponsors in putting forward candidates for vacant offices. He was clearly also a scribe of music: the fabric account of 1490/1 includes a payment to him 'pour avoir notte' a Gospel book.[72] His connections as a singer seem further to have helped him when in October 1489 he received a chaplaincy at the altar of 'Beata Maria de Vigellis' through the recommendation, in his turn, of the former papal singer and canon of St Omer Guillaume Decault.[73]

While the first rung, that of subdeacon, was the highest point up the ladder of holy orders to which most vicars would expect to progress, by December 1490 Fabri had assumed the position of 'vicar with the office of deacon' at the high altar vacated by the death of Nicolaus Fuyron. At the same time his own vicariate (attached to the canonry of Johannes de Le Caroulle) became a promotion, from the 'parva vicaria' he had been occupying, for Johannes Dergny.[74] In August 1491 Fabri picked up another chaplaincy, that of the altar of St Katherine in the (still surviving) parish church of St Sepulchre, and in the fabric account of 1491/2 he was still listed, in a payment for saying daily Masses for the soul of the deceased canon Baugois Le Beghin, as 'prestre et vicaire'.[75]

Fabri's trajectory was not invariably set on an upward course, however. Designated 'bursarius', and clearly tasked with the distributions of tokens to those singing at services in the choir (for the redemption of which, following standard practice, they would be paid), he appeared before the chapter at its meeting of 31 October 1492. Fabri proffered the customary thanks to the canons and returned the purse and keys of his office, apparently expecting to relinquish them. After deliberation the chapter decided to keep him on as bursar 'provided that henceforth he will give

---

Jacques Barre at Notre-Dame of Paris, who, apparently like Fabri, seems to have risen to that position in his twenties (see Wright, *Music and Ceremony*, 173). For the advancement of various former choirboys to the rank of master of the boys at the cathedral of Rouen see Adolphe Bourdon and Armand Collette, *Histoire de la maîtrise de Rouen* (Rouen, 1892; repr. Geneva: Minkoff, 1972), 106–12.

[72] 1490/1, f. 22v. Presumably work on books was what led to his possession, as noted in his executors' account, of 'Une presse a lier livres' (II. G. 482, no. 7, f. 6v).

[73] II. G. 355, f. 76v (26 October 1489). This act by its nature shows that Decault was now in good grace: a similar turn of nomination on 23 June 1480 had not been permitted due to his being under sentence of excommunication, and hence unable to enter chapter: 'G. Decault ut intellexerat erat in sententiam excommunionis etc litteris exinde confectis occasione certi debiti et ad instantiam Magistri Nicolai Rembert quarum non veniebat admittendus in capitulo.' (II. G. 354, 243v).

[74] II. G. 355, f. 81r (10 December 1489).

[75] II. G. 355, f. 85v (3 August 1491) and 1491/2, f. 25v.

due diligence to the divine office'.[76] Perception of Fabri's insufficiency may not have been confined to his conduct in this role. This is suggested by a notice in February the following year in the context of a fracas over the appointment of the master of the boys whose story will be picked up in Chapter 3. On presenting to the chapter both Fabri and Malin Alixandre as possible replacements in this post for Johannes Thorion, Hemont, the cantor, is informed

that although the one [clearly Alixandre] had been sacked from his duties for being inadequate, the other did not have sufficient burden of duty in the church, protesting, in his defence, that he was not known for being negligent.[77]

The prolix nature of the latter remark resists a confident interpretation; but given that the discussion concerns the role of master of the boys, it may be that Fabri had also been found wanting in his prior tenure of that post, perhaps through inexperience or insufficient personal application.

Whatever ill wind had blown over Fabri, however, it clearly dissipated: on 31 October 1496, four years to the day after his earlier admonishment in this position, he again presented himself as bursar with a purse of 'marellae'.[78] The chapter, 'considering his probity and diligence', confirmed him in his position as bursar, but admonished him that 'henceforth he apply diligence in exercising his office and be sparing with no one'.[79] In a sign perhaps of greater confidence in his abilities, the copy in the chapter acts of the 'bulle conservatoire' of 1492 names Fabri as having served as procurator for the resignation of the cantor's canonry by Johannes de Hemont. In the same connection we learn that Fabri had himself ascended to the

---

[76] Eadem die Dominus Robertus Fabri bursarius exhibuit in capitolo bursam et claves regraciando dominos. Post maturam deliberacionem continuaverunt eundem ad bursam regendum proviso quod de cetero faciat diligenciam erga divinum officium. (31 October 1492; II. G. 355, f. 93v)

[77] . . . dominus cantor . . . illico presentavit Dominos Robertum Fabri et Malinum Alexandre / tunc et illico domini responderunt quod tamquam non sufficiens ab exercio fuit unus eorum deportatus / alter non in ecclesia habebat onus sufficiens etc. protestans expresse non reputari negligens etc. (II. G. 355, f. 94r; 24 February 1493)

[78] 'Marellae', or 'mereaux', are the tokens 'distributed' to vicars for attending Mass and office, and redeemable for currency or, internally to the church (or even externally), for goods. On their use at St Omer specifically see Jules-Adrien Blanchet and Adolphe Dieudonné, *Manuel de numismatique française*, vol. 3: *Médailles, jetons, méreaux* (Paris: Auguste Picard, 1930), volume 3 (*Le méreau en France*), 516.

[79] Robertus Fabri bursarius comparuit in capitolo et consignavit bursam cum marellis[.] Domini considerantes probitatem et diligenciam ipsius continuaverunt eundem in eodem officio monendo ut de cetero faciat diligenciam in exercendo suum officium nemini parcendo. (II. G. 355, f. 122r; 31 October 1496)

canonicate, though by this point only of the collegiate church of St Pierre in Aire-sur-la-Lys rather than of his mother church.

But his advance was far from over: a key moment came on 24 April 1495, when he assumed the canonicate at St Omer of no less a figure than Simon Godeffroy, the former dean whose position of leadership had recently passed to Nicolas Rembert, and for whose actual act of resignation, intriguingly, Fabri had been the procurator.[80] Striking also is the fact that he gained Godeffroy's canonicate by permutation with the latter of his own canonry in Aire-sur-la-Lys, surely something of a comedown for the former dean. Indeed this canonry was not the only spoil to come Fabri's way following Godeffroy's departure: the following month he acquired via permutation a chaplaincy at the altar of St Louis in the church of St Martin from Burtius Allehoye, who had just obtained the same post from Godeffroy and who, as his side of the deal, took Fabri's chaplaincy of St Katherine in the church of St Sepulchre. Membership of a wealthy confraternity was always a sound career move for an upwardly mobile cleric, and in 1495/6 Fabri, curiously still styled 'vicaire', is named as 'receiver of the confraternity of St John the Evangelist'. Finally on 7 June 1504 he is referred to as cantor and canon of St Omer, a position he was to retain until his death on 31 December 1536 at what must have been, for the time, the uncommonly advanced age of around eighty-five.[81]

Something of Fabri's status (at least as perceived by himself) can be divined from the nature of the funerary epitaph that he had fashioned, the contract for which survives. Anticipating his death by more than seven years, this was issued on 12 June 1529 to Mathieu de Horst, a brass founder in Tournai, 'to make an epitaph in brass similar to that made and placed in the church for the late Sire Anthoine de Luxembourg, the images and figures according to the design that my said lord the cantor sent to him'. The scale alone of this epitaph – its weight of 606 lb exactly equaling that of its grandiose model – makes a clear statement about the kind of lasting impression Fabri aimed to make.[82] His executors' account permits the

---

[80] Cum itaque postmodum decanatus ecclesie Sancti Audomari ... per liberam resignationem dilecti filii Simonis Godeffroy nuper ipsius ecclesie decani de illo quem tunc obtinebat per dilectum filium Robertum Fabri ... procuratorem suum ad hoc ab eo specialiter constitutum in manibus nostris spontanea factam ... (II. G. 355. f. 100v)

[81] Fabri's date of death is clarified in his executors' account, II. G. 482, f. 9v.

[82] 'Au jour dhuy xii^e de juing anno xvc et xxix a este fait marchie par Mathieu de Horst fondeur de letton demourant a Tournay a Monseigneur Maistre Robert Le Febure prebstre chantre et chanoine de leglise de St Omer de faire ung epitaphe de cuyvre / pareil a ceste fait et mis en ladite eglise de St Omer pour deffunct Sire Anthoine de Luxembourg les ymaiges et personnaiges dicellui selon le patron que monditseigneur le chantre lui ennvoiera. Et ce pour le

inference that, as in so many analogous cases, the tablet must have been in place in the church before its subject's death, presumably inviting – implicitly or otherwise – prayers for his soul before his term in purgatory began. A certain George Monnoier is paid 'for having engraved the writing of the epitaph', for which purpose it had to be taken down before being restored to its place.[83]

But Fabri's posthumous provision in the church was not of course restricted to things immovable: it extended also to his foundation of the annual performance, discussed in the previous chapter, of the *Aurea missa*. Music clearly featured significantly in his funeral, at which 23s. 6d. was paid 'to the singers for having sung the Mass in music', surely in this case a reference to polyphony. Further payments 'to six vicars singing the chorus', to the choirboys and to no fewer than twenty-seven further vicars, besides the dean and as many as nineteen canons, gave ample scope for a resounding send-off.[84] His executors' account reveals an estate of some substance including, among his books, a copy of the *Cronica cronicarum*, a history of the world in the manner of Schedel's famous Nuremberg Chronicle, but from the perspective of France, England and Brabant. Originally issued in 1521 on thirty-two separate leaves, it was first published in book form in 1532, either way suggesting, in Fabri's case, a purchase late in life, and one of sufficient substance to command, at the sale of his effects, the sum of £4 from the dean.

To achieve the status of cantor, one of the highest offices of the church, was no mean feat, and stands as eloquent testimony to the advancement possible for a talented choirboy. But to gain broader recognition meant being able to attract the attention of high-ranking patrons beyond the city walls. An encounter with another Fabri, Johannes (who may or may not

---

pris de cincq sols chacun livre de tel pesanteur que lepitaphe dicellui Maistre Anthoine . . .' (II. G. 481). The full document is transcribed in Marc Gil and Ludovic Nys, *Saint-Omer gothique* (Valenciennes: Presses Universitaires de Valenciennes, 2004), 393.

[83] Monnoier's total costs of 40s. were partially (20s.) met by de Horst through his son Pierre du Dam, the rest coming from Fabri's estate. The removal and replacement were presumably a skilled job, since payment is made 'A Guy Touset fondeur de letton pour avoir demonte ledit epitaphe pour le graver et le remis en son lieu xiis. viiid.' (II. G. 482, f. 12v)

[84] Aux xix chanonnes presens audit service a chacun xii s selon le testament sont xi l viii s. A xxvi vicaraires et le petit vicaire chacun vi s selon ledit testament viii l ii s. A xi escottiers a chacun iii s xxxiii s. Item aux vi vicaires chantans le chorus a chacun iii s xviii s. Aux cure chapelains et habitues audit service qui furent en nombre [sic] de lvii a chacun xii d lvii s . . . Aux enffans de coeur ung karolus dor xxiii s vi d. Aux chantres pour avoir chante la messe en musique ung karolus dor xxiii s vi d. (II. G. 482, f. 8r)

have been a relative), demonstrates one of the ways in which this could transpire.

In late December 1485 a chantry was founded by Anthonius de Atrio, knight and 'magister domus' of Philip the Fair, Duke of Burgundy and captain of the castle of Saint-Omer, for his and his family's souls. Johannes Fabri and Johannes Dergny, 'priest vicars of this church', were assigned the keys and administration of the chapel of St Andrew, at the carrel where the Masses were to be sung. For the fulfilment of the foundation, the vicars were charged with 'performing the due service and celebrating Masses on the days on which they both, or the surviving one of them, would decide'. The record tells us that the Masses were to be discanted, suggesting that Fabri and Dergny were to lead the singing as well as to officiate.[85]

Clearly these vicar-singers, both of whom we have encountered already, were well connected: this was the Fabri 'alias Macque' who had served the 'lord' (presumably abbot) of St Albans as chaplain, and on whose behalf in 1481 the dowager Duchess of Burgundy, Margaret of York, had advocated for a vicariate. Dergny, meanwhile, was the vicar whom Johannes Rogier had that same year attempted to manipulate into a vicariate ahead of Balduin Le Sage.[86]

But the most ironclad route to choirboy fortune was through having word of one's talent reach noble ears. In July 1492 Baudin 'laprentiz' ('the novice') 'who in his youth had been a choirboy in this church', arrived before the chapter, presumably from the service of Philip the Fair, and

---

[85] Nobilis vir Anthonius de Atrio scutifer magister domus illustrissimi principis Domini Ducis Philippi Burgundie etc. ac capitaneus castri huius ville Sancti Audomari michi Nicasio Ernout in mandatis dedit ut dominis meis decano et capitulo capitulariter in loco hac capitulari congregatis iuxta tenorem fundationis certi cantuarii per ipsos Anth[onium] et suos nuper fundati prout superius in hac registro et eo amplius in litteris originalibus desuper confectis una in thesauraria huius ecclesie altera vero in manibus dicti fundatoris et suorum remanentibus plenissime habetur nominarem et presentarem suo nomine discretos viros Dominos Joh[annes] Fabri et Joh[annes] Dargny [sic] presbiteros vicarios huius ecclesie ad debite deserviendos et missas dicti cantuarii celebrandos secundum textum et contentum huiusmodi fundationis diebus quibus ipsi ambo adnuerent seu alter eorum viveret[.] Quibus sic per me nomine quo superius nominatis et presentatis prefati domini mei benivole annuerunt decernentes eisdem capellanis claves et administrationem capelle Sancti Andree in carola in qua missas decantari conclusum est deliberari facere quod illico fecerunt[.] (II. G. 355, f. 63r)

[86] The latter move was presumably unsuccessful: it was not until 1490 that Dergny moved up from 'small' to full vicar, in the wake of Robert Fabri's advancement to vicar/deacon of the high altar. This was far from Dergny's most serious stroke of misfortune, however: the fabric account of 1490/1 (f. 28r) recounts how he had been sprung from prison in Calais where he had been held at the pleasure of the king of England. Success was the result of 'plusieurs diligences faites par ledit [Robert] Peppin ... a Callays vers le Roy dEngleterre pour la deliverance de Sire Jehan Dergny lors prisonnier audit lieu ... et sacquista tellement que ledit Dergny fu delivrez'.

presented certain letters of Monseigneur the Archduke Philip ... in order that his place in line for the provision of a vicariate or escoterie be maintained. To the which my said seigneurs, for honour and reverence of Monseigneur the Archduke, told him that, when the opportunity arises, they will be pleased to take care of the matter.[87]

This particular 'novice' was clearly the Balduinus Beghin who in June the following year was duly granted the escoterie of the deceased Petrus Galant, 'in contemplation and at the request of the most illustrious prince the lord archduke of Austria, and of the merit of Lord Balduinus Beghin, who was in his time a choirboy'.[88]

A series of letters to the collegiate church from the early sixteenth century testifies to its dealings with Charles V and his regent in the Netherlands, his sister Mary of Hungary. Among these are, by some miracle of survival, three (presented in full in the Appendix below) that address in very direct fashion issues involving choirboys. Two letters from 1534 recount what, from the point of view of musical advancement, must surely count as an epic missed opportunity.[89] On 29 March of that year, Mary of Hungary, still fairly new in her post as regent of the Netherlands and in the process of building the chapel choir for which she would become renowned,[90] wrote to the chapter of St Omer concerning a certain Michelet de Cobrize, choirboy. The letter relates how she has heard of this boy and commands that he be sent back 'with this messenger' so that she can hear him sing. Sadly, however, Michelet failed to make the grade: less than a month later, as we learn from a letter returned with the boy himself (see

[87] Au jourdhui xxvii de jullet jour de Sainte Anne presenta certaines lettres de Monseigneur lArchiduc Philippe / Sire Baudin laprentiz presbtre lequel en son josne eage a este enffant de coeur en ceste eglise affin que son tour de provision de vicarie ou escotterie luy soit gardee / Auquel mesditsseigneurs pour lhonneur et reverence de Monseigneur lArchiduc luy dient que volontiers quant le cas escherra / le auront par recommande etc. (II. G. 355, f. 91v)

[88] 'Die prima iunii vacante scoteria per obitum quondam Domini Petri Galant in contemplationem et [ad] requestam Illustrissimi Principis Domini Archiducis Austrie / meritisque Domini Balduini Beghin qui puer chori tempore suo fuit / domini eidem Domino Balduino providerunt.' (II. G. 355, f. 95r). Things had originally looked more swiftly propitious, since he was at first to have been assigned – less than a month after his approach to the chapter – the parish of Zoutenay, but this had clearly been in error: the record is scored through with a marginal note reading 'non vacent'. This Balduinus is clearly to be differentiated from the Balduinus laprentiz / des Grousilliers who (as discussed above) was assigned distributions for attendance at Mass and office in September 1492.

[89] Since the year in Brussels changed at Easter, the date 'ce xxix^e de mars anno xxxiii avant Pasques' would mean our 1534, not 1533.

[90] On Mary's noted love for music, and particularly her cultivation of the Netherlands court chapel see Glenda G. Thompson, 'Music in the Court Records of Mary of Hungary', *Tijdschrift van de Vereniging voor Nederlandse Muziekgeschiedenis* 34/2 (1984), 132–73.

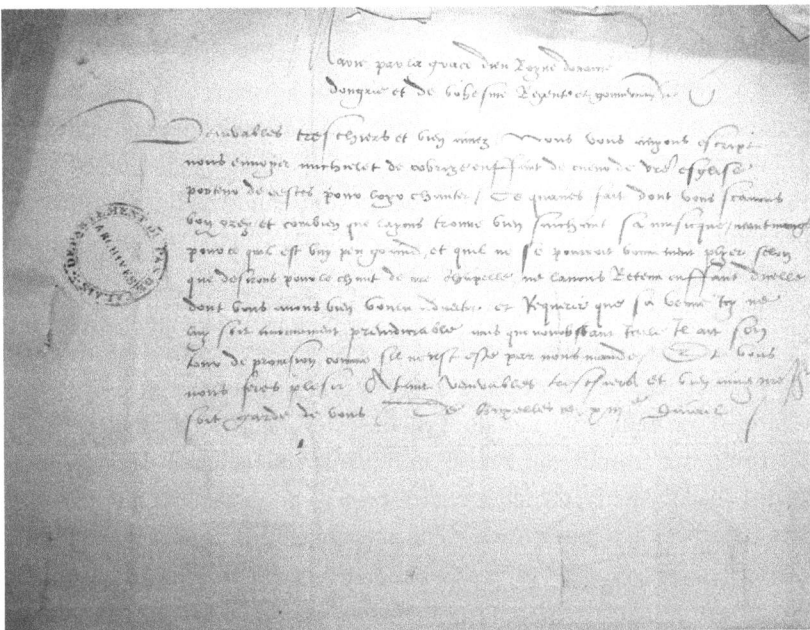

Figure 2.1 Letter to the chapter of St Omer from Mary of Hungary concerning the choirboy Michelet de Cobrize

Figure 2.1), he was packed off back to Saint-Omer. The queen relates how, 'although we have found him to be well versed in his music, because he is a little old/tall ["grand"] and because he could not well adapt himself to what we desire for the song of our chapel, we have not retained the child'. She goes on to request that this decision not stand against Michelet at his home church, and that he will be granted his regular income as if he had not been summoned to Brussels.

It seems highly likely that such occurrences were commonplace, and that Mary, who is known to have supported choirboys in schools through-out the Low Countries,[91] kept a keen eye out for new young talent and auditioned choirboys in this fashion on a regular basis. It may be that, as elsewhere, boys in her court chapel were normally admitted at a certain age, one that Cobrize, being 'un peu grand', may have exceeded.[92] Equally, the considerable feat, which was surely demanded, of memorising new

---

[91] Ibid., 135.

[92] See for instance the stipulation of the chapter of Lyon Cathedral that, as noted by Jean Marie H. Forest, 'the habit of the church would not be given to boys more than eight years of age or to those who could not read well' (*L'école cathédrale de Lyon* (Paris, 1885), quoted in Becker, 'The Maîtrise', 139).

chants and new liturgical practices,[93] and the virtuosity – particularly in tackling such difficult items of chant as the matins responds mentioned already – demanded for their performance, must have rendered such a trial situation severely challenging to a young child. Equally, though, this level of interest, from one of the most powerful political figures in Europe, gives some measure of the cachet – in terms not just of musical but also of visual devotional and indeed political display – that attached to the skill of a gifted choirboy during this period.[94]

The potential rewards for choirboy success in such a forum as this could be considerable, as is amply revealed by a final example. On 16 June 1516, the chapter was sent a demand from Brussels from the sixteen-year-old Charles V on behalf of a certain 'Ernoulet du Broeuck'. This figure, clearly the composer Arnold von Bruck, and at that time a 'clerk of our private chapel', had formerly, the letter relates, been a choirboy at St Omer, in what was apparently his home town.[95] On account of this familial background, Charles, desiring 'his apt promotion and advancement in the holy church', now required that the chapter grant him 'the first vicariate that as from now will become vacant in your said church at your collation and disposition'. Charles went on to request that the chapter fulfil his wish

without hesitating to do this under the pretext that he departed from the same your church without your seal or licence of leave, the which, as we understand, he did more through youth than out of any malice, and, moreover, at the urgent pressing and request of certain of our special servants, and to enter into our service.

---

[93] On the feats of memory demanded of choirboys at Notre-Dame of Paris, see Wright, *Music and Ceremony*, 174–6.

[94] The frequent documentation of the impressment of choirboys into royal chapels reveals that Mary's interest, if rather more nurturing than what seems to have been the norm, was far from unusual among crowned heads. Examples include the story of a choirboy of Chartres who so impressed Anne of Brittany on a visit there in 1510 that she asked to take him with her, in return providing the cathedral with an inscribed bell, and the rather more brutal abduction, in 1517, of two choirboys of Rouen Cathedral who had impressed Francis I. (See Jules Alexandre Clerval, *L'Ancienne Maîtrise de Notre-Dame de Chartres* (Chartres, 1899), 107, and Bourdon and Collette, *Histoire de la maîtrise de Rouen*, 50–1.)

[95] The statement of Othmar Wessely that von Bruck had been a choirboy in Charles's own chapel may therefore need correction (see 'Bruck, Arnold von', *Grove Music Online*, 2001, www.oxfordmusiconline.com/grovemusic/view/10.1093/gmo/9781561592630.001.0001/omo-9781561592630-e-0000004124, accessed 5 December 2015). For an alternative possibility, however, see below. It seems clear from the archives that Arnold/Ernoult came from a family of long local tradition. The fabric account of 1431/2 records the appointment to an escoterie of a 'Maistre Brixe du Broeuc' (f. 2v). The numerous payments, in the second decade of the sixteenth century, to 'Pierre du Broecq drapier', possibly the boy's father, for clothing for the choirboys, suggest that he may have come from a family of tailors.

The latter suggests that von Bruck had earlier, perhaps while still a choirboy, been impressed into Charles's own choir. At any rate his service under Charles clearly provided a substantial early boost to his future career, and it must have been this early association with a Habsburg chapel that allowed him ultimately to assume his major post at the court of Charles's brother Ferdinand I. This case is reminiscent of the similar care taken by Leo X on behalf of Jean Cunsel, or Conseil, one of a number of French choirboys he had acquired from Louis XII. In a case exactly analogous to that of von Bruck, Leo wrote, in 1517, to Francis I to request a canonry for Cunsel in the Sainte-Chapelle of Paris, the institution in which the boy had received his training.[96] Such instances suggest that a certain obligation was felt to be implicit in the impressment of choirboys, and that such efforts to safeguard their future progress in the institutions from which they had hailed may have been more commonplace than the known documentation suggests.

Impressment of the better choirboys into more eminent and wealthy chapels was a hazard for ecclesiastical institutions across fifteenth- and early sixteenth-century Europe, especially those in northern France and the Low Countries, where the effectiveness of maîtrise training was widely acknowledged and admired.[97] In another sense, though, it was an acknowledgment of success: that boys from St Omer could attract the attention of the royal and imperial chapels was a clear sign of the efficacy of its training. If St Omer was no Cambrai Cathedral or St Donatian, Bruges, the success of its choirboys nonetheless proves, as do other aspects of its musical establishment, its high professional standing and the possibility for its choirboys of a bright future.

But such success, and the skilled training that led to it, in turn relied on cultivation and, crucially, investment from above. In the next chapter we shall consider the work of the masters of the boys and the role models embodied in some of the more famous and successful resident singers. In the inevitable absence (for northern Europe) of surviving music manuscripts we shall also enter the more hypothetical territory – based on the copying of music and records of its performance – of what may have been sung, and in what contexts and settings.

---

[96] See André Pirro, 'Leo X and Music', *Musical Quarterly* 21 (1935), 8.

[97] For a discussion of the effect of this practice in Liège and elsewhere see for example Antoine Auda, *La musique et les musiciens de l'ancien pays de Liège* (Brussels and Liège: Librairie Saint-Georges, 1930), 49–50.

Appendix: | Documents Concerning Choirboys and the Court Chapels of Charles V and Mary of Hungary

II. G. 112

1). Marie par la grace de dieu royne douairiere dHongrie et de Bohesme Regente et gouvernante

Mary by the grace of God dowager Queen of Hungary and Bohemia, Regent and Governor

Venerables treschiers et bien ames[:] Pource quentendons / quaves ung enffant de cueur appelle Michielet de Cobrize / que desirons oyr chanter / Nous vous requerons le nous envoyer avec ce porteur / Et vous nous feres plesir[.] A tant venerables tres chiers et bien amez nostre seigneur soit garde de vous. De Bruxelles ce xxix^e de mars anno xxxiii avant pasques

Venerable, dear and well-beloved: Insofar that it has come to our attention that you have a choirboy called Michielet de Cobrize, whom we desire to hear sing, we require that you send him with this messenger, and you will give us pleasure. To [our] so venerable, dear and well-beloved, may Our Lord be your protector. From Brussels this 29 March in the year [15]33 before Easter [i.e. 1534 new style.]

Marie

Mary

2). Marie par la grace [de] dieu royne douairie[re] de Hongrye de Bohesme regente et gouvernante

Mary by the grace of God dowager Queen of Hungary and Bohemia, Regent and Governor

Venerables tres chiers et bien aimes / Nous vous aiyons escript nous envoyer Michelet de Cobrize enffant de cueur de v[ost]re esglise porteur de cestes pour loyr chanter / Ce quaves fait dont vous scavons bon grez et combien que layons trouve bien saichant sa musicque / neantmoings pour ce quil est ung peu grand et quil ne se pourroit bonnement plyer selon que desirons pour le chant de n[ost]re chapelle ne lavons retenu enffant dicelle dont vous avons bien voulu adverter / Et requerir que sa venue icy ne luy soit aucunement preiudiciable avis que nonobstant Icelle Il ait son jour de provision comme sil ne eust este par nous mande[.] Et vous nous feres plesir.

Venerable, dear and well-beloved: We have written to you to send us Michelet de Cobrize, choirboy of your church [and] carrier of this [letter] to hear him sing. The which you have done and of which we know you to be well consenting. And although we have found him to be well versed in his music, nevertheless because he is a little old/ tall and because he could not well adapt himself to what we desire for the song of our chapel, we have not retained the child, whom we have wished to return to you. And we require that his coming here will not in any way count as a prejudicial judgement towards him, [and] that notwithstanding the same he may have his provision as if he had not been summoned by us. And you will give us pleasure.

A tant venerables tres chiers Et bien amez n[ost]re seigneur soit garde de vous[.] De Bruxelles ce xiii^e davril

To [our] so venerable, dear and well-beloved, may Our Lord be your protector. From Brussels this 13 April

Marie

Marie

II. G. 110

De par le Roy

From the King

Venerables chiers et bien amez[:] Pour ce que avons en singuliere Recommandacion n[ost]re bien ame Ernoulet du Broeucq a present clerc de n[ost]re chappelle domestique et lequel a parcidevant este enfant de cueur en v[ost]re eglise / et desirons son bien promocion et avancement en sainte eglise / Nous vous requerons bien affectueusment et acertes que en faveur de nous et a ceste n[ost]re requeste vous luy vueillez liberalement donner et accorder la premiere vicairie que derienavant [dorenavant] vaquera en v[ost]re dit egliese a v[ost]re collacion et disposicion par quelque moyen que ce soit et en contemplacion de nous le preferer a ce avant tous autres sans differer de ce faire soubz umbre quil se seroit parti dicelle v[ost]re eglise sans v[ost]re sceu congie ou licen[ce] ce que comme entendons il fist plus par jonesse que sans aucun malice et aussi a linstante poursuyte et requeste daucuns nos esp[ec]eaulx serviteurs et pour venir en n[ost]re service / Parquoy vous requerons y avoir regart et nous accorder n[ost]re dit requeste[.] Et vous nous ferez singulier honneur service et Plaisir[.] Ce scet dieu qui venerables chiers et bien amez vous ait en sa sainte garde[.] Escripts en n[ost]re ville de Bruxelles le xviii^e jour de juing anno xv^c xvi

Venerable, dear and well-beloved: Insofar that we have in singular esteem our well-beloved Ernoulet du Broeucq, presently clerk of our private chapel and who heretofore was a choirboy in your church, and we desire his apt promotion and advancement in the Holy Church, we require that, with apt affection and in good earnest, you, in goodwill to us and to this our request may wish freely to give and accord to him the first vicariate that as from now will become vacant in your said church at your collation and disposition by whatever means that this may be, and in deep consideration of us to prefer him for this before all others, without hesitating to do this under the pretext that he departed from the same your church without your seal or licence of leave, the which, as we understand, he did more through youth than out of any malice, and, moreover, at the urgent prosecution and request of certain of our special servants, and to enter into our service. Wherefore we require you to take this into account and accord us our said request. And you will render us singular honour, service and pleasure. This God knows; may he hold you, venerable dear and well-beloved, in his Holy protection. Written from our city of Brussels the eighteenth day of June, in the year 1516

Charles

Charles

3 | Masters and Master Singers

The sixth of June 1491 was a day of high drama. At a chapter meeting that day the chapter officially sacked Malin Alixandre from his post as master of the boys and ordered his removal from the house that he shared with them. This action stimulated a quick and strident response from the cantor, Johannes de Hemont, who was emphatic that the right of hiring and firing the master of the boys was his alone. For its part, the chapter claimed that the cantor's business was limited to overseeing the instruction of the boys and their house, and that the governance of the boys and their house was down to the chapter. Enraged at what he perceived as an infringement of his rights of office, the cantor walked out of the chapter meeting saying that he would resort to the process of law.[1]

In reality, though, the chapter was within its rights: the church statutes stated clearly that while the presentation of the master of the boys, or 'succentor' (literally 'sub-cantor'), was the business of the man for whom he deputised in ruling the choir – namely the cantor – his admission was the prerogative of the dean and chapter.[2] But the reason for the sacking, as recorded in the minutes of the next chapter meeting, held just four days later, takes the issue out of the realm of petty legalese. Here the 'animus' of

---

[1] 'Le vi^e de juing messeigneurs advertis [d']animus du gouvernement de Sire Malin Alixandre soubz chantre / et presente par Monseigneur le Chantre Maistre Jehan de Hemont messeigneurs deporterent ledit Sire Malin du gouvernement des vi enffans de coeur et maison duquel deportement monseigneur le chantre soy sentant greve et voeullant maintenir a luy appartenir linstitution et destitution du maistre de chant // Au quel mesdits seigneurs respondirent que quant au regime de lescolle et instruction en chant ne entendoyent point touchier mais seullement du gouvernement desdits enffans et maistrye(?). Lors monseigneur le chantre en soy partant du chapitre respondit quil se pouruerroit par justice[.]' (II. G. 355, f. 84v). For the nature of the relationship between the offices of cantor and succentor in the period generally, see for example Otto Frederick Becker, 'The Maîtrise in Northern France and Burgundy during the Fifteenth Century', unpublished PhD dissertation, George Peabody College for Teachers, Nashville, TN (1967), 189–95.

[2] This division had been made crystal clear the previous August in Hemont's own instrument of the renunciation of his canonry. The document speaks of the 'master of the school of song or music', '... cuius presentatio ad ipsius ecclesie pro tempore cantorem et successores suos dicte ecclesie cantores admissio vero ad dominos decanum et capitulum vel capitulum decano absente iuxta ipsius ecclesie statuta et ut consuetum est spectabunt et pertinebunt ...' (II. G. 355, f. 78v)

Alixandre's rule that had occasioned his removal casts the decision in a more starkly human light: it emerges that he had violently beaten one of the choirboys and, as the document says, hated him ('quemdam de sex pueris violenter verberaverat et [in] odio ipsum habebat'). Even given the ostensibly solid grounds for their actions, the chapter was careful to emphasise that it 'would not be harming the cantor in any right pertaining to his *cantoria*, nor wished him to be harmed'. For his part, Hemont 'wishes to please, but having not been consulted in this dismissal felt himself to have been aggrieved'. He offered to do whatever he could to content the lords, provided that they recall Alixandre and reinstall him in his prior position and lodgings. The chapter, however, stuck by its decision, affirming that Hemont should provide a suitable master and, failing that, that they would do so themselves 'according to the form of the statute'.[3]

As it turned out from a report presented to a chapter meeting on 13 July, the cantor had resisted evicting Alixandre, and still three days after the chapter's edict, and following repeated requests to Alixandre to leave, had failed to remove him from his post and replace him. In the face of this recalcitrance, the chapter had decided to take things into its own hands, replacing him with a man who will shortly figure more prominently in our story: the tenorist Grigoire Bourgois.

In the event, however, Bourgois's 1491 tenure of this post was short-lived: as so often in such cases, after copious disagreement and vituperation the injured parties decided to bury the hatchet, and in this same meeting they accepted Hemont's alternative candidate, Robert Poilly. The account affirms that Hemont had acted contrary to the express command of the chapter in seeking to maintain Alixandre in his position.[4] Yet in spite of this, and

---

[3] Die decima eiusdem mensis dominis in capitulo capitulariter congregatis / in eorum capitulo evocaverunt Dominum ac Magistrum Johannem de Hemont eidemque remonstraverunt qualiter Dominus Malinus Alixandre succentor quemdam de sex pueris violenter verberaverat / et [in] odio ipsum habebat quare ipsum Dominum Malinum ab eadem domo et alimentatione puerorum deportaverunt / expresse protestantes nec intendentes ipsum cantorem in aliquo suo iure adtangenti(?) sue cantorie gravare nec gravari ~~iure~~ velle quare fraternaliter requirebant ut eundem sic ammotum teneret et ratum haberet / Quiquidem dominus cantor respondit quod dominis ~~in gravumque tam~~(?) bene vellet complacere sed a dicta ammotione ipso non vocato sentiebat gravatum offerens eisdem dominis facere tantum quod deberent contentari proviso quod ipsum in eadem domo ut prius revocarent et restituerent. Ad quod domini acquiescere non voluerunt. Et ob hoc dominum cantorem [infor?]marunt quod de succentore habilem sufficientem et ydoneum qui scolas cantus regeret provideret / Alias domini protestati sunt / quod si non providerit domini providebunt etc. secundum formam statuti etc. (II. G. 355, f. 84v)

[4] It would appear that the dust took a while to settle: on 28 July (i.e. some two weeks after the matter had been decided), a stipend of twelve livres per annum was requested by the provost to be provided to Alixandre '... proviso quod comparebit et serviet ecclesie horis diurnis et

notwithstanding the protestations of both sides at being 'offended in our proper rights and dues', the injured parties decided to revert to the situation as it had been before the dismissal, although, perhaps prudently, they are unspecific about what the precise nature of that situation had been. Neither do the stated reasons for the cessation of hostilities – a claimed desire to cultivate peace and love, and the difficulty, in a time of prevailing war, of conducting the necessary legal proceedings – seem especially persuasive, much less unforeseeable. Certainly this is far from the only surviving record of violence towards a choirboy, and harsh treatment seems to have been relatively commonplace.[5] Perhaps, then, there were other dynamics in play here: the office of master of the boys, which changed hands frequently at this period, was a focus of frequent dispute during Hemont's tenure as cantor, with masters not uncommonly failing to meet the requirements of their post or being absent without having made proper provision. Clearly Hemont's position in the chapter was not a harmonious one, and there are hints, as Chapter 6 will elaborate, that he may have been a generally difficult figure; plus the problems that, as we saw in Chapter 2, he apparently suffered in trying to ensure his future financial security following the relinquishment of his prebend surely did nothing to foster a positive rapport with his colleagues.

On the other hand it is possible that the chapter considered itself on some level indebted to Hemont over the establishment of the 'conservatoire' and that he, reeling from the Alixandre fracas that followed shortly thereafter, felt a measure of righteous indignation. He had been to some degree instrumental, and clearly took some pride in, the negotiations that had led to the suppression of his canonry for the upkeep of the master and boys. At a chapter meeting on 31 December 1490 he had himself announced the suppression to the assembled company:

On the last day of the aforesaid month [of December], when the dean and canons were gathered in chapter, having received certain apostolic and legal letters sent down from on high via the venerable man Lord Johannes de Hemont, cantor, concerning the reservation of the suppressed fruits and revenues of the canonry and prebend that he was accustomed to receive, that are to be received on the chapter

---

nocturnis ac vaccabit instruentem pueris chori sub Domino R. Poilly usque ad beneplacitum dominorum et non alias' (II. G. 355, f. 85v). In other words he was to provide the customary service singing in the choir, for the payment customary for a vicar, but to leave the tutelage of the boys to Robert Poilly.

[5] For some particularly egregious examples of both at Rouen Cathedral see Adolphe Bourdon and Armand Collette, *Histoire de la maîtrise de Rouen* (Rouen, 1892; repr. Geneva: Minkoff, 1972), 107–10.

table by the said cantor for as long as he shall live, in manner and form as if he held the canonry in person, for the use and maintenance of the master of song and the six choirboys, as one can establish concerning these and other matters in greater detail through the apostolic letters and processes received from above. These apostolic letters he, appearing in person in the said chapter in the presence of myself the notary, reported, made known and published to the said lords the dean and canons, according to the form and process of moving the suit. The lords, wishing to proceed in the correct manner, held the said letter to have been reported, made known and published, and decreed themselves to have been duly informed.[6]

Hemont likely also felt buoyed by the fact that the cantor's right of nomination to the office of master of the boys was of venerable tradition, as indeed was the church's exclusive right, within the city of Saint-Omer, to run a school of music. This is affirmed in the 1438 Statutes issued, like so many other song school foundations, under Eugenius IV,[7] which by the way affirm the relative roles of cantor and dean and chapter. Here the situation is laid out thus:

We establish and ordain that for the ruling of the school of singing, or music, each year on the Monday after the first Sunday of Lent, the cantor of the church of St Omer may present to the dean and chapter a suitable person who, if he should prove appropriate, and useful and well disposed to the church, shall be held to be accepted, so that no one nearby in the town, borough, suburbs and districts of Saint-Omer may presume to run or hold a school specifically of music, unless by special licence of the aforesaid master of music or song.[8]

---

[6] Die ultima mensis prefati dominis decano et canonicis capitulariter congregatis / receptis certis litteris apostolicis et processibus de super fulminatis per venerabilem virum Dominum Johannem de Hemont cantorem super reservatione fructuum reddituum et proventuum canonicatus et prebende quos obtinere solebat suppressorum ad opus et interventionem magistri cantus et sex puerorum chori super mensa capitulari per ipsum cantorem percipiendorum quoad vixerit modo et forma quod si personaliter se canonicus existerit prout hec et alia per litteras apostolicas et processus de super habitos latius constare potest[.] Quasquidem litteras apostolicas ipse personaliter comparens in eodem capitulo coram me notario eisdem dominis decano et canonicis insinuavit notificavit et publicavit ipsas secundum formam et tenorem processus movendi[.] Quiquidem domini rite procedere volentes dictas litteras pro intimatis instructis et publicatis habuerunt et monite se debite reputaverunt etc. (II. G. 355, f. 83r)

[7] The widespread foundation of song schools generally at this time was motivated to no small degree by the need to provide voices appropriate for the burgeoning role of polyphony as well as being part of an organisational and didactic response to the turmoil of the Avignon exile of the papacy and subsequent schism. It was an important platform of the reforms of Eugenius IV, elected pope in 1431, and widely supported by funds provided by ecclesiastical benefices. See Osvaldo Gambassi, *"Pueri Cantatores" nelle Cattedrali d'Italia tra medioevo e età moderno* (Florence: Olschki, 1997), especially chapter 2, 53–65.

[8] 'Statuimus et ordinamus quod ad regimen scolarum cantus seu musice, quolibet anno, lune post brandones presentet cantor ecclesie Sancti Audomari decano et capitulo personam idoneam, quam

The comings and goings of the various masters under Hemont's cantorship together weave an intriguing web: obviously the chapter was acutely aware of the linchpin significance of the master in its musical provision and went to considerable lengths to attract – and keep – its favoured candidates. A promising early appointee under Hemont's leadership (which began following the death in late 1478 of his predecessor Antoine de Tramecourt) was a certain Johannes Tectoris, but in fact – as we learn from the chapter act of 2 May 1481 – his tenure had ended before it had even begun:

> The Bishop of Liège had written to the lords that he had retained to himself Johannes Tectoris alias Boulet for his own church in Liège; whom however the lords had recently admitted as succentor and master of the school of song. He [Tectoris] came on the same day to the lords in order to excuse himself and, thanking them, take his leave.[9]

Given its similarity to a much more famous name, that of the epochal music theorist Johannes Tinctoris, this is a name likely to make musicologists' blood race, and indeed an attempt was made in 1954 by José Quitin to tie both names to the same individual.[10] We know that Tinctoris had been in Liège at least some time before 1484 because he says so in the dedication, penned that year, of his *De inventione et usu musice*. More suggestively, he dedicates the volume in question to none other than Johannes de Stokem, *liégois* composer, whose service in the city's cathedral of St Lambert partially coincided with that of Tectoris. Thickening the plot is the fact that there is a lacuna in our knowledge during this period of the more famous man's whereabouts. However, while Quitin makes strenuous efforts to find a philological link between the two names, a conclusive case has clearly not been made and, as Ronald Woodley has pointed out to me,[11] the two personal signatures reproduced at the end of Quitin's article

---

si idonea et ecclesie utilis et propicia fuerit, recipere teneatur; adiicientes ne quis in villa, burgo, suburbiis et banleuca Sancti Audomari particulares scolas musice regere aut tenere audeat, nisi de magistri musice seu cantus predicti licentia speciali.' See Albert Legrand, 'Réjouissances des écoliers de Notre-Dame de St-Omer, le jour de St-Nicolas, leur glorieux patron (6 décembre 1417)', *Mémoires de la Société des antiquaires de la Morinie* 7 (1844–6), 201.

[9] Episcopus Leodiensis scripserat dominis se retinuisse Johannem Tectoris alias Boulet ~~pro~~ in sua ecclesia Leodiensis quem tamen nuper domini admiserant pro succentore et magistro scolarum cantus. Venit eatenus ipso die ad dominos se excusans eosque regracians licenciam accepit. (II. G. 355, 17v)

[10] 'Les maîtres de chant de la cathédrale St. Lambert, à Liège aux XVe et XVIe siècles', *Revue Belge de Musicologie* 8 (1954), 5–18. The confusion is still further enhanced by the fact that Nicolas Rembert acted as procurator for both Tinctoris and Tectoris in paying charges (annates) at the papal curia on canonries held by them (for more on this see p. 210).

[11] E-mail correspondence, 5 April 2015.

unambiguously read 'Tectoris'. At any rate, following an earlier stint in 1474–5, Tectoris's year as maître de chant in Liège in 1481/2 appears to have been his last, and his whereabouts – assuming, as we surely must, that he and Tinctoris were indeed two individuals – are thereafter unknown.

Fortunately for the chapter, their appointment directly following Tectoris's departure proved more propitious. Having held the same post the previous year, though, it is hard to imagine that Martin de Lavenne (or 'Lavesne') cannot have felt like a poor substitute following the chapter's attempt to woo Tectoris. This may partly explain why, on his reappointment, the chapter gave him

tunics of the colour of [those of] the boys, but these were given to him freely as an injunction to him that he should provide for them two young boys for the choir of tender age whereby it might conveniently happen that they may for a long time be able to serve in the church.[12]

In other words they were supplying him with a set of smart new clothes for his cohort, but on the apparent assumption that he would do some useful recruiting, bringing in boys who would serve for long enough to give the church a good return on its investment in them. The going was clearly not always easy for Lavenne; before the end of the year he found himself asking for a raise in his allowance for feeding the boys:

the lords, considering the high expense of grain and provisions agreed by special grace to the Lord Martin de Lavenne, master of song, for the sustenance and maintenance of his choirboys beyond the six livres granted, on each day one patard [a low country coin worth a livre tournois] until a more plentiful supply of food and improved weather arrives.[13]

Generally though this seems to have been a time of stability in the maîtrise, with Lavenne remaining in post until September 1486, when he was succeeded by Alixandre. His relationship with the choir had already been of long standing by the time he had assumed the position of master: in 1469/70 he had acquired his

---

[12] ... tunicas de colore puerorum sed hec de gracia dantur ei preceptum quod sibi provideat de duobus iuvenibus pueris pro choro tenerioris etatis quo fieri commode poterit ut diutius valeant in ecclesia deservire[.] (II. G. 355, f. 18r). The meaning here of 'provideat de' is not entirely unambiguous: although the explanation given seems the most likely one, it is also possible that the chapter is asking Lavenne to provide *for* two young boys who are already recruited (i.e. to provide them with bed and board out of his stipend).

[13] ... domini considerantes caristiam frumenti et victualium annuerunt de speciali gracia Domino Martino de Lavenne magistro cantus per sustentatione suorum puerorum chori ultra sex libras concessorum [sic] quolibet die unum patard donec et quousque uberior frugalitas et melioratio temporis advenerit. (II. G. 355, f. 25r)

vicariate from a certain 'Bassee' (Jehan de Herlines, *dit* Bassee, whom we shall meet later), the latter taking on his vacated escoterie.[14] His payment two years later for having 'written, ruled, noted and provided the parchment of twenty-four responses set in six of the books of processions' can only have been for copying four responses in processionals allocated to each of the six boys.[15] Since he relinquished his role as master halfway through the usual year-long cycle it would appear that Lavenne had decided for whatever reason that he no longer wished, or was no longer able, to serve in this capacity. A touching detail is recorded when, on 28 April 1487, the lords passed his resigned vicariate on to 'Guillebert Boursier their former choirboy'.[16]

Nothing in the records prior to 1491 suggests anything untoward in Malin Alixandre's relationship with either the chapter or the maîtrise up to that point, and the history is a long one: his ascent to the vicariate occurred as far back as September 1463, when he stepped into the shoes of the deceased vicar, noted music copyist and former master of the boys at Cambrai Cathedral Vincent Breion, whose epitaph can still be seen (Figure 3.1).[17] Having assumed the role of master of the boys in 1486 Alixandre held it uninterruptedly until the 1491 debacle discussed above. It seems likely that there was some fallout from that year's events: at the provost's annual visit on 5 July he admonished the canons, vicars and escotiers that they should apply themselves to the divine office with greater diligence than they had lately done.[18]

---

[14] De Martinet de Lavesne pour le vicarie que fu a Bassee xv s; De Bassee pour lescoterie dudit Martinet a lui conferee xi s (1469/70, f. 5v). Why 'Bassee' should have been prepared, via this transaction, to be demoted from vicar to escotier is unclear.

[15] 1471/2, f. 15v: A Sire Martin de Lavense pour avoir escript rieulle notte et livre le parchemin de xxiiii respons assis en vi des livres des pourcessions xii s

[16] ... vicariam huius ecclesie vacantem per simplicem resignationem Domini Martini de Lavesne contulerunt Domini Guilleberto Boursier eorum quondam corali ... (II. G. 355, f. 72r)

[17] For Alixandre's first appointment see II. G. 353, f. 58r. Breion had first appeared at Cambrai Cathedral as a chaplain in 1408; his tenure as master of the boys extended from ?1418 to 1421, and he seems to have left Cambrai in 1423. He held chaplaincies also at Arras, Lille and Noyon and, like his fellow cleric at Cambrai, Du Fay, was illegitimate, a condition for which he filed for papal dispensation in 1427. For full details see Alejandro Enrique Planchart, *Guillaume Du Fay*, 2 vols. (Cambridge: Cambridge University Press, 2017), vol. 2, 785–6. Breion's epitaph, of Tournai work, seems originally to have been located in the chapel of St Nicaise but is today embedded in the wall to the left of the last chapel in the north aisle. For details see Marc Gil and Ludovic Nys, *Saint-Omer gothique* (Valenciennes: Presses Universitaires de Valenciennes, 2004), 235, 379. For details of Breion's copying and binding work for St Omer see ibid., 379–80.

[18] Dominus Johannes prepositus in propria visitavit. Primo in choro. vicarios. scoterios / ac deinde in capitolo dominos monendo ut si caritative temporibus preteritis dixerimus ad huc perseverando in melius de cetero vivamus sicut confratres et etc. in officiis divinis meliorem adhibeamus diligentiam quam fecimus etc. Ac omnia que ad visitationem pertinent fecit ut moris est / (II. G. 355, f. 85v)

Figure 3.1 Funerary epitaph for Vincent Breion

Comments in the dealings with Johannes Thorion, who assumed the position of master in February 1492 following what was apparently only a six-month 'caretaker' role on the part of Poilly, suggest that circumstances continued to be rocky under his tenure. Three months after his appointment Thorion, like Lavenne before him, approached the chapter for more money due to the high price of provisions. The lords provided it, 'so that the said Lord Johannes will apply himself more vigilantly in the study and instruction of the said boys and be more often present at the daily and nightly hours'. In contrast to the extra payments detailed for Lavenne, however, Thorion's are specified 'to be distributed at the individual hours, that is to say at matins, Mass and vespers, on each of which four deniers parisis, amounting to twelve deniers for each day'.[19] The chapter was apparently keen, in other words, to ensure the solidity of its investment. The proviso at the end of this record states that the funds will continue to be supplied in this way until such time as Thorion is provided with a benefice that will guarantee him an income. It may be that, as occurred elsewhere,[20] the chapter was holding off on providing Thorion with a benefice pending the fulfilment of a trial period; or, alternatively, it may still have been playing catch-up following the unscheduled departure of Alixandre, with no vicariate yet being available to support the new appointment.[21]

Whatever the attitude of the chapter to his employment, an absence of fifteen days early the following February suggests, in hindsight, that Thorion was quickly in search of pastures new. Timing was clearly of the essence: later that same month his tenure for the year was up, and Hemont appeared before the chapter 'wishing to present, as is the convention, Lord Johannes de Thorion to the school of song, hoping that the same Thorion would wish to continue his service'. Thorion himself, however, had other ideas: 'within two days of this, prompted by certain motives, he said to the lord cantor that he should provide another master, and that it was not his intention further to serve in the capacity in which he had served'. This obviously came as a shock to Hemont, who responded 'that he did not now have time to find an alternative so quickly, and that he would make diligent effort to find someone adequate and suitable as soon as possible'. It was thus in desperation and as a stopgap that he at this point proposed Robert

---

[19] Dominus Joh[annes] Thorion magister puerorum chori in capitolo supplicavit ut sibi de alicuius subventionis auxilio atten[dentes] caristia[m] victualium sibi providere de gracia domini dignarentur[.] Ad cuiusquidam supplicationem pluribus consideratis que consideranda sunt prefati domini[.] Ut ipse Dominus Magister Johannes de cetero vigilentius studio et doctrina dictorum puerorum insistet ac frequentius horis diurnis et nocturnis intersit / ordinaverunt eidem distribui singulis horis. videlicet in matutinis missa et vesperis quilibet dicta bonarum. iiii d parisiensis. ascendentes qualibet die xii d. donec et quousque eidem provisum fuit de aliquo beneficio etc. (II. G. 355, f. 90v; 23 May 1492)

[20] As for instance – as Robert Nosow points out to me – was the case at St Donatian, Bruges.

[21] This lack was made up when, some four months later, the death of Mattheus Dostin freed up the vicariate attached to the canonry of Hugo de Monchy, which duly passed to Thorion. (II. G. 355, f. 92v; 17 September 1492)

Fabri and Malin Alixandre, who were both, as we learned in Chapter 2, rejected as unsuitable.[22]

But the lords were not giving up so easily and, as recorded in the next entry in the chapter acts, Thorion appeared before them again less than a week later to be sworn in, clearly as the outcome of some serious arm-twisting.[23] Even after this their success was only temporary, however: in July Thorion petitioned – again successfully – for fifteen days' absence, and then, less than three months later, canvassed for leave for an entire year. This he was permitted to take, starting on 1 October (the Feast of St Remigius). What is most striking in all this is that, having been significantly and repeatedly inconvenienced by Thorion, the chapter took such obsequious pains to encourage his return: acknowledging his 'sufficiency and suitability and hoping that he will afterwards give himself diligently in service to this church', they pledged that 'the year having passed, if it will please him, the lords guarantee to give him back his vicariate as formerly'.[24] Either Thorion was a talent of unusual proportions or the chapter was desperate to find a competent master of the boys. Their indulgence of him is particularly striking since he must at this point have been quite young: as we shall shortly see, he did not die until 1547, in which year he was buried in the chapel of St Nicholas in the very church he had, in his younger years, struggled so hard to leave.

---

[22] Johannes de Hemont comparens in capitulo volens presentare ut moris est Dominum Johannem Thorion ad scolas cantus sperans quod ipse Thorion vellet continuare suum servicium / nichilominus certis de causis ad hac animum suum moventibus citra duos dies dixit eidem domino cantore quod provideret de alio magistro et quod non erat intentionis amplius servire in ea facultate qua serviebat / hiis dictis dixit dominus cantor prefatus quod non habebat spacium nunc temporis ita celeriter se querendi alium / et quod faceret diligentiam quantotius inveniendi alium sufficientem et ydoneum et illico presentavit Dominos Robertum Fabri et Malinum Alexandre / tunc et illico domini responderunt quod tamquam non sufficiens ab exercitio fuit unus eorum deportatus / alter non in ecclesia habebat onus sufficiens etc. protestans expresse non reputari negligens etc. (II. G. 355, f. 94r; 24 February 1493)

[23] Consequenter prima mensis martii Dominus et Magister Johannes de Hemont cantor postquam certas remonstrationes fecerunt dicto Domino Johanni Thorion et tandem post multas altercationes non obstante excusatione per eum habita medio dominorum dominus cantor prefatus consultus in capitolo representavit predictum Dominum Johannem Thorion / quem domini protestantibus consuetis expositis et declaratis et factis admiserunt / protestantes etc. (II. G. 355, f. 94r; 1 March 1493)

[24] ... considerantes sufficientiam et ydoneitatem ipsius et sperans quod inposterum diligens in serviciis huius ecclesie se dabit domini concesserunt inde quod non obstante statuto possit se absentare ab uno festo Remigii usque ad alium festum anni sequente perdendo tamen emolumenta sue vicarie / Et quod anno revoluto si sibi placet redire domini eundem recipient ut inantea vicarius. (II. G. 355, f. 98r; 27 September 1493)

All this begs questions concerning Thorion's whereabouts before his appearance in the Saint-Omer records, and in particular where he may have received the training that apparently made him such hot property. Records found by Bruno Bouckaert and David Fiala place him in the collegiate church of St Amé, Douai, where, in 1485–6, 1486–7 and again in 1490–1 and 1491–2, he is cited as responsible for Masses on Tuesdays, though not necessarily for celebrating them himself. Since the relevant lists for the intervening years are missing, it seems likely that Thorion was in Douai continuously from 1485 until his arrival in Saint-Omer, though a similar lacuna in the accounts from 1479 to 1485 deprives us of documentation of his year of arrival. It is clear, however, that he did not spend the entirety of the year 1491–2 in Douai (where the accounting year began on 24 June, as opposed to St Omer's 10 September): in addition to his role as master of the boys beginning in February 1492, his time at St Omer was further occupied in 1491–2 by singing the *Salve* at the chapelle sur le marchiet, and by celebrating weekly two of the daily Masses at the chantry of Antoine de Wissoc. Since mentions of him in Douai do not presuppose a permanent chaplaincy or even necessarily regular employment, it may be that he was already searching for brighter prospects elsewhere, or perhaps combining his work at St Amé with other as yet unknown activities. Details in the chapter acts at Douai suggest that Thorion's dissatisfactions at St Omer were not a new phenomenon: complaints by him to the chapter (unfortunately unspecified) are logged in each year from 1487 to 1490, with all of them apparently being resolved.[25]

While everything known about Thorion this far back places him unequivocally in the north, however, documents from the earlier 1480s locate a man of the same name in a very different setting. Assuming this is the same singer (and the name is not a common one), his biography becomes at this point suggestive of much more than local significance. A notebook complied by Antonio Alabanti, prior of the Florentine Servite friary church of Santissima Annunziata from 1477 to 1485, studied by Valente Gori and Darwin Smith,[26] and also addressed by Giovanni

---

[25] My thanks to David Fiala for these details on Douai.

[26] Valente Gori, 'La musica alla SS. Annunziata di Firenze dall'origine alla fondazione della cappella musicale', *Academia Musicale Valdarnese, Bollettino d'informazione semestrale, Badia di Soffena* (Castelfranco di Sopra), [1981], no. 1, 9–22; no. 2, 4–23; Darwin Smith, 'La réforme musicale à la Santissima Annunziata de Florence (1478–1485) et la politique religieuse de Lorenzo de'Medici', *Drammaturgia* 14 (2017), 7–52, at 18; Darwin Smith, *"Memoriale" de maestro Antonio Alabanti prieur de la Santissima Annunziata de Florence (1477–1485), Édition,*

Zanovello,[27] places a 'Jo. Torion' there in 1483. Here he is described as a 'contralto' and as one of four 'magistri musice', three of whom are each assigned an aspect of the tutoring (in Torion's case supervising the contralto line) of what was evidently an ensemble comprising friars and novices of the friary. This group is tasked with singing the conventual round of music, including polyphony, in the choir, ranging from settings of the *Salve regina* through laude, motets, psalms, hymns and Magnificats to full Masses.

This function of the magistri, including Torion, in coaching a choir of non-professional singers was part of a considerable expansion in the use of polyphony, both vocal and instrumental, during Alabanti's tenure as prior. By the early 1480s a group of internationally recruited professional singers was in place. At first these 'singers of the house' were tasked with singing in the usual round of Mass and office, but by January 1484 we encounter a group of four whose role at SS. Annunziata had been restricted to the Saturday Lady Mass beside the church's miraculous image of the Annunciation, while the majority of their work, and indeed salaries, came from the baptistery and cathedral. By this point, music in the church had reached a level that was exceptional not just in Florence but throughout the peninsula. Singers employed between the three institutions, a grouping that Frank D'Accone dubbed the 'Florentine Chapel',[28] included some of the most celebrated musicians of the day, including Agricola, Isaac and Ghiselin Verbonnet. Darwin Smith notes that their emoluments in the later 1480s, drawn from the three partner institutions, equalled exactly those of singers in the papal chapel, and it seems likely that the papal model was very much in Alabanti's mind. A document of 26 May 1483 records reimbursement to the prior of costs he had incurred in Rome for having works – including five Masses and three motets – copied by the papal

---

introduction, index et glossaire, 2 vols. and facsimile, Habilitation à diriger des recherches (HDR), Université de Paris I, 2010; Darwin Smith, 'Greban, Arnoul', in Ludwig Finscher (ed.), *Die Musik in Geschichte und Gegenwart* (Kassel: Bärenreiter, 2002), 7, cols. 1542–5; Darwin Smith, 'Le budget de maître Antonio Alabanti, prieur de la Santissima Annunziata de Florence (1477–1485)', in Olivier Mattéoni (ed.), *Classer, dire, compter. Discipline du chiffre et fabrique d'une norme comptable à la fin du Moyen Âge* (Paris: Comité pour l'histoire économique et financière de la France, 2015), 217–47. My grateful thanks are due to Darwin Smith for an extended and fascinating e-mail discussion of this topic and for sharing with me his own and Gori's published studies.

[27] '"In the Church and in the Chapel": Music and Devotional Spaces in the Florentine Church of Santissima Annunziata', *Journal of the American Musicological Society* 67 (2014), 379–428.

[28] 'The Singers of San Giovanni in Florence during the Fifteenth Century', *Journal of the American Musicological Society* 14 (1961), 307–58.

singers, and for treating them to a meal. In this connection, as Smith notes, the recording in Alabanti's notebook that the choir had among its music a Mass on *L'homme armé* suggests a tantalising link with what must at that point have been the freshly copied Cappella Sistina MS 14, which includes no fewer than five such Masses. The five Roman cycles were part of a haul of no fewer than eleven new Masses acquired in 1483, earlier the same year as the formation of the coached conventual choir, including further cycles brought from Rome and others copied, and even composed, on the spot.[29]

This, then, was the sophisticated and richly endowed musical world of which Torion was a part. The fact that he is the only individual named in connection with the conventual choir without the title 'frate' would certainly support the notion that he was young, since even novices (typically in their upper teens) were addressed as 'brothers'. Gori's statement that he 'subsequently took the habit of a brother'[30] may mean simply that he assumed the role of a novice, rather than necessarily taking vows. While it is not possible, at least at present, to be certain of the full extent of Torion's presence at SS. Annunziata, Darwin Smith has traced payments to him (nowhere naming him as a 'frate') in the church's *ricevuti* from July 1482 to October 1483, the latter about the time when, according to Smith's dating, his name appears in the prior's notebook.[31]

How, then – if this was indeed the individual who went on to a distinguished musical career elsewhere and who died in Saint-Omer as late as 1547 – did Torion, a boy or at most a young man from the north, come to be singing in Florence in 1483? While solid evidence may yet be lurking in the archives of SS. Annunziata, the most likely hypothesis surely points in the direction of one of the four singing 'heavyweights' (to use Darwin Smith's term) who from January 1484 comprised the rump of the church's professional choir and who were resident in the priory itself. This group, of

---

29 Smith, "*Memoriale*", 87–8, and Gori, 'La musica', no. 2, 14 and 17. See also Zanovello, '"In the Church"', 390, 401, 407. On composition, note the payments to 'Janes Utrijch (Janes Witinc), cantore, per due messe recò da Roma et per più canti compose qui in convento', and 'Frate Andrea di Giovanni francioso a dì 19 dicto [1484], lire 44 s. 7 sono della sua messa novella'. (See Smith, "*Memoriale*", 87.)

30 Gori, 'La musica', no. 2, 19. Unfortunately Gori gives no source for his information, though the general reliability of his citations and the fact that he was himself a Servite prior at SS. Annunziata surely lends it credence.

31 See Smith, 'La réforme', 44–5. Zanovello (384) equates him with the Johannes Comitis [sic, not 'Comitus', as in Zanovello] who turns up frequently as a singer in 1482. However, as Smith points out to me, neither 'Torion' nor 'Comitis' is a sobriquet: both are in fact surnames, strongly suggesting two distinct individuals, a conclusion supported by the fact that no fewer than eight singers named Johannes are documented as singing in the convent between 1480 and 1485 (on this see also Smith, 'La réforme', 43–4).

two native and two northern singers, included an 'Arnolfo di Francia', whom Smith has plausibly equated with the polymathic figure of Arnoul Gréban, former magister (of both song and grammar) and organist of Notre-Dame of Paris, and author of a monumental mystery play *La nativité, le passion et le resurrection de nostre Sauveur Jhesu-Crist*.[32]

Arnolfo, described in 1477 as a cleric of the diocese of Cambrai, arrived in Florence with a group of companions in 1473. The fact that none other than Lorenzo de' Medici *Il Magnifico* personally (in a rare gesture) obtained a papal dispensation for him to take holy orders so that he could be installed as a chaplain in the Medici church of San Lorenzo suggests already that Arnolfo was a man of far more than average talent. In January 1478 he was one of five singers hired to form the choir of the cathedral of Santa Maria del Fiore. However, following the Pazzi conspiracy which saw Lorenzo's brother Giuliano murdered in the cathedral only some three months later, Arnolfo, now personal singer to Lorenzo, was assigned to teach music to the novices of the SS. Annunziata, and the following year he was dispatched to France to recruit singers. While Arnolfo did not himself return to his position at the priory until 1484, it seems a reasonable supposition that Torion/Thorion may have been one of the talented choir-boys that he, following common practice at the time, recruited and had sent to Florence as a musical adornment of the Medici and of the friary church that they closely patronised.[33] At any rate, the return of Arnolfo to Florence coincided with the musical high point of the choir of SS. Annunziata, run now by the four resident singers who, in addition to singing the weekly Lady Mass, were tasked with hiring the singers to fulfil all the friary's musical needs. In the event the musical achievements of the church were apparently short-lived, since Alabanti's relinquishing of his post in July 1485 coincided with the departure from the records also of many of the professional singers, including Arnulfus, who followed the former prior to Bologna. It is possible that Torion left around the same point, giving enough time for him to arrive in Douai for his first documented appearance there that year.[34] But the likely Italian sojourn of a musician closely

---

[32] For the following details on Arnolfo see Smith, 'La réforme', 28–32, and Smith, *"Memoriale"*, 98–9.

[33] For a detailed consideration of the close patronage of SS. Annunziata by Lorenzo see Smith, 'La réforme', 32–9.

[34] Of course this is not the only possible scenario whereby Torion may have returned to his native north. David Fiala has pointed out to me the possible coincidence between the presumed departure of Torion and the appointment as master of vicars in St Amé, Douai, of Simon Attaignant. Attaignant, who according to the Douai vicars' accounts received his appointment,

associated with Saint-Omer opens up a further hypothesis that appears, based on the aggregate of information, extremely suggestive. To address this takes us to the incipient sixteenth century and the abbey of St Bertin.

In 1501 Antoine de Berghes, then abbot of St Bertin, directed a missive to Cardinal Giovanni de' Medici (the future Pope Leo X) in Rome. The letter is of more general interest because it was written for the abbot by none other than Desiderius Erasmus, then lodging at the abbey under the abbot's patronage, a fact that has guaranteed its survival and publication among Erasmus's works.[35] The letter was composed in response to one sent the previous year by Giovanni himself, in which he had expressed thanks for the generous welcome he had received at St Bertin during his travels through Europe.[36] It discusses two songs sent to the cardinal – he being 'most deeply learned in this ancient and divine art' – along with the letter, recently composed by an unfortunately unnamed composer who claims to have been nurtured in the family of the Medici.[37] This man, says de Berghes, is the prince of the art of music of our town:

But it has pleased me, in the meantime and in this instance, to revive an ancient custom, so that I should bestow upon your Excellency something in the way not only of a thank-you letter of hospitality but also of a guest-gift. I am sending two little musical songs; a gift that, though exceedingly meagre and even slenderer than Cicero's 'slendiferous'[38], nonetheless I am confident will not be unpleasing, both since you yourself are most deeply learned in this most ancient and by universal

---

on 26 May 1483, while in Rome serving under Ferry de Clugny, could plausibly have brought Torion with him on his journey from Italy to Douai, where he presented himself for residence on 24 June 1484.

[35] The letter is widely published in editions of Erasmus' epistles.

[36] Henri de Laplane claimed in 1855 that Giovanni's letter 'was long conserved in the archives', apparently implying that it had been lost; at any rate I have not been able to trace it, and if it had lasted through Laplane's time it would surely have been destroyed with the loss of the St Bertin archive in 1915 (*Les abbés de Saint-Bertin* vol. 2: 1450–1791 (Saint-Omer: Fleury-Lemaire, 1855), 74). On the young cardinal's travels see Johannes Burchard (ed. L. Thuasne), *Johannis Burchardi: Diarium sive rerum urbanarum commentarii* (Paris: Ernest Leroux, 1883–5), 41–2. See also Scipione Ammirato, *Ritratto d'huomini illustri di Casa Medici*, in *Opuscoli del signor Scipione Ammirato*, vol. 3 (Florence: Amadore Massi and Lorenzo Landi, 1642), 63–99, particularly 66.

[37] It will be remembered that Du Fay, in his one surviving autograph letter, sent to Piero and Giovanni de' Medici in 1456 (see for instance David Fallows, *Dufay* (revised ed., London and Melbourne: Dent, 1987), 71), announced that he was sending them some of his own recently composed songs. Perhaps this was a common method whereby the Medici received new music. My thanks to Barbara Haggh-Huglo for this suggestion.

[38] Henry Howard adds: 'of slight or poor construction'. The reference is to a letter of Cicero that refers to a 'levidense munusculum' (*Ad familiares* 9.12.2). It may be a word made up by Cicero; if not it is clearly meant to be a playful almost-neologism.

agreement divine art, just as in all others; and since the cantilena is fresh and very newly born, and born moreover of him who proclaims that he was once nurtured in the most renowned family of the Medici; [a family] which seems to me to have been without doubt a gift from heaven for the incitement of genius and the enrichment of studies. This man is the chief of the art of music in our city.[39]

The letter has been known to musicology since Edmond Vander Straeten published the relevant extract in 1882. As he tantalisingly put it, 'there will be very interesting work to be done in the archives of Saint-Omer to recover some trace of this great musician, brought up as an intimate of the Medici and who later became one of the glories of composition'.[40] Johannes Thorion – assuming the singers in Florence and St Omer were indeed one and the same – surely emerges as the most likely candidate to have been this unnamed figure. As a young choirboy, especially as the putative protégé of Lorenzo's musical amanuensis, he could well have been housed and nurtured by the Medici before, as a brilliant young musician, finding employment in their favoured friary church. If the identification is accepted, Thorion would be unique among musicians linked to Saint-Omer in being traceable, in his youth, to Florence: for this indeed to be the Thorion who died in his adopted city in 1547 he can scarcely, in 1483, have been much out of his teens. If this in itself adds to the likelihood of his being in Florence already as a boy, then his employment as a youth in a Florentine church under powerful Medici patronage can surely only augment the possibility of an early presence in that dynastic household. On the other hand the duration of his residence in Saint-Omer – including, by the way, the period of the Medici visit – was such as to imply that he was probably native to the town in which he sang, taught, worshipped and was buried.

[39] My thanks to Henry Howard for this translation. The original reads as follows: Libuit autem interim et hac in re priscum referre morem, ut tuae praestantiae non solum hospitalis epistolae verumetiam xeniorum vice nonnihil adderem. Mitto autem cantiunculas musicas duas; quod ego munus, tametsi perquam exiguum ac Ciceroniana etiam levidensa levius, tamen haud ingratum fore confido, vel quod es ipse huius artis antiquissimae omniumque consensu divinae longe scientissimus, itidem ut aliarum omnium; vel quod cantilena recens est et nuperrime nata, et ex eo quidem nata qui se quondam in clarissima Medicum familia praedicat alitum fuisse; quae mihi nimirum ingeniis excitandis ornandisque studiis coelitus data fuisse videtur. Is est in nostra urbe musicae artis princeps.

[40] Edmond Vander Straeten, *La musique aux Pays-Bas avant le XIXe siècle. Documents inédits et annotés*, 8 vols. (Brussels: C. Muquardt, etc., 1867–88; republished in 4 vols., New York: Dover, 1969), vol. 6 (1882; Dover reprint vol. 3, part 2), 323–4. Smith also makes the link between the Florence Torion and the figure alluded to in the letter; see "Memoriale," 82–3.

For the Thorion of the 1490s, though, the bond that putatively drew him back to Saint-Omer was yet to be set, and for the time being his ambitions led him elsewhere. The permutation through which he dispensed, in July 1494, with his vicariate at St Omer may give some indication of where his outside interests, at that point in his career, were directing him: he exchanged it for the perpetual chaplaincy at the altar of St Denis in the crypt of the Augustinian monastery of St Genevieve in Paris, with one Michael Le Gay, who will re-enter our story later in connection with none other than the composer Jean Mouton. Whatever the attractions of Paris, and whatever youthful dissatisfaction Thorion may have felt with St Omer, however, he clearly took little time to overcome them: only three years later the chapter was awarding him another vicariate 'in consideration of the service he performs', and, because he was currently in Saint-Quentin and unable to make it to the city to take up residence immediately, they allowed him until the Feast of St Remigius (1 October, and hence three and a half months later) to return and swear the requisite oath in person. The word used for his role at St Quentin, 'ruoram', would appear to be a local corruption of 'ruarius', a rank peculiar to that church set somewhere between vicar and canon and involving responsibilities singing the daily round of Mass and office.[41] To have been the holder of such a post in this wealthy royal collegiate church surely reflects considerable professional status for a singer-cleric, and one wonders why he would have abandoned it to return to St Omer. Still more strikingly, among other services – including singing for the daily Masses of the foundation of Antoine de Wissoq and (as we shall see) for the daily *Salve* foundation of Nicolas Rembert– he again became master of the boys, either singly or in tandem with another cleric, uninterruptedly between 3 November 1497 and 1513.

If the importunity of the chapter's efforts in the 1490s to lure Thorion back may indeed smack of desperation, it was surely as nothing compared to that which led to their next appointment. However scandalous his assault on the hapless little soul he had so vigorously beaten, it was clearly

---

[41] See David Fiala, 'La collégiale royale de Saint-Quentin et la musique', in Camilla Cavicchi, Marie-Alexis Colin and Philippe Vendrix (eds.), *La musique en Picardie du XIV͏ᵉ au XVII͏ᵉ siècle* (Turnhout: Brepols, 2012), 190–1. The document reads as follows: Die xiiii͏ᵃ eiusdem mensis [June 1497] domini . . . considerantes obsequia per Dominum Johannem Thorion impensa ecclesie vicariam vaccantem per obitum Domini Mathei le Roy eidem contulerunt et sibi cum suis iuribus et pertinentiis providerunt / Sed quia ruoram trahit in Sancto Quintino et non possit honeste ita celeriter venire ad residenciam domini secum dispensaverunt usque ad festum Remigii et pendente tempore litteras non habebit / sed sub data presenti cum venerit ad residenciam expedientur . et etc. Iuramentum solitum prestare tenebitur in propria / (II. G. 355, f. 126v)

insufficient to discourage the reinstallation, in the old job he seems variously to have misused, of Malin Alixandre. On 27 June 1493 he was reinstalled in his former post, and in February the following year was duly admitted to another full year's tenure. The notes appended to the usual reappointment formulas – that the chapter should be 'informed of his experience and suitability' and that his appointment is for 'as long as he can be found to be suitable'[42] – may bespeak a certain nervousness, but in the event business seems to have proceeded as usual. Indeed it would appear that Alixandre gave every satisfaction. When, at reappointment time in 1495, another possible candidate was put forward for the office he was summarily passed over in favour of the incumbent, 'in consideration of the services he has expended'.[43] Whether or not this alternative master, a certain Philippe Bunoys, was related to the composer Antoine is unknown, though both probably hailed from the hamlet of Busnes, some thirty kilometres south-east of Saint-Omer.

At any rate, a change in personnel was not far off, since on 22 November of the same year Alixandre died, his position and associated vicariate passing to a certain Johannes Clerici.[44] Like others before him, Clerici took liberties that bespeak limited options on the part of the chapter. Having asked, on 19 October 1497, to take time off to go to Bruges and been warned against doing so, he proceeded to ask on the 31st of the same month for a year's leave. The chapter replied that he was allowed three months' statutory leave per annum, and no more. If the lords had smelt a rat in connection with this request, their judgement, as it turned out, would have been sound: on 11 November Clerici was appointed succentor at St Donatian, Bruges, a position that he was to retain until 23 December, 1498. Nearly four months later and still not back in post, the chapter reminded him that according to the statutes that he had sworn to uphold, after three months' leave without special permission he was bound to resume his post,

---

[42] II. G. 355, ff. 95v and 100v.   [43] II. G. 355, f. 108r.

[44] There are no serious grounds to associate this figure with a man of the same name who according to Guillaume Crétin had copied, at the behest of Okeghem himself, the composer's legendary motet in thirty-six parts. This Clerici (or 'Jean Le Clerc'), who died in 1511, was a singer in the papal chapel in 1450, member of the French royal chapel, canon of St Martin of Tours as well as of Noyon and Soissons, and already in 1472 archdeacon of Reims. The same can be said of the (clearly related) individual of the same name who, on his death in 1536, donated a large number of books of music (including the famous motet) to the cathedral of Amiens (on these two figures see Georges Durand, *La musique de la cathédrale d'Amiens avant la Révolution* (Amiens: Yvert et Tellier, 1922), 452–3; summarised by Grantley McDonald in Cavicchi, Colin and Vendrix (eds.), *La musique en Picardie*, 394–5). The name is common and widespread.

'under penalty of privation'. Yet after all this they inexplicably granted him an extension up to six months. Finally on 3 March the chapter allowed that the income from the vicariate of Clerici, 'absent by grace of the lords', be diverted to the needs of the choirboys.[45] His financial incentive thus dissipated, this latest recalcitrant disappeared altogether. It seems clear that, building on his post at St Donatian, Clerici did not neglect to make further contacts in Bruges: he is recorded as having spent a year from 1499 to 1500 as succentor at the church of Our Lady in the same city.[46]

With Clerici's departure, temporary at first and later permanent, on 3 November 1497 Johannes Thorion embarked, against all prior odds, on what was to prove a period as master of the boys of exceptional, perhaps even unique, duration. Indeed his tenure was far to outlast that of the man who had fought so hard to keep him, since Johannes de Hemont himself passed away in 1500, to be succeeded as cantor by Robert Fabri. Ironically, the chapter was, in the end, highly fortunate in its choice of Thorion: in a situation in which demand plainly far outstripped supply he showed unusual steadfastness to the church and to the boys who, a full half century later, he would remember in the inscription on his painted epitaph which, by some miracle, has survived.

The reading in chapter on 6 May 1547 of Thorion's testament (the latter is dated only two days earlier) and the announcement of his burial directly following High Mass presumably occurred, following standard convention, the day after his death.[47] His funeral exequies proceeded, with unusual dispatch, five days later.[48] Agreement as to the desired placing of his epitaph, adjacent to his place of burial as revealed in his will,[49] followed on 17 October:

---

[45] II. G. 356, ff. 2r, 3r, 6r, 7v.

[46] For the Bruges details see Reinhard Strohm, *Music in Late Medieval Bruges* (2nd, rev. ed., Oxford: Clarendon Press, 1990), 183, My thanks to Robert Nosow for further details.

[47] See II. G. 358, f. 110r. Hence the conjectural 'quinto' in the wording of his epitaph, below.

[48] Mensis maii die ix^a domini mei annuerunt fieri in choro huius ecclesie exequias quondam Domini Johannis Thorion die mercurii proxima. (II. G. 358, f. 110r). The ninth of May was a Monday in 1547.

[49] 'Mon corps recommandant a sepulture saincte laquelle je reslis sil plaist a messires doien et chapitre dudit St Omer lacorder en la chapelle St Nicolas fondee en ladite eglise et ce aupres de lhuis dedens ladite chapelle[.] Pour laquelle sepulture je donne a la fabricque dicelle eglise dix carolus dor[.]' (Dainville (Arras), Archives départementales du Pas-de-Calais, Justice échevinale de Saint-Omer, 15B3, f. 48v). While Thorion's will gives the customary detail on his obsequies and desired posthumous observances, it contains, as Gil and Nys note (*Saint-Omer gothique*, 128), disappointingly little detail concerning his possessions (beyond money and furniture to be donated), in particular providing no details of any books he possessed at death. It does inform us, however, that he donated to 'Jehan Dostremoulle procureur de ladite ville de Saint-Omer ung tableau paint estant sur mon dreschoir en ma chambre nomme ung *Ecce homo* affin quil aye memoire de moy' (f. 49v).

On 17 October my lords assented, insofar as it is in their power, that the epitaph of the former learned man Lord Johannes Thorion, at the time of his death vicar of this church, may be affixed in the chapel of St Nicholas of this said church.[50]

The epitaph takes the form of a panel-painted triptych, of very fine workmanship and likely by a local painter.[51] Dating, to judge by its style, from several decades before its owner's death, the panel was almost certainly – typically for such images – first mounted in Thorion's home before, as Douglas Brine notes, 'transfer to the church with its commemorative inscription added'.[52] It depicts the donor, presented by his patron saint John the Baptist, on the right wing, facing St Jerome on the left, these two flanking a central depiction of the Virgin enthroned on a rainbow in a mandorla surrounded by cherubim (see Figure 3.2 for the complete open triptych, and the front cover for a detail of the donor). In closed position it presents an elegant depiction of the Annunciation on a red ground. The identity of the donor himself is defined by his coat of arms above St John's shoulder and by the inscription beneath the central panel (Figure 3.3). The latter, typically for funerary purposes in elegiac couplets, informs the viewer that:

In this ground lies Johannes Thorion, a corpse,
    who gave much musical teaching to the boys;
whom on the [*fifth*] of May, loosening the hard bonds
    [*of his body*], pale death took from sight.
For him therefore let crowds of young and old weep,
    as they wet their breasts too with doleful tears.
Into the Father's kingdom on high let him soar [*to reach*] the stars,
    and, I beseech it, let none be ashamed to pour out prayers.[53]

---

[50] Mensis octobris die xvii^a domini mei annuerunt inquantum ipsos tangere potest affigi epitaphium quondam discreti viri Domini Johannis Thorion tempore sui obitus huius ecclesie vicarii in capella Sancti Nicolai huius dicte ecclesie. (II. G. 358, f. 119v)

[51] On its style and execution see Gil and Nys, *Saint-Omer gothique*, 256–9 and Christian Heck, Hervé Boëdec, Delphine Adams and Astrid Bollut, *Collections du Nord-Pas-de-Calais: La peinture de Flandre et de France du Nord au XVe et au début du XVIe siècle*, 2 vols. (Brussels: Centre d'étude de la peinture du quinzième siècle dans les Pays-Bas méridionaux et la Principauté de Liège, 2005), vol. 2, 385–90.

[52] *Pious Memories: The Wall-Mounted Memorial in the Burgundian Netherlands* (Leiden and Boston, MA: Brill, 2015), 105–6.

[53] Translation by Henry Howard. The following transcription includes (due to a few lost words) some minor conjectural completion:
    Hac Joannes inest Thorion tellure cadaver
    Musica qui pueris dogmata plura dedit.
    [*Qui[n]to*] quem maii dissolvens vincula dura
    [*Corpor*]is eripuit pallida mors oculis.
    Hu[n]c igitur plangant juvenumque senumque caterv[a]e
    Cum madeant lacrimis flebilibusque sinus

Figure 3.2 Triptych of Jean Thorion © Carl Peterolff

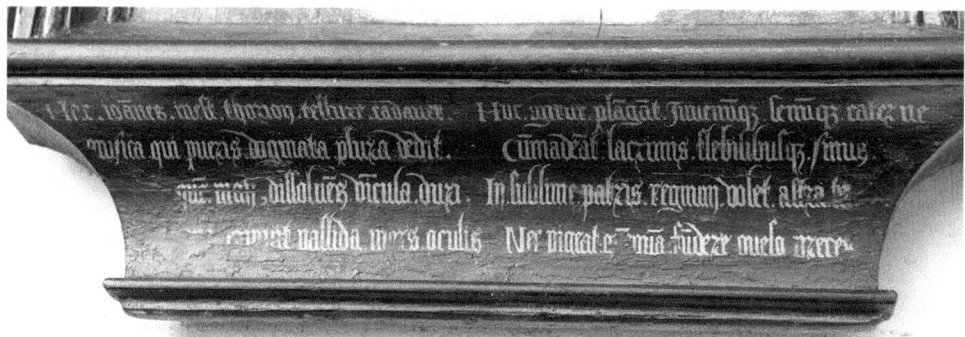

Figure 3.3 Triptych of Jean Thorion, inscription © Carl Peterolff

It is surely unsurprising that Thorion, for so many years a mentor of choirboys, should have chosen as his burial place the chapel dedicated to their patron saint.[54] Here, following convention, his painted epitaph would have been positioned adjacent to an actual tombstone, now lost.[55]

In sublime patris regnum volet astra ten[endo]
  Nec pigeat quemquam fundere qu[a]eso preces.
[54] As pointed out to me by an anonymous reviewer of this book.
[55] For details of the analogous arrangement for Toussains de Le Ruelle see p. 255.

While, presumably, Thorion's body rests in the chapel to this day, his painted epitaph has led, at least for the last two hundred years or so, a more peripatetic existence. This surely began when, following the destruction in 1785 of its original home on the marketplace, the icon of Notre Dame des Miracles was removed to the cathedral, where its chapel supplanted that of St Nicholas. At any rate the triptych is recorded in the late nineteenth century as occupying a position above the tomb of Antoine de Wissoc in the latter's chapel in the fifth bay of the south aisle, an apt placement for a priest once among those paid to celebrate Wissoc's commorative Masses.[56] Following restoration in 1971 the succession of its moves is murky;[57] but after spending several decades in the treasury of the cathedral of Arras it finally returned, through the good offices of the indefatigable sacristan Benôit Meens, to the cathedral of Saint-Omer where, since June 2019, it has again hung in the chapel of Antoine de Wissoc.

Master Singers

Clearly the position of succentor in a major ecclesiastical institution was a seriously onerous one: as the cantor's musical factotum he was tasked with the general functioning of music in the church. Some sense of the extent of that responsibility can be had from the wording of the instrument whereby, in 1503, Robert Fabri, in his role as cantor:

presented the distinguished man Johannes Thorion, most expert in the art of music, to instruct the choristers of the said church in the same art, to direct the school of song; and also to teach the rituals of the choir and church and good behaviour and to do the other things that arise from his post, as is customary.[58]

---

[56] See Henri Loriquet, *Épigraphie du département du Pas-de-Calais*, Tome V, 1er et 2e fasc. (*Ville de Saint-Omer*) (Arras: Laroche, 1892), 18–19.

[57] An exhibition catalogue from 1992 states that it was thereafter placed 'for reasons of security and better conservation' in the treasury of the cathedral of Arras before, in 1981, moving to the Musée Henri Dupuis (in Saint-Omer) in expectation of the opening of a treasury of the cathedral of Saint-Omer in the octagonal tower (the medieval location of the treasury) (see the entry by F. Foucart in *Trésors des églises de l'arrondissment de Saint-Omer*, catalogue d'exposition sous la direction de Guy Blazy, Saint-Omer, Musée de l'Hôtel Sandelin, 26 septembre–13 décembre 1992 (Saint-Omer: Musée de l'Hôtel Sandelin, 1992), 141–2). The plan never materialised and at some point the triptych clearly returned to Arras.

[58] ... discretum virum Dominum Johannem Torion in arta [sic] musica maxime imbutum / ad choristas dicte ecclesie in eadem arte instruendum scolas cantus regendum / Necnon cerimonias chori et ecclesie ac mores bonos edocendum aliaque faciendum que huiusmodi suo officio occurrunt / prout moris et consuetudinis est presentavit / (II. G. 356, f. 77r)

Thus his responsibility embraced not only the running of the maîtrise and tutorship of its boys, but also more general musical direction, including the activities of the vicar-singers and, at St Omer, the tuition and performance of the scholar-singers of the escoterie. It may perhaps be in recognition of the heaviness of this load that, in the first decade of the sixteenth century, payments begin to be made to two masters instead of the single one as hitherto, though how the labour may have been divided between them, and whether consecutively or simultaneously, is unknown. At any rate it is easy to see that the presence of singers capable of assuming a degree of their own responsibility would have been a major boon.

This is nowhere more obvious than in the case of the genre of singer known as the tenorist, essentially a singer/director who apparently led from his own singing of the chant line, whether in chant *tout court*, or in composed or improvised polyphony. Rob Wegman has surmised that the tenorist's role was fundamental in guiding and shaping the texture of counterpoint. This would surely have had its most fundamental impact in the vast majority of the polyphonic music of the time that was per-formed *ex tempore* by improvising, in more or less formulaic fashion, on chant. From his position in the midst of the texture, the tenorist would thus have been expected to be able to hear, and by some means presumably to direct, the progressions of musical intervals going on around him. His function in his apparently defining musical setting would thus have com-bined roles that we today would see as the province of conductor and composer. Such skill, as Wegman also points out, would have made such individuals highly sought-after and often also highly paid.[59] One might add indeed that it says something very significant about the achievement of tenorists, as indeed of succentors, that even the hothouse cultivation of the northern European maîtrise was able to produce so comparatively few men deemed capable of taking on such roles.

---

[59] 'From Maker to Composer: Improvisation and Musical Authorship in the Low Countries, 1450–1500', *Journal of the American Musicological Society* 49 (1996), 444–9. See also Barbara Haggh, 'Music, Liturgy and Ceremony in Brussels, 1350–1500', 2 vols., unpublished PhD dissertation, University of Illinois at Urbana–Champaign (1988), vol. 1, 189–91. The role of the vocal tenorist would thus share significant characteristics with the 'tenorist' in the contemporary practice of lute duos as described in connection with Pietrobono of Ferrara, and, by analogy, in the similar practice in German-speaking lands (though there without use of the epithet). Here also the player of the lower part was responsible for maintaining the solid foundation of a pre-existent line, with or without embellishment or added simultaneities, over which the soprano lutenist would extemporise (see Keith Polk, *German Instrumental Music of the Late Middle Ages: Players, Patrons and Performance Practice* (Cambridge: Cambridge University Press, 1992), 25–7).

Saint-Omer, as elsewhere, had its tenorists, and none more notable than the next major player in our story, Grigoire Bourgois. We have already encountered Bourgois, sometimes known as 'Scripure', in connection with the choirboy-cleric Pierre du Hecq, and with the firing in 1491 of Malin Alixandre. The fortunate discovery of a completely unrelated document from June 1472 supplies valuable information concerning his position prior to arriving in Saint-Omer, allowing us in turn to determine the means via which he came to be there. The record, found by Rob Wegman, recounts how Bourgois had appeared before a magistrates' court in Ghent, trying to sue a certain Arend vanden Couden for selling him an unruly horse; indeed the horse had been so intractable that it had injured several of Bourgois's companions. Bourgois's suit, which demanded that vanden Couden take back the horse, return his money and pay for the injuries, was unsuccessful, but the record tangentially supplies an important piece of information, because it names him as a tenorist of the king of Naples.[60]

There are grounds to speculate that this was not Bourgois's first illustrious posting: a 'Gregorio', named 'tenorista' and in one instance (along with the composer-singer Johannes Sohier *dit* Fede) 'contratenorista', appears among the singers of St Peter's, Rome, between 1461 and 1466. Usually receiving a salary of 3 ducats (though 4 one year and 2 another) rather than the 1½ or 2 typically paid to the other singers, Gregorio's valued role in the ensemble was apparently reflected in his superior remuneration. Since absences taken by him in 1462 and 1464 were each followed by the arrival of new singers, it has been plausibly suggested that he had been given leave for the purposes of recruiting. One of these singers, Guillaume Rosa, plus Gaspar van Weerbeke, who took on his role as tenorist during his absences, and Fede, Gregorio's only singing colleague whose salary matched his own, all received benefices – whether or not actually taken up – at St Omer, thus together weaving a tissue of interconnections that strengthen the likelihood that this Gregorio and Bourgois were one and the same.[61]

The process that led to Bourgois's move northward probably began when, at Saint-Omer in November 1471, a treaty was proclaimed between

---

[60] For this information see Rob C. Wegman, *Born for the Muses: The Life and Masses of Jacob Obrecht* (Oxford: Oxford University Press, 1994), 67–8.

[61] For the payments see Franz Xaver Haberl, *Bausteine für Musikgeschichte* vol. 3: *Die römische "Schola Cantorum" und die päpstlichen Kapellsänger bis zur Mitte des 16. Jahrhunderts* (Leipzig: Breitkopf und Härtel, 1888; repr., 'drei Bände in einem Band', Hildesheim and New York: Georg Olms, 1971), vol. 3, 48–9. See also Christopher Reynolds, *Papal Patronage and the Music of St. Peter's, 1380–1513* (Berkeley and Los Angeles, University of California Press, 1995), 45, 46–8. On Weerbeke's St Omer benefice, see p. 209.

the Kingdom of Naples and the Duchy of Burgundy, and simultaneously between the latter and the Kingdom of Aragon.[62] It seems reasonable to assume that the chapter of St Omer and Bourgois, who was surely present in King Ferrante's chapel, engaged in mutual wooing at that time. But the ultimate trigger came from his own employer: as we learn from a letter from the Milanese ambassador in Naples dated 20 March 1473, 'Gregorio de Fiandra' became one of a number of Ferrante's singers embroiled in a significant diplomatic scandal involving Galeazzo Maria Sforza, Duke of Milan. The duke had been attempting, via duplicitous methods, to poach singers from the Neapolitan choir for his own. Part of the fallout from this was that three singers, including Gregorio, were 'given licence to return to their homelands', probably at this point their only recourse since the duke was warned, under threat of possible diplomatic reprisals, to renege on his plans to take on any of the unfaithful singers himself.[63]

The unscheduled permission 'to spend more time with his family' surely explains the scramble over benefices that, later that same year, eased Bourgois's move to Saint-Omer (though what he was doing horse-trading in Ghent the year before remains a mystery). The alacrity with which matters were stitched up in his favour surely had much to do with local networks and family ties. The name (along with his additional epithet 'Scripure') was one of local currency: the fabric accounts record the presence of a Stephanus Bourgoys (who had recently died) in 1388/9 and of a Jacques Bourgois who received a chaplaincy at the Saint-Omer church of St Aldegonde in 1458/9, and died, vacating it, on 10 February 1473. In July 1458 a certain Nicasius Scripure, as procurator for Emanuel Loste, resigned a chaplaincy that passed to the vicar Ingerand du Tielt.[64] Familial bonds surely explain why, fifteen years later, Nicasius swung so effectively into action on behalf of his illustrious namesake. On 4 May 1473, the same Loste acquired the altar of St Maurice in the church of St Aldegonde, which he promptly exchanged by permutation with Nicasius for the latter's vicariate and chaplaincy of St Andrew. From here the pieces fell quickly into place: three days later Bourgois picked up the perpetual chaplaincy at the altar of St Louis, which he the same day exchanged with Loste for the

---

[62] See Richard J. Walsh, *Charles the Bold and Italy (1467–1477): Politics and Personnel* (Liverpool: Liverpool University Press, 2005), 48–9. Walsh's account clears up some ambiguity in earlier descriptions of this event. See also Richard Vaughan, *Charles the Bold: The Last Valois Duke of Burgundy* (repr. Woodbridge: Boydell, 2002 (first published London: Longman, 1973)), 75.

[63] Paul A. Merkley and Lora L. M. Merkley, *Music and Patronage in the Sforza Court* (Turnhout: Brepols, 1999), 51, 57.

[64] II. G. 354, f. 5r.

latter's position in the chapel of St Andrew.[65] If not actually earmarked for him, this must at least have been precisely the kind of post Bourgois was seeking, since he kept it until, more than two decades later, he died and was buried in the same chapel. Bourgois's gain became, in short order, someone else's loss: at the very next chapter meeting just a week later on 14 May, the canons informed 'Anselmo Doublier tenoriste' that he 'should seek his employment elsewhere since they now had no need of him'.[66] Bourgois's connections with singers of an altogether higher profile are reflected in his role, on 27 June 1474, as procurator for canon Guillaume Decault in presenting the latter's privilege to be in Rome for the year as a papal singer.[67]

By the end of the same year, 'Gregorio le Scripure tenoriste' is recorded as receiving twelve deniers per day (six deniers for each) for singing Mass and vespers, twice the sum paid to a regular vicar for attending the full day's observances.[68] This payment was rescinded, however, the following 29 May for unspecified reasons.[69]

Bourgois's responsibilities at St Omer included stints (in 1478/9, 1479/80 and 1480/1) as master of the boys. This overlap of the roles of tenorist and master of the boys seems to have been exceptional, however, suggesting that the former role made Bourgois a more valuable commodity than anything he could offer in the latter capacity. The same consideration may also account for the fact that in each of the above years he was accepted into the role only if assisted by someone else.[70] Whatever the profile of his activities and their perception by the chapter, he was clearly not lacking in

---

[65] II. G. 354, f. 164v.

[66] Eadem die xiiii[a] maii domini mei exposuerunt Domino Anselmo Doublier tenoriste quod quereret suum profectum alibi quod eo iam non indigent[.] (II. G. 354, 164v)

[67] Hac die xxvii mensis junii post festum Nativitatis Beati Johannis Baptiste anno lxxiiii[to] discretus vir Dominus Gregorius Bourgois procurator Domini Guillelmi Decaut canonici presentavit privilegium sub nomine Latini Cardinalis de Ursinis de datta anno lxxiiii[to] ... continens quod dictus Guillelmus resedit cantorcapellanus in Romana curia a die sue creationis usque prefatam diem quod domini admiserunt ... (II. G. 354, f. 180r). Decault's advocacy by a cardinal of the Orsini family speaks clearly of the level of influence available to him.

[68] II. G. 354, f. 172r.

[69] ... pensio duodecim denari quod cottide Domino Gregorio tenoriste per ipsam ecclesiam seu capitulum dari consueverunt a modo in totum cassantur et annullantur[.] (II. G. 354, f. 188r)

[70] See II. G. 354, respectively ff. 215r, 229r and 241r. 'sub tamen conditione hac viz quod secum habeat aliquem ydoneum submonitorem / et habilem ad pueros ipsos instruendos / ergo de consensu tamen capituli[.]' (f. 229r; the wording in the earlier instance is similar.) The wording in the latest case supports the notion that Bourgois's contribution was seen to be of particular value and his time at a premium: the lords kept him on in this role provided 'se ipsum regat et pueros instrui faciat ut honor ecclesie et puerorum bonum utilitatem et honestatem exinde resultent caveatque de cetero a laycorum consortio'.

disposable income: the fabric account for 1480/1 records his having purchased a diamond from the estate of Jacques de Houchin.[71]

It seems evident that the fallout from the Milan–Naples scandal that led
to the arrival of Bourgois represented quite a windfall for St Omer. Hiring
Bourgois was one thing, however; keeping him was quite another. The
chapter acts reveal that by 1482 he was getting itchy feet: while St Omer
was a fine setting by most standards, to the former tenorist of the king of
Naples and (putatively) St Peter's, Rome, grander opportunities may have
beckoned. His efforts to shake loose seem to have begun early in 1482,
when, on 7 January, he asked the chapter for leave to depart

due to the continually active encroachment of wars in these parts and the consequent high costs of corn, crops and victuals, such that he will not henceforth be
able satisfactorily to pay his creditors, since all told he can make only four pounds
in the course of the year from his vicariate, which is scarcely enough even for bread
for him and his household.[72] And thus fearing that in delaying his situation may
become worse, he thought to seek his provision elsewhere. As a result he asked
leave from the same lords to absent himself for one or two years, until they can
enjoy tranquilities of peace.[73]

The lords, however, were having none of this, replying that

his vicariate is a benefice of service restricted to personal residency, which they had
as a special favour bestowed on him, and he had of his own free will promised to
serve the church for the rest of his days, fulfilling the role of tenorist, which had
brought him many favours. For they had given him first two and then one [more]
advances; and a little later they had for several years made him director of the song
school. Neither has he had so much occasion for complaint as many of his
colleagues, since he has six livres in groats annually from his parish of Adinquerke,
considering which, in order that no similar occasion of departure may be given to
the others, nor the divine worship of the church be defrauded of his due services,
they declared to the same Gregory that they would give him no permission beyond
that which was set out in the statutes of the church.[74]

---

[71] 1480/1, f. 32v.   [72] The word used – 'familia' – likely refers in this case to servants.

[73] . . . Dominus Gregorius Bourgois huius ecclesie vicarius declaravit dominis quod propter
inffractus guerrarum in hiis partibus assidue vigentes et subsequenter exinde granarum
frumenti et victualium caristiam se sustentare. et suis creditoribus a modo satisfacere commode
non posset. cum ex omnibus in totum complexis quo ex vicaria sua huiusmodi emergerent
prout annuatim termino quatuor libras grossorum percipiat quod vix sibi sufficiunt pro solo
pane sui et sue familie[.] Et sic formidans ne tardo huiusmodi in deterius ingravescat excogitavit
alibi suam provisionem exquerere. quapropter petiit ab eisdem dominis licentiam se absentendi
ad tempus unius vel duorum annorum et donec pacis tranquilitate fruantur[.]

[74] Domini habita deliberatione responsum ei dederunt quod sua vicaria huiusmodi est beneficium
servile astrictum ad personalem residentiam. quam tamen ex speciali gracia eidem contulissent
sua sponte promisit totis diebus suis ecclesie servire etc vices tenoriste exercendo quod que

Not easily put off, Bourgois approached the chapter again the following Friday, renewing his plea and, if they should again deny it, asking to exchange his vicariate via permutation with an escoterie held by Johannes Franchois. Bourgois's desire to exchange his post for something inferior is a mystery, unless he felt that the position of escotier was one from which he could more easily extricate himself. The chapter's (less bullish) mood this time is revealing both of Bourgois's perceived status and that of the church's music more generally: the lords profess to 'having had the greatest regard for the beauty of the choir since the time when the said Gregorius, as was previously related, was, out of respect for music and his voice, admitted to the said vicariate, by right of which he would serve the church as tenorist'. What they go on to propose gives some indication of a possible cause of irritation with Bourgois: 'if, nevertheless, the same Gregorius proceeds to apply himself more diligently than has been his wont, and devotes himself actively as he is duty bound and has promised, the lords will not be ungrateful, and indeed the possibility may arise for him'. But – for now at least – they turned down his requests.[75]

In September Bourgois was back before the chapter, asking for an extension to his statutory period of absence. The answer was a predictable no, but clearly one not necessarily expecting compliance since, as the entry reveals, they bribed him with 'every possible manner of favour, as it might be by giving him certain Masses, or letting him off all the hours except Mass and vespers'.[76] Whatever details are lost between these lines, Bourgois

---

eidem perplurimas gratias fecerant[.] Nam primo duos deinde unum stuferum eidem de excrescentia dederunt[.] Et postmodum ipsum ad regimen scolarum cantus ~~restituerunt~~ pro aliquot annis instituerunt[.] Neque sibi est tanta occasio querimonie quanta pluribus aliis suis convicariis cum habeat sex libras grossorum ex sua parochiali de Adinquerke annuatim. quibus attentis ne etiam detur aliis similis occasio recedendi. neve divinus cultus ecclesie predicte suis debitis fraudetur obsequiis dixerunt eidem Gregorio nullam licenciam se daturos praeterquam eam que in statutis ecclesie exponuntur[.] (II. G. 355, f. 26v)

[75] Die vero veneris sequenti quod fuit xi^a dicti mensis iterum accessit ad eosdem dominos similiter capitulariter adunatos et eis ut prius iterum licenciam requisivit alias si renuerent quod admittere dignarentur quidem permutationem conceptam inter eum de dicta vicaria. et Dominum Johannem Franchois de sua scoteria. ad meram eorundem dominorum dispositionem spectantium[.] Domini habito respectu maxime ad venustatem chori ex quo dictus Gregorius ut prefertur ex respectu musice et sue vocis fuit ad dictam vicariam admissus ea sc[ilicet] lege ut pro tenorista ecclesie serviret. si tamen ipse Gregorius de cetero se applicuerit diligentius solito et operam adhibuerit efficacem quemadmodum tenetur et promisit. domini non erint ingrati. verum sibi facietur ad possibilitatem. Tamen licentiam dare et permutationem predictam admittere renuerunt[.]De quaquidem refutatione omnibusque et singulis petiit Gregorius hu[iusmodi] fieri actum. (f. 26v)

[76] ... suadentes eidem ut remaneret et omnimodam graciam sibi possibilem facerent puta sibi tradendo certas missas aut ipsum tenendo liberum ab omnibus horis praeterque missa et vesperis quodque sibi super hoc consideret. (II. G. 355, f. 35r)

had indeed, on 4 August, been granted six months' absence (without pay) along with his colleagues Guillaume Didier and Eustache Maistresse (or 'Manessier'), a former singer of St Donatian, Bruges. Whatever the extent of the favours the chapter had offered him, Bourgois was still around in 1484, when he extracted the further concession that he be paid his full dues, as if he had been present at all the hours, provided he would turn up for all High Masses and vespers, and for all hours on major feasts, 'making a point of conscience about it', and losing one sol parisis for any of these that he should miss.[77]

Besides his brief tenure as master of the boys, Bourgois was able to extract an extraordinary range of concessions from the chapter which, for its part and notwithstanding its obvious annoyance, it obviously felt obliged to satisfy. The prospect of having Bourgois's services on high days was obviously enough to encourage the chapter to do everything in its power to retain him, something which – whatever his contractual obliga-tions – it would in reality have had little chance of enforcing.

Perhaps in the end Bourgois's familial ties were what kept him in Saint-Omer; or perhaps, as witnessed by what was clearly an ongoing connection with the former choirboy Philippe du Hecq, he felt a tie to the boys and/or to his other singer workmates. Whatever the truth, he remained with the church until his demise in 1496, whereupon he was buried, according to his wish, in the chapel of St Andrew. The terms of his will, dated 19 March that year, detail his annual obit service, to be paid for, as was conventional, by the rent for his house. It also illustrates the standard function of a canon's house in his posthumous welfare: it was to be sold on to the next cleric in line for a house, on whom was also levied, in addition to an annual rental of four livres twelve deniers, a further charge of sixty sous to pay for his predecessor's obit; that same cleric could then in turn expect the same privilege for himself on his own death and the passing on of his house to the next occupant.[78] Bourgois's other, fairly modest, posthumous provision

---

[77] Ad humilem supplicationem Domini Gregorii Bourgois vicarii huius ecclesie domini audita sua querimonia sibi annuerunt et secum dispensaverunt de gracia speciali quod interessens magnis missis et vesperis perciperet lucrum de omnibus horis / ita tamen quod in magnis solemnitatibus deberet adesse et aliis horis / suam quidem conscienciam super hac onerando / et si contingeret ipsis proviso abesse dictis horis praeter licencia / pro qualibet absentia perdet unum sc. parisiensem. (II. G. 355, f. 54r)

[78] 'Eadem die [19.10.1496] domini disposuerunt quod domus quam inhabitare solebat Dominus Gregorius Bourgois nunc pertinentem ecclesie onerata iiii libris xii d p[arisis] quod canonicus primus in optione si voluerit poterit optare eandem solvendo annuatim unacum dictos iiii libros xii d sexaginta solidi parisis pro obitu prefati Domini Gregorii quam sommam poterit idem habitans redimere more solito' (II. G. 355, f. 121v). The same mutually beneficial financial chain

was for the saying, daily after Mass, of the 'De profundis' in the chapel where he was buried. For this he provided the sum of 39s. 2d., from which the chapter agreed to meet his wishes from one six-month period to the next as long as funds would permit.[79]

While Bourgois is the church's best-documented tenorist, the chapter acts bear periodic witness to others. The advancement in 1458/9 of the organist Jehan Caignart to vicar in its turn opened up his vacant escoterie to 'Pierot Thenoriste'. This was presumably the 'Pierquin Bart teneur' who had been accorded the position of 'vicariot' (presumably something akin to 'small' or 'half' vicar) the previous year.[80] A notice concerning an unnamed tenorist in 1487 underscores the comparatively high level of investment (in both time and money) entrusted in potential tenorists: this 'arriving young tenorist' was assigned an annual subvention of twenty livres d'Artois for bed and board 'in the house of the succentor so that he may become more proficient in singing' as well as for money for his vestments, assigned from 'the remainder of the vicariate of master Johannes Derviler'.[81] Perhaps he was being groomed ultimately to take over the role from Bourgois; if so he might conceivably have been the Petrus Sommelart who acquired an escoterie in 1494 and, as we shall see shortly, is first flagged as 'thenorista' in a 1495 document alongside the composer Jean Mouton. Like Bourgois before him, Sommelart continues to appear in the records thereafter in

is well illustrated in a series of entries on payments due on claustral houses made in late 1463. Here a marginal note clarifies how 'the successors [in tenure of a house] only pay £12 parisis from which the said lord [predecessor] will have an obit of 100 shillings [=£5] parisis. The £7 remaining will be paid for by the successor of the said lord in paying for the profit of the obit masses, 140 shillings parisis [= £7].' ('A modo les successeurs nen payeront que xii libs parisis dont ledit magister ara ung obit de C s parisis que les vii libs du residu se raccateront par le successeur dudit magister en paiant au pourfit de le masse des obis vii^xx s. parisis') (II. G. 353, f. 59v). The charges vary to some extent from case to case, presumably in reflection of the size and rental of the house concerned, though the 100s. (£5) portion for the payer's obit remains, for this year at least, constant.

79 Eadem die xv^a eiusdem mensis Julii iiii^xx xvii executores testamenti quondam Domini Gregorii Bourgois insequentes voluntatem testatoris pro dicendo cothidie psalmum de profundis post missam per Anth[onium] Delattre fundatam per cappellanos in capella Sancti Andree in circuitu chori in quo iacet prefatus Gregorius obtulerunt xxxix s ii d par[isis]. per duas litteras super certis dotibus ut in litteris continetur quam sommam domini acceptarunt quam diu pignus durabit et ad recipiendum dictam sommam et solvendo capellanis pro quolibet die idem habebit onus receptor burse communis qui solvet ut ei videbitur expediens de vi mensibus in sex mensibus[.] (II. G. 355, f. 127v)

80 See 1458/9, f. 4r; 1457/8, f. 5r.

81 Decima tertia eiusdem / [February] cuidem advene iuveni tenoriste de gratia et liberalitate concluserunt domini dare pro anno viginti libros arthesios ad subveniendum sibi in expensis quas capiat in domo succentoris ut in cantu melius proficiat et pro vestimentis habebit residuum vicarie Ma[gistri] Joh[annis] Derviler[.] (II. G. 355, f. 69r)

connection with private foundations, including regular citations over about a decade up to 1513 as one of the singers of Rembert's *Salve* foundation. But in contrast to Bourgois, the records are silent regarding anything beyond payments; one might be led to conclude (as in the case documented in Chapter 6 of Enguerrand Le Quien) that fractious behaviour was more fruitful for historical detail than straightforward attention to duty. Whatever the full extent of the role of the tenorist, it would appear that – at St Omer if not everywhere else – it was typically occupied by one individual at a time, who divided his activities between services at the high altar and the celebration of private Masses and other devotions.

What Did they Sing?

While the (albeit fragmentary) thirteenth-century ordinal discussed in Chapter 1 gives considerable detail on the prescriptions and layout of Mass and office for the feasts it contains, survivals of the collégiale's chant repertory are extremely limited. A thirteenth-century antiphonary contains the readings and chants for the offices of the day (lauds, vespers and little hours) for the *estival* (summer) half of the year, covering the temporal from Easter vigil until the day before Advent Sunday.[82] The feasts of the sanctoral for the season include the two key feasts, discussed in Chapter 1, of St Omer: his *translatio* ('Saint Omer en fleurs') of 8 June and his *depositio* (the anniversary of his death) of 9 September. Saints particularly venerated at the collégiale but not from the locale include St Benedict, St Denis, St Martin, St Quentin and Sts Gervais and Protais.[83]

Beyond this the sole notated book is a magnificent manuscript antiphonary from the mid-sixteenth century, the only survivor of a commission, described in detail in the chapter acts and fabric accounts,[84] by the chapter from 1550 to 1561 to renew its choirbooks. The charge for this ambitious

---

[82] Bibliothèque de l'Agglomération de Saint-Omer, MS 205.

[83] For this and further detail see Jean-François Goudesenne and Marc Gil (eds.), *L'antiphonaire de la Paix des Princes chrétiens: Calligraphié à Saint-Omer par Sire Michel Reymbault, enluminé à Lille par Soeur Françoise de Heuchin ca 1550–1561*, Publications of Medieval Music Manuscripts, 30 (Ottawa: Institute of Medieval Music, 2003), x–xx.

[84] The relevant documents are transcribed in full in Goudesenne and Gil, *L'antiphonaire*, xxxix–xliii. This publication comprises a study and complete facsimile of the volume. While attention to the book was first drawn by Georges Coolen in 1960 ('Un antiphonaire de la Collégiale de Saint-Omer', *Bulletin de la Société des antiquaires de la Morinie* 19/363 (1960), 324–30), it remained little known until it was sold at Christie's in London in 1986, whence it has since disappeared into a private collection in the United States. It is therefore a cause of great relief

project fell to the munificent canon Lambert de Caverel, otherwise known for establishing a general procession for the Feast of St James to commemorate the peace signed between the Emperor Charles V and Henry II of France. As for so much concerning musical life at the collégiale, the preservation of its documents has afforded access to detailed knowledge of the manuscript's production, including its scribe, illuminator and binder. We learn from these entries that the surviving volume was originally one of two or three covering the *pars estivalis* of the year, while another pair (now lost) dealt with the *pars hiemalis*. The enormous cost – more than 550 livres – incurred by the production of the set suggests, especially in the age of printing, a prestige project. That conclusion is supported by the pristine state of survival of the existing volume which, as Jean-François Goudesenne notes, speaks against the notion of actual use for the divine office.[85] The manuscript is complemented by a sole surviving copy of the unnotated St Omer breviary that was published in 1518.[86]

Noteworthy in the temporal cycle of the antiphonary are the feasts of the Five Joys of the Virgin and, unsurprisingly given the status of the local icon, Notre Dame des Miracles. The book embraces both the temporal and the sanctoral, with the latter (some two-thirds of the total length) receiving the lion's share. Comparison with the thirteenth-century ordinal permits identification of celebrations that were introduced in the interim, mostly in response to newly founded chapels and their attendant ritual, much of it privately sponsored by the church's canons.

Unsurprisingly the feasts of the church's patron St Omer occupy important places in the calendar. Chief among these is the *depositio*, marking the notional anniversary of his death on 9 September, which receives its own office in the antiphonary and is the only saint's day assigned a quadruple rank in the thirteenth-century ordinal. The chant of the *translatio* ('Saint Omer en fleurs') of 8 June, whose colourful celebration was addressed in Chapter 1, draws for much of its material on the *depositio*, which latter in its turn shares material with the liturgy of St Martin and (to a lesser extent) those of St Amand, St Vincent, St Stephen

---

that it was completely photographed before disappearing from public view and published in facsimile.

[85] *L'antiphonaire*, xiv.

[86] *Pars hyemalis [-estivalis] breviarii ecclesie collegiate sancti Audomari* (Paris, per Didier Maheu [et] Jacques Ferrebouc, 1518). The single surviving copy is preserved as Brussels, Bibliothèque Royale de Bruxelles, Réserve Précieuse, Van Hultem 653; discussion in Edouard Fournier, 'Les bréviaires imprimés de Saint-Omer et d'Aire-sur-la-Lys', *Bulletin de la Société des antiquaires de la Morinie* XII (1908), 303–14.

and – more surprisingly – the eleventh-century St Olaf of Norway.[87] Though likewise of duplex rank, the 21 October *inventio*, marking the recovery of St Omer's relics after being hidden during the tenth-century Norman invasion, is musically marked in the antiphonary only by the widely used antiphon 'Intercede pro nobis beate pontifex', drawing for the remainder of its chants from feasts elsewhere in the volume.

Other locally important celebrations include (unsurprisingly) the *depositio* of St Bertin and the Feast of the little-known St Austreberte. Unknown outside Saint-Omer except in Rouen, doubtless due to the departure of this seventh-century abbess, following her consecration by St Omer, to Normandy, Austreberte is celebrated by a liturgy heavily reliant on that of St Katherine. While a full examination of the antiphonary's musical and textual contexts would constitute a study in itself, the overall pattern seems to be one of general conformity with these examples, showing a broad-based interconnectedness with the wider traditions of the Western chant repertory.[88]

At a more local level, clear distinctions can be drawn between the earlier and later surviving antiphonaries, with the later not only including new feasts but also enhancing the ranking of established ones. Many instances of the latter involve private foundations. The new Feast of the Visitation of the Blessed Virgin Mary, gradually established in the West in the fifteenth century, occurs only in the later books, in line with trends elsewhere in Europe. At the collégiale, though, introduction of the observance was the

---

[87] My thanks for this and other information concerning inter-feast connections and rankings are due to John Harper. The connection with the Feast of St Olaf can easily be seen via comparison of the St Omer Antiphonary, ff. 129v–130r with Lenka Jiroušková, *Der heilige Wikingkönig Olav Haraldsson und sein hagiographisches Dossier*, 2 vols. (Leiden: Brill, 2014), vol. 1, 399.

[88] A striking example among later additions to the St Omer liturgy concerns the Feast of St Claude, a Benedictine bishop of Besançon. The dedicatee of a chapel, situated next to that of his successor Nicolas Rembert, founded by Dean Simon Godeffroy, Claude is celebrated, with a feast assigned major double status in the antiphonary, in a liturgy drawn wholesale (though not in the same sequence) from that of St Edmund Rich, otherwise known as Edmund of Abingdon. See Andrew Hughes, 'British Rhymed Offices: A Catalogue and Commentary', in Susan Rankin and David Hiley (eds.), *Music in the Medieval English Liturgy: Plainsong & Medieval Music Society Centennial Essays* (Oxford: Oxford University Press, 1993), 262–3; see also Andrew Hughes, *Late Medieval Liturgical Offices: Resources for Electronic Research*, Subsidia Medievalia 23–24. 2 vols. (*Texts* and *Sources and Chants*) (Toronto: Pontifical Institute of Mediaeval Studies, 1994–5). The data accompanying these volumes is available at: http://hlub .dyndns.org/projekten/webplek/CANTUS/cgi-bin/LMLO/index.cgi. The raw text supplied on the office for Edmund Rich is available as follows: http://hlub.dyndns.org/projekten/webplek/ CANTUS/cgi-bin/LMLO/LMLO.cgi?X=%5BED52%5D&raw_text=true.
Though a thirteenth-century archbishop of Canterbury, Rich died in exile in France and was buried at the Cistercian abbey of Pontigny, where miracles were quickly reported.

direct result of a private foundation, of major double rank in line with the levels of the other Marian feasts, in 1455 by Dean Simon Bocheux (d.1462). Bocheux also provided for a second foundation to the Visitation for the chapel of the Holy Trinity, founded initially in 1336. He endowed an annuity of £12 in rents, divided into two parts: £7 to fund the distributions to the canons and other clerics attending the offices of prime, matins, High Mass and second vespers on the feast itself, plus £5 for a single chaplain 'of good life and conduct' ('de bonne vie et honneste conversation') to celebrate a weekly Mass of the Holy Trinity.[89] The following March he added a further endowment of 4s. 6d. to fund a procession and *Salve* service on the same day. Disbursements for the feast are carefully specified: 36s. is to go on lights, 60s. in distributions to be divided between resident canons attending matins, Mass and vespers, plus 12d. to each vicar, 6d. to each of the fourteen escotiers, 6d. to each of the celebrant, deacon and subdeacon at Mass, 6d. to the cantor or other canon leading the choir, 12d. for the organist, 12d. for the senior churchwarden and 6d. for the minor churchwarden, 2s. for the bell-ringer, and so on. Additions to earlier foundations, at St Omer as elsewhere, need not necessarily come from the founder of the earlier office (or of the augmentation of an older one). A document included as part of the bundle II. G. 1776 details rents added according to the will of Toussains de Le Ruelle to the profit of the major double Feast of St Barbara founded by Pierre Pauchet.

In similar fashion the Feast of St Claude, absent from the earlier antiphonary, is ranked major double in the sixteenth-century manuscript antiphonary and triplex in the 1518 print, a clear reflection of the new chapel dedicated to the saint founded by Dean Simon Godeffroy (d.1499).[90] An inscription on two sides of an octagonal pillar of the former chapel of St Nicholas (still there but now concealed by panelling associated with the chapel of Notre-Dame-des-Miracles which superseded it) details the 1487 foundation by Wallerand Peppin of a double Feast of Sts Cosmas and Damian (27 September). The feast, the inscription asserts, is to be 'similar in all respects to the doubles of St Anthony and St Julian', and its celebration (in the same chapel of St Nicholas) is to be adorned by twelve 'tiercerons' of wax (a set size of candle), burning around the chapel

---

[89] On the two foundations see Emmanuel Wallet, *Description de l'ancienne cathédrale de Saint-Omer (Pas-de-Calais, ci-devant Artois), autrefois Notre-Dame de Sithiu, et Morinie, maintenant paroisse Notre-Dame* (Saint-Omer/Douai: Baclé/author, 1839), 31. See also Loriquet, *Épigraphie*, 4. Bocheux's foundation documents are preserved as a bundle in II. G. 2727.

[90] On the foundation of this chapel see Wallet, *Description de l'ancienne cathédrale*, 32.

throughout the feast day, and by 'the six choirboys', though in precisely what fashion is not stated. The two saints are to be further honoured by two (votive) Masses for Peppin's soul and those of his family and friends, to be celebrated after matins respectively on the Thursday following the Feast of Sts Simon and Jude (28 October) and the Sunday after Ascension (forty-three days after Easter), with 'priest, deacon and subdeacon and the master and said choirboys, organ and the usual "sonnerie" [presumably bell-ringing]'. In fact the feast was not raised in rank until 1495 when, the fabric account for the year relates, Peppin endowed the tithe (*dime*) of Arnyck for the purpose.[91] Sure enough, the feast is ranked (like those of Anthony and Julian), in both the sixteenth-century antiphonary and the 1518 breviary, as major double, superseding the three-lesson ranking of the thirteenth-century ordinal.[92] Likewise referencing the Feast of St Anthony, assent was given at a chapter meeting of 19 September 1472 to Crestien Le Vasseur 'that he may found a grand double of the Feast of St Nicholas like that of the Feast of Anthony, provided he can found it properly'; in other words presumably provided he has sufficient funds.[93]

More speculatively, although the chapel of Notre-Dame de Pitié was not established until around the mid-sixteenth century, the observance of the Five Joys of the Virgin on the Saturday after Ascension Day may perhaps reflect the new cult and related *confrèries* of Notre-Dame de Pitié emerging during the reign of Louis XII (1498–1515). If this is so, the apparently unique texts found only in the 1518 breviary (plus whatever associated chants they carried) may have been newly composed.[94] Though limited in scope, the surviving volumes, along with documentary evidence, indicate that the liturgy and chant of the collégiale continued to accrue new observances

---

[91] 'Item ung double le jour Saint Cosme et S Damien samblable en tout aux doubles S Anthoine et S Jullien et avoec ce audit jour . xii . tyercerons de cyre que seront mis et alumes audit jour autour de la dite capelle . et aux . vi . enfans de coeur a chacun . xii . d . p[arisi]s[.] Item deux messes desdits sains que se celeberont audit lieu apres matines par prebtre diacre et soubdiacre le maistre et lesdits enfans orghes et sonerie acoustumee lune le joeudi prochain S Symon S Jude et lautre le dymenche prochain apres lascencion[.] Et pour ce faire et acomplir a prins la cerge leglise de chiens pries Dieu pour son ame parens et amis que leur faice pardon[.] Amen.' Quoted and discussed in Loriquet, *Épigraphie*, 27–9.

[92] See the calendar in Goudesenne and Gil, *L'antiphonaire*, xiv–xv.

[93] Le xixe jour de septembre messeigneurs de capitle ont accorde a Maistre Crestien Le Vasseur leur confrere quil fonde ung grant double de le feste de Saint Nicolay ad instar festi Anthonii / pourveu quil le fondera suffiss[ammen]t[.] (II. G. 354, f. 158r)

[94] On the foundation date of the chapel of Notre-Dame de Pitié see Wallet, *Description de l'ancienne cathédrale*, 34. On the five joys see Gérard Gros, *Ave Vierge Marie: Études sur les prières mariales en vers français (XIIe–XVe siècles)* (Lyon: Presses Universitaires de Lyon, 2004), 30–55.

and revisit old ones, especially as a result of enhancements in private expressions of piety in the fifteenth and early sixteenth centuries.

Regarding polyphony, as in most other centres of late medieval musical excellence across northern Europe, all trace of written polyphonic music has been erased. Due to the extent of documentary survival for St Omer, though, it is possible to draw significant inferences concerning the scope of singing in parts, at least at the high altar. Both public and private devotions with 'deschant' are widely attested, as already noted, from at least the early fifteenth century. Much of the music so designated was surely sung extempore on the book, a conclusion supported by the absence in the earlier stages of any records concerning notated music.

That situation changed in the year 1462/3, when a certain Jehan de Herlines *dit* Bassee was paid for 'a large book of paper and seven quires of large size, noted in discant containing a number of Masses, bought from him'.[95] The sum paid for this volume – 110 sous – was very considerable: to put it into perspective, this is six sous more than the organist of the day was paid for the whole year, and more than four times the sum paid annually to the youth who operated the organ bellows. Even thirty years later the payment for copying a single Mass ranged between three and five sous. In short, this must have been a huge quantity of music, and it is tempting to speculate as to where it might have originated.

Since Bassee was clearly paid for supplying notated music rather than for copying it, it seems reasonable to postulate that it came from outside Saint-Omer. The most likely sources for such a large quantity of Mass music must surely be the large establishments with which the collégiale enjoyed close relationships, musical and otherwise. Among musical contacts in the early 1460s the master of the boys, Eustache Maistresse, or Manessier, had until recently been a singer at St Donatian, Bruges, while Toussains de Le Ruelle, well known to musicology from his long service at the Burgundian court and elsewhere, was a prominent member of the chapter.[96]

---

[95] A Sire Jehan de Herlines dit Bassee pour ung grant livre en pappier et sept coyers de du [sic] grant volume nottez en deschant contenant plusieurs messes a lui achetez du sceu et commandement de messeigneurs en plain capp[it]re pour ce paie comme appert par quittance c x s (f. 23 r–v)

[96] The first appearance of Maistresse that I have been able to trace occurred on 15 July 1459, when he received a vicariate vacated by the death of its prior incumbent Ansel Heynneman. He was first presented by the cantor as master of the boys on 23 February 1461 (II. G. 353, f. 48r and f. 51v), retaining the post for the following two years. Further appointments are recorded for 1466–7, 1475–6, 1476–7 and 1477–8. For a detailed discussion of Toussains's life and career see pp. 248–56.

The most likely source for such a large body of music would surely have been the Burgundian court, with which, as we shall explore later, the chapter acts detail frequent and regular contacts throughout the period and beyond.

A Jean Lambert *dit* Bassee was a member of the Burgundian court chapel from 1436 to 1469,[97] but while it is not inconceivable, prima facie, that 'Jehan de Herlines *dit* Bassee' could be the same man with a toponymic, it would be hard to square work as a Burgundian chaplain with the vicariate held by the 'Jehan de Herlines' at St Omer. Besides brokering the book of Masses, the St Omer Bassee had dealings with the same church at least from the mid-1450s until 1469/70. In 1455/6 and subsequent years he is listed in the fabric accounts as having borrowed a breviary in two volumes, which he finally, in 1462/3, purchased for fifty sous, surely, given the date, from the proceeds (or commission) from the sale of the Mass book. The same year 'Jehenne Herlins', a seamstress and likely a female relative, received twelve sous for work on 'several aubes'. More curiously, and as already noted, in 1469/70 the future master of the boys Martin de Lavenne acquired Bassee's vicariate in exchange for his own escoterie. Why the latter would have settled for a demotion of this nature is unclear, though he proceeded the same year to pass the post on to another cleric.[98]

Perhaps the most striking thing about the acquisition of the volume of Masses is its isolation. A great advantage of the remarkably good state of survival of the archives is the largely uninterrupted perspective it offers. Although only two and a half years of fabric accounts are missing between the early 1460s and early 1490s, the documents of the period otherwise contain not a single unequivocal mention of notated polyphonic music. This seems at first blush a curious situation, which will be addressed shortly; but for the moment we will move on to the next such record that does appear. This entry, which reads as follows, is dated 25 August 1494, and is of great interest for other reasons: 'Item, the 25th August to Master

---

[97] See Jeanne Marix, *Histoire de la musique et des musiciens de la cour de Bourgogne sous le règne de Philippe le Bon* (Strasbourg: Heitz, 1939; repr. Geneva: Minkoff, 1972), 242–60. For the period from 1466 to 1469 see David Fiala, 'Le mécénat musical des ducs de Bourgogne et des princes de la Maison de Habsbourg, 1467–1506', unpublished PhD dissertation, Université de Tours (2002), vol. 2, annexe 1.

[98] It would surely be prudent to assume that the 'Johannes Lambert' who appears in the records between the late 1480s and mid-1490s was a different individual.

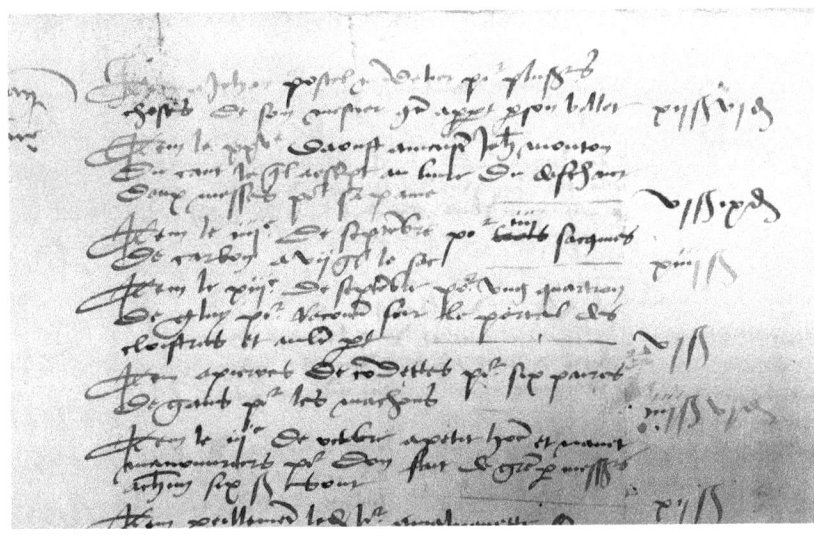

Figure 3.4 Payment to Jean Mouton for copying Masses

Jehan Mouton for the music that he has written in the book of discant, two Masses, for his pains 6s. 9d.' (see Figure 3.4)[99]

Clearly the chapter was happy with Mouton's work: the fabric account for 1494/5 details substantial further copying undertaken by him. In these he is referred to by his toponymic 'de Holluighe', resolving any reasonable doubt that this was indeed the composer Jean Mouton. The first payments are again for copying Masses:

Item, to Master Jehan de Holluighe for a quire of *carte realle* paper to write several Masses in the large book of discant in the choir, 4s.

Item, to the said Master Jehan de Holluighe for having ruled the said paper and written three new Masses, 16s.

Item, to the said Master Jehan for having written, again in the said book, three more Masses, 15s.[100]

---

[99] Item le xxv^e d'aoust a Maistre Jehan Mouton du cant lequel a escript au livre de deschant deux messes pour sa paine, vi s ix d (1493/4, f. 37v)

[100] Item a Maistre Jehan de Holluighe pour une main de pappier Carte Realle pour escripre aucunes messes au grant livre de discant au coeur: iiii s
Item audit Maistre Jehan pour avoir regle ledit pappier et escript trois messes nouvelles: xvi s
Item au dessusdit Maistre Jehan pour avoir escript encoures audit livre trois autres messes: xv s
(1494/5, f. 31v)

The first of these records thus reveals the size ('carte reale') of the paper used for the 'grant livre': at 44.5 × 61.5 cm this would have divided into a folio size of roughly 30.75 × 44.5 cm, clearly more than adequate for reading by the assembled choir.[101]

More tantalisingly still than these records, though, on the next page of the same account Mouton is paid for producing a complete manuscript:

Item, to Master Jehan de Holluigues for a quire of paper which he ruled, and composed a book of Magnificats on all the tones, Te Deum and other things in discant, put in the choir of the said church, the which by order of Messires G. Decault, R. de Monte and R. Poilly, assigned by chapter to inspect the said book, pay 28s.[102]

Uncoincidentally, the fabric account for the following year includes a payment

for having had made an oak cupboard bearing a lectern, placed at the end of the choir on the side of monseigneur the provost, [in which] to place the books of discant that are in the choir, by agreement made with Jehan Hussier.[103]

Costing forty-eight sous, this must have been an impressive item, and it surely bespeaks a certain pride in the new musical acquisitions. The description fits the kind of layout depicted in contemporary images such as the famous illumination of Okeghem and the French royal choir in performance. It also affirms the position of the choir, at least when singing composed polyphony, *in medio chori*, a setting whose convention is confirmed by earlier payments from 1443/4 and 1475/6.[104]

---

[101] This is assuming the standard Bolognese size for carta realle: see for instance Jane Bernstein, *Music Printing in Renaissance Venice: The Scotto Press (1539–1572)* (New York and Oxford: Oxford University Press, 1998), 63.

[102] Item a Maistre Jehan de Holluighes pour une main [twenty-five sheets] de pappier le avoir regle / et compose ung livre de Magnificat sur tous les tons Te Deum et autres choses en discant mis au coeur de ladit eglise duquel par lordonnance de Messires G. Decault. R. de Monte et R[.] Poilly commis a viseter ledit livre par capitle paye xxviii s (1494/5, f. 32r)

[103] Item pour une aulmaire dallemarche mise au bout des quayeres au lez de monseigneur le prevost portant ung pupiltre pour mettre les livres de dischant qui sont audit coeur par marchie fait a Jehan Hussier (1495/6, f. 31r, in both the surviving copies of the account for this year.)

[104] 'Item audit Sire Vincent [Breion] pour pluseurs aultres peaulx de parchemin pour faire ung livre escript et note des respons servans a doubles au long delan pour mettre au moillon [centre] du coeur' (1443/4, f. 9r); 'Pour une peau de parcemin a faire les viii neupmes au popitre des chantres au millieu du coeur paie a Sire Martin de Lavenne' (1475/6, f. 28v). The latter record clearly refers to the untexted festal neumes, copied onto a single leaf and sung (according to mode) as conclusions to antiphons for Benedictus, Magnificat, Quicunque vult, and the final antiphons of vespers, lauds and the nocturns of matins (see David Hiley, *Western*

Besides his copying activities it appears that Mouton was also singing for the church during at least the two years he was copying music, and the aggregate of information in Saint-Omer prompts an excursus into newly known aspects of his early career, and speculation arising from them. A record in the chapter acts dated 18 September 1495 accords him and 'Petrus Sommelart thenoriste' 12d., along with 9d. to another unspecified Petrus, 'continuing the grace of the previous year'. These were surely daily sums to be distributed (as typically) in lots of 4d./3d. at each of matins, Mass and vespers, though why Sommelart, who, as already noted, was by now an escotier, would have been receiving extra payments is unclear. The fact that 12d. amounts to double the fee typically assigned to vicars, and is equal to what Bourgois had been accustomed to receive as tenorist, surely bespeaks the perceived quality of the services provided.[105] It appears likely, then, that this group of three singers was being paid as a small ensemble of polyphonists, presumably taking a line each with the six choirboys on the top line of four-voice music.[106]

On the same day the lords, extending the favour done for the tenorist Petrus Sommelart the previous year to Masters Johannes Mouton and Petrus ~~Sommelart~~, allowed them the same favour, viz to Petrus 12d. parisis, to Johannes 12d. parisis and to Petrus 9d. until All Saints', and to the others, i.e. the tenorist and Mouton, for the whole year, or to the said Mouton until the return of Lord Michael Le Gay, vicar etc.[107]

In Mouton's case the wording suggests that this work was as a temporary replacement, since the record specifies that he is to be paid until the return of the vicar Michael Le Gay who had been given several months' leave of absence. It is clear, however, that his involvement with the church continued, since on 12 May 1497 we read that

the lords promised to Master Johannes Mouton the vicariate vacant through the death of Matheus Regis, according to the conditions and agreements made at the

---

Plainchant: A Handbook (Oxford: Clarendon Press, 1993, 331–3). My thanks to John Harper for this information.

[105] As, for example, the six deniers daily paid to 'Balduino Laprentis'; see above, p. 81.

[106] My thanks to Robert Nosow for this suggestion.

[107] Eadem die domini continuando gratiam anno preterito facto Petro Sommelart thenorista Mgr Joh Mouton et Petro ~~Sommelart~~ concesserunt eisdem gratiam eandem videlicet Petro xii d par[isis]. Joh xii d par[isis]. et Petro ix d usque ad Omnium Sanctorum et aliis videlicet thenoriste et Mouton. per totum annum / aut dicto Mouton usque ad adventum D[omini] Michaelis Le Gay vicarii etc. (II. G. 355, f. 113r)

time of his return. For the setting in order of his situation/property(?) in Aire they granted him three weeks.[108]

'De statu suo Arie' may refer to dealings regarding an unknown benefice in Aire-sur-la-Lys, most plausibly associated with the collegiate church of St Pierre in that neighbouring town, where other St Omer clerics – including (see below) Mouton's likely kinsman Franciscus de Holluigues – also held benefices. Alternatively it might concern property, as in the case of his 1506 return to the region (see below) to sell a house. Mouton was presumably being granted a favour, allowing him to earn an income while sorting out whatever affairs he had locally, and before the vicariate was passed on to a more permanent incumbent. At any rate he was soon on the move: from 16 February to 26 June the following year he surfaced as a *parva vicaria* at the cathedral of Cambrai,[109] and by 1500 was master of the boys at the cathedral of Amiens.

Mouton's presence in Saint-Omer is hardly surprising: the family name 'de Holluigues' presumably refers to the village of Haut Wignes near Samer, a town only a few kilometres from Saint-Omer, where many of its scions resided then, as they still do today.[110] Mouton is himself referred to in the dedicatory preface of the 1555 motet collection of Le Roy and Ballard as 'Sameracensis', while a document of 1506, giving the name of his mother and her husband, details, as mentioned, his sale of a house in Samer. His citation, by Leo X, as apostolic notary calls him 'clericus Morinensis' (cleric of the diocese of Thérouanne), a connection that is further cemented by the fact that, as we learn from the inscription of his (now lost) tombstone at Saint-Quentin, he was 'chanoine de Thérouanne et de cette eglise'.[111]. If, as for Josquin and Compère, a benefice at the collegiate church of Saint-Quentin

---

[108]   ... domini promiserunt Magistro Johanni Mouton vicariam vaccantem per obitum Domini Mathei Regis sub conditionibus et permissionibus fiendis in regressu suo / ad disponendum de statu suo Arie concesserunt eidem tres ebdomada[.] (II. G. 355, 125r)

[109]   My thanks to David Fiala for this information, and for sharing with me his image of Lille, Archives départementales du Nord, 4G 6791, f. 7r, where 'Jo Holluighe' is listed along with the other twelve petits vicaires present in Lent 1498. Fiala also drew on the unpublished documentation concerning the 'small vicars' of Cambrai circulated by Alejandro Planchart; my thanks are also due to the late Professor Planchart for kindly sharing this document with me (research now published in his *Guillaume Du Fay*, 316–17). Fiala further notes the inclusion of 'Mouton' among the Cambrai petits vicaires in Jean Molinet's poem *Ceux qui sont convocquiés aux nopces Magdelaine de Laidin*.

[110]   My thanks to Mouton's modern-day family member and local historian Gérard Holluigue for these and other details.

[111]   Text for example in David Fiala, 'La collégiale royale', 213.

was a mark of more general professional distinction, one at Thérouanne, whenever it was acquired, more likely reflects local connections.

At least two other clerics of the same name, surely relatives, emerge from the St Omer accounts in the later fifteenth century. Franciscus/Francois de Holluigues was appointed to both a chaplaincy and a curacy in January 1459.[112] If his styling, in the fabric account, as 'Francequin de Hol[luiges]' suggests someone fairly junior at this point, his progress was rapid: already in 1465 he was granted, via the authority of letters submitted by the provost, the minor canonry and prebend of the deceased canon Nicolaus de Aula.[113] Having resigned this on 14 September 1472, a year later Franciscus was admitted to a major prebend which, the following January, he in turn exchanged via permutation with Philippe de Mailly for a canonry at the collegiate church of St Pierre, Aire-sur-la-Lys.[114] Clearly an advance even on his major prebend at St Omer, the post at Aire carried with it the role of scolasticus (or 'écolâtre'), meaning head of education in the church and wider community, a post that, with the positions of dean, cantor and treasurer, was one of the four major offices of the church. With this latest step up the hierarchical ladder, Franciscus disappears from view, but April 1475 sees the arrival of a 'Jacobus Moton', appointed to the chaplaincy of St Maurice in the church of St Aldegonde.[115] The 'Jacobus de Holluigues' who on 26 January 1478 assumed the chaplaincy of St Kather-ine in the church of St Sepulchre (via permutation with Petrus Stallin for the chaplaincy of St Louis in the church of St Martin) was surely the same man.[116] Further evidence of likely family members comes from the Saint-Omer *comptes des argentiers*, which record the names of individuals admitted as bourgeois of the city. Thus 1455/6 saw the arrival of Noel Mouton; 1489/90 Baudechon Hellewischs; 1498/9 Ancelot de Hollewicq; 1505/6 Guilbert de Holluigues; and 1540/1 Charlot de Hollewighe.[117] Copies of wills for an Ancel de Hollewicq (presumably the 'Ancelot' just named) and a Katherine Mouton, 'widow of Clay Ledreu' (the latter dated 31 August 1504), are included in a volume of Saint-Omer wills for the dates

[112] Fabric account of 1458/9, f. 4r; II. G. 353, f. 46r.

[113] On 1 May. See II. G. 353, f. 63 r, and also the fabric account 1464/5, f. 5v.

[114] II. G. 354, ff. 157r, 172r–v.

[115] II. G. 354, f. 186v. This post was the subject of fairly rapid musical chairs that saw it fall only two months later into the hands of Guillaume Decault (f. 188r).

[116] II. G. 354, f. 215r.

[117] My thanks for this information to Dr Philippe Derieux, who compiled a list of arriving 'Bourgeois de Saint-Omer' from the above-mentioned records.

1496–1504 preserved in the Archives Départementales du Pas-de-Calais at Dainville (Arras).[118]

Besides their implications concerning Mouton's home *terroir*, of more general interest is the fact that the copying records cited above provide evidence of another known fifteenth-century composer being employed as a scribe. Mouton's name is thus added to those of Obrecht – a prolific scribe during various phases of his life – Binchois and (putatively) Busnoys, Tinctoris and so on. For present purposes, though, their chief importance lies in what they can tell us about the provision of polyphony at St Omer and, by inference, what they might suggest about such provision in other institutions of similar size. A number of general observations are prompted. Perhaps the most striking of these concerns the pattern of acquisition: while the use of books of composed polyphony in private chantries can certainly not be ruled out, provision for the high altar involved two major bouts of buying in notated polyphony separated by thirty years in which there is no clear evidence that any new polyphony was acquired by the church at all. Given the virtual completeness of the fabric accounts for the period in question, it would be difficult to explain the situation any other way. But in any case, this conclusion is supported by the nature of the Mouton documents, which also show a revealing discrepancy of attitude to music for the Mass on the one hand and music for the office on the other. While the records for copying Masses are for additions to the 'grand livre de deschant', either written directly into the book or copied on new quires to be sewn in later, that for copying office polyphony is for a brand-new book. The implications seem clear: the 'grant livre' into which Mouton copied Masses must have been none other than the big book of Masses that had been bought from Bassee in 1462–3; and the creation from scratch of a volume of office music surely suggests that the choir had not hitherto possessed a volume of office polyphony at all.

But again, this does not seem unduly surprising: on the one hand it is reasonable to suppose that even much of the office polyphony of Du Fay and Binchois – music sufficiently impervious to fashion still to have been being copied seventy or more years after its composition – represents the stylised tip of a vast iceberg of improvised office discant in the fifteenth century. On the other hand it may well be that, as elsewhere in the region, the church was at this time instituting a more regular polyphonic provision for the office, something here, as elsewhere,[119] likely reflected in the

---

[118] Justice échevinale de Saint-Omer MS 15B2, respectively ff. 195r–v and 220r–v.
[119] A point made to me in this connection by Barbara Haggh-Huglo.

payments for daily singers of which Mouton was himself a beneficiary. As far as the performance of polyphonic Masses is concerned, though, the fact that the chapter chose in the 1490s to have new Masses added to a volume which was by then more than thirty years old, rather than starting a new book, must imply that the old Masses were still being performed. Rapid musical expansion after about 1480, and more sustained patterns of copying documented at a few institutions of the highest importance, may perhaps lead us to expect a faster turnover of Mass music in large churches than was in fact generally the case.

In this context it is worth remembering that a number of surviving choirbooks copied for major institutions up to about 1480 contain music several decades old. Domarto's *Missa Spiritus almus* and Du Fay's *Missa Se la face ay pale* must have been some thirty years old by the time, around 1480, that they were copied into Rome, Cappella Sistina manuscript 14. Similarly Christopher Reynolds's suggestion that Rome, San Pietro B80, dating apparently from 1474 to 1475, encompasses Masses first copied in earlier choirbooks for the same choir between 1458 and 1463 makes sense only if their use was still envisaged; and some of the Masses in San Pietro B80 must in any case have been some twenty-five years old by the time their surviving copies were made.[120] The great book of Masses in St Pietro probably finds its closest surviving parallel in the Brussels manuscript Koninklijke Bibliotheek 5557, again a source composed of fascicles stitched together at various stages, with extra pieces added later on blank openings between them. But in the later fifteenth century there must have been similar books in the choirs of all the great cathedrals and collegiate churches.

The next phase of copying began in 1507/8, when Robert Doudeville was paid ten sous 'pour avoir notte deux nouvelles messes en discant pour servir au coer de ladite eglise'.[121] The sum of five sous per Mass, as paid to Mouton the previous decade, was clearly still the going rate. A hand of 'lombard' paper was supplied for the purpose but, in contrast to Mouton's case, not by the scribe himself: 'Item pour une main de grant pippier lombart pour notter lesdits messes payet ale femme Henri du Four iii s.'[122] Since no further detail is given, it cannot be known if these new Masses, and their hand of paper, had joined Mouton's in the 'grant livre de discant'. What does seem clear, though, is that the next batch of

---

[120] Reynolds, *Papal Patronage*, 98–104.   [121] 1507/8, f. 37r.

[122] F. 37r. 'Papier lombard' from the fourteenth century was a term apparently used widely in reference to Italian paper sold by merchants from the peninsula; the term came to be applied more generically to a thick 'cartridge' paper.

Mass-copying in 1509/10 – coming almost half a century after the acquisition of the 'grant livre' – was for a new volume and one, to judge from the payment for 'grandes lettres' (presumably painted initials), of some stature:

Item, for having had ten Masses in discant noted by one named Bonnet living with the master of song. Paid for each Mass 6s., and for the paper 10s., which is for the whole 70s.

Item, to the said Micquelot [Le Cras] for having bound the said book of Masses and made the large letters and other things as appears in the bill, 8s.[123]

Since this new book had been bound only the previous year, a payment in 1510/11 'for having refastened and rebound a big book of discant' ('pour avoir recolle et reloyet ung grand livre de deschant') must have been either for Mouton's vespers volume or, conceivably, for the only book so described hitherto, namely the 'grant livre' of 1462/3.[124]

Whether or not this venerable volume was still in use in the 1510s, however, the church had clearly entered a much more liberal phase in its attitude to the acquisition of composed polyphony. 1510/11 also saw a payment (detailed on the same page) 'a Sire Jehan Cambelin a son presentement achetay aluy v livres a motes payet xlv sc'. The number of volumes and the comparatively modest price paid to Cambelin (one of the two masters of the boys from 1508 to 1511) may suggest the purchase of a set of five part books rather than five volumes in choirbook format. Still more striking is the payment (again on the same page), scarcely more than fifteen years after the payment for Mouton's vespers volume, of twenty-eight sous for a book comprising thirteen Magnificats and a Te Deum.[125] Micquelot Le Cras was again paid (eight sous) 'for having provided a quire of Lombard paper and bound the said book of Magnificats in parchment'.[126] The implications of this, since Mouton's volume of vespers polyphony was by this point only some fifteen years old, are hard

---

[123] Item pour avoir faict noter dix messes en deschant a ung nomme Bonnet demourant aveuc le maistre de chant payet pour chacune messe vi s et pour le papier x s est icy pour tout lxx s. Item audit Micquelot [Le Cras] pour avoir lyet ledit livre a messes et faict les grandes lettres et aultres parts comme appert par billet viii s (1509/10, f. 26r)

[124] 1510/11, f. 26r.

[125] Item a Sire Betremieu Le Moisne vicaire pour avoir notte xiii Magnificas et le Te Deum en ung livre a part payet xxviii s (1510/11, f. 26r). Betremieu is named as one of the two masters of the boys from 1516 to 1518, and, in 1516/17, 1517/18 and 1520/1, is paid for singing for Dean Nicolas Rembert's *Salve* foundation. He seems to have been the Betremieu Thibault who, in his will of 1544, made bequests to his brother Georges Thibault (also a copyist: see below; for this information see Gil and Nys, *Saint-Omer gothique*, 389).

[126] Item audit Micquelot pour avoir livre une main de papier lombart et lyet en parchemin ledit livre a Magnificas [sic] viii s (1510/11, f. 26r)

to fathom: perhaps the balance in vespers polyphony was shifting away from improvised discant in favour of composed polyphony; perhaps tastes were moving towards the potentially greater sophistication of composed music; or maybe the church was simply cultivating a desire for greater variety. Whatever the case, the copying of new Masses also continued, with 'Sire Betremieu' paid the following year for a further 'deux messes en deschant' (at five sous each) and in 1518/19 'Sire George Thibault' paid 'for having had rebound the book at the high altar and a legendary of the choirboys ... [and] for writing two new Masses in the said book'.[127]

The flurry of copying in 1509/10 also included the (plainsong) Mass of 'Recordare', copied 'in the two large graduals in the choir of the said church'.[128] Named for its Introit, 'Remember, O Lord, thy covenant, and say to the destroying angel, stay now thy hand', this is a votive Mass celebrated in time of plague, still a recurring blight on the city in the early sixteenth century. More intriguingly, a further payment (of twelve sous) to 'Jan de Le Venne for the Masses of Recordare for "sonnerye" was paid by order of the lords'.[129] What manner of 'sonnerye' was intended, whether from the bells, organ and/or from a larger array of instruments, is unknown. What is for sure though is that the sounds of the church of St Omer extended far beyond those produced by human lungs. From at least the fourteenth century a vital agent in extending that sound beyond the choir and side chapels and into the wider building was the organ, the subject of Chapter 4.

---

[127] A Sire George Thibault pour avoir fait reloyer le livre du grand autel et ung legendier des enfans ...[et] pour lescriture de deux messes nouvelles audit livre (1518/19, f. 28r)

[128] Item audit Micquelot pour avoir notte le messe de recordare ens les deux grans grels estans au coeur de ladite eglise xxiiii s (1509/10, f. 26r)

[129] Item a Jan de Le Venne pour les messes de Recordare pour sonnerye a este payet par lordonnance de messeigneurs xii s (1509/10, f. 37v)

4 | The Organs

Weaving through the accounts, threading in and out of the story of the church's vocal traditions and the larger impulses to which they gave expression is the equally ramified story of the instruments that supported them, and that amplified the church's corporate voice through the larger building and beyond: the bells and – the concern of this chapter – the organs. As elsewhere, the church's organs developed in tandem with the changing morphology of the building that housed them and whose authority and grandeur they were fashioned to reflect, in physical stature as well as in sound. If such grandeur is overwhelmingly expressed by the immense eighteenth-century organ, reworked by Cavaillé-Coll in 1853, that today dominates the west end, the arrival of that huge behemoth contributed to a tradition that was by then already centuries old.

Other eyes have traced the threads of this development in the past: while the death in 1890 of Louis Deschamps de Pas may have deprived us of earlier scrutiny of the church's maîtrise, this indefatigable antiquarian did pursue the history of its organs.[1] The continuous run of the St Omer accounts starting in the late fourteenth century is remarkable for the insight it offers into the provision and maintenance of organs in a large ecclesiastical institution beginning in the late Middle Ages, and of the individuals who gave them utterance. I will begin by following the building of organs from the late fourteenth to the sixteenth century, before broadening the lens to consider their players, and what can be deduced of the nature of the musical practice in which they partook.

---

[1] 'L'église Notre-Dame de Saint-Omer, d'après les comptes de fabrique et les registres capitulaires', *Mémoires de la Société des antiquaires de la Morinie*, vols. 22 and 23 (Saint-Omer: H. d'Homont, 1892–3), ch. 5, 'Les orgues', vol. 23, 82–110. I have given a briefer outline of the organ-building in this period in 'Organs and Instrumental Performance at the Collegiate Church of Saint-Omer, Northern France, in the Later Middle Ages', in Timothy J. McGee and Stewart Carter (eds.), *Instruments, Ensembles, and Repertory, 1300–1600: Essays in Honour of Keith Polk* (Turnhout: Brepols, 2013), 101–9.

First Signs

The earliest surviving records of substantial work on an organ, from the fabric account for 1391–2, bear witness to a considerable building campaign, occupying at least three months of that fiscal year.[2] The account specifies expenses 'for the repair and positioning of the organs and for the stone masons' ('pro reparatione et locatione organorum et per lathomos'), rather than for a completely new build. Earlier records clarify the prior existence of an organ: an entry in the earliest surviving fabric account of ?1378 details payment for the 'repair of the organ shutters and two keys for the same'.[3] A payment detailed in the account for 1385/6 'for the repair of the glass window next to the organ that is called "O"' permits the deduction that the organ was at this point positioned on the north wall of the north transept.[4] De Pas notes that the 'window called "O"' can only refer to the rose window at the end of the north transept, the lengthening of the south transept being by that point incomplete. The same author sees support for the notion of a thoroughgoing repair rather than enlargement of an existing instrument in the absence of direct mention of the provision of new pipes. But payments for lead totalling at least 132 lb. surely implies at least some new pipework, either to expand ambitus or (more likely) to increase the numbers of pipes for individual keys,[5] if not on the scale of the donation of 600 lb. of lead that in 1478, for example, supported the building of a new instrument for St Vulfran, Abbeville.[6] One record, following a payment for 52 lb of lead, detailing further payment 'for fat/oil with a hand (quire) of paper for founding the said lead by the said stonemasons' ('pro pinguedine cum una manu papiri pro fundendo dictum plombum per dictos lachtomos') is surely suggestive, and while the reason

---

[2] II. G 2802 (roll).

[3] Item pro refectione hostii organorum et duabus clavibus eiusdem (II. G. 2797 (roll))

[4] Item pro refectione fenestre vitree iuxta organa que vocatur . o . quam fecerunt maiores et scabini ville facere (II. G. 2798 (roll)). Discussed in Deschamps de Pas, 'L'église Notre-Dame', 84, and Emmanuel Wallet, *Description de l'ancienne cathédrale de Saint-Omer (Pas-de-Calais, ci-devant Artois), autrefois Notre-Dame de Sithiu, et Morinie, maintenant paroisse Notre-Dame* (Saint-Omer/Douai: Baclé/author, 1839), 46.

[5] Robert Bates has pointed out to me that the term 'ranks', though commonly used in connection with organs of this period, is properly speaking a misnomer, since there were at this time no separable ranks; rather the number of pipes per note increased with ascending pitch. He further notes that lead could have been required also for weights on the bellows and lead tubing.

[6] Marcel Degrutère, 'De l'orgue . . . des instruments et des hommes', in Camilla Cavicchi, Marie-Alexis Colin and Philippe Vendrix, *La musique en Picardie du XIVe au XVIIe siècle* (Turnhout: Brepols, 2012), 276–7.

for supply of paper is unclear,[7] succeeding payments for materials includ-ing sand, firewood and even a forge show that, stonemasons though they were, the 'lachtomi' were clearly founding something. The records are silent as to details concerning the pipes at this early stage, but it seems almost certain that whatever the nature of their distinction across the range in terms of numbers and pitches per key, they would have comprised a *Blockwerk* without scope for registral variation.[8]

While the organ's position following this work remained on the north wall of the north transept,[9] new pipework would be of a piece with a project significant enough to entail, as did this one, substantial and heavy con-struction involving considerable effort, expense, materials and man-hours. The latter involved as many as seven stonemasons, most of them paid for work covering twenty days or more. Johannes Noel, who constructed a completely new case, a new set of shutters and all the other woodwork, was paid for thirty-four and a half days spent on the task, in which six further carpenters were also engaged.[10] Payment for production of new keys (fashioned, we are told, from figured burr or root wood) might also suggest an extension of range *vis-à-vis* the earlier organ, though it could of course refer simply to replacement of existing keys that had worn down.[11] Con-siderable quantities of new stone, ironwork and different kinds of wood, plus payment for painting and sculpted wooden figures all reinforce the impression that whatever its earlier state, the organ became in the last decade of the fourteenth century an instrument of substantial dimensions, and one perceived to be of major importance for the fabric as well as the functioning of the institution. Clearly its construction was a signal (and

---

[7] Robert Bates has, however, commented to me that paper was used for lining bellows boards and wind trunks.

[8] See Barbara Owen and Peter Williams, 'Organ, IV: the classical and medieval organ 6: The church organ, 1100–1450', *Grove Music Online*, 2001, www.oxfordmusiconline.com/grovemusic/view/10.1093/gmo/9781561592630.001.0001/omo-9781561592630-e-0000044010, accessed 11 September 2016.

[9] See Deschamps de Pas, 'L'église Notre-Dame', 82–4. For an illustration of a similar positioning see the image by Simon Bening of the celebration of a Mass on the cover of my book *The Cultural Life of the Early Polyphonic Mass* (Cambridge: Cambridge University Press, 2010). The source is a Book of Hours (*c.*1535–45) from the Rothschild Collection, Waddesdon Manor (The National Trust), MS 26, folio 154v.

[10] Item Johanni Noel qui cassam et totum opus ligneum existentem in dictis organis composuit pro xxxiiii. diebus cum dimidia qualibet die ix sc valent xv l x s vi d (1391/2)

[11] 'Item pro uno assere nuncupato cnolhout quo claves organorum facte sunt' (1391/2). Synonyms for 'cnolhout' include 'wortelhout' and 'figuratie', the latter on account presumably of the attractive figure of this particular wood that made it suitable for organ keys. See www.termenvanboheest.org/k#knolhout, accessed 9 October 2019. My thanks to Henry Howard for tracking this down.

highly expensive) event in the life of the church: rather akin to the laying of a foundation stone, the installation of the first pipe was toasted in wine, and marked by further drinking, apparently of mulled wine ('wine with spices') at a visit from clerics of St Bertin.[12]

As so often, if the progress of building can be traced in some detail, ideas concerning the actual practices – and logistics thereof – in which the organ was engaged rely much more on inference and speculation. This will be considered more fully below; for now, though, it will be sufficient to note that, typically for the time, the primary roles of the organ surely concerned not, as is most characteristic today, accompanying, but rather interjections of various kinds within the ritual. Besides short solo items this would have involved diverse manners of alternation with chant or polyphony, either directly in alternatim performance, most obviously (but not exclusively) of items conducive to such practice, for instance Kyries, psalms, canticles (especially the Magnificat), hymns, sequences and of course the *Te Deum*, or in separate numbers such as antiphons, adding grandeur to the liturgy and/or providing relief for the singers.[13] Use of the organ surely did not per se, at St Omer any more than anywhere else in the later Middle Ages, necessarily imply vocal polyphony, albeit that enhancements in organ and polyphony here, as elsewhere, probably coincided. As for the singing participants in the liturgy, its staple was likely the monophonic performance of chant, probably enlivened by two-voice items involving chant plus treble elaboration (see below); and whatever vocal polyphony took place, at Mass, vespers or in votive observances, it seems unlikely to have included simultaneous involvement of the organ.

For devotions at the high altar, which during this period stood at the east end of the chancel, not (as today) much further west at the crossing,[14] what was possible was clearly contingent on geography. As discussed in

---

[12] Item pro vino dato ipsis magistris quum apposuerunt primam pipam orghanorum
Item pro vino et spe[cie]bus quum dominus grenarius Sancti Bertini venit visitatum dicta organa cum quodam alio religioso et eorum familia (1391/2)

[13] In the words of Arnolt Schlick, 'Attending in churches to God's praise / relief from choral song / and refreshment of the human temper [from] vexation.' ('Pfleglich in kirchen zum lob gottes / erleichterung Chorgesangs / vnd erquickung menschlichs Gemüts vnd verdruß'), from *Spiegel der Orgelmacher und Organisten* (Speyer, 1511), quoted in Franz Körndle, '"Usus" und "Abusus" organorum" im 15. Und 16. Jahrhundert', *Acta Organologica* 27 (2001), 223–40, at 223. As examples of the (considerable) German use of organ during Mass, Körndle recounts the detailed fifteenth-century stipulations for the monasteries of St Sixtus, Merseburg, St Bartholomäus, Frankfurt am Main and St Emmeram, Regensburg (see ibid., 224–6). Körndle (*passim*) also notes the degree to which organ performance in some German settings actively replaced (sometimes considerable) portions of the otherwise sung Mass.

[14] Wallet, *Description de l'ancienne cathédrale*, 23 and plate 1.

Chapters 1 and 3, singing at high altar observances took place from a lectern placed in the centre of the choir. The payment, in the fabric account for 1433/4, 'for a little bell hung in the choir to make the organ play' ('pour une cloquette pendue ou cuer pour faire jouer des orgues') likely gives some indication of the exigencies of conducting high-altar ceremonies involving an instrument placed in the north transept, and a further reference in the same account to 'le cloquette des orghes' suggests that, as elsewhere, this was a standard item in the liturgical toolkit.[15] In the absence of a sight line, the organist would surely have relied, in determining when to come in, on the keen sense (which we shall explore in the next chapter) of the distinctive timbres of bells that would have been customary in this period and milieu.

The investment in time and effort on organ renovation seems to have been well judged: no repairs are recorded until 1441–2, when 'Sire Bertin capellain en leglise de Terrewane' was paid fifteen livres 'pour remettre apoint les orghenes de leglise'. Repairs performed by an assistant, Durant Le Sieure (and his daughter), included, as was frequent, work on the bellows (for which new leather was provided) plus attention to their boards and to the wind chest.[16] Clearly this was enough to keep things on track for ten years, until, in 1451/2 and again the following year, Jehan de Louvain 'organiste et faiseur dorghes' was paid for maintenance work.[17] New bellows are installed every decade or so: presumably, in spite of tanning, the leather would crack over time, and rats would do their worst to similar effect. More interestingly, in 1464/5 substantial work on the bellows was also accompanied by the purchase of tin to cover (presumably) the pipes, and boxwood to cover keys of the keyboard.[18] Further bellows work followed in 1475/6, when 'Marc Sproukof organ worker' was paid £36 for five new bellows.[19] In this same ledger we encounter for the first time a figure who will be key to the next phase of organ development in the

---

[15] 1433/4 f. 6r.

[16] Item paiet a Durant Le Sieure pour refaire le sommier les souffles les foeulles et pour aider audit Sire Bertin . . .; Item paiet encore ale fille dudit Durant . . . (1441/2, 5v)

[17] Respectively f. 15r and f. 16v. The 1451/2 entry reads 'A Jehan de Louvain faisseur dorghes pour avoit refait et remis apoint les orghes de leglise par le commandement de messeigneurs xxiiii s.' In the entry for the following year, which reads the same except for naming Jehan as 'organiste et faiseur dorgues', he is paid twenty sous.

[18] . . . pour deux douzaines de feulles destain pour brunir les tuyaux iii s. pour buisset pour couvrir le clavier ii s. (f. 15v). The word 'brunir' ('to polish', or 'to burnish') must here refer to beautifying the pipes and/or to polishing subsequent to the covering with tin.

[19] A Maistre Marc Sproukof ouvrier dorgues pour avoir fait .v. nouveaulx soufles aux orgues de leglise par marcie [= marché] fait a lui par messeigneurs a este paie xxxvi lbs. (f. 22v)

church: that year Victor Langhedul, organ-builder of Ypres, was hired for maintenance work on the organ of the chapel of Notre-Dame sur le marchiet. Presumably motivated by propitious opportunities on the horizon, Langhedul, following common practice, clearly ingratiated himself with the chapter by doing far more work than he had been paid for. His reward was not only to be reimbursed for his pains anyway, but to become, within five years, the architect of a major new instrument.[20]

'Les Grandes Orgues'

The major building work of the late fourteenth century had paid off handsomely, since the organ kept its position for almost a century. By 1481, however, it had clearly become insufficient for the church's demands: in that year it was joined – though not replaced – by a completely new instrument. The fact that almost half the expense entailed was borne by money from the estate of the recently deceased canon Jacques de Houchin is, for the history of music in the life of the church, of more general interest, to which I will return in the Epilogue.[21] The construction of the new organ was bound up with larger developments in the building that was to house it: Deschamps de Pas notes that by 1481 the church had been considerably enlarged compared to its state a century earlier, with the ceiling of the nave now raised to its current lofty height. Whatever their respective functions, the old organ was clearly not thought adequate to fill this expanded space, and it also seems likely that a grand voice was felt to be necessary for the newly grander body.

In 1480/1 Victor Langhedul visited the old organ and presented the chapter with his design for its replacement.[22] Langhedul, clearly a man of impressive gifts, was – as far as can be determined – the founder member of a long-running dynasty of organ-builders,[23] the most celebrated being his

---

[20] A Victor Langhedul ouvrier dorgues demourant a Yppre [sic] pour avoir refait et mis apoint les orghes de ladite cappelle par marcie fait a lui par mesdits seigneurs au pris de six l[.] Et pour ce quil ya fait plus douvraiges que il ne devoit faire par don de grace lui a este ordonne par mesdits seigneurs ix lbs font les deux parties ensemble xv lbs. (1475/6, f. 29v)

[21] For details of the Houchin donation see below, note 29.

[22] 1480/1, f. 21r and 21v respectively (Deschamps de Pas erroneously assigns the latter to the account of 1481/2). 'A Maistre Victor Langhedul pour avoir aporte et monstre a messeigneurs ung patron pour faire unes nouvelles orghes pour lequel luy este paiet par lordonnance de messeigneurs xxv s. et pour ce xxv s.' Quoted in Deschamps de Pas, 'L'église Notre-Dame', p. 85.

[23] See for instance Patrick Roose, 'Langhedul', in Malou Haine and Nicolas Meeùs (eds.), *Dictionnaire des facteurs d'instruments de musique en Wallonie et à Bruxelles du 9ᵉ siècle à nos jours* (Brussels: Mardaga, 1986), 242–3.

great-grandson Matthijs, a highly influential figure in the development of the seventeenth-century classical French organ, most signally through his reconstruction of the 'grandes orgues' of Saint-Gervais-et-Saint-Protais in Paris, famously played over more than a century by members of the Couperin family. In a satisfying turn of the wheel, this later Langhedul was also commissioned in 1617 by the St Omer chapter, for the sum of a thousand florins, to make extensive repairs and augmentations (to be carried out within two years) of the sixteenth-century Crignon 'petites orgues' (on which more below).[24] The relationship of his fifteenth-century ancestor with Saint-Omer, as was usual in such cases, entailed at least annual returns for maintenance and repair until, with the payment for organ work to a 'Maistre Anthoine organiste de St Michiel dAnvers' in 1508/9, one should probably assume that he had passed away.[25]

Planning concerning the new organ, as was usual in such matters, was careful: the 1480/1 account records the sending of an emissary to Bergues to vet one of the prospective builder's instruments there:

To Jacques de Haudricourt for having been in Berghes to the prior of the Dominicans to find out if the organ of their monastery is fashioned by the hand of Master Victor Langhedul and to find out if the said Master Victor was the man to build and complete a construction such as that he had undertaken to have made for the said monastery, where he [Jacques] spent three days; for each day 4s., totalling 12s.[26]

Langhedul's handiwork was clearly held to be sufficiently satisfactory for the lords to dispatch the same Jacques, as we learn from the following record, to Ypres to invite the maker to come to Saint-Omer to discuss the project.[27] The story unfolds in the account for 1482/3, with the hard bargaining taking place at the house of the organist Simon Caignart, and the dean and canon Hughes de Monchy coming in to seal the deal.[28] The

---

[24] Deschamps de Pas, 'L'église Notre-Dame', 100.

[25] This is to suggest that he died rather earlier than the ?1513 hypothesised in Roose, 'Langhedul', 242. Roose notes the difficulties of reconstructing details of the history of Langhedul dynasty on account of the loss of the Ypres archives in the First World War.

[26] A Jacques de Haudricourt pour avoir este a Berghes devers le prieur de Jacoppins pour scavoir si les orghes de leur monastere estoient faictes de le main de Maistre Victor Langhedul et de scavoir se ledit Maistre Victor estoit homme pour faire et achever une telle ouvraige quil avoit entreprins de avoir fait audit monastere ou il vacqua trois jours pour chacun jour iiii s. sont xii s. (1480/1, f. 21v; not 1481/2, as stated in Deschamps de Pas, 'L'église Notre-Dame', 85.)

[27] Audit Jacques pour avoir alle a Ypre pour aler querir ledit Maistre Victor pour venir en ceste ville devers messeigneurs pour marchander pour faire unes nouvelles orghes ou il a vacquiet trois jours pour chacun jour iiii s. sont xii s. (1480/1, f. 12r).

[28] Item quant on marchanda pour faire lesdit orghes a lostel de Sire Simon Caignart fut paiet xx s.; Item depuis presens monseigneur le doyen et Maistre Hughes de Monchy a lostel dudit Sire Symon fut paiet xxviii s. (1482/3, f. 12r)

following entry from the chapter act of 16 May 1481 would appear to indicate that the decision had in any case by this point been virtually if not conclusively made, though the blanks at the points of the maker's name may suggest, at this early stage, some lingering equivocation:

The lords corporately ordered that the organ of this church be renewed and that funds remaining from the testament of Master Jacques de Houchin be used for the same, and that these things be done according to an agreement and contract made between those deputed from among them and a certain Victor [blank space], organ-builder of Ypres, with a new *Rückpositiv* behind and separate, and with a variety of sounds as defined in the written account of the contract, namely as agreed, and for the sum of thirty livres of groats ordering Master Matheus Advisse, master of the fabric, to write to the same [blank] and initiate the work.[29]

At any rate, further bargaining presumably took place when, on Christmas Day and Night of 1481, Langhedul and two of his assistants were entertained by the chapter for dinner.[30]

While no written agreement has survived, it seems clear from this record that, as might be expected, the new instrument was both larger and more sophisticated than the earlier one, including a separate *Rückpositiv* situated behind the player of the main instrument. No additional keyboards are mentioned besides the positif, probably suggesting that the main organ was, like (presumably) its predecessor, a single-manual instrument. It is unclear from the wording whether its 'diversitas sonorum' refers to the main organ or the positif, but contemporary norms suggest that any separable stops were on the *Rückpositiv*, with the main organ comprising a large *Blockwerk*, perhaps divided, containing principals and mixtures.[31] A further chapter entry for November 1481 would seem to imply, in addition to various elaborations of the case, the bass-ward extension by a note, a common addition to organs in the later fifteenth century:[32]

---

[29] ... domini ordinarunt inter se quod renoventur organa huius ecclesie et exponantur ibidem pecunie remanentes ex testamento Magistri Jacobi de Houchin. fiantque juxta pactum et conventionem habitam inter deputatos ab eis et quemdam Victorem [blank space] organificem de Ypres. cum novo positivo posteriori et secreto ac diversitate sonorum in cedula pacti expressorum scilicet pro pacto et somma xxx librorum grossorum ordinantes Magistro Matheo Advisse magistro fabrice quod eidem [blank] scribat et opus incipiat. (II. G. 355, f. 18r; also quoted in Deschamps de Pas, 'L'église Notre-Dame', 85.)

[30] A Maistre Victor Langhedoel et a deux de ses varles pour avoir este au disner le jour et nuyt de Noel pour chaqun disner xii s. sont xxiiii s. (1481/2, f. 43v/f. 44r of the other copy.)

[31] My thanks to Kimberly Marshall for this inference.

[32] My thanks to Franz Körndle for this observation. We learn from the contract for the Waghers organ work of 1515 (see below) that the prior organ (i.e. the condition in which it was left by Langhedul) had a range from G to a''. Indications of a standardised range in the early to mid-fifteenth century from low B to f'' are suggested by the attestation of that range in the famous

The same day [the lords] ordered that for the beauty and decorousness of the new organ there be made a pact and agreement with Master Victor the organ-builder; and – if it may be done for a reasonable price – let it [the organ] be augmented by a further key and [corresponding] pipe and that additionally two angels be fashioned on the side according to the figure and form supplied by him, as long as he will not demand anything excessive and that it may not exceed six livres in groats or thereabouts.[33]

Intriguingly there may have been some recycling of the old organ in the production of the new one: we read of the transport of the old instrument and its lead pipes to the Haut Pont and thence by water to the Languedul workshops in Ypres.[34] Over the following year the various parts of the new organ made their way to Saint-Omer via the reverse route, steadily bringing the project to fruition under the watchful eye of Simon Caignart.

Records walk us through the piecemeal arrival of certain 'huysserie' (door frame or casement work), two bellows, a box full of lead (presumably pipes) and (as still occurs) the positif organ in its already complete state, held in place in its cart en route from the Haut Pont by pots of wine.[35] The

treatise of Arnaud of Zwolle of *c.*1440, and by the specification of the same lowest note in a surviving 1445 organ contract from Leuven (see Jean-Pierre Félix, 'L'orgue gothique dans les Pays-Bas méridionaux', in Marcel Pérès (ed.), *Les orgues gothiques: actes du colloque de Royaumont, 1995* (Paris: Créaphis, 2000), 86). See also the treatise on organ polyphony in Munich, Bayerische Staatsbibliothek Cod. Lat. 7755, which notes that 'Claues in organis modernis sic formantur: prima claues [sic] est b durus [sic] secundum manum b mi, et significat mi, cui correspondet prima in pedalibus et eciam b mi. Secunda clavis dicitur [c] ffaut, [3a] desolre et sic deinceps …'. Quoted in Theodor Göllner, *Formen früher Mehrstimmigkeit deutschen Handschriften des späten Mittelalters* (Tutzing: Hans Schneider, 1961), 157–97. My thanks to John Caldwell for this reference. Extensions in years subsequent to Arnaud's treatise led (as in the case of the Waghers work on the St Omer instrument) down to F and up to a" (see Hans Fidom, 'Placement of Large Medieval Organs in Churches in the Netherlands: Reflections on a Large Medieval Organ to Be Built in the City of Groningen, the Netherlands', (also in Pérès (ed.), *Les orgues gothiques*), 110). Ranges in later years quickly pushed further in both directions. My thanks again to Franz Körndle for discussions on this point.

[33] Ipso die ordinarunt quod pro venustate et decore novorum organorum fiat conventio et pactum cum Magistro Victore organifice. et si pro rationabili precio fieri possit augeantur de una grossiori clave et fistula. fiantque duo angeli lateraliter alias iuxta figuram et formam per eum traditam dum non nichil excessive poposcerit et non excedat sex aut circa libras grossorum. (II. G. 355, f. 26r, 25 November, 1481; also quoted in Deschamps de Pas, 'L'église Notre-Dame', p. 86.) On the development of the construction of organs generally, and registration in particular, in the Low Countries during this period see Félix, 'L'orgue gothique', 69–106.

[34] Item a quatre brouteurs pour avoir mene les vielles orghes et ploncq jusques au haultpont vi s.; Item a ung maronnier pour avoir mene lesdits vielles orghes du hault pont jusques a Ypre lx s. Item a Baudin Le Prevost pour ung pouchon a mettre le ploncq des vielles orghes pour mener a Yppre iii s. (1482/3, f. 12r–v)

[35] Item a Sire Symon Caignart pour avoir paiet les bateliers qui avoient emene aulcune huysserie dYppre au haultpont vi s.; Item audit Sire Symon fu bailliet argent pour acheter du fil darcal

inclusion of three separate or divided chests ('huches de secret') certainly requires comment: two of these must respectively have served the main and positif organs, though it is unclear what the third 'huche' may have been for: perhaps for pedals on the main organ; or perhaps a separated rank on the positif such as was available on at least some later fifteenth-century instruments for the lowest rank or a cymbale.[36] The latter technology was certainly available by this time, and a useful practicality given the man-power involved in wind supply.[37]

Details concerning the decoration of the case and doors show that the finished article must have been a thing of considerable beauty, not to mention a riot of rich colour:

To the painter to paint the positif was paid three escus, which is worth £4 16s.

Item, paid to make the pine cones [the insignia of the chapter] to engrave the large pipe, both for the mould [itself] which made it and for the man who cast it, 40s.

Item, to Jehan Martin, carver, for having made four wooden figures for the said organ, 42s.

Item, to Jehan des Chocques, painter, for the painting of the organ shutters, 42s.

Item, to the said Jehan for painting the wall behind the organ, 40s.

Item, to the said Jehan for having added the blue on the said shutters and for having painted all around the said organ, £7.[38]

Meanwhile the chapter act of 8 August 1483 similarly informs us that:

[latten wire] pour ledit organiste xxii s. vi d.; Item baillet audit Sire Symon pour paier le batellier lequel avoit amene deux souffles dYppre a St Aumer ix s.; Item paiet a ung batellier pour avoir amene trois huches de secret des orghes dYppre jusques au haultpont ix sc. Et pour les amener du haultpont jusques a leglise xii d sont x s.; Item paiet a ung batelier nomme Anthoine van Dorne pour avoir amene ung laye [wooden box] plaine de plonc dYppre jusques au haultpont comme appert par cedulle xl s.; Item aux brouteurs qui amenerrent ledit laye du haultpont jusques a leglise l s.; Item paiet a ung batellier pour avoir amene le positif dYppre jusques au hault pont lxxv s.; Item paiet aux brouteurs pour avoir amene ledit positif du haultpont jusques a leglise vi s.; Item pour trois lots de vin a assir ledit positif a ii s. vi d. le lot sont vii s. vi d. (1482/3, ff. 12v–13r)

[36] See for instance Felix, 'L'orgue gothique', 94, and Fidom, 'Placement of Large Medieval Organs', 108. Peter Williams notes that separable ranks occurred earlier on small chests (*Rückpositiv* or *Brustwerk*) than on main organs (*The European Organ, 1450–1850* (London: Batsford, 1966), 18).

[37] Barbara Owen and Peter Williams, 'The Organ V, 1, and 2: Developments, 1450–1500', accessed 11 September 2016.

[38] Au paintre pour paindre les positifs fu paiet iii escus qui valent iiii lb xvi s; Item paiet pour faire les pommes de pin pour estoffer le grant tuyau tant pour le forme qui le fit comme pour celuy qui le gette xl s; Item a Jehan Martin entretailleur pour avoir fait quatre ymaiges de bos servans ausdits orghes xlii s; Item a Jehan des Chocques paintre pour le faicon des foeulles des orghes xlii lb; Item audit Jehan pour paindre le mur derriere les orghes lx s; Item audit Jehan pour avoir adiouste lasur ausdits foeulles et avoir paint tout autour desdits orghes vii lb. (1482/3, ff. 12r, 13r; also quoted in Deschamps de Pas, 'L'église Notre-Dame', 86–7.)

The lords ordered that the shutters or cover of the newly renovated organ be furnished in blue on its surfaces and coverings and that its walls on every side be painted and honourably perfected in every respect to the beauty and decorousness of the church.[39]

Further painting work by Jehan (now named 'de Dunckerke') detailed in the following year's fabric account allows us to identify what would appear to be another level of 'diversitas' to the organ's sound:

To Jehan de Dunkerke, painter . . . for having painted in black behind the organ . . .
    To the said Jehan for a gilded sun serving the large organ.[40]

Such a 'gilded sun', clearly visible in the case, would have made a tinkling sound when rotated, akin to the still familiar 'Cymbalstern'.[41]

Presumably, like his counterparts today, the maker made further visits to the site following the preliminary discussions; such putative forays may be concealed among the general payments recorded,[42] and it may be that the visit of 'the organist and his entourage' from Ypres on 13 December 1482 actually refers to the organ-builder of the same town.[43] The record may equally refer to the actual 'organist' of the maker's home town, however, following the usual procedure of inviting outside players to vet the new construction: the same fabric account records further payments 'to the organist of Thérouanne for having come to examine the said organ' ('a lorganiste de Therouanne pour avoir venu visiter lesdits orghes') and 'to several singers of Thérouanne who came with the said organist' ('a aucuns chaintres de Therouanne qui estoient venus avec ledit organiste'). No reason is given as to why the organist of Thérouanne brought singers with him. Perhaps he brought his own singers due to a perceived need, in trying out the new instrument, for a familiarity of performance interaction that was felt possible only between a player and singers used to working closely together and/or steeped in a particular, localised practice; or perhaps the Thérouanne singers came simply out of curiosity.

---

[39] . . . domini ordinaverunt quod follia seu cooperture organorum de novo renovatorum muniantur azure in planicie et superficie quodque parietes circumquoque pingantur et honorifice omnia perficiantur ad venustatem et decorem ecclesie (II. G. 355, f. 44r; also quoted in Deschamps de Pas, 'L'église Notre-Dame', 87.)

[40] A Jehan de Dunckerke paintre . . . pour avoir paint de noir derraere [sic] les orghes . . . Audit Jehan pour ung solleil dorey servant aux grandes orghes (1483/4, f. 34v)

[41] My thanks for this information to Robert Bates, who notes that such figures were conventionally made to resemble the sun, moon or stars, and in the former case, for obvious reasons, were frequently gilded.

[42] As for instance the following: 'A Victor Languedeul facteur dorghes a este paiet a plusieurs comme il appert par cedulle iiii^{xx} vii lb 6 s' (1482/3, f. 12r).

[43] Item le xiiie jour de decembre quant lorganiste [in this case clearly the organ-builder] et son maingnaige vindrent dYppre en ceste ville paiet audit organiste xl s. (1482/3, f. 12v)

Whatever the case, the instrument, following checking by the organist of Thérouanne and (unspecified) 'others', was judged a triumph:

The 16th day of the month of July in the year [14]83 Victor Langhedul, organ-builder, who had sometime past undertaken to build a new organ and a positif with diversity of sounds, as is more amply declared in the agreement and papers thereto pertaining, has today delivered the said organ and affirmed it to be in the required state, and such as to go before all cognisant in such things. Accordingly my lords had it played by the organist of Thérouanne and others, who affirmed it by their oath to be a magnificent and truly excellent construction, such that its like as far as what it contains will not be found. This notwithstanding, the said Victor has pledged to come once or twice a year for six to eight years as may be required and if necessary at the expense of the church to visit the said organ and to adjust such things as may need to be adjusted.[44]

The 'grandes orgues', hailed as peerless of its type, was situated (like the present organ) at the west end of the building, beneath the tower concurrently being rebuilt to house, as we shall see in the next chapter, the newly cast peal of bells. The old organ, meanwhile, remained in the north transept and hence much closer to, though still at some distance from, the choir.

The chapter lost no time in putting the organ to use, to the considerable pecuniary advantage of the organist. A chapter act of 9 February 1482 instructs that:

The lords ordained that now that the organ has been renewed, for the enrichment of divine observance of this church, it shall be sounded more often from now on, that is on double feasts of Apostles and every Saturday and on feasts of the Virgin at the *Salve*. And for increase of his salary they ordained to the organist Symon Caignard eighteen livres d'Artois for each year.[45]

Whatever the extent of use of the earlier organ, the new regime would appear to have represented a significant augmentation. Just how significant

---

[44] Le xvi^e Jour du moys de juillet an lxxxiii Victor Langdul facteur dorgues lequel avoit piecha empris de faire nouvelles orgues. et positif. en diversite de son. comme au marchiet et escript sur ce est plus amplement declaire. a aujourdhui livre lesdits orgues et les a affirme estre en point deu. et tel que pour passer devant tous ad ce cognoissans sur quoy messeigneurs les ont fait touchier par lorganiste de Therouanne et aultres qui les ont afferme par leur serment estre ung magnificque et fort excellent ouvraige. et tel que de pareil ne sera point trouve de ce quil tient. Nonobstant cela. ledit Victor a promis de venir tous les ans une fois ou deux jusques a vi ou viii ans. aux depens del eglise se requis en estoit et mestier feist pour viseter lesdits orgues et amender ce quil seroit a amender. (II. G. 355, f. 43r; quoted in Deschamps de Pas, 'L'église Notre-Dame', 87–8.)

[45] … domini renovatis organis huius ecclesie ordinarunt ad augmentationem divini cultus quod a modo sepius sonentur videlicet in duplicibus festis apostolorum et singulis diebus sabbati ac festis Beate Marie ad Salve.

Et pro augmento salarii ordinarunt Domino Symoni Caignard organiste singulis annis decem et octo libras Arthesii (II. G. 355, f. 27r)

seems clear enough from the newly elevated salary of the organist: paid at the rate of five livres per annum since 1475, when his salary had been raised from four, his new salary of eighteen livres was quite a shift, and one, moreover, that was maintained in subsequent years. A record of 11 August 1484 clarifies the distinction between the payment for his new tasks *vis-à-vis* his traditional responsibilities:

> It was concluded by the lords that Lord Simon Caignart, organist of this church, for Masses solemnly discanted with the organ outside the choir, should receive a salary for his labour per se and separately from his contract agreed for other Masses discanted within the choir as has been customarily paid to him in other times and years.[46]

Specification of the use of the new organ for all double feasts of Apostles and all Marian Masses would seem to imply that other needs were addressed by the earlier organ in the north transept; in other words that the choice of organ for a given devotion was governed by hierarchy and function.[47] Perhaps the unaccustomed distance between new organ and choir explains the visit of the singers from Thérouanne, the enhanced spatial disparity requiring the testing out of a kind of coordination unfamiliar to the singers available on site;[48] or perhaps the new organ's functions were aimed partly or even principally at 'public' Masses celebrated at altars on the west front of the screen.

The 1484 record provides some specific information, referring as it does to performance of Masses not just 'within choir' but outside it. Quite how this might have functioned cannot be determined with precision, but it must in at least some cases have involved the separate positif which, whatever the astringency of its component pipes, seems unlikely to have had the carrying power to function in any meaningful way in the context of observances conducted at great distance, and especially within the choir at the opposite end of the church. It seems possible that such singing may on at least some occasions have involved singers in the organ gallery (space permitting). Circumstances of this nature would offer the possibility not

---

[46] ... conclusum est per dominos quod Dominus Simon Caignart organista huius ecclesie / de missis solemniter decantandis cum organis extra chorum recipiet salarium sui laboris seorsum et per se / a suo pacto causa aliarum missarum infra chorum decantandarum sicuti aliis temporibus et annis solitum est sibi solvi (II. G. 355, f. 54v)

[47] As documented, for example, in the case of three separate instruments in the Rites of Durham. See Joseph Thomas Fowler (ed.), *The Rites of Durham, Being a Description or Brief Declaration of all the Ancient Monuments, Rites, & Customs Belonging or Being within the Monastical Church of Durham before the Suppression*, Publications of the Surtees Society, 107 (Durham, Edinburgh and London, 1903), 34 and 220.

[48] My thanks to John Harper for this suggestion.

only of organ interjections, most obviously at the offertory (though also possibly at the elevation and Agnus Dei) and in alternatim items with the voices, but even of its use in full ensemble, especially, one might propose, in playing the tenor in polyphony based on *cantus prius facti*. At any rate it could easily have been co-opted to play preludes and postludes for Masses of all kinds. The celebration of such Masses 'outside choir' – whether with the positif or 'grande' organ – could at least in theory have embraced many of the private Masses being celebrated at subsidiary altars around the building, including those in lateral chapels adjacent to the organ itself, where signalling from bells would have been quite adequate to permit the required interaction with organist and, putatively, singers in a loft. While the choreographic challenges entailed in a space housing so many private observances can hardly be overestimated, neither can the potential impact in such situations of performance on a new and impressive instrument. Given the scale and – as will be revealed in Chapter 6 – the emphasis on shows of one-upmanship that characterised privately founded observance, here as elsewhere, the potential appeal of the display offered by the church's new 'voice' can hardly be doubted.

Looked at more globally, a large west-end organ such as this, standing at the western extremity not just of the church as a whole but of the 'public' space of the nave, suggests a wider purview than could have been marked out by the sound of its earlier confrère in the north transept. Its moniker as 'the organ outside the choir' might well imply as much, and it is tempting to speculate whether a corollary of its all-encompassing scope would have been to forestall devotions at other altars in the church for the duration of Masses in which it partook. It seems likely that the new organ would have been called into service also for such public events as *Te Deum*s for grand entries (occasions frequently recorded in the chapter acts) by visiting dignitaries entering the building from the west end. A pointed implication of this nature may be gleaned from a detail concerning the organ's decoration. In 1487, Saint-Omer having in May of that year been conquered by French royal forces, Fremin Martin was paid to remove from one of the organ pipes the fusils (emblematic of the Order of the Golden Fleece) and crosses of St Andrew of the House of Burgundy, replacing them instead with the royal French fleurs-de-lis.[49] This action, and the speed of its execution, surely implies a particular visibility of the great organ to visiting

---

[49] A Fremin Martin plommier pour avoir oste a ung buhot des orges qui estoit pave de fussils / et remis au lieu desdits fussils. et de croix St Andre fleurs de lis que aparoit par se quittance cy rendue. xxiiii s (fabric account for 1487, copy 1, f. 26r). See also Deschamps de Pas, 'L'église

magnates and officials, and says something significant about the degree to which a large instrument of this nature could be emblematic of more than local, institutional pride. But the instrument's scale and location would also suggest involvement in other kinds of public observance intended to embrace participation far beyond that simply of the resident clergy, including processions and other 'out of choir' activities that stood to benefit from a powerful instrument capable of filling the entire space with sound.

* * *

Given the lifespan of the previous organ and the expense of, and pride taken in, the new one, it comes as something of a surprise to find it being taken down within little more than thirty-five years. But the organ, given its location at the west end, was caught up in larger forces: the considerable heightening and restructuring of the west end tower necessitated the vacating of the space beneath it to facilitate structural strengthening work. In 1508/9 a certain Antoine [Mors], 'organiste' at St Michael's, Antwerp, was paid to arrange the dismantled instrument in order in the cloister.[50] The concurrent loan (detailed on the same page) by the organist of St Bertin of that institution's 'petites orgues' was clearly made to provide a substitute for the 'grandes orgues' for the duration of the building work.[51]

An entry in the chapter acts for 20 April 1514 sums up the situation: 'the lords ordered ... that the organ be taken down so that the newly commenced doorway may more easily be finished and fulfilled'.[52] The organ was re-erected on the north wall of the north transept. Since this had also been the position of the fourteenth-century organ, this earlier instrument must at this point have been dismantled. The fabric account for the year 1513/14 reveals that work on the new portal was proceeding in tandem with the reassembly of the organ: payments for carpentry interweave detail on the construction of the new door with extensive work on the 'dossal' of the organ, presumably its gallery or balcony. The new installation, which

---

Notre-Dame', 88. On this aspect of the greater territorial history of Saint-Omer see the Prologue, 15.

[50] A Maistre Anthoine organiste de St Michel dAnvers pour avoir mis les grandes orgues jus et les mis par ordre sur les cloistres payet ung florin vaillissant xxviii s (1508/9, f. 35r). On Mors see Bernard Hédin, *Les Orgues du Pas-de-Calais* (Lille: Domaine Musiques Région Nord-Pas-de-Calais, 1996), 379.

[51] Item a lorganiste Saint Bertin pour avoir preste et apporte les petites orgues luy a este donne vi s (1508/9, f. 35r)

[52] ... domini ordinaverunt ... quod instrumentum organicum deponatur ut portale noviter inceptum facilius confici et adimpleri possit (II. G. 356, f. 179v; not 379v, as stated in Deschamps de Pas, 'L'église Notre-Dame', 99.)

involved masonry work including making holes in the wall to take the beams to sustain the organ and to allow for a door for access to the console, clarifies the location of the instrument as the 'wall towards the cloister'; in other words, the north wall of the north transept which gave out onto the cloister before the latter's demolition following the Revolution. While a further payment entered on the same page is for 'opening and closing the cavity above the portal to the cloister for the placement of the organ',[53] surviving remnants clarify the actual location as to the left of the present north door, the current setting for the sculptural ensemble known as 'Le Grand Dieu de Thérouanne'.[54] The floor-level 'door to access the said organ' is clearly visible in Figure 4.1, while the aperture now to the right of the kneeling Evangelist surely once afforded access to the organ loft.

The accounts suggest that early work on the organ uncovered a need for more than simple reassembly. The process began with extensive work on the loft. Payment to the carpenter 'Maistre Jacques [Yons/Youtz]' for ten days 'pour mettre jus le dossal des orgues'[55] was quickly superseded by outlay to the joiner Jan Daspere and his labourer for work, beginning on Wednesday 12 July 1514, on the same 'dossal' and an associated door (presumably that giving access to the loft) of between four and five days per week for five weeks. While work hit a hiatus when, sometime around mid-September, the hapless joiner (as noted in Chapter 1) succumbed to

---

[53] Item a Guillaume et Olivier Hermel machons pour avoir ouvre et fait les troues au mur devers les cloistres pour y mettre et assir les poutres du dossal des orgles et pour perchier ledit mur pour faire ung huys pour aller ausdits orgles ... lxxii s vi d

Item ausdits Maistre Jan et Guillaume son fils pour avoir ouvre et restuppe le creux deseure le portal du cloittre pour y mettre les orgles ... xxxviii s vi d

(1513/14, f. 35r). For a series of records from this year see Deschamps de Pas, 'L'église Notre-Dame', 90–1.

[54] Transported to Saint-Omer in 1553 from the cathedral of Thérouanne before the latter's total destruction at the hands of imperial troops, this ensemble, comprising a colossal thirteenth-century figure of a seated Christ flanked by the Virgin and Saint John, was intended originally for relocation on an exterior wall. Such plans never in fact coming to fruition, it remained within the building, finally coming to rest, on floor level, against the south wall in the south-west corner of the building until, in 1962, it was transported to the Louvre for display as part of an exhibition on the cathedrals of France. On its return it was rehoused, again at floor level, in the north transept before being lifted, in 1966, into its present vantage point some three metres up the same wall. See Georges Coolen, 'Le Grand Dieu de Thérouanne', *Bulletin de la Société des antiquaires de la Morinie* 19/372 (September 1962), 636–7 and Emmanuelle Opigez, 'Le deesis de Thérouanne et sa place dans la sculpture française du XIIIe siècle dans le nord de la France', *Bulletin de la Société des antiquaires de la Morinie* 25/465 (March 2005), 138. My thanks to Rose-Marie Pasquier for these details and references.

[55] Item audit Maistre Jacques [variously Yons or Youtz, carpenter] pour avoir ouvere x jours et une prime pour mettre jus le dossal des orgles a vi s le jour sont lxi s vi d[.] Et ung jour pour sa corde vi s[.] Et pour son varlet pour deux jours a iiiis vi d sont vii s[.] (1513/14, f. 31v)

Figure 4.1 North transept, north wall, with Grand Dieu de Thérouanne © Carl Peterolff

plague, there had clearly by that point been considerable progress on the organ loft and other woodwork.[56] The following year's account details the work's continuation in the form of the construction of a scaffold to erect the instrument itself. This was followed by woodwork on new bellows and on a separate chamber to house them, along with an air duct through the wall to accommodate iron fixings to access the bellows chamber itself, which was situated over the cloister.[57] While the chamber in question, like the cloister on which it sat, is long gone, a surviving hole with a brick surround in the pillar on the west wall of the north transept, adjacent to the great north window (Figure 4.2), allows us to locate the duct's likely point of entry.[58]

With this work a new organ-builder, Charles Waghers of Hazebroucq,[59] enters the scene, at first seemingly to oversee the (re)construction but in the event assuming a more fundamental role.[60] By a stroke of good fortune, the

---

[56] Item le xxvᵉ jour daust je fis ma[r]chie audit Jan Daspere huchier de parfaire et achever le custode des orgles. et frumer lesdits dossal a deux cottes de faire . . . le cassis et l[h]uys en partye et deliveray a deux fois xxiiii s. et se devoit recepvoir la reste a mesure que ladite ouvraige se parferoit lequel est mort de peste et a laissiet ledit ouvraige a parfaire pour ce ici xxiiii s (1513/14, f. 32v). Whether the 'huys' and 'cassis' refers to the door to access the loft or to the organ shutters themselves is unclear. Their referents in this case may be contingent upon the sense here of 'custode': Robert Bates has suggested to me that this may refer to a piece of cloth stretched inside a frame, with both together forming shutters closing off the front of the organ case.

[57] Item a Jehan Jourdain et a Jehan Wyon soyeurs dhaes pour avoir soyet les achelles des souffles et aultres bos pour le cambrette desdits souffles ou il [sic] vacuerent xi jours et une prime a quatre s. le jour chacun sont iiii lb x s. (1514/15, f. 29v)
Item audit Maistre Jacques [Yons/Youtz, carpenter] pour avoir ouvre au plancq[ue]r [floor] et chambrette des souffles pour les orghues ou il a vacquiet deux jours sont xii s. (1514/15, f. 30r).
Item audit Maistre Jehan machon pour avoir faict les trous es murs pour mettre les fers des orgues et buze [duct] du vent ou il vacquiet vi jours une prime mains(?=matins, i.e. early morning) sont xxxiiii s vi d (1514/15, f. 33v)

[58] This location would seem to be supported by the general heading for payments for 'wood purchased to prop up the scaffold to pierce the great pillars of the said church and also for the organs' ('. . . des bois achetes pour estanchonner les hours pour perchier les grans pillers de ledit eglise et ausy pour les orgles'). See also a specific payment over the same page: 'Item le xxvᵉ jour d'octobre fu achete a Mahieu Labitte .l. sapins a xxi piece pour les hours dentre les grans pillers de ledit eglise sont faicts iiii lb vii s vi d' (1514/15, 29r-v).

[59] In other encounters, Waghers is credited with construction of a large organ plus a positif for St Jean, Valenciennes, in 1515 (see for example Barbara Owen, *The Registration of Baroque Organ Music* (Bloomington and Indianapolis: Indiana University Press, 1997), 8–9. A record from the church of St Martin, Courtrai/Kortrijk, from 1524 details the engagement of Waghers for the repair of the great organ and delivery of a new positif ('herstelling van het groot orgel en levering van een nieuw positiforgel'). See Anton Deschrevel, 'Het orgel in de St-Maartenskerk te Kortrijk', *Koninklijke Geschieden Oudheidkundige Kring van Kortrijk* 33 (1963–4), 229–62.

[60] See 1514/15, ff. 29r–30r, 31v, 32v–3v, 35r–v for these details; also Deschamps de Pas, 'L'église Notre-Dame', 91.

Figure 4.2 Putative hole for bellows duct, north wall of north transept

contract for Waghers's work survived, and it is worth quoting it *in extenso*.[61]

All should know that before the aldermen of the town of Saint-Omer appeared in person Charles Waghers, organist and organ-builder, and acknowledged that he had concluded an agreement with messeigneurs the dean and chapter of the church of St Omer to repair, rebuild and put in good order the organ of the said church. That is to say the large instrument that is at 11' or thereabouts, starting at gamma *ut* [G] and extending up to the octave of high A *la mi re* [a"]. The said person appearing will be held to repair it and put it in its original state, and to add F *fa ut* at the bottom and fully to provide it with a piercing fourniture as befits such an instrument, and to make it much better than it was formerly, in the judgement of workers and individuals cognisant in such things. Item, for the positif, the same person appearing will be held to fashion it entirely anew, harmonising with the *montre* [facade] of the large

[61] See Norbert Dufourcq, 'Les orgues de Notre-Dame de Saint-Omer', *Bulletin trimestriel de la Société academique des antiquaires de la Morinie* 17 (1948), 214–18. My thanks to Robert Bates for supplying me with a copy of this article. See also Hédin, *Les Orgues du Pas-de-Calais*, 379. Neither source gives a call number for the contract and I have not been able to trace the original.

case, with five registers, to wit a *sourt* at 6′, the second a *flahuttes* sounding an octave above the said *sourt*, the third a positif at 1½′ [an octave higher still], the fourth a triple octave, the fifth a good *cimballes* sounding with all the other registers on the said positif in whatever way it pleased the player to incorporate it [or 'in such a way that the player will want to incorporate it']. The said person appearing will be held to put back the shutters, boards and other things at his expense, except for the large components of the said organ like the large pipes that two individuals cannot conveniently lift or carry. Also the scaffold to access and build the said construction within and without, ironwork and new bellows will be at the expense of my said lords of the chapter, as also will be the painting, if they wish to have anything of the said pipes repainted. And my said lords will provide workspace to the person appearing. All the said work on the organ must be well and sufficiently fulfilled and completed, as is said, to play by the Feast of St John the Baptist [24 June] 1516 at the latest. And all to the agreement of workers and individuals cognisant in such matters. And to achieve this the said person appearing must receive the sum of twenty-eight livres grossorum that my said lords of the chapter or their deputy and receiver are bound to pay him at the point that the said work shall be complete. And if the same person appearing does any work concerning the said organ beyond this present contract and work order, he will expect payment at the discretion of my said lords of the chapter. And the said person appearing has undertaken to maintain, supply and accomplish at every stage [in respect of] all that which is indicated above, and he offers as security all his goods and possessions and those of his heirs, present and in future, and for greater security Jehan de Gheusere, tailor, bourgeois of this town, has constituted himself as guarantor for the said Charles, pledging on his own behalf as principal merchant to supply and complete the transaction in case there is fault with the said Charles Waghers, and to render and make good all interests and damage that my said lords may have and incur on this account, under similar obligation of goods and possessions. And the same Charles under the same obligation as he has pledged above, to discharge, acquit and render invalid his said security, renouncing, through the faith and oath of his body, never to proceed against the effect and tenor of these documents.

Witnessed by the seal of the said town to the acknowledgements here given, the 20 February 1513 [1514 new style].

And on the payment for the said letters is signed: A. Mondreloiz[62]

---

[62] Sachent tous que pardevant Eschevins de la ville de Sainctomer, comparut en sa personne Charles Waghers, organiste et facteur d'orgue, et a recognut qu'il a fait marchié a Mess. Doien et Chapitre de l'église de Sainctomer de repparer, reffaire et mettre à point les orghes de ladite église. Assavoir le grant instrument qui est de unze piez ou environ commenchant à game *ut* en enssievant [ensuivant] jusques à la double de *A la mi ré* en hault, ledit comparant sera tenus de les reparer et mettre en leurs premier estat et de y adjouster F. *fa ut* en bas et le furnir plainement de bonne furniture trenchant comme il appartient à ung tel instrument, et de la faire beaucoup milleures qu'elles n'estoient auparavant, par le dict de ouvriers et gens en ce cognoissans. Item pour le positif sera tenu icelluy comparant de le faire tout nouveau contenant

The first material detail supplied by this tract concerns the range of the existing, Langhedul instrument, from G at the bottom of the bass stave (gamma *ut*) to a" ('the octave of high A *la mi re*'), encompassed in an instrument with a longest pipe of '11′ or thereabouts'. Waghers is to augment the lower range by a note, down to F (resulting in a 12′ instrument), giving a new composition to the main interior division (*fourniture*) which nevertheless remained without stops, to produce a piercing, brilliant tone as was expected.

But his most substantial task concerns the positif, which he is instructed to rebuild from scratch, with its facade in visual harmony with that of the main organ. The scale of the undertaking suggests that there had been a substantial advance in standard approaches to building a positif in the three decades since the delivery of the Langhedul instrument: Waghers's new positif is to be equipped with five registers: a *sourt* 'of 6″ – which Dufourcq suggests would actually have comprised a stopped 3′ rank; a *flahuttes* stop (a facade principal?) sounding an octave higher; a positif

le montre du grant ouvraige avecq cincq registres: est assavoir ung sourt de six piez, le second flahuttes sonnant l'octave dudict sourt, le tiers ung positif de piet et demy. Le IIIIe ung triple octave, le Ve unes bonnes cimballes sonnant avecque tous autres jeuz estans aud. positif ainsy qu'il plaira au joueur de la mesler. Sera tenus ledit comparant de remettre les custodes feullez et aultres choses à ses despens, saulf que pour les gros membres desdites orgueles comme les grosses buzes que deux gens ne scaveroient bonnement lever ne porter. Aussi le hourdaige pour aller et faire le dit ouvraige par dehors et pardedens ferraille et nouveaulx soufflez et sera aux despens de mesdits seigneurs de Chapitre comme aussi sera le painture se ilz veullent aucune chose faire repaindre desd. buhos. Et se livront mesdits seigneurs le lieu pour ouvrer audit comparant. Tout lequel ouvraige de orghes doit estre bien et souffisament fait et parfait comme dit est pour jouer en dedans le sainct Jehan Baptiste, que l'on comptera mil cincq cens et seize du plus tard. Et tout au dict de ouvriers et gens en ce cognoissans. Et pour ce faire, doit avoir ledit comparant la somme de vingte huit livres de gros que mesdits seigneurs de Chapitre ou leur commis et receveur luy seront tenus de paier à lavenant que ledit ouvraige se fera, et se icelluy comparant fait aucun ouvraige touchant lesdites orghes au dehors de ce présent marchié et devis, attendera à la bonne grace de mesdits seigneurs de Chapitre. Et à tout ce que dessus est dit de tenir, furnir et acomplir [sic] de point en point a ledit comparant obligié et obleige tous ces biens et hiretaiges et ceulx de ses hoirs présens et advenir, et pour plus grant sceurté Jehan le Gheusere, parmentier, bourgeois de ceste ville pour ce comparant s'est constitué caution pour ledit Charles en promectant en son nom privé, comme principal marchant de furnir et acomplir le marchié en cas que faulte y ait oudit Charles Waghers et de rendre et de restituer tout interests et domaige que mesdits seigneurs porroient avoir et encourir à ceste cause, soubz pareille obligacion de biens et hiretaiges et icelluy Charles soubz le meisme obligacion que dessus a promis deschergier, acquitier et rendre indempne sa dicte caution renonchant par les foy et serment de son corps de jamais aller contre l'effect et teneur de ces présentes.

Tesmoing le scel de la dicte ville aux recognoissances cy mis le XXe de febvrier XV^c et XIII [1514 new style]

Et sur le ploy desdites lettres est signé: A Mondreloiz

[principal] of 1½'; a triple octave; and a *cimballes* stop, available in any desired combination with the other registers, or perhaps 'sounding with the other registers in such a way that the player would want to use it'. This latter would have contained one or more breaks, meaning that the pitch was not fixed throughout the keyboard's range. Dufourcq notes that this constitutes a standard composition for an early sixteenth-century positif, albeit lacking the expected reeds.

Waghers is charged to refashion – at his own expense – the shutters (typically comprising stretched canvas over wooden frames), 'boards' (for what is not specified) and 'other things', though the lords graciously give him a pass on the heavier items including the large flanking groups of (presumably free-standing) bourdons or 'trompes' (here designated simply 'buzes'). The chapter will foot the bill for the necessary scaffolding (both inside and outside) and ironwork, plus new bellows and any required repainting of pipes. For the entire undertaking he is assigned two years, with the expectation that he will finish his work by St John's Day (24 June) 1516, the tailor Jehan de Gheusere, bourgeois of the town, standing as his guarantor. Satisfactory completion will be recompensed by payment of £28 in groats, with supplementary fees accruing for any additional work.

Folio 35r of the fabric account for 1514/15 announces the first stages of this grand project, in the form of:

Other expenses for the organ of the said church, to restore it to good condition to be used for the honour of God and the divine service, through an agreement made with Master Charles Waghers, for the sum of £28 in groats, on the conditions and agreement made and agreed before the aldermen of the town.[63]

Besides payments for drawing up the agreement itself and the first instalment – of no less than £86 15s. 6d. – to the builder for construction costs, work on the instrument begins to unfold. Further work on the chamber for the bellows would seem likewise to bespeak a substantial construction to house the six bellows, for which horse hides are purchased and sewn.[64]

---

[63] Aultres mises pour les orgles deladite eglise pour les remettre en leur estat pour en user a lhonneur de dieu et du service divin par marchiet fait a Maistre Charles Waghers pour la somme de xxviii lbs de gros sur les conditions et marchiet fet et passe pardevant eschevins de la ville.

[64] Item payet a Anthonie de Le Moire paintre pour avoir entamme les buizes destaint xii s; Item payet a Michiel du Val et a Jehan de Le Helle tanneurs pour chacune piaulx de cheval a xviii s le piau iiii lb x s.; Item pour deux aultres cuiers de cheval achetes xx s le piece a Ernoult Le Scacth xl s.; Item payet a Charles Blommart pour avoir cure lesdits cuyrs de cheval l s; Item payet a Lambert de Berghem pour avoir fait les bois et achelles desdits souffles et pour avoir aidiet a mettre le custode desdits orghes payet pour tout (1514/15, f. 35r).

Payment is made to 'Anthoine de Le Moire, painter, for having coated the pipes with tin' while coating of further pipes is also attested by payment for 'six and a half dozen sheets of tin'.[65]

The following year's account offers further detail on the construction. Key here is what appears to have been the installation of the new positif organ, which occupied the carpenter for six and a half days. Payments are entered for plumbing work on the bellows (lead was used to weight them) and on founding what were clearly two substantial organ pipes. Further payments to 'Anthoine de Le Moure, painter' cover his work 'painting twelve pipes of the said organs and the large blue pipe', clearly facade pipes, with the latter, given its stand-out colour, likely destined to be the centre-piece. Meanwhile a payment for making the 'iron' (clearly some form of ducting) to conduct the air to the instrument from the bellows chamber over the cloister completed the connection between the machine and its lungs.[66]

Whatever ambition was harboured for Waghers's craftsmanship, it would quickly be dispelled. On 8 February 1516 the church's messengers were dispatched to Magister Jacques Le Corte, 'curé de Locquere, organis-tre', and Mahieu Leleu, organist of Ypres and organ-builder, to invite them to assess the new workmanship. Whatever the verdict from their inspection on 15 February, it was not sufficient to reach a conclusion: four days later the messenger was on his horse again, this time to Bruges to summon the

---

[65] Item a Guillaume Gauwalle pour avoir livre certaines achelles pour faire le chambrette des souffles a este paye comme appert par son billet vi lb xiiii s x d; Item audit Pierre [Baillet] pour six douzaines demye de foeulle destain a xviii d le douzaine sont xiiii s x d (1514/15, f. 35v). While the facade pipes would most likely have been of pure tin, some interior ones would have used lead, coated with tin for protection. My thanks to Robert Bates for this information.

[66] Primes a Maistre Jacques Youtz carpentier lequel le xv^e de jenvier vint rasir le chaiere des orghes et y ouvra vi jours demi sont xxxix s (1515/16, f. 31r).

A Franchois Lascere plommier de ladite eglise pour avoir fonde les plons pour mettre sur les souffles des orgles ou il vacca ung jour vi s

Audit pour avoir fait les deux buisses [sic] pour lesdits orgles pessant ensemble viii^{xx} xix lb ou il vacca luy et son varlet chacun ung jour x s (1515/16, f. 32r).

Aultres mise pour les orgles de ledit eglise tant au Maistre facteur Me Charles comme a aultres

Primes a este paiet a Bertin pour faire foiet un piece de bois pour reposer les souffeles ix d

Item paiet A Gomaire orloighe macquere [clockmaker] pour avoir fait ung fer pour perchier le mur deriere les orgheles pour conduire le vent paiet audit x s

Item le dernier jour de jenvier a este paiet par lordonnanche messeigneurs a Carles [sic] Waghers la somme de xviii lb

Item ledit dernier jour fut fait marchiet a Anthoine de Le Moure paintre pour paintre douze buzes desdits orgheles et le grande buze dasur et doibt pour le tout avoir vi l (1515/16, f. 35r).

organists Laneulle à Claiquin and Maistre Josse Bus.[67] Clearly some behind-the-scenes wrangling ensued, since on 25 August Masters Corte and Bus (the latter now dubbed 'facteur dorgheles') were back, this time at the behest not only of the chapter but also of Waghers himself. Finally, at the command of the provost (who was also bishop of Arras), an organ-builder from Arras visited and judged the finished work to be insufficient. At this point the chapter decided to pursue the matter before the magistrate.[68]

As often in such cases, this was just the beginning of what was to prove a long tussle between the opposing parties. Presumably at the request of the magistrate, the following year Jacques Corte and Josse Bus were back again, this time along with another Bruges organist, Jacques Onye. De Pas notes that this latest deputation coincided with Waghers's request to finish the work on the organ that he had begun, a request assented to on condition that he would allow ongoing inspections and would pay the fines that had already been levied against him.[69] The inspection concluded, the three arbiters met with a clerk of the town's court to deliver their verdict.[70]

The series of payments connected with the case against Waghers the following year (1517/18) allows us to infer the outcome. Here we learn that the same clerk of court has concluded from the act decreed by the town that the builder must have the organ finished before the end of August.[71] Continuing to push his case, Waghers's petition on 7 April for more money

---

[67] The Bus (or 'Buus') family embraced a long and distinguished line of organists and organ-builders including Jacques de Buus, composer and organist of St Mark's, Venice in the 1540s, as well as Josse, who was responsible for the 1505 building of the organ for the hospital of Notre-Dame in the family's home town of Audenaerde (see Félix, 'L'orgue gothique', 102).

[68] For these arrangements see 1515/16, ff. 35r–36r.

[69] Mensis septembris die decima octava comparens in capitolo coram dominis meis capitulariter congregatis discretus vir Johannes Blancquemain laicus tabellio presentatus requisivit ex eisdem dominis meis nomine et vice Magistri Caroli Waghers organificis ibidem presentis instrumentum organicum huius ecclesie per eundem Carolum Waghers alias inceptum iuxta ordinationem dominorum maiorum et scabinorum huius oppidi posse perficere et adimplere qua requisitione facta(?) Domini mei mature deliberantes concluserunt eundem Magistrum Carolum debere perficere huiusmodi instrumentum sed quo ad visitationes ipso perfecto et completo fiendas dixerunt se velle stare ordinationi et interpretationi dictorum dominorum oppidi Sancti Audomari percipientes(?) quorum interest velle dictum Magistrum Carolum Waghers compellere ad satisfaciendum expensas in quibus fuit iudicialiter condempnatus necnon quasdam alias expensas causa et occasione dicti instrumenti prius factas (II. G. 356, 219v). See also Deschamps de Pas, 'L'église Notre-Dame', 92.

[70] Item a Jacques Chevalier greffe [clerk] de la ville pour avoir examine lesdits Onye Bus et Corte a scavoir se par leur visitation faicte desdits orghes elles estoient dewement faictes xxx s. (1516/17, f. 30v)

[71] Primes a Jacques Chevalier pour tires de lacte de lordonnance de messeigneurs de la ville quil [Waghers] debvoit avoir parfait lesdits orghes en dedens le my aust ii s. (1517/18, f. 31v)

to complete the work was given the brush-off, the chapter informing him that he would receive his money when his task was sufficiently fulfilled and not before.[72] Clearly this time the chapter meant business: the first two weeks of August saw further organ visits (and considerable wining and dining) by Josse Bus and Jacques Corte, along with a certain Mahieu Wolf and his brother.[73] More poignantly, one can only imagine the dismay of Matheus, son of the deceased Victor Langhedul, original builder of the instrument, when, on 7 August, he visited to review the transformed state of his father's instrument.[74]

Throwing (at least in hindsight) good money after bad, the chapter on 7 August agreed to pay Waghers ten scuta in money of Artois in order to complete the necessary work by the deadline that had been imposed.[75] Yet a note in the fabric account suggests that, even at this late stage, the errant builder was failing to address the work so widely – and expertly – perceived to be outstanding: the last entry on the topic for that year records his being summoned to explain the reasons for his (unrecorded) appeal when he had still, since his sentence, done nothing to complete the assigned work.[76] It is hard not to conclude that, in reality, the chapter's decrees had no teeth: the deliberations continued in subsequent years, with another round of inspections and legal proceedings occurring in the year 1519/20,[77] and a still larger one the following year.[78] By 1521/2 the chapter had finally realised

---

[72] Eadem die [7 April 1518] Magister Karolus Waghers petiit ex dominis meis pecuniam propter perficere possit [recte: posse] instrumentum organicum[.] Domini mei super sui petitione deliberans dixerunt quod opere adimpleto eidem totale satisfacient et non antea[.] (II. G. 356, f. 226v)

[73] 1517/18, ff. 31v–32r.

[74] Eadem die [7 August 1518] domini mei pro sua parte denominarunt ad visitationem organorum huius ecclesie Dominum Jacobum de Corte curatum de Locquere et Magistrum Matheum [Langhedul] filium quondam Victoris eorum ultimi factoris (II. G. 356, f. 229r)

[75] Eadem die ordinarunt Magistro Karolo Waghers factoris organorum huius ecclesie decem scuta monete currente in Arthesio ut opus per ipsum inceptum infra terminum in sententia de super enarratum completum reddat et hoc in diminutione maioris sibi debite ratione [sic] dicti instrumenti organici si ipsum bene et sufficienter perficiat (II. G 356, f. 229r)

[76] Audit Jacques Widoit pour aller signifier audit Charles quil venist en viestare [sic] dire ses raisons de son apel/pourtant que riens navoit este fait de nouveau depuis la sentence ii s. (1517/18, f. 32r)

[77] This involved a return visit by Jacques Corte from Locre (Loker), along with Jan de Berlettes from Arras (ff. 39v–41r).

[78] A Maistre Jacques Wallart pour avoir solicite la fin dudit proces ou il a vacquiet pour plusieurs journees ad fin de rajourner les visiteurs eslus pour revisiter ledits orgles xxxii s.
Item fu ordonne par messeigneurs maieur et eschevins de envo[i]ere [sic] Tassinot de Le Helle a Aras devers adjourner Jehan de Berletes a Locquere adjourner Monsieur Jacques Corte a Ypre Monsieur Mahieu le Leu facteur dorgles a Brughes Maistre Jacques organiste de Notre Dame de Brugleyes [sic] par commission de mesditsseigneurs ... (1520/1, f. 37v)

the game was up and, however defective its state, agreed to accept the organ as it stood, even paying Waghers a settlement.[79]

The Crignon Organ

Not until 1546 was this regrettable situation addressed, when the chapter drew up a contract with Jean Crignon (or Crinon) of Mons for a new organ.[80] Clearly afraid of being burned again, the chapter took great pains to ensure that this instrument would reach the required standard. The contract was detailed in a meeting of the chapter of 25 August following vetting by imperial notaries and signing by the builder, and was read out in chapter the following day in the latter's presence.[81] The fabric account of

[79] Messeigneurs doien et chapitle veant que lon se scavoit avoir raison de ce M. Charles organistre et faiseur dorghes conclurent de faire appointement avecq luy et furent deputez M. Pierre Michau et M. Nicole Hanicque pour communicquier avec ledit M. Charles en la presence de aucuns de messeigneurs de la loy en la maniere que senssuit. Est que iceulx de chapitle prendent icelles orgues en tel estat quelles sont presentement en paiant comptant audit organiste la somme de xxvii l[ivres] c[ourants] et moiennant ce ledit M. Charles accorde que messeigneurs de chapitle lievent et prendent xv l[ivres] c[ourants] par lui mis et consignez es mains de Jacques Widoit lors amman du marchiet. Lequel Jacques pour ce comparut et promict paier lesdits xv l. en dedens le S. Jehan Baptiste comme le tout appert par laccord passe par devant messeigneurs de la ville pour ce ycy xxvii l. (1521/2, f. 11v) Quoted in Deschamps de Pas, 'L'église Notre-Dame', 93.

[80] Deschamps de Pas's report on Crignon's work is essentially paraphrased also in Comte (Arthur) de Marsy, 'Jean Crignon, facteur d'orgues à Mons, et les petites orgues de l'église Notre-Dame de Saint-Omer', *Annales du cercle archéologique de Mons* 27 (1896–7), 63–7. See also Hédin, *Les Orgues du Pas-de-Calais*. Besides that at Saint-Omer, Crignon's work is documented at other northern cities including Mons, Brussels and Leuven, where, at the church of St Pierre, an organ constructed by him in 1556 survived until destroyed by Allied bombing in 1944. He seems to have died sometime after 1585 (see Malou Haine and Nicolas Meeùs, *Instruments de musique anciens à Bruxelles et en Wallonie: 17ᵉ–20ᵉ siècles* (Brussels: Centre culturel de la Communauté française Wallonie-Bruxelles, 1986), 28).

[81] Contractus organorum: Mensis augusti die xxvᵃ domini mei convenerunt cum Magistro Johanne Crinon artifice organorum pro uno instrumento organorum pro hac ecclesia secundum certam figuram et declarationem eiusdem instrumenti scriptis redactam signis manualibus eiusdem artificis signatas [recte: signatis] pro summa mille centum quinquaginta florenorum carolinorum // et ultra hoc de gracia eidem solvetur summa quinquagenta aliorum florinorum carolinorum casu quo aliquid registrum ut vocant ultra huiusmodi declarationem in eodem instrumento fecerit / sub conditionibus in contractu desuper confecto latius specificatis. Deputan[tes] venerabilem virum Magistrum Lambertum de Caverel canonicum fabrice huius ecclesie receptorem ad sollicitationem obligationem huiusmodi contractus coram notariis imperialibus expedientem. Necnon ad deliberationem et solventem eidem Johanni Crinon ad bonum computum du[e]centa lb ex pecuniis in cista capituli existen[tibus] et ad fabricam pertinentibus. Quequidem obligatio die sequente coram dominis meis capitulariter congregatis / eodem Crinon presente fuit lecta de verbo ad verbum et per dominos meos eadem in omnibus suis clausulis approbata. Necnon expensas cum eodem Crinon durante huiusmodi contractu factas. (II. G. 358, f. 95v)

1545–6 reiterates its contents and expands on it considerably.[82] Payment, agreed at 1,150 carolus d'or as detailed in the contract, was to be paid in instalments: 200 on the day the deal was struck, followed by a series of payments of 100 each time, with the final 450 forthcoming on the delivery of the finished instrument. On top of this, a further 50 carolus d'or would be payable for 'quelques registres' in addition to the agreed specification of 'quinze registres avec ung positif'. In other words, this instrument incorporated considerable registral variety presumably operated by either sliders or (possibly by this time) a spring chest.[83] It is reasonable, though, to assume that, as was becoming standard in the sixteenth century, ranks of reeds, along with flutes and mixtures including at least fourniture and cymbale, multiple keyboards and so on, would have featured on the Crignon instrument.

An intriguing detail concerns a payment, of no less than twenty sous, to 'Anthoine Framery paintre' for producing a blueprint for the prospective organ. The following (surely linked) payment 'for two skins of parchment' ('pour deux peaulx de parchemin') suggests a design of substantial dimensions. Whatever its merits in permitting an impression of the prospective instrument *in situ*, this image may well have been used in soliciting opinion from outside arbiters. The next entry after the records just mentioned seems likely to be a case in point: here a certain Mahieu Le Febure is paid for having 'taken letters to an organ-maker living in Ypres', an initial overture that, on 20 July, resulted in a return visit to Saint-Omer of the said maker, now named as 'Maître Michel', along with an unnamed organist.[84] In a more explicit indication, the receiver of the fabric (Lambert

---

[82] Ff. 70v–2v. The first account essentially reiterates the Latin document recorded in the chapter acts:

> Aultres mises et despensse pour les nouvelles orgues que messeigneurs doien et chapitre le xxv^e daoust xv^c xlvi ont fait marchie avec Me Jehan Crignon facteur dorgues demeurant a Mons en Hainault et doibvent contenir quinze registres avec ung positif selon que plus au long est contenu en la declaration dudit instrument. Et ledit Crignon doit aussi livrer toute lescrinerie et ce est moiennant ce mesdits seigneurs sont tenus luy bailler unze cens chinquante carolus dor a scavoir au jour du marchie faict deux cens carolus dor. Item aultres cent carolus dor trois mois apres ledit marchie. Et apres de trois mois en trois, aultres cent carolus jusques a sept cens, et la reste montant a quatre cens chinquante carolus quant ledit Crignon aura livre ledict instrument. Et si ledit Crignon fyt quelques registres oultre les xv que dessus mesditseigneurs luy ont promis bailler chinquante carolus dor comme est plus a plain contenu au contract sur ce passe devant notaires imperiaulx. (1545/6, f. 70v). See also the transcription of the documentation in Deschamps de Pas, 'L'église Notre-Dame', 95–6. A newer, more complete reading of the series of documents can be found in Marc Gil and Ludovic Nys, *Saint-Omer gothique* (Valenciennes: Presses Universitaires de Valenciennes, 2004), 403–4.

[83] As suggested to me by Robert Bates.

[84] A Anthoine Framery paintre pour ung patron quil a fait pour lesdites orgues xx s

de Caverel) is paid to travel to Amiens to consult organ-builders on the appropriate cost of an organ 'like that of the design of the said Crignon'.[85] The following payment, made in Amiens, to 'a sculptor and joiner' to produce 'a design in the old style' may suggest a need on the part of the arbiters for something more three-dimensional in order to make a judgement.[86] Consultation while there focused not only on the projected instrument at St Omer, but on local points of comparison: de Caverel's fact-finding involved demonstrations by organists on instruments of the Amiens churches of St Martin and St Germain, and was followed by the dispatching of letters concerning organ-building back to St Omer.[87] Clearly all was judged satisfactory since on 13 August the chapter's messenger was in Mons setting up the agreement with Crignon which, we learn, was finalised on the 25th of the same month.[88] The usual round of banquets and wine drinking, at the end as at the beginning of the negotiations, sealed the deal.[89]

Item pour deux peaulx de parchemin viii s (1545/6, f. 71r)

A Mahieu Le Febure pour par ordonnance de messeigneurs le vii[e] de jullet avoir porte lettres a ung facteur dorgues demourant a Ypre viii s

A messagier de chapitre pour avoir le xviii[e] de Jullet apporte le[ttre]s de monseigneur le chanchelier contenant son advis touchant les orgues vi s (1545/6, f. 71r)

Le xx[e] de jullet messeigneurs ont faict venir en ceste ville M[e] Michel facteur dorgues demeurant a Ypres avec ung organiste pour communicquer avec eux sus le fait desdits orgues ausquelz messeigneurs ont ordonne pour leur paines et vaccations trois escus sol[eil] valent v l. xiiii s (1545/6, f. 71r–v)

[85] Ce recepveur par ordonnance de messeigneurs en datte du xxi[e] de jullet a este [a] Amiens pour soy informer aux facteurs dorgues combien polroit couster ung instrument tel que le patron dudit Crignon / et sa devise ou il a vacquis chincq jours a xxiiii s sont vi l (1545/6, f. 71v)

[86] 'A ung tailleur et menuisier audit Amiens pour faire ung patron a lantique, x s.' Robert Bates has pointed out to me that 'design in the old style' referred in France at this time to 'in the style of the Renaissance' (i.e. of classical inspiration) as opposed to the Gothic; hence in fact, in other words, a design in the modern style.

[87] A deux organistes audit Amiens pour avoir monstre les secrets des orgues tant de leglise St Martin comme St Germain x s

A Baudechon messager de Paris pour avoir aporte lettres dAmiens touchant le faict des orgues (1545/6, ff. 71v–72r)

[88] Au messagier de chapitre pour par ordonnance de messeigneurs le xiii[e] daoust avoir este a Mons querir Maistre Jehan Crignon pour faire marchie avec luy desdites orgues ou il a vacquie viii jours a vi s. chacun jour xlviii s

Le xxv[e] daoust messeigneurs doien et chapitre feirent marchie audit Maistre Jehan Crignon pour faire les dites orgues come plus au long est contenu au foeullet precedent auquel Crignon ce recepveur delivra presens les deux notaires imperiaulx deux cens carolus dor portant icy ii[c] lib.

Audit Crignon pour le denier a dieu iii s (1545/6, f. 72r)

[89] Le xix[e] de jullet pour despensse de bouche faicte au logis monseigneur le doien avec M[e] Jehan Crignon facteur dorgues pour communiquer du marchie des orgues ou estoient presens messeigneurs le doien, le chantre, Werhel, Cousin, Caverel, et Le Riche xxv s vi d

Beyond these consultations, subsequent to the contract messengers were sent periodically to visit Crignon in Mons to ensure – since the work was taking place in his workshop, not on site – that he was hard at work on his commission, that his efforts were meeting required standards, and to pay him his due instalments.[90] Clearly this time the chapter was taking no chances, and it must have been with some relief as well as gratitude that, on 11 May 1547, the chapter paid (at an outlay of no less than forty sous) for a banquet in Mons for Crignon and his workforce, 'to encourage him, and for his workers for working so well'.[91]

By 25 July, as we learn from the fabric account for 1546–7, building work on the organ was sufficiently advanced for preparations to begin on the masonry and carpentry work necessary for its installation, following which everyone was served supper 'in order better to discuss the business'.[92] One signal advantage of the documentation on this point, which details the particular walls of the building on which work was to be carried out, is that it allows us fairly closely to locate the position the organ was to occupy. Reference to 'the vault above the altar of St Julian, the wall on the side of the chapel of St Andrew, the walls on the side of

Le lendemain avec les dessus nommez fors Monseigneur Cousin, despendu au cellier de chapitre xx s (1545/6, f. 71r)

Item pour le vin du marchie que fut but en la maison Monseigneur Le Riche presens messeigneurs Werhel, Doslerel, Caverel, ledit Crignon et les deux notaires imperiaulx avec le notaire de chapitre xl s

Item pour despensse de bouche audit lieu au soupper presens messeigneurs le doien, Le Rice, Doslerel, Tilly, Caverel, ledit Crignon et le notaire de chapitre xxxi s vi d (1545/6, f. 72r–v)

[90] Le xxiii^e de decembre au messagier de chapitre pour avoir seiourne ung jour a Mons pour veoir et visiter si ledict Crignon besongnoit ausdites orgues et soy informer sil estoit solvent pour servir leglise vi s

Le xxiiii^e de janvier ce recepveur a envoie par ordonnance de messeigneurs cent carolus dor a Maistre Crignon facteur dorgues demourant a Mons tant moins et a bon compte des orgues quil fyt pour leglise portant icy ladite somme de c l.

A Jehan Cointel messagier de la ville pour par ordonnance de mesdits seigneurs avoir porte ledit argent a Mons xii s vi d (1545/6, f. 72v)

[91] Le xi^e de may messeigneurs ont ordonne a ce re[ceveur] aller en la ville de Mons vers Me Jehan Crignon facteur dorgues veoir en quel estat estoient lesdites orgues auquel par lordonance de mesditseigneurs il delivra la somme de c l.

Item apres avoir veu le tout en bon train pour luy donner couraige et a ses ouvriers de bien besongner, ce re[ceveur] (par ladvis Monseigneur Cousin present) leur donnist le bancquet, ou fut despendu xl s (1546/7, f. 69v)

[92] Ledict jour [25 July] furent prinses les mesures pour mectre et asseoir lesdites orgues ou estoient presens ledit facteur, Hugues de Le Chievre Extasse Balle carpentier de leglise, Agnieulx Clement machon et son homme[.] Et apres quil eut baillet a chacun ses mesures ce re[cepveur] leur donnist a soupper pour mieulx deviser de laffaire ou fut despendu la somme de xxx s (1546/7, f. 69v)

the choir [and of] Notre-Dame des Clocques' situates the organ's position in the south-east corner of the north transept, and thus almost adjacent to the choir. Its position was almost certainly on the east wall of the southernmost chapel of the north transept, that of 'Little St Andrew', otherwise known, due to the foundation in the same chapel by canon Baugois le Beghin of the chantry of Sts Julian and Basilisse, as the chapel of St Julian.[93]

Work required for this installation was substantial, including major new construction to make space for the organ and carry its weight. Payments in the fabric accounts reveal that masons were occupied for considerable periods building new walls, vaulting and an arch above the organ placement, while carpenters were busy with planking, building steps to afford access to the instrument, and so on.[94] Likewise a chapter act for 27 September 1547 details the building of stone walls, plus wooden flooring, for the support of the organ.[95]

By this point the organ, albeit still in sections, was already in the city, whence it had arrived, curiously, from Aire-sur-la-Lys, rather than from the builder's home town of Mons. We learn that on 18 March 1547 'the

---

[93] 'Touttes les pierres, tant pour larcure, la vaulse dessus lautel St Jullien, la muraille du coste de la chapelle St Andrieu, les murailles du coste du coeur, et Notre Dame des Clocques, que pour ladite montee desdites orghes ont estees prinses a la provision de leglise, et estimees par ledit Agnieulx [Clement] machon a la somme de xl lib par tant icy reseing' (1546/7 f. 72r). See also Deschamps de Pas, 'L'église Notre-Dame', 97. For the location see Wallet, *Description de l'ancienne cathédrale*, 46 (description); plate 1 (plan of the building). While Wallet proposes that the organ was situated on the south wall of the chapel, it seems more likely, given the work that was required on all three of its walls (facing respectively north, east and south), that the organ was affixed to the chapel's east wall.

[94] See for example the following, all from the fabric account for 1546/7; similar proceedings are detailed in the account for the following year:
   ... les ouvraiges detaille faicts par Agneaulz Clement [mason] et ses compaingnons pour larchurre et vaussure pour les orgues nouvelles. Et portoient lesdits ouvrages detaille faicts durant chincq sepmaines es mois de novembre et decembre ... en ce comprins le mur faict du coste de la chapelle St Andrieu xxiii l v s (f. 69v)
   A Anthoine Colbrant carpentier pour ung petit cerifier quil a vendu pour soustenir le chintre [underside ('soffit') of an arch structure] de larcure desdites orgues ... (f. 70r)
   Audict Agnieulx pour avoir ouvre a la vaulte de la chapelle St Jullien desoubz lesdites orgues, vi jour en la ii^e sepmaine de janvier ... (f. 70v)
   A Maistre Eustasse Balle m^e carpentier de leglise pour avoir ouvre xxxi^e journee, tant pour avoir hourde pour les machons, fyt les chintres pour larcure et vaulse, appoincte les gittes [joists], et foeully les esselles pour le plancquier, fyt ledit plancquier, et fyt une montee avis pour lesdites orgues ... Touttes les esselles pour ledit plancquier, et pour les pas de la montee ... (f. 72r)

[95] Eadem die domini ordinarunt venerabili viro Magistro Lamberto de Caverel canonico fabrice huius ecclesie receptori ut faciat edificare muros lapideos ac tabulata lignea necessaria pro novis organis huius ecclesie expensis fabrice. (II. G. 358, f. 117v)

said organs were transported into the town on seven carts',[96] and duly installed in the assigned setting. The usual preoccupation with visual impact and decoration is highlighted by further payments to the painter Anthoine Framery, this time 'for having painted and gilded with burnished gold an image of Our Lady which is placed up high on the said organ and also for having painted four little statues and a monkey, the whole placed on the positif of the said organ'.[97] Perhaps the figurines and monkey, like the figures on the organ of Strasbourg Cathedral, provided public entertainment by incorporating movement of some kind.[98] Similarly the joiner Jehan Collard was paid for supplying the wood 'beneath the organ' (presumably for the gallery), and for carving wooden mouldings and roses.[99] The mason Agnieulx Clement is paid for carving decorative pipe shades for the tops of pipes ('clerevoies'), while payment is also made for four poles of 7′ in length to function in some unspecified method of tuning.[100] A chapter act for 11 May 1547 details an order for lavish curtains for the organ of red silk and cloth-of-gold.[101] Payments for substantial ironwork including mention of 'two pillars sustaining the said organ' confirm support of the instrument off the ground, as is standard in contemporary iconography and surviving instruments of the period.[102]

Finally, by 4 June 1548, the completed work had been examined by the organists Jehan Lescallier from Bailleul, Jehan Rogier from Arras, Maillart Erkemboude from Comines, Pierre de Le Haye (*dit* Perot) from Furnes and

[96] Le xviiie de mars xvcc xlvii furent amenees lesdits orgues en ceste ville en sept chariots et fut donne par ce re[ceveur] aux cartons [carters] loges au logis du Chingne pour eux refereer [sic] deux lots de vin . . . (1547/8, f. 59r); Audit Crignon pour linterest quil a eut sus les chariots qui ont amene lesdites orgues depuis Aire iusques en ceste ville . . . (1547/8, f. 63r).

[97] Le xie dapuril [sic] a Anthoine Framery paintre pour avoir painct et dore a lor bruny une ymaige de Notre Dame laquelle est mise en hault desdits orgues ensamble avoir painct quatre petis mennequins, et ung singe, le tout mis sus le positif desdites orgues de marchiet fyt avec ledit Framery, present Me Jehan Crignon facteur desdites orgues viii l. (1547/8, ff. 59v–60r).

[98] My thanks to Kimberly Marshall for this suggestion.

[99] A Jehan Collard huch[i]er demeurant a St Aumer pour avoir lambroussiet, et livre larmarche du plancher dessoubs lesdites orgues et y mis plusieurs mollures et grandes roses de bois tailliees et ce de marchiet fyt avec ledit Collard, present ledit Crignon, la somme de xiiii l. (1547/8, f. 60r).

[100] A Agnieulx Clement, machon, pour avoir commenche a ouvrer pour tailler les clerevoies desdites orghues . . . (1547/8, f. 58r); Item pour iiii bastons de vii piets de long pour touchier sus le clavier pour accorder lesdites orgues . . . (1547/8, f. 59v).

[101] Ordinan[te] etiam eidem ut emat cortinas sericeas rubei coloris ac pannum auratum (II. G 358, f. 110v)

[102] A Maistre Henry Tonnoire serrurier de leglise pour avoir livre ung grand ancre de vingt piets de long et deux grandes clefs le tout de fer de buissiere, pour fermer les deux pilliers soustenans lesdites orgues, pesans ensamble ciiiixx iiii l de fer a xii d chacune lib. Et plusieurs autres parties douvraige de fer que a fallut pour lesdites orgues . . . (1547/8, f. 60r–v)

Philippe Compère from Hazebroucq,[103] receiving a universally clean bill of health. Similar visits, resulting in similarly unreserved approbation, were made to inspect the wood and pipework.[104] Following painting of the shutters, inside and out, by the painter Anthoine Framery the organ must have been a thing of considerable beauty.[105] Ongoing maintenance was assured by regular visits from Crignon and, following his presumed demise, in 1596–7 by Pierre Ysoré, a builder from Bergues whose work is documented also at Arras, Bourbourg and Veurne.[106]

The chapter was evidently more than satisfied with the state of the new 'petites orgues', even making a gift of £11 8s. to Crignon's wife when she visited the town.[107] But there could be no greater compliment on the instrument of an organ-builder than the request to build another. A surviving note in Crignon's hand, dated 21 May 1551, records his receipt of a down payment of "fifty florins, of forty groats per unit' towards an eventual total of 365 florins for a new organ for Notre-Dame sur le

---

[103] 1547/8, ff. 60v–62r. Interestingly, on 17 August of the same year, an 'honestum juvenem Mattheum Compere clericum morinensis diocesis' was appointed as organist at St Omer and the chapelle sur le marchiet (II. G. 358, f. 128v). The presence of these two organists both named Compère must raise the question as to whether they were related to the composer Loyset Compère. Since the latter was designated both in Milan in 1476 and, a decade later, while a member of the French Royal Chapel, as of the diocese of Arras, the possibility of a local connection seems strong. (See, respectively, Leeman L. Perkins, 'Musical Patronage at the Royal Court of France under Charles VII and Louis XI (1422–83)', *Journal of the American Musicological Society* 37 (1984), 552, and Paul Merkley and Lora L. Matthews, *Music and Patronage in the Sforza Court* (Turnhout: Brepols, 1999), 133.)

[104] A Jehan Collard et George Hanon escrigniers et tailleurs danticques, demeurant en St Aumer, pour par ordonnance de messeigneurs avoir visite toutte lescrignerie et taille desdites orgues, scavoir si le tout estoit aussi bon que le patron[.] Lesquels apres avoir le tout visite ont declaire le tout tant en escrignerie que en taille estre beaucoup meilleur que le patron . . .; A Jehan de Le Nefz et Andrieu Bissoit estangniers [metal (tin) workers] demeurant en St Aumer pour . . . avoir visite le parement [front pipes] tant du grand jeu que positif et aulcuns registres desdites orgues pour scavoir sil estoient de fin estaing de Cornoaille [Cornish tin: considered the best and purest] comme et selon que le marchiet parloit[.] Lesquels ont declairet ce que dessus est dict, estre de fin estaing de Cornoialle [sic], comme appert par acte signee de leurs mains icy exhibee . . . (1547/8, f. 72r–v)

[105] Le vi^e de juing a Anthoine Framery paintre pour avoir painct dehors et dedens les grands foeullets desdites orgues[.] Et ce de marchie fyt avec ledit Framery par ce recepveur present Me Jehan Crignon a somme de xxii l. (1547/8, f. 73r)

[106] It seems that, as today, the new instrument took some 'bedding in': on 24 September 1548 a request was sent to Crignon 'ut huc veniat pro dissonantia organorum'. The situation must have been considered to be of some urgency, since, already on the 28th, payment (in wine) was made to the builder 'qui huc venit corrigendum dissonantiam organorum' (II. G. 358, both on f. 131r). On Ysoré see Deschamps de Pas, 'L'église Notre-Dame', 101.

[107] Audict [Crignon] pour don faict a sa femme estant en ceste ville (par messeigneurs) six escus sol[eil] valent xi l viii s (1547/8, f. 73r)

marchiet.[108] In 1549/50 the chapter apparently attempted to sell Waghers's 'grandes orgues' to the abbey of Blangy. Given the absence of further detail, however, it seems likely that the negotiations fell through, and that (as Deschamps de Pas surmises) the instrument was dismantled when, in 1602, a pre-existent positif was installed 'in place of the great organ of this church for use of the same on ferial days'.[109]

Not until the eighteenth century, with the installation of the present instrument in its original form (before the major rebuild in 1853 by Cavaillé-Coll), did the fifteenth-century Langhedul instrument finally find a worthy replacement at the west end.[110] The absence of intervening evidence of an instrument in that location suggests that performance involving organs was restricted, for two centuries or more, to the choir and north transept.

* * *

The documents at St Omer provide a remarkable insight into the preparations, politics and general machinations attendant on the provision of organs for this great collegiate institution. As usual in such cases, however, the questions to which they give rise outnumber the answers. What, most signally, was the nature of the music played by the organs, and how did they interact (or not) with singing?

While documentation is limited, it seems likely that, as noted above in connection with the first documented organ, a major part of the organ's role at St Omer, as elsewhere, was fulfilled by the playing of chant or interaction with the choir, often in direct alternatim performance. As for other genres and as for most other establishments, written music is lacking; but we can

---

[108] That this single leaf, part of a bundle of documents pertaining to the chapel combined under the call number II. G. 2724, has not been lost must count as a minor miracle, not least since little further information on this instrument seems to have survived. Two brief entries in the relevant volume of chapter acts are all I have otherwise been able to trace. On 30 April 1551 Lambertus de Caverel, receiver of the fabric, is instructed to summon Crignon in connection with the plan for the new organ (II. G. 358, f. 166v). On the following 13 September, in a damaged part of this seriously desiccated manuscript, Caverel is again invoked in an entry concerned with the contract of 1551, though not enough is readable to infer much beyond that it concerns some degree of payment (II. G. 358, f. 185r). Since further documentation seems to be lacking, this record may have addressed final reckoning; at any rate the limited extent of information where one might expect it suggests a much more modest instrument than that for the collégiale.

[109] Domini mei ordinarunt accommodari certa organa vulgo *positif* dicta ad domum mortuariam R^{mi} J. de Vernois spectantia in loco majorum organorum hujus ecclesie ad iisdem utendum in diebus ferialibus (Deschamps de Pas, 'L'église Notre-Dame', 99 and 102.)

[110] Deschamps de Pas, 'L'église Notre-Dame', 101–4.

surely assume that, as elsewhere, performance of improvised and written polyphony in Mass and office was integral to the instrument's function from its first appearance. Solo organ performance in this early phase, as documented in theoretical sources and by such codices as Robertsbridge and Faenza, would as elsewhere typically have involved a sustained-note, chant-based tenor with busy treble figuration above, a format that, as Kimberly Marshall notes, relates directly to the standard construction of contemporary organs, pitting long, flanking 'bourdon' pipes against shorter, higher-pitched pipes characteristically arranged in a central mitre formation.[111]

General trends would likewise suggest that the organ's use was extended and diversified with the passing of time, and it is tempting to speculate that the enormous hike in the organist's salary that accompanied the arrival in the 1480s of the Langhedul organ at least partially reflected an enhanced role for organ polyphony within ritual observance. In common with the new level of sophistication of the instrument itself, this would have reflected desires to add greater elaboration to the ritual, as well as to provide relief for the singers in the fulfilment of a long and sophisticated liturgy. It is likely that organ 'versets' alternated variously with singing in most items of the Ordinary and some of the Proper, along with canticles at lauds, vespers and matins, plus hymns and the various psalmodic and responsorial chants.[112]

Any more directly interactive type of ensemble, if indeed it was desired or expected, would have been contingent on spatial considerations. The presence with their organist, on a visit to assess the organ installed in the late fifteenth century, of singers from Thérouanne might imply a close degree of interaction perhaps extending to direct ensemble, a practice that may be suggested also by the presence as part of the same build of a separate *Rückpositiv*. The distance of the organs from the altars at which devotions were being conducted was surely too great to allow any such

---

[111] For this and general repertorial discussion see her 'The Creation of Late Medieval Organ Music', in Pérès (ed.), *Les orgues gothiques*, 125–42.

[112] On *alternatim* performance in France from the fourteenth century on, see Edward Higginbottom, 'Organ Music and the Liturgy', in Nicholas Thistlethwaite and Geoffrey Webber (eds.), *The Cambridge Companion to the Organ* (Cambridge: Cambridge University Press, 1998), 130–47 and Benjamin van Wye, 'Ritual Use of the Organ in France', *Journal of the American Musicological Society* 33 (1980), 287–325, especially the summary of earlier practice on pp. 289–99, and the older literature referred to there. For a discussion of *alternatim* procedures in the context of speculation on the possible role of the organ in choral accompaniment, albeit in sixteenth-century Italy, see Gary Towne, 'Music and Liturgy in Sixteenth-Century Italy: The Bergamo Organ Book and Its Liturgical Implications', *Journal of Musicology* 6 (1988), 471–509, particularly 489–90.

ensemble unless the singers were themselves positioned with the organist rather than next to the officiating clergy; and in the case of singing at high altar services 'in medio chori', even the sixteenth-century instrument, which was closest in proximity to the choir, must have been too distant from singers in the chancel to allow for direct ensemble or indeed uninterrupted sight lines, though signalling by bells could have afforded reasonably close alternation between music sung and played. This must have been especially so between the mid-fifteenth and mid-eighteenth centuries, when the choir – an enclosed space – extended as far as the west wall of the crossing, where it was closed off at its western extremity by a *jubé* (screen).[113]

The invariable placement of large instruments of the period high on the wall surely reflected acoustical concerns arising from the architectural situation: a raised source of sound affords the transmission of direct sound waves to more, and more widely dispersed, listeners; it allows access to the flat (and hence most effective) reflectors of sound above the level of the pillars; and – perhaps crucially – it permits simpler sound reflections from the vaults of the building into side chapels and chancel, whose access to organ sound is thereby uninterrupted by their (much lower) masonry screens, stalls and *jubé*.[114] Whatever the nature of their interaction with the choir, however, the dimensions of the organs, at least beginning with the late fifteenth-century instrument, surely imply much more than simply monophonic performance, and the references to 'out of choir' observance open up considerably more diverse possibilities for interaction.

---

[113] Wallet, *Description de l'ancienne cathédrale*, 45 and plate 1. As noted on p. 40, six columns, each surmounted by an angel, surrounded the choir. These were linked by curtains, as described in the church inventory of 1557: 'Six pendans de courtines de damas cramoisy rouge, avec les voies tout du long de drap d'or rouges avec armoiries de feu Monsr d'Arras.' See Louis Deschamps de Pas, 'Inventaire des ornements, reliquaires, etc., de l'église collégiale de Saint-Omer en 1557', *Bulletin archéologique du Comité des travaux historiques et scientifiques* 1 (1886), 87. Deschamps de Pas notes that 'Monsr d'Arras' refers to Eustache de Croy, bishop of Arras from 1521 to 1538 (as well as provost of St Omer). On the *jubés* of St Omer, of which the earliest evidence dates to the late thirteenth century, see Georges Coolen, 'Les jubés de la collégiale de Saint-Omer', *Bulletin trimestriel de la Société des antiquaires de la Morinie* 403 (1970), 321–34. This book's frontispiece image of St Omer from the missal of Oudart de Bersacques shows, behind the saint, the *jubé* erected in the fifteenth century under the deanship of Simon Bocheux.

[114] Full assessment of this complex topic is clearly beyond the scope of this study. For valuable considerations see, however, Dorothea Baumann, 'Acoustics in Gothic Cathedrals: Theory and Practical Experience in the Middle Ages', in Pérès (ed.), *Les orgues gothiques*, 37–48, especially 42, and Dorothea Baumann (trans. Barbara Haggh), 'Musical Acoustics in the Middle Ages', *Early Music* 18/2 (May 1990), 199–210, especially 203–8.

The Organist

If discourse surrounding the organs – and especially, as we shall see, the bells – tends at times to stray into the anthropomorphic, their voices nevertheless remain mute in the absence of human hands. Yet if human agency drove all the church's sound-sources, fairly clear lines seem to have been drawn between their supporting organisational structures. While we know that at least some choirboys received keyboard tuition of some kind, evidence that the church's organists came up through the structure of the maîtrise is limited.

There is some indication that organ-playing was a family affair, which would itself go some way to explain logistics for the passing on of skills: Jehan Caignart, paid annually as organist in the 1450s and 1460s, is followed in the same role from the 1470s until his death in 1493 by Simon Caignart.[115] Also noticeable, in contrast to the musical chairs that characterises, as we saw in Chapter 3, the role of master of the boys, is the longevity typical of incumbents of the organist's chair, for which continuity is frequently measurable in decades. In contrast to the bell-ringers, however, organists could also be paid, as vicars, for celebrating Masses: Simon Caignart himself occupied a vicariate and was paid for celebrating Masses founded by Baugois le Beguin.

As noted already, the role of the organist underwent considerable augmentation when, during the tenure of Simon Caignart, it received a boost through the installation of the Langhedul organ in the 1480s. At this point a large number of responsibilities 'outside the choir' ('extra chorum') were added to an already significant roster of services in the choir, perhaps suggesting, among other things, that the growth in the number and complexity of private devotions was accompanied by a similar growth in demand for the organ. By a decade or so later, its institutional role had expanded still further: the fabric account for 1495/6 includes payment to the then organist, Alleannie Gerin, for playing at all greater and lesser double feasts, general processions and on all Saturdays (for the *Salve*) and vigils of Our Lady at Notre-Dame sur le marchiet, along with all other offices involving processions.

---

[115] The two may have been brothers: in his will (Dainville (Arras), Archives départementales du Pas-de-Calais, Justice échevinale de Saint-Omer, 15B1, f. 152r–v) Simon asks for his burial to be cited 'au plus pres de Messire Jo Caignart mon frere'. Of course it is also possible that there were two Jehan Caignarts of successive generations.

As for the instruments themselves, however, information concerning when they played is sadly not accompanied by specifics about what they played – knowledge that, beyond general inferences, seems likely to remain locked in the past. In this respect, knowledge of what was played would appear to share its characteristics with the sounds that made it a reality: even in the few organs surviving from this period the degree of modification over the intervening years makes direct access to their late-medieval timbres elusive. Only one family of instruments from the time has surviving members that can still reasonably be said to transmit the actual sounds of half a millennium ago: these instruments, the church bells, form the subject of Chapter 5.

5 | The Bells

... harmonieux interprètes de nos joies et de nos douleurs ...[1]

When Baugois le Beghin, canon of St Omer, died in 1475, he endowed a bell 'called Julienne' to be rung at specified moments in specified ways.[2] It was to be heard seven times on each of a series of occasions: every day both at matins and at the beginning of his personally founded daily Mass in his chosen chapel and, further, every Saturday and on the vigils of all Marian feasts, while the *Salve regina* was being sung in the nave. Like Nicolas Rembert (as Chapter 6 will detail), Baugois was keen to associate his personal plea with that of the High Mass, the central focus of community devotion; therefore he also decreed that it be rung every day during High Mass at the precise moment of the elevation, 'as is customary in notable churches of this kingdom'. With this foundation Baugois was thus able to embed his personal plea in a wide network of devotions, and to have it resound through the building, out into the surrounding city and beyond.

Records beginning in the late thirteenth century detail the use of a large church bell, of which this (as we shall see) was certainly one, to signal the elevation in addition to, or in place of, the smaller bell that had been part of the history of the elevation since its inception.[3] As the key moment in the celebration of Mass, at which the transubstantiated redeemer became flesh in the form of the raised host, the elevation carried special significance for the potential endower: material association with it offered – in the form of a proxy presence – personal linkage to the moment of grace and the benefit of the prayers of those present. From a late medieval perspective, therefore,

---

[1] Oscar Bled, 'La Bancloque de Saint-Omer', *Bulletin de la Société des antiquaires de la Morinie* 7 (1882–6), 169.

[2] Baugois was received as a canon of St Omer on 22 February 1462. His executors' account is preserved in MS II. G. 473. The document founding his bell-ringings and daily Mass survives in II. G. 1776.

[3] See Joseph Jungmann, *The Mass of the Roman Rite: Its Origins and Development* (translation, by Francis A. Brunner, of *Missarum Solemnia*), 2 vols. (Westminster, MD: Christian Classics, 1986), II. 209–10, 131. To judge from the many records of payments for bells in church fabric accounts of the period, only the large, cast bells hung in church towers or belfries were dignified with names such as that given by Baugois to his bell.

Baugois's bequest was a masterstroke: by imprinting his sounding proxy on the crucial moment of the principal devotion of his own church he was able not only to harness the prayers of those present in the building, who would immediately have turned to face the anticipated elevation, but to 'kindle charity' in anyone within earshot in the surrounding city and beyond.[4] The ringing of such elevation bells would serve as an announcement to anyone in the environs of the church, who could then rush into the building in time to view their maker, and to instruct those working round about to pause, face the church and worship the risen Christ being made present within its walls.[5]

Some indication of the perceived efficacy of bells to extend the power of the transubstantiated host comes, paradoxically, from instructions to keep them silent. Durandus, in his thirteenth-century (but ubiquitous throughout the later Middle Ages) *Rationale divinorum officiorum*, admonishes that 'during a time of interdict, the bells are silent because often on account of the crime of those under interdict, the tongue of the preachers is obstructed, according to what the Prophet says: *I will make your tongue stick to your palate because this house* – that is, the people – *is rebellious* – that is, disobedient [Ezekiel, 3:26]'.[6] Times of interdict were signalled in churches of Arras by a single toll from a medium-voiced bell and the symbolic closing of the church doors of the great abbey of Saint-Vaast.[7] Similarly in 1216 Pope Honorius III instructed an abbey in southern Albania to refrain from using bells during Mass lest they should 'involve' people beyond the walls who were under interdict and hence denied the benefit of the sacraments.[8] A more general statement of deprivation, like the so-called 'Lenten array' according to which religious images were covered and deprived of their attendant succour, can be seen in Durandus's call for the silencing of bells on the three – especially penitential – days before Easter.[9]

---

[4] For the latter function see John H. Arnold and Caroline Goodson, 'Resounding Community: The History and Meaning of Medieval Church Bells', *Viator* 43 (2012), 122.

[5] For a series of examples of this from thirteenth-century England, Italy and France see ibid., 122–3.

[6] Timothy M. Thibodeau (trans.), *The Rationale divinorum officiorum of William Durand of Mende: A New Translation of the Prologue and Book 1* (New York: Columbia University Press, 2007), 53.

[7] Carol Symes, *A Common Stage: Theater and Public Life in Medieval Arras* (Ithaca, NY, and London: Cornell University Press, 2007), 141.

[8] For this and other examples see Arnold and Goodson, 'Resounding Community', 123.

[9] Thibodeau, *Rationale*, 53.

At St Omer the message of penitence was heightened on these days, as we learn from the thirteenth-century ordinal, by the sounding from the tower, in lieu of all the otherwise expected soundings of bells, of a loud rattle made with pieces of wood.[10] The sound, heard first to herald Thursday matins must, as Deschamps de Pas notes, have been carefully orchestrated to prove powerful enough to be clearly audible on the ground. In other words, on these penitential days of the triduum not only were those within earshot deprived of the sound of bells signalling the key moments of divine worship, they were assailed instead by a non-tonal 'noise'. Tonal deprivation mirrored the deprivation of light being symbolically enacted simultaneously within the church, where on each of the three days twenty-four candles were lit and successively extinguished following the performance of each psalm until the church was left in total darkness.[11]

At the opposite extreme, the pealing of bells – of a number and range barely imaginable in these days of post-Revolutionary depletion – must at times of celebration have been almost overwhelming. This can scarcely have been more powerful than when, following triduum privation, the full complement of bells swung into action at the 'Gloria in excelsis' at Mass preceding vespers on Holy Saturday. Carol Symes's evocation of the full force, on major feasts, of bells in nearby Arras would surely have applied equally well to Saint-Omer:

Holy days could be heard as well as observed, since nothing but the clamor of bells was heard in the streets from which traffic had been cleared. The synodal statutes of 1280 reiterated the custom observed in the diocese: on feast days all worldly labor should cease, and on the most important holidays the use of carts, carriages, and horses was also forbidden. In this way, the very soundscape of holidays reminded the town dweller, inured to worldly racket, of their special character.[12]

---

[10] '. . . campane non pulsantur, sed ante quod procedatur ad officium diurnum, totiens pulsantur signa lignea super turrim quotiens pulsarentur campane in festo sollempni in feria quadragesimam usque ad altam missam.' Louis Deschamps de Pas, 'Les cérémonies religieuses dans la collégiale de Saint-Omer au XIIIe siècle: Examen d'un rituel manuscrit de cette église', *Mémoires de la Société des antiquaires de la Morinie* 20 (1886–7), 163.

[11] '. . . hora pulsationis a matutinas, ascendit turrim et percutiuntur ibi signa lignea ad hoc appropriata, et notandum est quod hac die et duobas sequentibus ad matutinas, ad majus altare accenduntur XXIIII cerei super lignum ad hoc ordinatum et semper (?[sic]) ad inclinationem [recte: inchoationem] uniuscujusque a[ntiphona] tam ad nocturnos quam ad laudes et similiter ad inchoationem cujus libet responsorii extinguitur unus cereus ita quod cum incipitur canticum "Benedicitus" extinguitur ultimus cum quo totum lumen quod est in ecclesia extinguitur.' See ibid., 161–2; description on 113–15.

[12] *A Common Stage*, 141.

Signifiers also of powers of this world, bells projecting multiple clamour from belfries en route would likewise have marked the civic entries of important personages, of power either ecclesiastical or terrestrial.[13]

Examples such as that of Baugois serve to remind us of the latent power of bells not only for celebration but also for jurisdiction. The sound of large bells marked out a radius that broadened the presence – and by extension the authority – of their users over a wide area, whether that was thought to embrace parish, city or indeed the surrounding region that contained them. If the loftiness of church towers could itself engender a sense of power and control, it also afforded access to sound that could make perception of that power all but unavoidable. At a time of a much more limited range of aural stimulation than that of today's world, people learned from an early age to recognise the voices of the individual bells in their city and the duration and frequency of their ringing, both singly and in combination. The extent of the use of the bells – far beyond that familiar today – is abundantly clear from the scope and regularity of their repairs, and especially payments for new clappers and the baldricks that connected them to their partners in sound.

Most obvious to us today of course is the bells' function to mark out the daily liturgical round of institutional, parish and community worship of which the elevation at High Mass was only the most signal aspect. But compared to our familiar striking of the hours and calling to daily services, the applications of bells even within the institutions that housed them were in the Middle Ages much more frequent and various. The thirteenth-century Norwich Customary gives a striking indication of the extent of the daily round of ringing required, in a pre-chronometrical era, for the running of that city's priory (now cathedral). Signals from the bells regulated not only the church's devotions and the comings and goings of the monks who manned them but also its meetings and the functioning of its lay workers. Messages were differentiated by numbers of bells, their (relative) size, methods of striking, and so on.[14]

While no detailed prescriptions for marking the hours survive for St Omer, manuals from elsewhere provide a strong indication of the kinds of procedures that were surely followed. A mid-sixteenth-century bell-ringers' manual from St Donatian, Bruges, provides meticulous descriptions of the

---

[13] See for example the description of Philip the Good's entry into Bruges on 11 December 1440 (see Reinhard Strohm, *Music in Late Medieval Bruges* (2nd, rev. ed., Oxford: Clarendon Press, 1990), 81).

[14] Paul Cattermole, *The Bells*, in Ian Atherton et al. (eds.), *Norwich Cathedral: Church, City and Diocese 1096–1996* (London: Hambledon Press, 1996), 494.

ringing required on different ranks of feast and at the component hours and Mass.[15] The general pattern is clear: smaller bells with simple successions of 'pulsings' for minor feasts, building, via increasing size and complexity, to the ringing of all the bells for Mass, matins and vespers on the most important days of the calendar. A similar pattern articulates the progression of individual devotions, from small/few at the beginning of an observance to (relatively) large/many at the end. Where this pattern is flouted, a special message is clearly intended, as when, at Easter Mass and Matins, the entire panoply of bells is rung directly and simultaneously. This full, festive marking of the arrival of the risen Christ provides a striking parallel to the similar sounding of all the bells for the 'joyeuses entrées' of visiting magnates (both temporal and ecclesiastical), for whom, reciprocally, such symbolism allies their terrestrial authority to a higher, heavenly one.[16] Another variation, with particularly festive connotations, is the practice whereby the clappers of groups of three bells (or sometimes even four) could be fastened to one another to be rung together in a pattern known as 'triplicare' ('batteler' (Fr.) or 'beyaerden' (Fl.)). Alternatively a skilled bell-ringer could manipulate a pair of bells with his hands while also striking two further bells via cords fastened to his feet. While multiple ringing of this nature involved the striking of stationary bells, it could be combined for special, especially festive, effects with other bells being sounded 'in flight' (i.e. swung). Such striking could involve inventive rhythmic combinations of stuck sounds, rhythmically articulated at the will of the player, and sounds created by swinging, their pace dictated solely by the mass of the bells producing them.[17]

Each city, each institution and each foundation had its own intricate conventions: an early-thirteenth-century processional from the cathedral of Soissons 'ad usum episcopi' gives detailed instructions for bell-ringing on days when the bishop was present. Distinctions between ringing bells in succession, 'bina et bina' (presumably pairs of bells rung in succession) and 'glassus' (a combination of bells sounded simultaneously[18]) clearly encoded

---

[15] A fascicle included as part of the bundle Bruges, Bisschoppelijk Archief, Reeks D 6. My grateful thanks to Robert Nosow for providing me with photographs of the entire manual.

[16] See the discussion of various such intended analogies in Andrew Kirkman, *The Cultural Life of the Early Polyphonic Mass* (Cambridge: Cambridge University Press, 2010), 86–93.

[17] See Luc Rombouts, *Singing Bronze: A History of Carillon Music* (Leuven: Lipsius Leuven, 2014) (transl. of *Zingend Brons. 500 jaar beiaardmuziek in de Lage Landen en de Nieuwe Wereld* (Leuven: Davidsfond, 2010)), 41–2.

[18] See John Neale Dalton, *The Collegiate Church of Ottery St Mary, Being the Ordinatio et statuta ecclesie sancte Marie de Otery Exon. Diocesis, A.D. 1338, 1339* (Cambridge: Cambridge

messages that were decipherable as necessary to the hearing of the local populace. A bell named 'Gloriosa' seems to have had particular associations for the laity, sounding before the sermon to the people on Ash Wednesday, and summoning them to church on Maundy Thursday. As at St Donatian, all bells were called into action to celebrate Christmas and Easter, and as (see below) at St Omer, the largest bell had its own special cachet, in particular for specified processions. It was rung, on each occasion, nine times: after Mass on Easter Day, after Terce for the octave of Easter, for the Mass of the Dead at the church of St Crispin, before the procession preceding Mass on Rogation days, for the procession on Pentecost, before the procession on the Feast of the Dedication of the Church, for the order for the installation of a new bishop, and so on.[19] Ringing of multiple bells would typically require enhanced workforces, hence the varying numbers of 'aydes' paid at St Omer to assist with ringing for all processions and on all feasts of semi-duplex or higher rank.[20]

Baugois's Bell

If the range of messages – still less the psychological effects – originally conveyed by the sounds of late medieval bells are hard to imagine today, bells represent a perhaps unique opportunity directly to share a sonic experience with our fifteenth-century forebears. In the majority of places – Saint-Omer included – most were at some point melted down, typically exchanging their tuned state for the very different sound of canon; and even many of those that did not meet this fate have at some point been

---

University Press, 1917), 232. See also Charles du Fresne du Cange, *Glossarium mediae et infimae latinitatis* (Niort: l. Favre, 1883–7).

[19] The manuscript is Paris Bibliothèque Nationale MS Latin 8898, available on Gallica: https:// gallica.bnf.fr/ark:/12148/btv1b8432463d/f1.image (facsimile) and https://archivesetmanuscrits .bnf.fr/ark:/12148/c(fc62427t (description). My thanks to John Harper for drawing my attention to this source and its contents.

[20] For example, 'Aux compaignons qui sonnairrent les grosses cloques la nuit de la nativite Nostre Dame / le jour / et le jour de la deposicion St Aumer ensemble qui font trois jours xxiiii s' (1475/ 6, f. 28r); 'A plusieurs aydes qui ait ayde a sonner tous les sollennes doubles et demy doubles et triples durant le cours de cest an et pour ce xxii lb xvii sc vi d' (1478/9, f. 23v). See below for the large numbers of 'aydes' paid for ringing the church processions. Tables detailing the feasts assigned such ranks at St Omer are provided in Jean-François Goudesenne, introduction to *L'antiphonaire de la Paix des Prince chrétiens: Calligraphié à Saint-Omer par Sire Michel Reymbault, enluminé à Lille par Soeur Françoise de Heuchin ca 1550–1561* (facsimile edition of a St Omer manuscript antiphonal of c.1550–61), Publications of Mediaeval Musical Manuscripts No. 30 (Ottawa: Institute of Medieval Music, 2003), xliv–xlvi.

recast. Yet there remain a significant number of actual bells cast in the sixteenth century or earlier, many of them still in use.[21]

While Baugois's bell was recast in 1920 it enjoyed a remarkable career to that point, and in its reincarnated state hangs in the belfry to this day, an uncanny fulfilment of its donor's device, 'pour tout tamps', which it bears. The fuller inscription with which it was cast gives notice of its origins:

The distinguished man, Master Baugois Le Beguin of Fauquembergues, doctor of canon law, canon of this church, devotedly gave me, Juliana, called hereafter Julia, to the church of St Omer; the smelters being the founders Gobelin Moer and Guillaume Carpet, in the year of our Lord 1474.[22]

One of only two of the church's bells to survive the Revolution, Julienne, or more prosaically 'le bourdon', put its grand sonic stamp on the great occasions of the city for half a millennium, its role in ringing out times of celebration in more recent times earning it the sobriquet 'La Joyeuse'. In the 1880s Oscar Bled could still claim that 'all the inhabitants of Saint-Omer know this magnificent bell, of a sound so full, at once so sweet and so solemn'.[23]

Julienne was a bell of awesome proportions. Measuring more than two metres in both width and height and weighing between 17,000 and 18,000 lb (or almost six tons) in its original state, it required the exertions of six men to swing into action. Annual records in the fabric accounts record outlay for this physical effort, such as the following from 1505–6:

To the said sacristan [Jehan de Le Venne] and five aides for having rung in flight the large bell Julienne given by the said deceased [Baugois], during the *Salve* each Saturday of the year, vigil of Our Lady and on the principal feasts [nataulx] during the time of [this] account, £4 10s.[24]

---

[21] For example, Toby Huitson estimates that 'over 1,970 medieval bells survive in England and are still in regular use'. See his *Stairway to Heaven: The Functions of Medieval Upper Spaces* (Oxford and Philadelphia, PA: Oxbow Books, 2014), 76.

[22] '+ me julianam vocatam hinc juliam ecclesie beati audomari devote donavit egregius vir magister baugelius beguini de falcoberga oriundus decretum doctor huius ecclesie canonicus. conflantibus gobelino moer et willelmo carpet fusoribus anno domini M⁰ cccclxxiiii.' See Bled, 'La Bancloque', 167.

[23] 'Tous les habitants de Saint-Omer connaissent cette magnifique cloche d'une sonorité si pleine, si douce et si grave à la fois.' Ibid., 166.

[24] 'Audit cloqueman et chincq aides pour avoir sonne a volee le grosse clocque Julienne donnee par ledit feu durant le Salve pour chacun samedy de lan veille de Notre Dame et des nataulx durant le temps de compte iiii lbs x s' (f. 29v). 'Les nataulx' was a term generally used in reference not only to Christmas Day but also to the principal feasts of the year more generally, typically Easter, Pentecost, All Saints and Ascension (see *Dictionnaire du Moyen Français*

The shuddering of the tower that resulted from swinging such a huge mass into motion meant that the church was ultimately forced to give up ringing the bell 'in flight'; for many years, therefore, its sound, including the ringing of the hour, was produced solely by being struck, as had from the beginning been the practice for all its specified uses except those named in the above record. Finally in 1852 a new system of suspension permitted its setting in motion by only two men; but degradation of the supporting structure after four centuries' exposure to the elements made it clear that it could not regularly support the strain of such a large weight in movement. Major structural work ensued, and on 17 July 1875 it was able (now bearing its modern appellation 'la Joyeuse') again to resound in its full glory, announcing to the populace the following day's festival of the crowning of the icon of Notre Dame des Miracles.[25] In the end, though, enthusiasm got the better of its surely fatigued metal: perhaps ironically – given the wholesale revolutionary destruction of bells – over-zealous ringing on Bastille Day, 1900, resulted in a crack from which, despite repair work four years later, it could not be saved, resulting in its refounding in 1920. From 1996 the recast bell was in abeyance due to the need to replace its two motors, though in 1999 permission was given for its occasional use on grand celebrations.[26] Following a full-scale restoration of the bells and belfry beginning in 2014, its wondrous noise nowadays again resounds every Sunday morning, when at 9:31 it announces the impending High Mass. Its sounds resonate deep within the church its patron so richly endowed, and where his mortal remains likely still remain buried in the north transept. Baugois was laid to rest in close proximity to the chapel of 'Little St Andrew' (today that of St Carlo Borromeo) in which he founded an altar to Sts Julian and Basilisse and a daily Mass, and near to which his badly worn funerary slab still lies (Figure 5.1)[27].

(1350–1500) (www.atilf.fr/dmf/)). At St Omer it embraced the four celebrations of Christmas, Easter, Pentecost and the patronal Feast of St Omer.

[25] See Bled, 'La Bancloque', 167–8.

[26] See *La Cathédrale de Saint-Omer*, www.cathedrale-saint-omer.org/?/architecture/description, accessed 4 October, 2019. Something of Julienne's magnificence can also be experienced via the sound of the 16,454-lb bourdon Salvator which, with those of its companions all dating from 1505, still emanates from the cathedral tower of Utrecht (see Rombouts, *Singing Bronze*, 48).

[27] Though much of the inscription, including Baugois's name, is no longer legible, enough was decipherable in 1839 for his funerary slab to be identified by Emmanuel Wallet: 'En face de cette chapelle, et à quelque distance toutefois, se trouve parmi les pavés une très-grande pierre bleue, sur laquelle est tracée en relief la figure entière dun prêtre. Le calice, la tête et les mains formés sans doute d'une incrustation de marbre et de cuivre, sont détachés; et autour de la pierre se

Figure 5.1 Baugois Le Beghin, funerary slab, north transept © Carl Peterolff

rencontrent encore quelques fragmens d'inscription, avec la date de 1475, le titre de canoine et une reste d'armoiries portant un chevron: circonstances qui témoignent que là fut la tombe de Bauduin-le-Begum [sic].' See *Description de l'ancienne cathédrale de Saint-Omer (Pas-de-Calais, ci-devant Artois), autrefois Notre-Dame de Sithiu, et Morinie, maintenant paroisse Notre-Dame* (Saint-Omer/Douai: Baclé/author, 1839), 39. See also Henri Loriquet, *Épigraphie du département du Pas-de-Calais*, Tome V, 1er et 2e fasc. (*Ville de Saint-Omer*) (Arras: Laroche, 1892), 53, and 281, where the author notes the then-readable name 'Bavgesius Beghini'. Of the name only one capital 'B' and a few descenders are legible today, though other details, notably 'canonicus necnon parochialis de Waurans', verifiable in Baugois's executors' account, are still apparent.

Proclamations of a New Church

The early history of Julienne was part of a more comprehensive plan for the provision of bells for the collégiale in the last quarter of the fifteenth century, which was itself bound up with major developments in the building for which it was cast. It coincided with the culmination of an extended programme of rebuilding during which the church assumed essentially the shape we see today. Only one significant part of the building in its current form was yet to emerge: its bell tower.

It appears that ambitions to upgrade the church's bells extended back some time before work on the new tower got underway: as far back as the 1440s money from tithes had been earmarked for the purchase of bells, and the fabric account for 1462/3 records the visit of a bell-founder from Bois-le-Duc ('s-Hertogenbosch) to examine the existing bells and make a proposal.[28] But there seems little doubt that motivation for a new, and newly lofty, square tower was heightened by knowledge of the imminent building of the – in the event much grander – likewise square tower of the abbey of St Bertin. Added to this, the 1470 blessing, by the abbey's monks, of five new bells must, for the chapter, surely have made the desire to match this with five new bells of its own a matter of pride. With the new, much larger and more solidly built tower supplanting the smaller, open-worked spire that had preceded it, this also became a possibility.[29]

But the realisation of that possibility, as will shortly emerge, was far in the future, in a time by which most of the bells' donors were already long dead. Any concerns about the housing of the bells were clearly insufficient to dissipate the head of steam (and financial muscle) that had got behind the idea of founding a new peal of bells, however, and 1475–6 saw the raising of substantial sums from the church's clerics. None was more generous than the cantor Thierry de Vitry, whose personal donation of £326 8s. covered the entire cost of the bell tuned to 'la', named Magdaleine:

---

[28] 1462/3, f. 23r: A ung fondeur de clocques du Bosleduc [sic] pour avoir este au clocquier avec moy N. de Le Salle viseter les clocques et avoir attendu le responce de messeigneurs sur ce quil se offroit a faire nouveller clocquee si leust pleust a messeigneurs baillie du commandement de mesdits seigneurs iiii s.

[29] For these building developments see Louis Deschamps de Pas, 'Essai sur l'art des constructions à Saint-Omer, à la fin du 15e et au commencement du 16e siècle', *Mémoires des Antiquaires de la Morinie* 9 (1851), 161–251. Deschamps de Pas sees this rivalry, rather than any prior ambitions concerning a more impressive array of bells, as the new tower's primary *raison d'être* ('Essai sur l'art', 163–4).

From master Thierry de Vitry, cantor, canon of Aire [sur-la-Lys] and canon of the said church of St Omer, for the gift of a bell tuned to the tone of la which he gave to the said church, the said bell weighing in metal 3,800 at the price of 26s. in groats per hundred, which amounts to the sum of £296 8s., and for the manufacture, to the workers to make the said bell £40, the said parts adding up to £336 8s.[30]

The weight of this bell – clearly itself a substantial instrument – of 3,800 lb offers some perspective on the behemoth (at 17–18,000 lb) that was Baugois's Julienne. Payments further on in the same account reveal the preparations for the testing of Magdaleine: we learn of a frame being constructed to hang it and sound it 'a volee', and directly thereafter of the acquisition of wood for the furnace for its founding, along with that of 'Omer', its companion on the pitch of mi.[31]

Before the end of 1475 the greater part of the church's collective response to the peal of St Bertin – the bells on mi, fa, sol and la – was already cast:

On the 16th day of November of the present account the four bells recently made and founded were baptised, one of the tone of mi named Omer, the second of the tone of fa named Marie, the third of the tone of sol named Austreberte and the fourth of the tone of la named Magdaleine for which several pieces of gold were received as a gift from the godfathers and godmothers, the sum of £22 3s., of which should be deducted and held back for the vicars and those who conducted the service 32s., for the sacristan and other officers who had set up the scaffolding and other needs required for this, 14s. And for incense, myrrh, fumigant and resin 63d. There remains current for the said fabric £19 15s. 6d.[32]

---

[30] De Maistre Thierry de Vitry chantre canone dAire et canone de ladite eglise de St Aumer pour le don dune cloque entonnee de ton de la laquelle il a donne a ladite eglise pesant ladite cloque en metal trois mil viii cens au pris de xxvi s de gros le cent qui montent a le somme de deux cens iiii^xx xvi lbs viii s et pour la faichon aux ouvriers pour faire ladite cloque xl lbs montent lesdites partiez a trois cens xxxvi lbs. et viii s. (1475/6, f. 12v)

[31] A Maistre Jaquez Blommart maistre carpentier de ladite eglise lequel a livre pluseurs pieces de bos pour pendre et sonner a volee la cloque nommee Magdalaine [sic] du ton de la donnee par Maistre Thierry de Vitry canone pendue en le carpenterie pres du celier de capitle et y avoir ouvre lui et ses gens par plusieurs jours comme appert par ung papier signe xiii lbs. ii s.
Audit Maistre Jaquez pour aulcunes blocqueaulx de bos et tronches pour mettre en la fournaise quant on fondit le my et le la et ung jour et demi de ung de ses varles pour couvrir et descouvrir ladite fournaise et faire ung tramel (1475/6, 26v)

[32] Le XVIe jour de novembre de ce present compte furent baptisies les quatre cloques desrenierement faictes et fondues lune du ton de mi nommee Omer la seconde du ton de fa nommee Marie la iii^e du ton de sol nommee Austreberte et la iiii^e du ton de la nommee Magdaleine dont fut recu en don des parrins et marrines en plusieurs pieces dor la somme de xxii^l iiii^s dont fault deduire et rabbatre pour les vicaires et ceulx qui firent loffice xxxii^s pour le clocquemant et aultres officiers qui avaient apointies les hours et aultres besoignes ad ce requises

Completing the hexachord, on 26 August 1488 the two bells tuned to ut and re, suspended for the purpose, were themselves baptised.[33]

This customary 'baptism' of bells, and involvement of 'godfathers' and 'godmothers', in addition to their quasi-human names and dedications in the first person, gives some measure of the level of personification assigned to these (however artificial) voices. The custom of blessing and naming of bells is first documented in the old Spanish liturgy prior to the Arab invasion of 712, and was probably already old by then.[34] The name could be provided by the donor, the 'godfather' (often naming the bell after himself) or even the founder; in other examples it could derive from a saint or simply its function or the time of its use. The baptismal ceremony typically involved purification with salt, water and oil in addition to the various kinds of incense detailed above, the chanting of psalms and reading of a series of blessings. The latter addressed the functions of the bells to summon the faithful, disperse the enemy, give protection against the wiles of the Devil, guard against storms and enhance devotion, including the standard comparisons between the bells and trumpets of war, those of Moses in particular.[35]

Like the building programme that had preceded it, progress on the tower, and installation of its new bells, was slow and deliberate, and informed by careful planning and consultation. In spite of the levying for the tower fund of a generous proportion of the income from each prebend, building work was greatly retarded by insufficient finances, particularly given the disruption in income from Flemish property due to protracted hostilities between the royal forces of France and the Flemish forces of the Duchy of Burgundy. The resulting civil strife, embracing several sieges and changes of jurisdiction over the city, apparently resulted in a long cessation of work: between 1477/8 and 1493/4 no further construction seems to have taken place. While it could scarcely have anticipated such an extended

xiiii[.] Et pour enchens mirre thimiama et olibane lxiii[d] demeure bon a ladite fabrique xix[l] xv[s] vi[d][.] (Quoted in Deschamps de Pas, 'Essai sur l'art', 219.)

[33] Item le jour du baptesme desdits deux clocques assavoir ut. re. et que Maistre Judo[cus Dausque] et Phi[lippe] de Mailly avoient alle pour les parins et marines qui fut le xxvi[e] jour daoust pour iceulx monseigneur le doyen et aultres au disner en me [sic] maison fu fait ung escot ou il y eut trois lots de vin de x s.[:] xx s. (1487/8, f. 33r)

[34] On the origins and nature of the ritual and its meanings see Rombouts, *Singing Bronze*, 32–5; also Jean-Daniel Blavignac, *La Cloche: Études sur son histoire et sur ses rapports avec la société aux différents âges* (Geneva: Grosset and Trembley, 1877), 33–54.

[35] See Arnold and Goodson, 'Resounding Community', 118–19. For a discussion of these associations in the late medieval Mass commentaries of Durandus and Honorius Augustodunensis see also Kirkman, *Cultural Life*, 104–6, 128–9.

hiatus, the chapter had in any case made plans to avoid subjecting the bells to extended silence. The novel solution chosen was to take down the existing spire and partially to rebuild it on the ground, with the new bells suspended therein. The location chosen was the castle motte (mound), for which an annual rent (only slightly above the notional peppercorn) of two capons was settled on with its proprietor the duke of Burgundy.

By 8 May 1476 the four bells already cast were hanging in their provisional setting and were swung into action for recreation. Thereafter the chapter seems to have missed no opportunity to use them for their intended purpose. The considerable number of processions for which they were rung suggests that, even without their intended vantage point and reach, their sound was sufficient to carry across the city. Perhaps it was in the interests of volume that, in 1478/9, they were fitted with new, larger clappers.[36]

The fabric account for that year provides an exceptionally long list of processions, all sonically cloaked, following standard practice,[37] in the ringing of all the bells. The likely motivation was surely the frequent presence that year of the (then) Duke of Austria and Burgundy, the future Emperor Maximilian I. Leaving no doubt as to the loyalty of the city in the conflict between the House of Burgundy-Habsburg and the Royal House of France, the new duke's entry into the city was clearly an affair of considerable lavishness. The payment to the cart-driver and two assistants who brought the 'covers' from the 'vironicke jusques a ledit eglise' (the 'vironicke' surely a reference to Notre Dame des Miracles, in its chapelle sur le marchiet) suggests the erection of a covered walkway for the duke between the collégiale and its satellite chapel.[38] The church must have presented quite a spectacle on Maximilian's arrival: a further payment is for a 'carpet of flowers [and/or foliage] in the church the day that our lord the duke came twice to hear Mass'.[39] The date in question appears to have been

---

[36] A Maront Corbillon fondeur de artellerie le quel a reffait et engrossit les v. battaulx des grosses clocques noeusues / et y mis du fit et achur nouvel par marchiet fait aueuc luy . . . (1478/9, f. 23r)

[37] Durandus notes that 'bells are rung in processions so that the demons who fear them will flee . . . They are so fearful when they hear the trumpets of the Church Militant, that is the bells, that they are like some tyrant who is fearful when he hears in his own country the trumpets of some powerful king who is his enemy.' Thibodeau, *The Rationale divinorum officiorum of William Durand of Mende*, 53.

[38] Au carton [cart driver] qui amena les cappes [covers?] de leglise depuis le vironicke jusques a ledit eglise le jour que monseigneur le duc vint en ceste ville et pour deux hommes qui luy aiderent (1478/9, f. 21v)

[39] Pour estramure en leglise au jour que monditseigneur le duc y vint oyr messe par ii fois (1478/9, f. 21v)

29 June: a later entry in the same account records 'paid to Martin the bellringer and to his assistants for having rung all the bells on the Feast of Sts Peter and Paul when my lord came to hear Mass at St Omer'.[40]

Clearly this was not the duke's only foray into city festivities: a further payment is to 'twelve companions who rang the procession that was made on the octave of the sacrament'.[41] More joyfulness was to follow: a further payment is 'to the assistants who sounded on the Saturday of the battle the bell of "mi", at the command of Master Hughes Monchy, canon'.[42] The Saturday in question was clearly that of 7 August, when the duke's forces defeated the French army at Guinegate, a victory that did not, however, prevent ongoing years of civil strife. The victory did in the end prove decisive, however, putting paid to Louis XI's claim to Burgundian territories under the Salic law that precluded succession through women, in this case Maximilian's wife Mary of Burgundy, the daughter of Charles the Bold. Why the records mention only the one bell on the occasion of this victory, for which typically all the city bells would have sounded out, and why the bell of 'mi', remains, however, a mystery.

Of the many other processions (invariably with bells) recorded for that year, most involved the carrying of relics:

f. 21r:

To four companions for having rung the general procession made on the first Sunday of Lent, 2s. [the first Sunday of Quadragesima (i.e. Lent) was 28 February 1479]

To the assistants who helped ring the procession that was made on the Feast of St Gregory in which was carried the head of Monseigneur St Omer, 2s. [the Feast of St Gregory was 12 March in Saint-Omer]

[Scored through:] To the assistants who assisted in ringing the procession on Easter Sunday, and the head of Monseigneur St Erkembode was carried, 2s. [Easter Day was 11 April 1479]

---

[40] Payet a Martin le clocqueman et a ses aydes pour avoir sonne toutes les clocques le jour Saint Pierre et Saint Pol present monseigneur vint oyr messe a SaintOmer (1478/9, f. 22r)

[41] A xii compagnons qui sonnerent le procession qui fut faicte es octaves du sacrement et y fut monditseigneur le duc present a chacun xii d (1478/9, f. 21v). While the 'sacrement' seems most likely to refer to Corpus Christi (which fell on 10 June), this is complicated by the fact that another procession is specified on St Margaret's Day, which in 1479 fell on the same day. Perhaps, as John Harper has suggested to me, 'sacrement' in this case refers to Pentecost, whose octave that year fell on 5–6 June.

[42] Aux aydes qui sonnerent le samedi de le bataille le clocque du my par le commandement de Maistre Hughes de Massy chanonne (1478/9, f. 22v)

To the assistants who rang the procession made on Easter Wednesday to St Bertin, 2s. [Wednesday after Easter Day was 14 April 1479]

To the assistants who rang the procession on Sunday 15 May, and the head of Monseigneur St Omer was carried, 2s. [15 May was a Saturday in 1479; perhaps this was for first vespers of Sunday, hence Saturday evening]

To the assistants who rang the procession on the last feast of Pentecost, at which the head of Monseigneur St Erkembode was carried, 2s. [Pentecost 1479 was on 30 May]

f. 22r:

To the assistants who rang the procession made on the Feast of St Margaret to St Bertin, 3s. 6d.[43]

A suite of processions with relics (and bells) began on the patronal feast day, that of the *depositio* of St Omer (i.e. the anniversary of his death). The processions, on subsequent days, with the church's relics of (respectively) St Erkembode and St Austreberte are unrelated to either saint's feast day, and were clearly in this succession subsidiary to the principal Feast of St Omer:

f. 22r:

To the assistants who rang the procession, which was on a Thursday, when the body of St Omer was carried, 2s.

To the assistants on the following Friday when the body of St Erkembode was carried, 2s.

The following Saturday when the body of St Austreberte was carried, 2s.

The following Friday when the reliquaries were carried and there were celebrations until after the processions, 4s.

To the said assistants for having rung on the said 9th the Tuam Crucem, 9s.

To the said assistants who rang the procession on Sunday [19 September] when the head and body of Monseigneur St Omer were carried, 2s.[44]

---

[43] A iiii compaignons pour avoir sonne le procession generalle faicte le premier dimence de quaresme ii sc; Aux aydes qui aiderent a sonner le procession qui fut faicte le jour Saint Grigoire ou fut porte le chief Monseigneur Saint Aumer ii sc; Aux aides qui aiderent a sonner le procession faicte dominica in passione et fut porte le chief Monseigneur Saint Erkembode ii sc; Aux aides qui sonnerent le procession faicte le mercredi de pasques a Saint Bertin ii sc; Aux aydes qui sonnerent le procession faicte le dimence xv^e de may et fut porte le chief Monseigneur Saint Aumer ii sc; Aux aydes qui sonnerent le procession faicte le derniere feste de le penthecouste et y fut porte le quief Monseigneur Saint Erkembode; Aux aydes qui sonnerent le procession faicte le jour madame Sainte Marguerite a Saint Bertin iii sc vi d

[44] Aux aydes qui sonnerent le procession et fut par ung joeudi que on porta le corps Saint Aumer ii sc; Aux aydes le vendredi ensuit que on porta le corps Saint Erkembode ii sc; Le samedi ensuit que on porta le corps Sainte Austraberte ii sc; Le vendredi ensuit [17 September] que on porta

The prevailing dynastic hostilities meant that it was not only the building of the tower that was long left in abeyance. Also, and concomitantly, on hold was the refashioning of the wood from the dismantled belfry (meanwhile serving to house the bells on the castle motte) into a smaller bell tower over the crossing of nave and transepts, such that existing work there was in danger of collapse. In this instance, though, help was at hand in the form of a bequest of three hundred livres from the canon Walleran Peppin. The condition for the donation was that, on recouping the expenses, the chapter would spend them on rents to support foundations for his soul, a provision that in fact transpired in 1490.[45]

While the tower project was revived in 1493/4, it was not until five years later that building actually commenced. In 1498/9, following long and exhaustive investigation and the weighing of the advice of various master masons on the bearing of the huge weight of the new edifice, the first stone of the new tower was laid, in a grand ceremony, by the abbots of St Bertin and Clairmarais. On this foundation of solid counsel, the building work

toutes les fiertres et fut feste jusques apres les processions, iiii s; Ausdits aydes pour avoir sonne par ledit ixme le Tuam Crucem. ix sc; Ausdits aydes qui sonnerent le procession au dimance que on porta le chief et corps Monseigneur Saint Aumer ii sc

[45] See Deschamps de Pas, 'Essai sur l'art', 170–1. All this is carefully detailed in the fabric account for the six-month period from 28 May to 1 November 1487, f. 14v (full record entered in only one of the two copies): De Maistre Walleran Peppin docteur en medecin et chanoine de St Aumer veant que messires au temps de ce present compte avoient fait mettre jus le grant cloquier de ceste eglise pour y mettre le beffroy et cloches qui sont en bas sur icelluy grant cloquier / et du boys venant dicelluy faisoient ung autre clocquier pour mettre sur le croisie de ladite eglise ainsi que il est advint que le xxviii^e de may ceste ville fu substraitte des franchois et mise en lobeissance du Roy de France par quoy furent exempts de recepvoir leurs rentes estans en Flandres qui est le principalle revenue de ladite eglise / Au moyen dequoy ledit clocquier estoit en dangier destre tout perdu et pery et demourer imparfait au grant vitupere et deshonneur de ladite eglise et des suppots / Il meu de devotion et singulierement pour subvenir a la necessite urgente bailla promptement comptant la somme de iii c libz courant a la fabricque de ledite eglise moiennant laquelle somme / mesdit seigneurs oblegerent et obligent tous les rentes et revenus de ladite eglise drois cents [sic] prouffis et emolumens y escheans que dor plusaplain est faite mention es lettres obligatoires sur ce faictes de faire dire et celebrer doresenavant perpetuellement et a toujours quel temps quil soit une messe en le chappelle St Nicolay le vendredi y furnir pain chire et vin a ii sol. par chacune messe avec ce tenir ardant jour et nuit une lampe devant ledite chappelle et toutes et quantes fois que lon fait stacion a heure de vespres le vendredi devant le crucifix les(?) jours dessusdits croix v torses ardans pesans chacune iiii libs tant que ladite stacion sera retraitte en coeur estans iii [libs?] devant le croix en hault sur le dossal / et deux devant lautel Notre Dame dessoubs ledit dossal sauf que le samedi ne seront allumes que les troys devant ledit crucifix a ce que ledit jour Sire Pierre Pauchet a fonde les deux autres, mais les jours et festes Notre Dame y seront mises les deux que lon fait chacun vendredy et lors en aura un devant Notre Dame et ainsi continuer les vies durant et de leurs successeurs depuis le tradicion et deliverance desdits deniers qui fut le premier jour daout anno IIII^{xx} sept pour ce icy en somme(?) iii^c libs

itself was executed in little more than a year, and the canons were finally able to install the bells that until then had sounded only from their provisional setting on the castle motte. Following on from this in its turn, the latter construction was dismantled and reassembled to assume its new role in the form of the smaller bell tower over the crossing. While further strengthening work to walls and foundations went on over the next several years, the tower, and its role in extending the church's collective new voice over the surrounding landscape, was essentially complete.[46] With the baptism and installation in 1507/8 of the bell 'Suzanne' in the tower over the crossing, the collective assemblage of bells seems to have reached completion, and what historically was surely its widest sonorous range.[47]

Beyond the Collégiale

It is in this range, and its very externalising nature, that the sound of the bells is differentiated most fundamentally from all other sounding media generated by the collégiale. No matter what the power of its interior reverberations, from the larynx of the smallest boy to the boom of its largest complement of organ pipes, all such sounds were directed within its walls, to those gathered there to receive them. Bells, with their sheer volume and the sonic reach afforded by high positions, always and essentially functioned to announce: joy and jubilation, yes, but also authority, warning and ultimately power. In ringing out across the townscape and beyond, the sounds of the church's bells inevitably imposed, and the potential was always there for them to do so in aural conflict with others. Their function, in other words, and however broadly conceived, was political. Thus their full meaning cannot be arrived at by considering them in isolation: it demands some sense of their relation to the others with which they harmonised or clashed, and to the different, and often competing, forces that swung them into action.

Besides their function as clarions for the institutions that housed them, bells were also, therefore, sites of intersection, and not infrequent rancour,

---

[46] L. Deschamp de Pas, 'Essai sur l'art', 171–6.

[47] 1507/8, f. 36r: Aultres mise pour le clocque nomme Suzanne estant au petit clocquier reffondue de nouveau par Tassin Baullet nouvelle poise iii c xii L de metal[.] Et la bieze pesoit iii c xxx L de metal par marchie a lui fait en tacque pour tout ledit Tassin a eu viii L x s et de fin estain qui font ensemble ix L[.] Sur quoy a rechept xviii L de metal restant de la vieze clocque a xxi d le livre prisie par Jehan Chiret qui val[ent] xxxii s[.] Auisy reste ichi a compter comme il appert par le signe dudit Tassin la somme de vii l ~~xii s~~ viii s.

between interacting powers, clerical and lay. Means of civic communication from time immemorial, certain key bells retained their importance for the larger community at least (within the confines of modern-day France) until the Revolution, when their association with the power structures of the *ancien régime* led to their wholesale destruction. Hence authority over them resided not only with the clergy in whose church towers they were hung, and to whose services they summoned the populace, but also with the civic administration whose functioning they regulated. Not surprisingly, therefore, their history was typically punctuated by disputes over authority and concerning costs for maintenance and recasting.

As elsewhere, a bell of particularly long and vital tradition in Saint-Omer was the lookout bell, or 'cloche du guet'. Hung in the tower of the parish church of St Denis, the most important function of this bell (called 'Marie') was to signal both violent incident within the city and attack from without. Its sounding, which would persist until the ringing of the contrary bell 'of retreat' ('de retraite'), summoned all men from fifteen to sixty years old to assemble for the lookout. But the bell also, besides its more expected devotional uses, had a range of other, quotidian applications. Primary among these was to ring (each time for the duration of a quarter of an hour) at sunrise, at noon and at 7.00 in the evening to mark the passage of the working day (hence its parallel designation as 'cloche de l'œuvre'). Under an alternative appellation as 'dining bell' ('cloche du dîner'), its noontime ringing also served to signal the time at which wool merchants were allowed to start buying.

Among other applications it also served to sound the curfew and, at least from 1559, to signal the times for opening and closing the city gates, for which latter it was rung for half an hour prior to the setting of the sun. Its functions, which trumped those of all other bells in the city, also serve to introduce the hierarchies according to which the use of bells was bound: no other bell was to be heard while the cloche du guet was running through its paces. Why, though, the church of St Denis, rather than the much wealthier and grander collegiate church or indeed one of the other parish churches? Part of the reason was its central position, allowing the bell to resound across the entire city; but another was surely the fact that this was the church customarily attended by the mayor and aldermen, who occupied stalls in the choir more prominent even than those of the clergy.[48]

---

[48] For information on the cloche du guet see Oscar Bled, 'Notice sur la cloche de l'église de Saint-Denis à Saint-Omer', *Bulletin de la Société des antiquaires de la Morinie* 7 (1882–6), 114–29.

The function of the St Denis bell as 'cloche de l'oeuvre' broaches the topic of what, for Jacques Le Goff, was a new role of bells as timekeepers, signs of the rise of the mercantile class and the regulated working day. Le Goff points out the express building in 1355 of a belfry in Aire-sur-la-Lys to regulate the commercial dealings and working day of the cloth trade, and hence as a tool of mercantile control.[49] A feature most obviously of textile centres, of which Saint-Omer was another, bells used to control work time became, before widespread access to the 'objective' time provided by clocks, a bone of great contention between fourteenth-century employers and workforce.[50] Jonathan Martineau points out how, in the aftermath of the Black Death when labour was at a premium, the most frequent demand made by workers – and sometimes, as at Thérouanne in 1367, met by their employers – was the silencing of the work bell.[51] Clearly, at the very least the sound of the work bell had, for merchant as for worker, to be clearly distinguishable from any others, and its control was a focus of particular power.

The role of the work bell as keeper of at least a notionally measurable time as opposed to the marker of events, or even of the cyclical but mutually variable succession of the church's 'hours', of course relates its function to that of the clock, its co-instrument of jurisdiction and eventual successor. Only with the installation of clocks could the strife inherent in the use of employer-controlled work bells realistically be settled, and the clock's influence gradually drew earlier, less mechanically regulated operations of time under its aegis.[52]

---

[49] Jacques Le Goff (transl. Christophe Campos), 'Church Time and Merchant Time in the Middle Ages', *Social Science Information* 9/4 (August 1970) (translation of 'Temps de l'Église et temps du marchand', *Annales* 15/3 (May–June 1960), 417–33), 159–60. See also Le Goff (transl. Arthur Goldhammer), *Time, Work and Culture in the Middle Ages* (Chicago, IL, and London: Chicago University Press, 1980) (translation of *Pour un autre Moyen Âge: Temps, travail et culture en Occident* (Paris: Gallimard, 1977)), 35–6.

[50] See *Time, Work and Culture*, 46, which comments also on the similar enactment, in 1335, by the bailiff of Amiens of 'the aldermen's desire that "the sound of a new bell" should serve as the new means of regulating the "three crafts of the cloth trade" – as then existed in Douai, Saint-Omer, Montreuil, and Abbeville'. See also Jonathan Martineau, *Time, Capitalism and Alienation: A Socio-historical Inquiry into the Making of Modern Time* (Leiden and Boston, MA: Brill, 2015), 58–9; Gerhard Dohrn-van Rossum (transl. Thomas Dunlap), *History of the Hour: Clocks and Modern Temporal Orders* (translation of *Die Geschichte der Stunde: Uhren und modernen Zeitordnungen* (Munich and Vienna: Carl Hanser, 1992)) (Chicago, IL, and London: University of Chicago Press, 1996), 296–300.

[51] Martineau, *Time, Capitalism and Alienation*, 59.

[52] Ibid., 59–63; on these developments see also Dohrn-van Rossum, *History of the Hour, passim*, particularly 299–305, and Le Goff, *Time, Work and Culture*, 48–52.

This same process saw a concomitant, and exponential, growth also in numbers of clocks and businesses connected with their production and maintenance, a change amply reflected in the St Omer accounts. Thus it comes as no surprise to discover the importance for the St Omer sacristan ('cloqueman'), of the maintenance of a clock. In 1462/3, for example, we read of a payment:

> To a clockmaker from Ath in Hainaut named Engoulant Le Bidau for having repaired the clock in the room of the sacristan, by agreement made: 19s. And another time to examine the said clock. 1 lot [approx. two litres] of wine of the chapter of 2s., total 21s.[53]

Clearly this man was judged well up to his onerous job: the next entry details how the chapter had a faulty clock sent to him in Ath to be fixed. By 1475 maintenance of clocks seems to have become one of the many sundry tasks (in addition to the obvious one of ringing and organising ringing) expected of the 'cloqueman'. That year he was paid 'pour mettre apoint et entretenir en estoit deu lorloge de leglise', and by 1495/6 his job description included 'pour avoir gouverne et conduit lorloge de ladite eglise durant ledit an', a requirement that, in addition to sweeping, cleaning, decorating the altars for major feasts, lighting lamps and putting up the banner on the tower on the church's dedication day, is detailed annually thereafter.[54]

Besides the cloche du guet, a further bell dubbed the 'cloche d'alarme', more particularly assigned to warn of attacking enemies, hung in the tower of the (now demolished) church of St Aldegonde, not coincidentally placed at the highest point of the city and with the best potential view of attackers. It took precedence only on the occasion of actual invasion, when its swinging into sound, and the great carrying power emanating from its lofty position, would call the inhabitants of the city to arms. Since the size of a bell was proportional to its volume it was decided in 1548 to found for this purpose a new, larger bell of 4,000 lb, 'et plus hault par son que possible sera'.[55]

---

[53] A ung orlogier de Aat en Heynau nomme Engoulant Le Bidau pour avoir mis apoint lorloge qui est en le chambre du clocqueman par marchiet fait xix s. Et une aultre ffois pour ledit orloge viseter .1. lot de vin de capitle de ii s. sont xxi s. (1462/3, 23r)

[54] 1475/6, f. 21v and 1495/6, f. 22v, respectively.

[55] Bled, 'Notice sur la cloche', 123. Robert Nosow has pointed out to me that while under siege the city of Bruges requested that the church of St Donatian refrain from ringing the hours, a state of affairs likely called for, he suggests, so that the alarm bell could be clearly audible across the city.

However vital the roles of 'le guet' and 'l'alarme' to the running and security of the city, however, they both ceded ultimately to the authority of the 'bancloque', or *campana banni*. This bell, traditionally the heaviest and with the greatest carrying power, was the instrument of the *bannen*, meaning the authority of the city government to call together the popu- lace.[56] The great Saint-Omer bancloque, suspended in the belfry of the collégiale, embodied functions that probably dated back to the origins of the town around its two great ecclesiastical houses. In the words of Canon Oscar Bled, it was the 'principal organ of the will of the city, or of the magistrates who administered it'. As elsewhere, the bancloque represented – and to no small degree embodied – the notion of civic community, to the extent that civil disobedience in Boulogne in the 1270s led to the king demolishing both the bell and the belfry from which it commanded the attention – and collective self-image – of the citizenry.[57] Its association with civic control and punishment was equally palpable, however, and surely the motivation behind the post-Revolutionary smashing of the Saint-Omer bancloque on 18 September 1792.

Unsurprisingly also, the bancloque was the site of regular power struggles between the magistrates and the chapter until, in 1487, control over it was ceded definitively to the town. Positioned in the tower of the collégiale, its distinctive tone marked out the hours and festivals of both sides of the community, and the long reach of its sound guaranteed the desire of both for its maintenance. Most signally, though, it functioned to summon the citizenry to the marketplace for the announcement of new laws or new decrees of the town council, or – via fast, repeated strikes – to call them to arms or to enact vengeance. Indeed without the summoning by the bancloque, or in the absence of sufficient numbers thereby assembled, laws could not officially be passed; hence, conversely, those failing to appear at its summons risked punishment. In calling together the bour- geoisie to enact retribution (during whose violent administering it con- tinued to sound out) on those deemed to have committed crimes, the bell played, moreover, a more direct role in enforcing discipline, and one conveying an unmistakable warning to potential transgressors. As Carol Symes has noted, 'Loud summons, raised voices' – whether from the metal of a bell or the larynx of a crier – '... were necessary for the delineation of

---

[56] See Rombouts, *Singing Bronze*, 40–1. For a detailed treatment of the Saint-Omer bancloque see Bled, 'La Bancloque '.
[57] Symes, *A Common Stage*, 139.

boundaries, the advertisement of authority, and the legitimacy of transactions'.[58]

Instantly recognisable in isolation, the bells accrued further meanings in combination: thus the simultaneous sounding of the bancloque with that of a smaller bell gave notice that it was ringing for the bourgeoisie as opposed to the chapter. Combined with the sound of the bells of 'le guet', 'l'alarme' and 'l'effroi', it signalled imminent danger, something akin, one imagines, to today's 'red alert'.

Bells were the instruments, par excellence, of medieval communication: marking the hours, summoning the faithful, warding off storms and other works of the Devil, warning of impending invasion, calling to arms, inciting punishment, facilitating the passing of laws and ordinances, and more generally structuring the lives of citizens and controlling and cementing perceptions of community, they were never simply neutral decorations of a city soundscape. But they were a good deal more than all this besides. In sounding forth their many and various voices from their grandiose, renewed edifice, the bells of the collégiale of St Omer were aiming their tones beyond the local citizenry in announcement to the wider world: that here was a church of regional and even wider consequence, one capable, as the next chapter will explore, of attracting the attention of great magnates – secular and sacred – and lofty talent wherever they happened to reside.

---

[58] Ibid., 142.

Loose Canons? Music and the Craft
of Ecclesiastical Power

An entry in the chapter acts of 4 December 1482 heralds the arrival of a
new man in town. Though not a composer nor even apparently – following
an early stint as a *contratenorista* at St Peter's, Rome – a singer, Nicolas
Rembert was surely the most influential figure in music at St Omer during
the later fifteenth and early sixteenth centuries. To appreciate how he could
have assumed such prominence involves understanding the role during this
period of intermediaries at the papal curia in the development of clerical
personnel across the reach of the Western church. Rather like key gallery
owners in the history of twentieth-century painting, a figure such as
Rembert was an *éminence grise* in the wake of whose machinations talent –
including musical talent – could rise or fall, lead to fortune or confine to
penury. In the process, such individuals could themselves accrue considerable wealth and assure, through the foundation of prominent posthumous
devotions, that their reputations would long exceed their earthly tenure.

The careers of such musical luminaries as Du Fay, Binchois, Okeghem,
Regis and Josquin remind us how musical skill could result in advancement
to high clerical positions, posts more normally reserved to the scions of
wealthy families and indeed of the nobility. Such advancement could, as
apparently in the case of Du Fay, allow more time for composing, perhaps
even a reason for such career moves on the part of prolific composers;
alternatively it might, along with increased distance from regular exercise
of the very skills that had enabled it, lead to a reduction in musical activity
as singers assumed higher office and their quotidian musical duties fell to
deputising vicars. But if much of the discussion that follows inevitably
moves us away from musical practice, it remains the case that it was
precisely such practice that enabled career advancement in the first place.
We have seen already in Chapter 2 how an excellent singing voice could
function as the passport of a gifted boy into service of a great court choir,
and how – in turn – fulfilment of that same skill could later be reciprocated
by the patron in finding his subject a position back on his home *terroir*.
Such cyclic career patterns could prove equally propitious at the other end
of a career, as amply demonstrated by the lucrative crowning assumption
of provostships by Binchois and Josquin. At the same time, such

appointments proliferated the links between the great courts and chapels and the smaller centres to which their employees later devolved. The later parts of this chapter will reveal the rather contrasting effects of such interchange in the cases of two canons who arrived at St Omer from earlier positions as members of no less a chapel than that of the Burgundian court.

Before following the progress of these individuals through the corridors of power, however, we need to grasp the nature of the system that sustained them: the network of canonries and higher offices of the church. In contrast to the appointments of chaplains, vicars, escotiers, masters of the boys and the choirboys themselves which, as earlier chapters have demonstrated, were in the gift, if not indeed at the whim, of the dean and chapter, canonries typically required the assent of the pope or of the magnate into whose rights of collation they fell.[1] As a result, this was a system hugely beneficial to clerics – including musicians – whose gifts had conducted them to positions of eminence at major courts and religious institutions.

The Dean and Chapter

The canons were the church's governing body, the 'college' that constituted the 'collégiale'; in short, its *raison d'être*. The building existed, in theory at least, for their spiritual, as well as physical, sustenance while, in its turn, standing as the beacon of their devotions. As instituted around the year 820, the chapter of St Omer comprised thirty canons, a number that, with a few fluctuations, remained stable throughout the Middle Ages. Each of these was appointed to a benefice with an attendant 'prebend', an income from property received in exchange for maintaining Mass and office. At least notionally, according to a thirteenth-century stipulation, the provost of St Omer – standing at the head of the chapter – was elected by the canons, while they in their turn were chosen by him.[2] In reality, however, collation of canonries became increasingly in the later Middle Ages the province of higher powers. This meant, in the first place, the papacy which, through an increasing process of acquisition beginning in the late twelfth century, had universally wrested control of appointment to benefices away

---

[1] For what remains the most comprehensive description of the system of papal control of church benefices as it pertains to the careers of musicians see Pamela Starr, 'Music and Music Patronage at the Papal Court, 1447–1464', unpublished PhD dissertation, Yale University (1987).

[2] For these details see Alain Derville, 'Les chanoines de Saint-Omer aux XIVe et XVe siècles', in Nicolette Delanne-Logié and Yves-Marie Hilaire (eds.), *La cathédrale de Saint-Omer: 800 ans de mémoire vive* (Paris: CNRS, 2000), 89.

from the local authority of bishops (in the case of parishes), and chapters (in the case of collegiate churches).[3] By the fifteenth century, however, a large proportion of canonries and higher offices were – via long-standing agreements with the papacy – in the direct collation of temporal magnates; and even those that were not frequently fell, following direct intervention, to appointees of the ruling *gens*.

One consequence was that the liturgy, initially performed by the canons themselves, came increasingly in the later Middle Ages to be maintained by lesser clerics, each replacing a canon and standing in, as 'vicar', for the actual beneficiary, for small pro rata payments made on the basis of attendance: a workforce already familiar from Chapters 2 and 3. While this was in one sense a function of the increasing complexity of the liturgy and in particular its musical demands, it was chiefly, especially in the larger cathedrals and collegiate churches, a reflection of the rising social and ecclesiastical status of the canons and their divorce from the real business of sacred observance. The cleavage between status and function, and its concomitant freedom from actual attendance, opened the way to what came to be seen as one of the great abuses of the medieval church: pluralism of benefices. This approach to ecclesiastical positions, and the fabulous wealth canons could accrue, led to strenuous efforts and frequent subterfuge in their pursuit, both through the papal machinery and, often, through courts of canon law.[4]

Clearly the best situated to benefit from this system were those at its centre, namely the pope and the cardinals, their relatives and familiars. But the favours and loyalties it could buy drew the practice also into the dealings of secular magnates, who sought the collation of benefices for their courtiers and favourites, with (implicit or otherwise) support for the papacy in return. This symbiosis worked with particular effectiveness for the dukes of Burgundy and especially Philip the Good. Philip's enthusiasm for a crusade and his direct support for the papacy, particularly that of the much-assailed Eugenius IV, brought with it substantial and widespread beneficial concessions. From 1428 the collations of the duke were even constituted in the form of 'rolls', with names of courtiers to receive

---

[3] For the progress of papal control over benefices from its beginnings to ubiquity see Starr, 'Music Patronage', 15–31.

[4] For a recounting of this process as it affected the composer Fede see Andrew Kirkman, 'Johannes Sohier *dit* Fede and St Omer: A Story of Pragmatic Sanctions', in Fabrice Fitch and Jacobijn Kiel (eds.), *Essays on Music and Musicians in Honour of David Fallows: Bon jour, bon an, et bonne estraine* (Woodbridge: Boydell and Brewer, 2011), 68–79.

benefices listed in pecking order for each institution under ducal control.[5] In 1436 the provost of St Omer was authorised to assign a hundred benefices to individuals named by the duke, while, among other permissions, in 1441 and 1442 the pope signed concordats limiting the extent of papal control over benefices in Burgundian territories outside the Kingdom of France. Ever-greater access to the system continued to flow from Eugenius's successors, especially following, in 1453, the fall of Constantinople and the resultant ambitions for a crusade, for which Philip was the most signal advocate. Installation of Philip's clients across the board, from the most politically significant bishoprics to legion canonries and chaplaincies, progressively cemented his political control while vastly enhancing the incomes (and pensions) of his courtiers and other adherents at no cost to his own treasury.[6]

The reach of Burgundian influence was extended especially by the bestowal on ducal favourites of many of the higher offices, particularly those of the rank of provost and dean, of cathedrals and major churches across Burgundian territories.[7] Provostships were in any case typically the preserve of members of the nobility: the position at St Omer, carrying a taxable income of eight hundred livres and entailing personal presence only on an official annual visit, was held from 1480 by Johannes de Burgundia, bastard son of John, Count of Nevers, the latter a stepson of Philip the Good.

As a result of this system of seigneurial patronage, canons were frequently unconnected to the regions in which their benefices were held and, given the increasingly permissive approach to residency, would more often than not have been absent.[8] Given, furthermore, the divorce of position from ostensible function, they need neither to have been clerics, nor even adult. Unsurprisingly this system led to widespread discontent, not least on the part of local clergy who might ostensibly have been eligible for

---

[5] See David Fiala, 'Le mécénat musical des ducs de Bourgogne et des princes de la Maison de Habsbourg. 1467–1506. Étude documentaire et prosopographique', unpublished PhD dissertation, Université de Tours, Centre d'études supérieures de la Renaissance (2002), 158–62.

[6] See Richard Vaughan, *Philip the Good: The Apogee of Burgundy* (London and Harlow: Longmans, 1970), 205–38.

[7] For details of this system see Vaughan, *Philip the Good*. For greater detail on its workings with regard to the Burgundian court chapel see Fiala, 'Le mécénat', 148–90. For more on the system as it played out in the appointment of members of the Burgundian chapel to benefices at St Omer, see below.

[8] According to the extant rule of 1227, to be deemed 'resident' a canon, following a first year of actual full residence, needed each year to spend twenty-four weeks either present, or away studying, on pilgrimage or at the papal curia (see Derville, 'Les chanoines', 90).

advancement, and for those who did obtain prebendary benefices but found their colleagues' positions occupied by outsiders, absentees, members of the laity or indeed children.

Notwithstanding all this, compared with earlier times the fifteenth century was at St Omer a period of proportionally high residence. Part of this was surely down to the relative stability of the city (discussed in the Prologue) *vis-à-vis* its surrounding regions; but a concomitant circumstance was its prosperity under Burgundian control and its cliental relationship to the ruling dukes. Local power structures also went hand in hand with the appointment of canons from local families, a situation broadly beneficial to singers since, however far afield careers were built, there was, as already noted, a widespread desire to return, in the fullness of time, to one's home locale.

Given the success of the northern maîtrises, therefore, it is unsurprising to see this career pattern giving rise to the clustering, in prominent northern cathedrals and collegiate churches, of singers or – as apparently in the case of Rembert, at least former singers – who had built their careers in illustrious choirs far from home. Nor, by the same token, is it surprising to find common patterns of employment linking the canonicates, and indeed the vicariates, of the most musically prominent establishments, shared bonds of skill and professional association leading then, as now, to intertwining patterns of employment.

Prominent in such cases are singers in the papal chapel: where better to display the skills that would oil the wheels of career advancement than at the epicentre of ecclesiastical preferment? Thus, as Craig Wright noted, a third of the musicians in the papal choir during Du Fay's tenure there – including Rembert – held (or would go on to hold) positions at Cambrai Cathedral.[9] Close connections with the papal chapel are revealed also by the surprising number of papal singers who gained prebends at St Omer, particularly in the 1470s: between June 1474 and March 1476 no fewer than three papal singers – Guillaume Decault, Guillaume Rosa and Johannes Hangion – became canons of St Omer, though only Decault seems to have taken up residence there, assuming the prebend of the deceased former Burgundian court chapel singer Toussains de Le Ruelle.[10]

[9] Craig Wright, 'Musiciens à la cathédrale de Cambrai, 1475–1550', *Revue de musicologie* 62/2 (1976), 223.
[10] Decault, dubbed 'cantor capellanus domini nostri Pape Pauli novissimi', was admitted via his procurator on 15 March 1473, having fought off a challenge for the benefice from Johannes Bultel. See II. G. 354, f. 161v; the documentation continues to f. 164r.

As a further example of the wheels-within-wheels operating in the appointment to such benefices, it is striking that Rosa and Rembert, who were both listed as singers at St Peter's in the 1470s, consecutively also held the same canonicate at St Donatian, Bruges, Rembert succeeding Rosa in 1489.[11]

The ties of home could scarcely be better illustrated than via the career of Rembert himself: canonries at Cambrai and St Donatian, Bruges, musically speaking *sans pareille*, were insufficient to lure this native of Doudeauville away from Saint-Omer, just forty-odd kilometres north-east of his birthplace. For the collégiale this was clearly a windfall: we have seen already how Rembert, papal familiar and, by 1493, notary of the sacred rota (the office that dealt with all benefices below the rank of bishop) and *abbreviator litterarum apostolicarum* (a scribal office in the apostolic chancery), was able in Rome to shepherd through the 'bulle conservatoire' and the further bull providing for Johannes de Hemont after his relinquishment of his prebend, though the 103 livres he received for his pains can only have burnished his sense of territorial loyalty. But Rembert's status and political acumen at the curia were exercised far more broadly across his musical network. Like the composer Johannes Puyllois, a papal singer earlier in the century, he clearly built up a lucrative practice as a procurator for benefices sought by a wide clerical clientele, the rump of which, it would appear, comprised his fellow singers.[12] Originally the task of the supplicant himself, the process of seeking admission to a benefice was by this stage of such complexity that anyone with the (considerable) resources necessary would employ a procurator with the legal, bureaucratic and – crucially – diplomatic skills to give his ambitions the best chance of success. Both Puyllois and Rembert were themselves, moreover, impressive collectors of benefices, surely an important calling card in acquiring supplicatory business on behalf of others. Procurators were likewise the conduit of choice for all manner of other curial processes, from exchanges of canonries by 'permutation' to dispensations of various kinds, whether concerned with plurality of benefices, permissions for absence, the waiving of the state of illegitimacy and so on.

Following, perhaps, the principle of true words being spoken in jest, some potential insights into Rembert's perceived skill as a procurator can be gleaned from the humorous poetic correspondence, long known to

---

[11] Reinhard Strohm, *Music in Late Medieval Bruges* (2nd, rev. ed., Oxford: Clarendon Press, 1990), 188.

[12] See Starr, 'Music Patronage', 38–62 for a detailed account of Puyllois's successful procuration of two benefices for Johannes Okeghem.

scholarship, concerning the singer and composer (of a single surviving rondeau) Jean Cornuel, *dit* Verjus.[13] Like Rembert a contratenor (in his case from 1466 to 1468) of the papal choir,[14] the famously wayward Verjus clearly did not share his vocal confrère's political skills. The subject of a verse 'Regime de Verjus, vicaire de Cambray' by Jean Molinet, Verjus was himself the author of a rhyming missive directed to Rembert in Rome, bemoaning his poverty and asking 'sien amy' to use his influence to find him a prebend in Cambrai ('Faictes moy donc(ques) vostre confrere En la prebende de Cambray'). He is wearied by being a petit vicaire (paid singer) of Cambrai Cathedral, and would love to have a canonry ('Je suis tané d'estre vicaire, Mieux aimeroie d'estre au grand Caire'). Appealing to Rembert's pity, he is also keenly aware of his musical colleague's skills at expediting papal bulls ('Je ne puis avoir pis que j'ay. Faictes mes bulles despeschier').

But whatever their professional connections, Verjus seems to have been in no doubt that his strongest suit with Rembert lay in the two men's shared roots, as 'two calves of the region of Boulogne' ('Deux veaux sommes de Boullenois'). According to his narrative at least, common experience, however rarefied, was easily trumped by blood and soil: 'Se la terre est nostre grand mere, Comme dit Virgile et Omere, Je tiens que vous estes mon frere Maternel, il n'est riens si vray.' Whether or not his harping on about consanguinity ('L'ung suis de vos pouvres parents' / 'Vous estes cousin au cousin') is to be taken literally, common origins, for Verjus, clearly implied duty of support.

Looked at from a broader perspective, we might alternatively view this emphasis on shared origins as a shrewd gambit, on Verjus's part, in seeking the attention of a man who clearly had much bigger fish to fry. From a musical perspective this is illustrated by Rembert's unsuccessful efforts, as witnessed by a document dated 9 September 1489, to obtain a benefice at St Omer for Josquin.[15] The nature of that hoped-for canonry begs further explanation of the nature of such appointments, since it was an 'expectative' grace: in other words the awarding to a position that had yet to fall

[13] Eugénie Droz, 'Notes sur Mᵉ Jean Cornuel, dit Verjus, petit vicaire de Cambrai', *Revue de musicologie* 7/20 (1926), 173–89 and André Pirro, 'Jean Cornuel, vicaire à Cambrai', *Revue de musicologie* 7/20 (1926), 190–203.

[14] Franz Xaver Haberl, 'Die römische "schola cantorum" und die päpstlichen Kapellsänger bis zur Mitte des 16. Jahrhunderts', *Vierteljahrsschrift für Musikwissenschaft* 3 (1887), 236–8.

[15] Jeremy Noble, 'New Light on Josquin's Benefices', in Edward E. Lowinsky and Bonnie J. Blackburn (eds.), *Proceedings of the International Josquin Festival-Conference* (London: Oxford University Press, 1976), 80–4.

vacant. Still more revealing of the nature of the jockeying for position involved in such appointments, the expectative was in this case backdated: a widespread concomitant of this cumbersome system was that the curia frequently issued competing graces for the same position, meaning that temporal priority was crucial in attempting to avoid the legal proceedings that frequently delayed – sometimes for years – the definitive filling of available openings.

A striking case in point at St Omer, one that I have outlined in detail elsewhere, concerns another composer-singer, Johannes Sohier *dit* Fede.[16] Fede, who had been resident at St Omer in the 1440s, including at least one year (1446–7) as master of the boys,[17] was granted an expectative benefice at the church dated 1 May 1462, at which time he was a singer in the chapel of the dowager Queen of France Marie d'Anjou. He lost this claim (and a good deal of money on his opponent's expenses) after a bitter canon legal battle with a rival claimant. In reality, as the full story reveals, he was on a hiding to nothing, his being one of no fewer than 1,045 claims to benefices relying on income from land at least theoretically under the aegis of the king of France issued with the same date. This unprecedented flurry of activity followed the repeal the previous year by King Louis XI of the Pragmatic Sanction of Bourges via which the French monarch had, since 1438, forbidden the right of collation by the papacy to benefices on French soil. The aim of the slew of benefices handed out on (at least ostensibly) the kalends of May was simply to appoint the king's own clients to as many vacant (or even not-yet-vacant) positions as possible before the pope had had the opportunity to do the same. Yet even given the somewhat scatter-shot nature of Fede's effort and, moreover, the extremely high places occupied by the backers of his slippery opponent Jean de la Mote, it still took the latter almost four years of legal wranglings to achieve his victory over the hapless Fede.

Fede's experience provides a case study in the challenges – and financial risks – that could face a claimant to a lucrative benefice; explains the value to such an individual of an advocate as adept and experienced as Rembert; and provides a clear illustration of the kinds of reasons that could motivate the backdating of an expectative benefice such as that bestowed on Josquin. To get some measure of the value of such positions, and the reasons why candidates worked so assiduously, and often viciously, to obtain them, a full prebend at St Omer was taxed based on an estimated income of eighty

---

[16] See Kirkman, 'A Story of Pragmatic Sanctions'.

[17] Fede's presence at St Omer is indicated in the fabric accounts for the relevant years.

livres per annum, a figure that, moreover, due to various attendant dispensations from taxation, was in reality a good deal shy of its actual value. Such a prebend, which was further linked in the case of the Josquin document to provision of another benefice in St Ghislain taxed at thirty livres (without cure of souls) or forty livres (with cure of souls) per annum, represented a handsome income. To get a sense of the desirability of a St Omer prebend, the 80 livres on which it was taxed compared (at least according to fourteenth-century tallies) to 62 at Arras, 60 at Thérouanne and Tournai, 45 at Lille, and 31.78 at Aire-sur-la-Lys.[18]

The case concerning Josquin was not Rembert's only dealing with a prebend at Saint-Omer linked to a singer associated with the papal choir: a record in the chapter acts dated only a month before the Josquin document details his involvement in appointments to a Saint-Omer prebend held fleetingly by Gaspar van Weerbeke. In this instance, though, the record clearly states that Weerbeke resigned the prebend, which was assumed by Rembert's favoured candidate and close associate, Robert de Monte.[19] And in 1488, as Jeremy Noble notes, he acted as procurator in paying the annate (the one-off papal tax, valued at half the first year's income) due on a prebend at St Gertrude, Nivelles, for 'Johanne Trutoris, clerico Camera-censis diocesis' resident of Naples, surely, as Noble points out, a reference to the great theorist and composer Johannes Tinctoris.[20] It seems likely that

---

[18] For these comparisons see Derville, 'Les chanoines', 92; but see p. 93 on the much greater actual income of a major prebend at St Omer, which was likely to have been more in the region of two hundred livres.

[19] Decima nona mensis augusti Galienus Polzone tamquam procurator Domini Roberti de Monte presbiteri certum dominis presentavit processum vigore cuius petiit instanter ipsius Robertum in possessionem realem et corporalem canonicatus et prebende recipere quos dum vixit obtinebat Magister Lu[dovicus] Toureti et post eius obitum de illis provisus extitit quidem Gaspar de Weerbeke per cuiusquidem Gasparis resignationem in manibus sanctissimi factam predictos canonicatum et prebendam ipso Ro[berto] dominus sanctissimus contulit prout in quodam processu ipsis dominis exhibito clare constat[.] Ad cuius petitionem prefati domini volentes ob honorem Magistri Nicolai Rembert eorum confratris ipsi Roberto inquantum possunt annuere responderunt quod ipsius Ro[berti] in confratrem recipient et concanonicum hac tamen conditione stante quod ipse Robertus diligenciam faciet exactam ut infra nativitate proxime litteras apostolicas ad huiusmodi receptionem necessarias et consuetas ipsis dominis decenter presentabit / aut alias receptio sua nulla. docuit sufficienter de omnibus et singulis requisitis ad adeptionem possessionis quam domini simpliciter concordarunt[.] (II. G. 355, f. 75r, 19 August 1489)

[20] Noble, 'New Light on Josquin's Benefices', 83; from Émile Brouette, *Les 'Libri Annatarum' pour les pontificats d'Eugène IV à Alexandre VI. IV. Pontificats d'Innocent VIII et d'Alexandre VI (1484–1503)*, Analecta Vaticano-Belgica, Documents relatifs aux anciens diocèses de Cambrai, Liège, Thérouanne et Tournai. Première série, vol. XXIV (Brussels: Institut historique belge de Rome, 1963), No. 193, p. 68 (20 July 1487, Cameracen.), which gives the following annotation: 'Die 27a februarii 1490 prefatus Nicolaus, procurator ipsius Johannis Trutoris, ut patet publico

the instance involving Weerbeke was a case of 'permutation', another widespread – and ultimately notorious – characteristic of the practice of appointments to benefices whereby beneficiaries would 'trade' them with one another for more mutually agreeable positions.

Rembert's role as 'fixer' in Rome was facilitated by his frequent, and often extended, periods of residence in the Eternal City. His connections there were of the highest order. The text of the bull appointing him to his first canonry at St Omer refers to him as a table companion ('commensalem') of the pope, while an entry in the chapter acts for 28 September 1491 notes, perhaps more tellingly, that he 'was and is a continuous member of the household and table companion' ('fuit et est familiaris continuus commensalis') of 'Raphael by divine mercy of the title of San Giorgio in Velabro of the holy Roman church deacon cardinal [and] chamberlain of the most holy lord our pope'.[21] A privilege for absence presented on Rembert's behalf by Robert de Monte on precisely the same day the following year implies that he had spent the intervening year (and would presumably continue to reside during the year to come) in the same household.[22] Cardinal Raffaele Riario, the 'Cardinal of San Giorgio', a grand-nephew of Pope Sixtus IV, was camerlengo, the officer in charge of all administration and legal proceedings concerning the property and income of the papal see. He was a noted patron of artists including Pinturicchio and Michelangelo, whom he was responsible for inviting to Rome, thereby paving the way for the creation of the artist's most monumental works. Beginning in the late 1480s he had built as his personal residence the vast palace, later the Palazzo della Cancelleria, where Rembert, at the expense of St Omer, would likely have resided as a

---

instrumento publicato manu Francisci Pappacode, notarii Neapolitensis in Neapoli, ubi ipse Johannes moram habet sub anno Domini 1488, indic. 7, die 18ª mensis septembris predicto anno 5° [= 1488], vigore dicti instrumenti obligavit ipsum Johannem principalem pro dicta annata.' The fact that Rembert acted in the same capacity for the canon of Cambrai Nicolas Tectoris makes the confusion that has existed between the latter and Tinctoris all the more palpable (for more on this see pp. 100–1, above).

[21] Raphaele miseratione divina titoli Sancti Georgi ad velum aureum sancte Romane ecclesie diaconus cardinalis sanctissimi domini nostri pape camerarius (II. G. 355, f. 87v). Starr notes that while most papal servants named as 'table-companions' of the pope did not, by the fifteenth century, actually dine with the pontiff, the term continued to denote privileged status ('Music Patronage', 56).

[22] Robertus de Monte procurator R[everendi] p[atris] Magistri Nicolai Rembert / presentavit dominis in capitulo capulariter congregatis privilegium impetratum a reverendo in Christo patre et domino Raphaele miseratione divina Sancti Georgii ad Velum Aureum sancte Romane ecclesie diacono cardinali sanctissimi domini nostri pape camerario de datis diei xiᵉ mensis Aprilis pontificatus sanctissimi domini nostri domini Innocentii divina providencia Pape octavi anno viii indictione decima / quidquid privilegium habuerunt pro debite presentato / et ipsum fore in curia Romana (II. G. 355, f. 93r, 28 September 1492)

member of his entourage in the 1490s. In Riario's circle he would have mingled with the great and the good of his time including quite possibly Michelangelo himself, a member of Riario's coterie in his first Roman phase of 1496–1501.

Small wonder, given his status, positions and evident skills, that Rembert was able at various stages to acquire for himself an impressive roster of benefices, at Cambrai Cathedral; St Géry, Cambrai; Notre-Dame, Antwerp; St Donatian, Bruges; and elsewhere as well as at St Omer. Yet it seems clear that, from the early 1480s on, it was to the latter, the wealthiest and most splendid collegiate establishment in the environs of his birthplace, that he chose to direct his ultimate ambitions.

Rembert's Prebendary Progress

As for many of the positions towards which he shepherded others, Rembert's own progress to his beneficial status at his chosen church was to have its twists and turns, though it is clear that from the start strong winds were blowing in his favour. If his designs on St Omer can be traced back to the early 1480s, it would still be some time before he would grace the town with his actual presence: the entry in the chapter acts detailing his 1482 appointment to a canonry notes that he is 'in Romana curia residente', and he is 'installed' in the choir via the person of his procurator Johannes Monicque.

This initial stage of his beneficial career sees his securing of a prebend that had been acquired, following long dispute at the papal curia, by one Olivier de Vledrezelle. Olivier's tenure was apparently brief, however, since he had by now died, allowing Rembert's procurator to petition, successfully, on his behalf. It is clear from the documentation, though, that the impetus behind the appointment was not local: the *procurium* was a general one at the collation of the pope, and hence valid for any available prebend becoming vacant; if, for whatever reason, this one had failed to go through, Rembert had leave to press his suit for a different position, currently in the hands of another candidate but of a status as yet not fully resolved:

But since the *procurium* was a general one without any specific reference to this prebend, the said procurator promised the lords that within six months he would have it set up for him as regards a specific *procurium* and for it to be sworn that the Master Nicolas is of legitimate birth, a specific and express avowal having been made by the same [procurator] that if on the day it should happen that Master

Nicolas be defeated concerning this prebend he would have recourse to the right indicated to him concerning the prebend which Jacobus de Bauchis holds, concerning which the case is unresolved as was explained in the letters of provision of the same Nicolas Rembert.[23]

Rembert had clearly been predestined to get a prebend at St Omer come what may. If anything were to go awry with the position formerly occupied by Vledrezelle he had another iron in the fire, namely the claim to a prebend currently occupied by, though not yet definitively assigned to, one Jacobus de Bauchis.

In fact Rembert never needed to fall back on this insurance package, but as it transpired de Bauchis was deprived of his prebend anyway, losing out in due course to still another candidate, one Johannes Maertan. Maertan's case, like Fede's already discussed, provides a vivid illustration of the ways in which the strings of local ecclesiastical preferment could be pulled – often by the agents of shifting political allegiances – and the sheer length of time such benefices could remain under dispute. Maertan appeared before the chapter on 24 April 1483 to proffer his case for de Bauchis's benefice. Clearly his claim went back a long way: it was based on the conferment of the erstwhile provost of St Omer, Simon de Luxembourg, by this stage some three years deceased. The chapter rebuffed him, first because the benefice had by this time been for more than three years in the possession of de Bauchis, who held it by gift of the duke of Burgundy, and the chapter was forbidden to disturb him in possession of it on pain of a fine of a hundred marks of silver; second because, according to the terms of the 1482 Treaty of Arras between the Houses of France and Burgundy, all benefices (expectatives included) were to remain in the possession of their holders at that time; but third, and most importantly, because bestowal of the benefice would have to have the support of the living provost. Hence if Maertan wished to press his case he would have to enlist the backing of the current provost, Johannes de Burgundia, a figure closely linked to the duke.[24]

---

[23] Verum quia procurium erat generale nulla facta specialitate de hac prebende dictus procurator promisit dominis infra sex menses facere sibi constare de speciali procurio et ad iurandum quod ipse Magister Nicholaus est de legitimo thoro natus. facta per eundem speciali et expressa protestatione quod si contingeret ipsum Magistrum Nicholaum in dies de prebenda huiusmodi evinci ipse nichilominus regressum habeat ad ius sibi pretensum in prebendam quam possidet Jacobus de Bauchis. super qua lis et causa pendet indecisa prout in litteris provisionis ipsius Nicholai Rembert exprimitur[.] (II. G. 355, f. 37r, 4 December 1482)

[24] The whole complicated situation is outlined at length in an entry in the chapter acts for 24 April 1483 (II. G. 355, f. 41v).

Clearly Maertan lost no time in pursuing matters, for on 10 October of the same year he again appears before the chapter. Referring to a petition submitted the day before, he cites a writ issued in judgement against the lords by Robert Tulleli, subdelegate of the conservator of privileges in Paris. In order to avoid the need to proceed to prosecution of the lawsuit on the appointed day, he requests that they admit him directly to the canonry. Intriguingly he also goes on to rebuff some of the chapter's prior reasons for rejecting his claim. First, he asserts that Johannes de Bauchis is not from the territory of the lord duke but is an alien and hence ineligible to enjoy the benefice according to the terms of the peace treaty of Arras (of which more shortly). More signally though – and this is where Rembert's claim re-enters the picture – he disputes the notion that de Bauchis had been in undisturbed possession of the benefice for three years, or indeed even for one. This is because two years previously a sentence had been brought against him in the Roman curia in favour of Rembert, the appeal against which by de Bauchis remained undecided and had long hung in the balance. In the event, and as so often in today's world, threat of litigation was on its own of sufficient menace for the chapter to rescind its objections, and Maertan was duly admitted to his stall, situated, since he was not ordained, in the lower ranks of the choir.[25]

---

[25] Die x^a mensis predicti Johannes Maertan iterum venit ad dominos rogans eos obnixe ut eum recipere vellent in canonicum et confratrem iuxta petitionem per eum ~~factam~~ iam pridie factam. de qua fit mentio retro xxiiii. mensis Aprilis absque prosecutione litis sive appellationis nuper per ipsos interiecte a quadam monitione per venerabilem et circumspectum virum Dominum Robertum Tulleli subdelegatum conservatoris privilegiorum Parisiensis contra eosdem dicto Johanne nuper concessa et contra ipsos executa. alias declaravit quod sibi erat necesse comparere contra eos ad diem assignatum quod tamen invite facere vellet si sibi possibile foret. In super declaravit qualiter Jacobus de Bauchis non erat de partibus domini ducis sed alienigena quare non debet gaudere beneficio articulis tractatus pacis nuper facte. Item allegavit quod dictus de Bauchis nunquam fuerat pacificus triennalis possessor y[m]o nec annualis sed iam biennio elapsa sententia lata fuit contra eundem [i.e. de Bauchis] in Romana curia et in favorem Magistri Nicholai Rembert quo tamen appellatione per eum emissa suspensa adhuc pendit et diu pependit indecisa. Quapropter hiis attentis humiliter requisivit ad tuitionem et conservationem sui iuris sese [i.e. Maerten] in possessione recepi et induci ut profertur. Domini hiis auditis intellectis et ponderatis maxime sententiis in dicta monitione comminatis licet nuper ut profertur se opposuerint et ab eisdem comminationibus appellandis duxerint non fuerint tamen opinionis ulterius eandem oppositionem persequendi sed eundem recipiendi proviso tamen quod ~~dictus~~ ipse Johannes promittet prout promisit et iuravit ipsos reddere et relevare indempnes. et nichilominus pro ipso Johannes Franchois fideiussit principaliter et in sua persona eosdem et ecclesiam a quocumque dampno dangerio et interesse relevare stipulatione solemni in manibus mei notarii subscripti emissa et passata.

Solutis igitur iuribus solitis et iuramento in forma prestito. eundem Dominum Johannem Martaen receperunt in canonicum et confratrem stallo sibi in choro in inferioribus sedibus quum non erat in sacris ordinibus constitutus assignato per vicarium domini prepositi et

Behind the raw personal ambition motivating this case, there lurk, as in the instance of Fede, larger dynastic rivalries, with Maertan, clearly a creature of the king (hence the epithet 'Johannes Franchois' which the document at one point casually assigns him), pitted against de Bauchis, a client of the Burgundian duchy. More specifically to the time, the events clearly played out against the backdrop of the Treaty of Arras, signed the previous year. This treaty, an agreement between the French King Louis XI and Maximilian I of Habsburg-Burgundy, was an attempt at resolution of the dynastic strife that had followed the death in 1477 of Charles the Bold, the last Valois duke of Burgundy, at the battle of Nancy. Since the lands ruled over by the dukes were at least nominally held as fiefs of the French crown, at Charles's death they were seized by the king. That might have been the end of the Burgundian Netherlands had Charles not, before his death, betrothed his daughter Mary of Burgundy to the Archduke Maximilian (the future Maximilian I), who vigorously defended his spouse's inheritance. Things became still more awkward, however, with Mary's own death in 1482, forcing Maximilian to defend his status as regent for their infant son, Philip the Fair. The terms of the treaty sought a resolution to this impasse via betrothal of the French dauphin to Maximilian's daughter Margaret of Austria, with attendant territorial agreements. As outlined in the Prologue, though, this quickly unravelled, with Saint-Omer caught up in the ensuing strife between the king and (future) emperor, including a brief period under French control, before settling down from 1493 to a Habsburg-Burgundian dominion that was to endure until 1678.

Unsurprisingly given the stakes, the provision under the terms of the treaty – mentioned a number of times in the St Omer documents – for benefices acquired before its signing to remain uncontested failed to hold any more firmly than the treaty itself. In the event it was not only de Bauchis who was unable to capitalise on its provision and was forced to succumb to a client of the king: far grander reputations were also in balance. This is clear from the dispute over a canonry between Claude Carondelet and Nicolas de Hacqueville, both dignitaries of an altogether different order. Carondelet, a future grand chancellor of Flanders and Burgundy under Maximilian I and dean of Besançon, was the scion of a family of high-ranking courtiers and the son of Jean Carondelet, also Burgundian chancelier and provost of St Donatian, Bruges, and perhaps

---

iuramento solito as[illegible] ut moris est emisso per eundem presentibus ad hec Balduino de Grouzelliers hostiario capituli et Petro Fin testibus ad promissa omnia vocatis[.] (10 October 1483, II. G. 355, f. 46r)

best known today as the subject of an important donor portrait with Virgin and Child by Gossaert now in the Louvre. His opponent, a client of the opposing force of the king, was Nicolas de Hacqueville, counsellor and president of the Parlement in Paris, provost of the royal abbey of St Martin in Tours and abbot of Livry, and brother of Jacqueline de Hacqueville, long thought to be the woman of that name who was the subject of songs by, and possible lover of, the composer Antoine Busnoys.[26]

Hacqueville's case, pressed by the king via his *sergent a cheval* Nicolas de Marly, is rebuffed, his backers being informed that 'by the statutes of the church, which Nicole de Hacqueville has promised and sworn to observe, it is expressly declared that when anyone has for a year and a day been the undisturbed possessor of any canonry, he cannot be disturbed or hindered in the enjoyment of its fruits'. Since, as the judgement states, Carondelet has already occupied the benefice since he was eight or ten years old (he was by now around sixteen) he would presumably have been thought to be on safe ground.[27] Yet all that notwithstanding, and while the chapter acts do not recount the full sequence of events, Hacqueville apparently succeeded in wresting Carondelet's canonry from him: an entry from 11 September 1485 sees Johannes de Hemont presenting a procuratorium of 'Master Nicholas de Hacqueville canon of this church, together with the privilege of receiving its fruits, because he is residing in the University of Paris'.[28] Only a few months later, on 16 February 1486, we witness the

---

[26] The identity of this Jacqueline has been complicated by the existence of another woman of the same name who demonstrably moved in poetic-musical courtly circles; it remains unclear which, if either, of them was the Parisian noblewoman in question. See Paula Higgins, 'Parisian Nobles, a Scottish Princess, and the Woman's Voice in Late Medieval Song', *Early Music History* 10 (1991), 145–200; on Nicolas de Hacqueville see p. 155.

[27] 'Est assavoir quils aoyent bien ce que dit leur avoit et quils se conderoient bien de mesprendre advertissant que ledit Maistre Claude des a viii ans. ou x. ans. a este receu en pacifique possession de la prebende et chanoinie de ceans vacant par la mort de Maistre Jehan Haguenin or est il que par les status del eglise lesquels M[aistr]e Nicole de Hacqueville a promis et jure entretenir est par expres declaire que quant aulcun est par an et jour possesseur paisible daulcune chanoinerie lon ne le poeult inquieter ne empester la joyssance de ses fruys . . .' (II. G. 355, f. 42v, 13 June 1483). Carondelet was already a canon when, on 18 November 1476, a privilege was presented in chapter by canon Theodoricus de Vitry for him to spend the year from 24 June 1475 (when he would have been barely eight) studying law at the University of Dole (in the diocese of Besançon) (see II. G. 354, f. 207r).

[28] '. . . Jo[hannes] de Hemont presentavit dominis procuratorium Magistri Nicolai de Hacqueville canonici huius ecclesie unacum suo privilegio de fructibus percipiendis quia resedit in alma universitate Parisiense ("Lovanense" crossed out)' (II. G. 355, f. 62r, 11 September 1485). This was not Hacqueville's first attempt at a St Omer canonry: he had been presented, again by Johannes de Hemont, on 29 March 1476 only to be rebuffed at the last minute for not being in holy orders. Since this deficiency did not (in the case just discussed) stand in the way of Johannes Maerten, who was

reception to a canonry in the gift of Maximilian I of 'Claude Carondelet, protonotarius of the holy apostolic see and dean of Besançon'.[29] Since this is precisely the date on which Maximilian was elected king of the Romans one should probably surmise that this collation, likely one of many, had become available via his elevation. The 'small print' in this instance would seem to fill in the intervening events: Carondelet has not, for this new post, provided the usual proof that he is of legitimate birth, but the requirement is waived 'because at another time in the past Carondelet had sent the lords a valid document with his oath when he was admitted to another prebend'.[30] In other words, Carondelet, a canon (albeit an absent and juvenile one) of some years' tenure, has been ousted from this prior position by a client of the king, and has been installed, on the availability of another vacancy in the gift of his patron, in an alternative prebend.[31]

Clearly any customs governing appointments to the chapter had little purchase in the face of shifting political control. Yet it would appear from the documentation in this case, as in that of Maerten, above, that – at least prima facie – a year represented some kind of statute of limitation for appeals against beneficial appointments, any objection, from any quarter, effectively putting the clock back to zero. It would surely be hard to overestimate the level of disruption, and extent of legal litigation, that could arise from circumstances of this nature. Such leeway for the possibility of appeal would likely have tempted anyone with sufficient means and the remotest chance of success to mount a case on his own behalf against a sitting candidate, presumably secure also in the knowledge that the very act of appeal would open up a year-long window during which any unsuccessful suit could be refashioned for a subsequent attempt.

Given the city's history within ducal territory and its attendant wealth under Burgundian control, such clientelism on the part of the king seems hardly likely to have been welcomed. Hence we should probably sense

---

likewise presented to a stall in the lower form, one is bound to suspect other reasons for the chapter's demurral in this case (the record is on II. G. 354, f. 199v).

[29] ... Claudio Carondelet sancte sedis apostolice prothonotarii ac ecclesie Bisuntinensis decani (II. G. 355, f. 63v, 16 February 1486)

[30] ... tamen quia aliis preteritis temporibus documentum suffici[ens] cum juramento suo dominis emiserat dum ad aliam prebendam fuerat admissus ipse Carondelet ob reverentiam sancte sedis apostolice recipere gratiose duxerunt ... (f. 63v)

[31] Given all this, the appointment on 22 September 1486 of one Cornelis Russart to a prebend 'vacant through the death of Claude Carondelet' presents a conundrum: Claude Carondelet, dean of Besançon, lived until 1518. Presumably the scribe simply mistook one non-resident canon for another, or, more likely, mistook vacancy through resignation for vacancy through death.

more than the chapter's habitual parsimoniousness in its equivocal response to the request of the aldermen that they provide a delegation to join with the city's own contingent to proceedings related to the peace treaty in Arras the following April. While the lords agree to send representatives, recognising the church's role in city governance as one of the three estates and hence feeling that their presence would be appropriate, if not actually essential, they do so only on condition that 'this be done at the city's expense, and not at their own'.[32] But the case of Carondelet vs Hacqueville reveals the direction of the political winds in the wake of the Treaty of Arras: the king and, as a corollary, his clients were – at least for now – in the ascendant.

Returning from the macro level of regional politics to its effects on the collégiale, we can see from Maertan's case that Rembert's interest in a St Omer canonry had extended back at least to the year before that in which his own supplications first emerge in the chapter acts (i.e. 1481). In the end, and notwithstanding the evident impact of his actions on the outcome of the struggle for de Bauchis's stall, Rembert himself had no need of it; but his securing of de Vledrezelle's erstwhile canonry was very far from the end of his beneficial designs on St Omer.

On 22 October 1483, not even a year after securing his first canonry, Rembert petitioned for a second, asking to unite it with his first. This time he had acquired leave via the curia to receive the revenue of the prebend of the 'altera portione' of the parish of St Aldegonde.[33] If the wind had been behind Rembert the previous year, however, on this occasion his experience was not such plain sailing. Demanding, through his procurator Robert

---

[32] Die xii^e dicti mensi Aprilis Balduinus du Longpre et Guillaume de Le Neeusuerue scabini deputati venerunt ad dominos ad eum finem quod deputare vellent certos e suis pro eundo Atrebatum. ad exhibendum ad manus illustrissimorum dominorum de Beaujeu et aliorum pro parte Christianissimi Regis eiusque illustrissimi domini Delphini nati dominorum deputatorum illustrissimam domicellam Margaretam ducissam Burg[undie] etc. iuxta tractatum pacis et fedus coniugii initi nuper et compromissi inter ipsos Delphinum et Margaretam requirens ut domini de capitolo tamquam de principali parte membri ecclesie sociare vellent et comitari eosdem de villa.

Domini habita deliberatione inter se responderunt quod licet ipsi de villa quam plura suo capite fecerint per se absque evocando dominos ut puta[tum] ponendo certos officiarios et scabinos et deponendo cum tamen villa et regimen eius sit posita in manibus trium statuum dicte ville responderunt se esse promptos et paratos ibidem deputare et comparere proviso quod omnia viagia huiusmodi et alia similia si que deinceps fieri contingat fiant communibus expensis ville et non suis propriis. (II. G. 355, f. 41r, 12 April 1483)

[33] See II. G. 355, 22 October 1483. St Aldegonde, its position marked by a fountain on today's Place Victor Hugo, was a parish church that, increasingly derelict following its fall into obsolescence at the Revolution, was demolished following the collapse of its tower in 1800.

de Monte, that the chapter release the prebend and its fruits to him within six days, his importunity was countered by obduracy. The problems begin with his paperwork (*procuratorium*), which is found by the chapter to be incomplete. Nonetheless, the lords agree that if Rembert returns with it in order, they will award him the prebend, with one proviso: that he accept it singly, not conjoined with his existing benefice. It is never made clear what the nature of such unification may be and hence why Rembert found it to be so desirable and the chapter so objectionable. It is possible, however, that the reason lies in the status of the dean, who (alone of the chapter members) from the eleventh century onwards was provided with a double prebend.[34] On the chapter's part, there may have been discomfort with an 'ordinary' canon occupying a position of privilege normally restricted to the dean; on Rembert's part, a unified double canonry likely represented an accelerated step towards the prize that, on securing the decanal stall some ten years later, he would ultimately attain.

At any rate, the strident nature of Rembert's efforts suggests that he fully expected to be successful, and in such circumstances it is tempting to speculate that he had in some sense been led to believe that the chapter was preparing to manoeuvre him into the position of dean. Whatever the case, the substance of which will likely remain obscure, the chapter tried various avenues to prevent him from achieving his goal. In the initial stages it granted a grace period for Rembert to get his *procuratorium* in order, meanwhile recommending that he be provided with the prebend but without uniting it with the one already in his possession. While the meaning of the documentation, at more than five centuries' distance, is in places opaque, it would appear that the lords are offering – provided Rembert supplies the correct paperwork and agrees to hold off for a period of six months from further appeals to the curia to have his two canonries united as a single benefice – to release its fruits to him from the moment he enters into possession of it; if he refuses, on the other hand, the dispute can continue indefinitely and the six-month deadline will have no force.

In the event the chapter's entreaties fell on deaf ears: the following 13 February we learn of a 'highly rigorous and penal' papal 'monitorium' – essentially a threat of (unspecified) penalties if the chapter fails to comply – that has been received at Rembert's behest. The chapter is clearly shaken by the severity of the pope's missive; nonetheless, they say, their legal representative (Petrus de Sancto Amando) cannot unambiguously establish

---

[34] See Derville, 'Les chanoines', 89.

from the monitorium what they are expected to obey, and neither the principal (Rembert) nor his procurator is present to give clarity to the situation. Thus the chapter is seeking out legal advice to mount an appeal. Fearful though they may be of the severity of the pope's threats, the principle at stake is clearly of sufficient moment to the chapter that they are not about to give up easily to Rembert's demands.[35]

By 23 April Rembert's procurator Robert de Monte has 'in his hands a satisfactory procuration' to replace the inadequate one first submitted, to which the lords assent. Thus Rembert has his second prebend, but not the desired unification with his first. The situation comes to a head on 1 July 1484. While again the detail is not easy to tease out, it appears that Rembert has accused the lords of failing to respond to the demands of the papal monitorium, on the alleged grounds that the pope has been badly advised. The chapter denies his interpretation, and cites advice, sought out from legal authorities by Nicaise Ernoult, to the effect that Rembert's case is not credible. Accordingly it declares that anyone troubled by Rembert or his representatives concerning this matter shall be compensated for all loss 'at the expense of the whole chapter and church'.[36]

The presentation on 28 August by Rembert's procurator, Robert de Monte, of Johannes de Quercu as his vicar for the new canonry suggests his acceptance of the status quo. But in reality this is far from the end of the story: barely two weeks later, on 11 September, the lords instruct their representative Ludovicus Touret, who is leaving for Rome, to face down at the curia the 'condemnations and penalties' (whose substance remains unstated) 'unjustly executed' by Rembert's procurators, in order that 'a restorative and timely solution may be provided'.[37] Touret is assigned a written procuration to take with him and packed off the next day with a satchel for the necessary lawsuits and apostolic letters, and four pounds in silver coins for his trouble.

Thereafter the issue disappears from the documents. The outcome being therefore unknown, the absence of written evidence of appointment of Rembert to a unified prebend nonetheless surely, on balance, suggests that he was forced to give way. All came good for him in the fullness of time, however: on 1 January 1494 he is sworn in to the post he had surely had in his sights all along, that of dean. As usual, he is absent for the occasion,

---

[35] II. G. 355, f. 51r.   [36] II. G. 355, f. 54r.

[37] ... domini solitis postpositis contulerunt mutuo super certis censuris et penis in eosdem per procuratores Domini Nic[holai] Rembert iniuste executis ut de remedio provideretur salubri et oportuno[.] (II. G. 355, f. 55r)

presumably in Rome and likely still in the entourage of Cardinal Riario. His procurator Robert de Monte swears his required oath and is installed in the decanal position by the vicar of the (likewise absent) provost.[38]

The deanship of St Omer was a substantial ecclesiastical plum, assumed by Rembert through the resignation of his predecessor Simon Godeffroy.[39] It may be that Godeffroy's departure was not entirely of his own volition: while Rembert's bull of provision, mostly formulaic in nature, seems to suggest that his predecessor's resignation was linked to illness, he was still alive when, some three and a half years later, arrangements were made with him for the provision of rents to support his obit.[40] More than a year after Rembert's assuming of his post as dean, the chapter acts detail Godeffroy's disposal of his benefices in the city, the most significant being his canonry at the collégiale exchanged, via permutation, with none other than Robert Fabri, for a canonry at the collegiate church of St Pierre, Aire-sur-la-Lys.[41] It seems curious, to say the least, that Godeffroy would have relinquished the deanship of St Omer, a dignity of a level typically vacated only by death, for a mere canonry at an inferior institution. Whatever the reality of the situation, details in Rembert's executors' account reveal lingering bad blood with Godeffroy whose origins extend back to this changeover of power. It appears from the relevant entry that the vacating of the deanship 'by pension' (as opposed to death) entails payments into that pension by the departing dignitary's successor. Rembert, it is alleged, had short-changed Godeffroy and, moreover, had deducted costs for the expedition of his bulls, which he should not have done, causing great and long-lasting

---

[38] ... Robertum de Monte tamquam procuratorem prefati Magistri Nicolai ad possessionem dicti decanatus receperunt et admiserunt ut moris est[.] Quiquidem de Monte nomine procurationis solitum iuramentum in forma prestitit et iuravit cum protestationibus solitis. solvitque iura etc. fuit etiam per vicarium domini prepositi in stallo decani installatus et in loco decani positus ut moris est etc. (II. G. 355, f. 100v)

[39] The bull of provision states: 'We allow [indulgemus] you, since if perhaps Lord Simon at the time of his aforesaid resignation was in a state of some infirmity and it chanced that he died of the same infirmity within twenty days of this resignation, that the said deanship should be considered to have been made vacant not by the death but by the resignation of the said Simon ...' ('... si forsan Dominus Simon tempore resignationis predicte in aliqua infirmitate constitutus foret et ipsum infra viginti dies post huiusmodi resignationem decedere ex eadem infirmitate contingat quod dictus decanatus non per obitum sed per resignationem eiusdem Simonis vacasse censeatur voluntate posteriori predicta ceterisque contrariis non obstantibus auctoritate apostolica tenore presentum indulgemus.') This passage, formulaic and cast in the subjunctive though it is, nonetheless, in the act of its provision, suggests that it was motivated by a specific circumstance (II. G. 355, f. 101v).

[40] II. G. 355, f. 118v (1 July 1496); f. 127r (16 July 1497); f. 127v (31 July 1497); f. 128r (11 August 1497).

[41] II. G. 355, 24/29 April 1495

resentment. In recompense Godeffroy's heirs request not direct compensation, but, out of respect for their relative's soul, the purchase of ornaments for his personally founded chapel in the collégiale. The executors, clearly accepting this as (at least in principle) reasonable, answer the request for expense of fifty-six livres with the actual outlay of a more grudging twelve livres.[42]

The bull appointing Rembert as dean makes the standard proviso that no more than two benefices held by a single appointee should be parish churches or their perpetual vicariates, a stipulation presumably required to ensure the safeguarding of pastoral needs. In the process, though, it details the impressive haul of benefices that Rembert was actually holding at the time: the parish church of Martigny in the diocese of Geneva, the archdeaconate of Hainault in the diocese of Cambrai, the provostship of the collegiate church of St Géry, Cambrai (albeit at that point still under dispute with another claimant), and the priorate of the Cluniac priory of Rumilly-le-Comte, some twenty-six kilometres south-west of Saint-Omer and around twenty kilometres east of his birthplace of Doudeauville.[43] This last post, which Rembert retained until his death, was occupied 'in commendam': in other words he held it 'in trust' as patron rather than 'in titulum' as a functioning officer of the priory. As commendatory abbot he would have drawn the abbot's income without, of course, being held to provide anything in terms of duties or residence. This strikingly egregious mode of patronage was a favourite of Philip the Good, whose assignment of senior courtiers to such posts began with the 1447 appointment as commendatory abbot of St Bertin of Guillaume Fillastre the Younger, counsellor of the duke from 1440 and, from 1461, chancellor of the Order of the

---

[42] II. G. 484, f. 47r.

[43] Evidence gathered by Dom Ursmer Berlière records further benefices held by Rembert: in 1481 he was rector of the church of St Martin outside the walls of Aire-sur-la-Lys, while *c.*1490 he is detailed as a canon of Notre-Dame, Arras (Ursmer Berlière, *Inventaire analytique des Diversa Cameralia des Archives vaticanes (1389–1500) au point de vue des anciens diocèses de Cambrai, Liège, Thérouanne et Tournai* (Rome, Namur, Paris: Institut historique Belge; Delvaux; Champion, 1906), 164, 170. Further evidence, found by David Fiala, reveals that he also held the chaplaincy of St Alexis at the beghinage of Bruges, which at his death passed to Philippe Haneton (Archives Générales du Royaume, Bruxelles, Chambre de Comptes AGR, CC 20398, 5th account of Maistre Philippe Haneton). My thanks to David Fiala for this information. Haneton, giving some sense of the stature of individuals with whom Rembert shared beneficial interests, was a significant figure at the Habsburg-Burgundian court: he was future first secretary of the Grand Council of Charles V (from 1518), treasurer of the Order of the Golden Fleece (from 1520), and donor, with his wife Marguerite, of a famous triptych of the pietà by Bernard van Orley now in the Musées Royaux des Beaux Arts, Brussels.

Golden Fleece.[44] Since responsibility for payment on Rembert's behalf of his annate for the Rumilly post had been assumed by Simon Godeffroy, it would appear that, at least by the point the bills were issued (2 May 1494), the two were still on reasonable terms.[45]

Finally on 9 July Rembert appears in person to swear his oath according to the statutes. He is formally installed in the choir by Philippus de Bricqua, vicar of the provost, before returning to the chapter, where he is seated, by Hugo de Monchy as longest-standing canon, in the dean's position and bestows on all canons present the kiss of peace. On the 30th of the same month he presented for his first residency; but even this, his statutory year of 'full' residence, is peppered with (albeit brief and local) absences, some in the company of the provost. On the 31 July following he was deemed to have completed his first year's residence, and on 15 June of the succeeding year he received certification from the chapter to the effect that he had been resident at that point for more than a year and intended to continue. Like so many other church dignitaries of advancing years, it seems likely that Rembert was now planning a more settled lifestyle; at any rate, save for one further journey to Rome for the great jubilee year of 1500 announced by Alexander VI,[46] his peregrinations across the Alps, at least to judge from the chapter acts, were now at an end.

Rembert and Church Politics

Sedentary though Rembert's lifestyle may have become, however, it was hardly one of uninterrupted tranquillity. As in ecclesiastical houses else-where, the close familiarity of cloistral existence often bred contempt from which not even the deanship could shield him. This erupted violently in

---

[44] See Vaughan, *Philip the Good*, 235.

[45] See Brouette, *Les 'Libri Annatarum'*, 122–3: 'Die 2ª (maii 1494) unum par bullarum pro Simone Ordefroy [sic] canon. ecclesie S. Audomari de Sancto Audomaro, Morinensis dioc., super fructibus 39 lib. gross. monete Flandrie super fructibus prioratus de Rumiliaco, dicte dioc., pro Nicolao Rembert solvenda.' *Pace* David Fiala ('Le mécénat', 189), it would not appear that Godeffroy was actually the holder of the priorate before Rembert. That Godeffroy was not the holder of the priorate for at least some of his tenure as dean of St Omer is confirmed by another entry in Brouette dated 19 May 1485, recording payments due from Ludovico Toureti for two annates, including that of the priorate of Rumilly, on behalf of the abbot of St Symphorian, Trier (*Les 'Libri Annatarum'*, 19).

[46] In festo Beati Mathei Dominus Decanus N. Rembert recessit ab hoc oppido ad perficien[dum] suam intentionem per[a]gendi et visitandi limina sanctorum Beatorum Petri et Pauli hoc anno iubileo[.] (II. G. 356, f. 42r, 21 September 1500)

1497 when, around two o'clock in the afternoon on 18 May his fellow canon Johannes Derviller burst into his house with another man and after launching 'many injurious words, in spiteful spirit attacked him furiously, wishing to cut him with a knife and, grasping the dean by the neck, tried violently to suffocate him'.[47] This turn of events is particularly shocking given the long association of the two combatants: some seven years previously, as scribe of the chapter, Derviller had accompanied Rembert on his negotiations in Rome over the 'bulle conservatoire'.[48] While the precise details of Derviller's grievance will probably never be known, the prehistory of this incident in the chapter acts allows us to retrieve at least their outlines. The story as recorded begins the previous 9 December. From a meeting that day we learn that 'the lords determined for the sake of peace and concord to communicate with Master Johannes Derviller concerning each of the differences and [to do so] in writing, and for this purpose the lord dean, [and the canons] Judocus Dausque, Philippus de Bricqua and Eugene Labitte were commissioned', also calling in some of the monks of St Bertin.[49] The 11th of the next month sees further efforts at mediation:

since the dispute that had begun between the dean and chapter and Master Johannes Derviller hung unresolved, for the sake of making and keeping the peace the lords ordered that the individual petitions be written down, and that [the case] be decided in accordance with the requirements of the law, with the rights of both sides being preserved. The same Derviller promised to recognise everything in the presence of a judicial authority, and to consent to the sentence.[50]

Sure enough, five days later following up on the decision made, the lords order that Derviller should articulate in writing his rights as he sees them concerning the differences between himself and the chapter so that a

---

[47] ... Magister Johannes Derviller die xviii huius post prandium circa horam secundam vel circiter intravit domum suam unacum alio homine intravitque cameram ipsius in qua post plura verba iniuriosa per dictum Derviller eidem decano prolata animo malivolo invasit furiose et voluit eum percuttere cultello accipiens eundem decanum per collum nisus est eum suffocare. (II. G. 355, f. 125v)

[48] See above, p. 34.

[49] ... domini decreverunt pro bono pacis et concordie communicare cum Magistro Joh[anne] Derviller super singulis differenciis et in scriptis et ad hoc commissi fuerunt domini decanus Ju[docus] Dausque Phi[lippus] de Bricqua et Eug[enius] Labitte et secundum scripta faciant responsum in scriptis vocansque dominos de Sancto Bertino[.] (II. G. 355, f. 122v)

[50] ... super controversia mota inter dominos decanum et capitulum ac Magistrum Johannem Derviller indecisa pendente pro pacificatione et pace habenda domini ordinaverunt quod de singulis peticionibus fiat scriptum. et secundum quod iuris ordo postulat servato iure cuilibet ordinetur[.] idem Derviller facere promisit omnia recognoscere coram iusticia et consentire in sententiam. (II. G. 355, f. 123r)

formal hearing on them may be held at the court of Montreuil-sur-Mer. Thereafter his own acknowledgement of what is agreed before the judicial authority should expeditiously be drawn up in the usual form and stored safely in the treasury.[51]

The next entry on this topic, on 20 January, gets to the nub of the matter: Derviller exhibits a written deposition 'concerning the different states between the lords and himself concerning the tithes of St Martin which the lords have received'. As may be expected, at the root of the dispute is money, with Derviller apparently believing himself overtaxed for the tithes on his prebend (of St Martin outside the walls) vis-à-vis the payments made by his confrères.[52] The source of the problem, linking back to the involvement, noted above, of monks of St Bertin, seems to have been his prebend's location, outside the walls and adjacent to the abbey. A chapter entry for 5 August 1496 reveals strife that has arisen from the fact that St Martin was responsible for 'levying in several places tithes belonging to my lords the dean and chapter and my lords the abbot and convent of St Bertin conjointly'.[53] A further notice demonstrating that, sure enough, Derviller was embroiled in this dispute turns up the following 2 June: here we learn that 'the lords have ordered Marandus Danvet to go to St Bertin to learn whether they may wish to agree concerning the lawsuit of the tithes of St Martin against Master Johannes Derviller and whether they are happy to send back expenses and corrections'.[54]

---

[51] Die xvi[ta] eiusdem mensis domini insequendo conclusionem factam die xi[a] predicta domini ordinaverunt quod Magister Johannes Derviller redigat in scriptis conclusiones et iura super quibus ipse se stare vult super differenciis exeuntibus inter dominos et dictum Johannem Derviller ut singula possint pacificari et ea omnia coram iusticia Mon[ster]oli recognoscente et super recognicione littere in forma debita prolate ea[dem] expediantur et in thesauria conserventur[.] (II. G. 355, f. 123r)

[52] The wording and lack of clarity of the document make it somewhat ambiguous, but the following would seem to allow access at least to its essence: 'Le xx[e] jour dudit mois Maistre Jehan Derviller exhiba en capitle ung intendit escript touchant le different estat entre messires et luy pour les dismes de St Martin lequel messires ont recette et ont commis a Maistre Josse G[eorges] Ricamez Eug[ene] Labitte et Ja[cques] Plurion faire ung intendit Ys[aac?] Lebrecq et honneur de l'eglise.' It would appear that his colleagues are being enjoined in response to put forward their own deposition, 'Ys[aac?] Lebrecq' presumably being a legal notary whose services will be enlisted for the task (II. G. 355, f. 123r).

[53] ... les censsiers du cure de Sainct Martin sefforcoyent de lever en plusieurs lieux les dismes appartenant a messires les doyen et cap[it]le et messires abbe et couvent de St Bertin coniounctement. (II. G. 355, f. 119r)

[54] ... domini ordinaverunt Domino Marando Danvet ut vadat ad Sanctum Bertinum ad informandum an velint consentire in concordiam quoad processum decimarum Sancti Martini contra Magistrum Johannem Deruiller et si sint contenti remittere expensa et emendas[.] (II. G. 355, f. 126r)

Whether or not Derviller had actually given an assurance to obey the final ruling, it is patently obvious from his assault on Rembert that – whatever its eventual constitution – he was of no mind to abide by it, and for his part the dean, following his ordeal, was not about to compromise. The offer, following the attack, of the abbot of St Bertin to intervene in mediation is politely turned down by Rembert, who avows himself to pursue the matter legally: no concord will reign unless through the consent of the chapter and of the dean.[55]

While the chapter has been deliberating on the object of their ire, Derviller himself has been languishing in detention at their pleasure. We learn on 29 May 1497 (11 days after the attack) that

my lords have resolved through common consent that monseigneur the dean, accompanied by Master Josse Dausque, Eugene Labitte, with the procurator of the church will assemble before monseigneur the provost on the assigned day against Master Johannes Derviller, requiring to have justice from the said Derviller. And in the event that he should wish to redouble his contempt, to make clear on his emergence from prison that neither the dean nor the chapter will ever consent to the release of the said Derviller except by consent of the assembled parties.[56]

Clearly the hearing was held this same day and, the opposing positions having been presented, the provost handed down his judgement. Derviller must seek pardon, first from the provost and then, at the next chapter meeting, formally from the dean and chapter. Thereafter he is to depart the city within eight days of the sentence to reside in a university or on the property of one of his other benefices; neither is he to return to the town within three years, on pain of suspension from divine office and privation of his benefices 'under our [i.e. the provost's] collation, unless by our

---

[55] Item dominus abbas Sancti Bertini per organum sui granetarii et sui ballivi Martini de Wyssocq supplicari fecit inducere pacem in facto Magistri Johannis Derviller se offerendo si in aliquo posset auxilium ferre libenter faciet[.] Quibus responsum fuit eidem humiliter regraciando de bona caritate quam habet inter nos inducere pacem supplicarunt quod sit contentus quod fiat iusticia / Et ad eandem iusticiam et reparacionem tanti excessus dominus decanus in capituli promisit iniuriam sibi illatam prosequi et nunquam ad aliquam concordiam aut pacem pervenire nisi de consensu dominorum et similiter capitulum in generali nunquam devenient ad pacem nisi eis de consensu et voluntate prefati domini decani. (II. G. 355, 26 May 1497, f. 125v)

[56] ... messires ont delibere de comm[une] consentement que monsieur le doyen accompagnie de Maistre Josse Dausque et Maistre Eugene Labitte avec le procureur deleglise seront present devant monseigneur le prevost a le jour qui est assigne contre Maistre Jeh. Derviller en requerant estre faite justice dudit Derviller / et ou cas quil le voulsist [sic] relargir desprison eulx exposer a son eslargessement accordans tant ledit doyen que cap[it]le de jamais consentir a la delivrance dudit Derviller que par consentement des partyes convenitement etc. (II. G. 355, 125v)

intervening grace and authority'. Two days later Derviller, now duly pleading for pardon, hears the provost's sentence read out before the chapter. He is to be permitted to keep the income from his prebend provided he stays away, so that he cannot 'by word or deed inflict any injuries or trouble on any of the canons or their subordinates'. The final sting, though, is that he is to reimburse the chapter for all its expenses.[57]

The judgement and its further corollaries clarify that 'there has long been dispute between the lords and the said Derviller over the sequestration of incomes';[58] long enough, clearly, to lead to breaking point. Even following the sentence, Derviller is to be kept on a short leash: he is allowed to retain his income, receiving it via an intermediary, but at the end of a year, and again at the end of the second, must apply for the same permission for the year to come. He is also required to abide by the authority of the lords and their chosen arbitrators regarding the conclusion they reach on the 'existing dispute', clearly a reference to the level of sequestered tithes that led to his violent outburst in the first place. Provided he behaves himself according to these terms he can look forward to being pardoned, at least for his insubordination, by the dean and chapter.

For his own part, Rembert will forgive the defamation to which his adversary has subjected him in writing, but, it would appear, intends to

---

[57] Die ultima eiusdem mensis Magister Johannes Derviller acquiescens cuidem sentencie per r[everendum] p[atrem] dominum prepositum comparuit in capitulo rogaturus veniam secundum dictam sententiam cuius tenor sequitur: prolata xxix^a eiusdem mensis in aula presente dicto Derviller Christi nomine invocato pro tribunali et ad iura reddenda in aula nostre prepositure sedentes visis articulis fama communi et publica referente per nostrum promotorem officii actorem contra Magistrum Johannem de Derouiller [sic] rectorem ecclesie parochialis Sancti Martini dicti oppidi Sancti Audomari et ea de causa nomine iustitiarium et subditum reum exhibitis responsionibus per ipsum reum ad eosdem facta consideratoque quod ipse reus vive vocis oraculo se obtulit stare super hiis omnibus nostre ordinationi dicimus declaramus et sententialiter pronuntiamus ipsum reum a nobis tamquam suo iudice ordinationem veniarii petere debere de omnibus fore factis per ipsum commissis deinde a dominis decano et capitulo collegialiter et in eorum loco capitulari congregatis proxima die capitulari a die date presentis sentencie computando / quodque presens oppidum Sancti Audomari exibit infra octo dies etiam a dato presentis sentencie computando ad residentiam faciendi in aliqua universitate vel super aliquo suorum beneficiorum nec antedictum oppidum revertetur tribus annis continuis durantibus sub pena suspensionis a divinis privationisque suorum beneficiorum ad nostram collocationem pertinentium nisi nostre gratia et auctoritate intervenientibus, proviso tamen quod de fructibus dicte ecclesie parochialis Sancti Martini gaudebit integre licet continuam residentiam debeat inhibendo insuper eidem reo sub eisdem penis, ne a cetero aliquas iniurias aut molestias cuiquam canonicorum aut aliquorum nostrorum subditorum verbo vel facto irroget ipsum reum in omnibus expensis taxatione nobis imposterum condempnantes. (II. G. 355, 125v-6r)

[58] ... iampridem questio sit inter domines et dictum Derviller super sequestratione fructuum ... (f. 126r)

proceed to prosecute him for the physical injuries he has sustained. Alternatively, he muses, 'perhaps God will forgive him everything'.[59] The dispute over the level of the tithes for the parish of St Martin will also be continued, with consultation proceeding with the abbey of St Bertin 'regarding the legal proceedings about the tithes' and further legal hearings promised in Montreuil. On 2 June Derviller appears before the chapter, agreeing to the provost's judgement. Various avenues for keeping the peace are explored, and the opposing parties agree to address all their disputes separately. Emotions still evidently running high, however, 'after hostile words blew up the same Derviller left'.[60] We then learn that he has the previous Monday appealed against his banishment and called the opposing parties to judgement 'before the lord dean of Thérouanne, commissary in this region and judge between the parties. The oft-mentioned Johannes Derviller said, with indignant and angry spirit and threateningly, that if an enforcement of law were made against him he would do everything else on his part to the prejudice of the said lords or any specific canons.'[61]

In the process Derviller singles out Dausque and Labitte, 'who had earlier been deputed and commissioned to concern themselves with and direct the aforesaid suits on behalf of the said chapter', accusing Dausque of double-dealing via recourse to secular courts.[62] All this bluster notwithstanding, however, and while not agreeing with the judgement handed out to him, Derviller – as we learn from a note in the margin – has nevertheless

---

[59] The script for this passage in the chapter acts is very unclear, with many superscript lines added (possibly suggesting entry as the proceedings were being formulated). The following is a diplomatic, but necessarily tentative, transcription of the relevant passage: 'Et de emendis se referunt eidem Magistro Johanni ut talem faciat diligen[ciam] quod ab eisdem absolvatur omnis res sua et agat. Insuper quod cumque(?) Derviller libellum famosum contra dominum decanum scripserat promisit et dixit se non velle prosequi nec sustinere procurio eidem renunciavit et renunciare promisit sed que ad lesionem et iniuriam testatus fuit ipsam prosequi inposterum vel forsan propter omnia deum remittere[.]' (f. 126r)

[60] ... Magister Johannes Derviller comparens in capitulo post oblationes factas acquiescendo sententie per r[everendum] p[atrem] d[ominum] prepositum et plures vias deductas in medium pro pacificatione omn[ium] process[uum] fuit per partes concedatur quod omnes dicte questiones separentur[.] Nichilominus subortis verbis recessit idem Derviller[.] (f. 126r)

[61] ... ad iudicium coram domino decano Morinense in hac parte commissario et iudice inter partes ipsas vocaret. seperepetitus Jo[hannes] Derviller animo stomacato et irato et comminando dixit quod si super(?) eum executio ipsa fieret ipse omnia de sua parte alia in preiudicium dictorum dominorum seu aliquorum particularium ~~perse~~ canonicorum faceret. (f. 126v)

[62] ... et ibidem prefatum Judocum et Magistrum Eugenium Labitte etiam canonicum qui pridem fuerant ad processus prefatos solicitandos et dirigendos pro sepedictum capitulum deputati et commissi excertaret seu excertatos declarari faceret, dixitque ibidem quod idem Judocus modum de impetrando mandatis regiiis sciebat et doceret eosdem male fecisse quia ad forum que dicebat vetitum ... (f. 126v)

departed the town. Although there are ensuing brief notices to the effect that Dausque and Labitte are pursuing the recalcitrant Derviller through the courts at Montreuil, insisting that he submit to the chapter's judgements, the trail, as so often in such cases recounted in the chapter acts, at this point dries up.

What continues to be clear, however, is that, although this was the only apparent instance threatening to his life and limb, the tussle with Derviller was far from Rembert's only run-in with his colleagues. Later the same year he was embroiled in chapter in a shouting match with Osto Machecler, the upshot being that the latter requested that the lords summon the dean to a hearing before them. As usual 'for the sake of peace and concord', the lords decided to appoint one legal expert to represent the chapter and another to speak for the dean, and if that failed to give satisfaction to appoint a committee of three for the appeal. Perhaps more intriguing, however, is the possible insight that this entry offers into levels of disquiet concerning Rembert in the chapter more generally, stating as it does that such a committee, if it transpires, will supersede 'the case now begun before the lord abbot of Clairmarais ... among particular canons wishing to act against the lord dean'.[63]

At any rate, whatever specifically had piqued Machecler's ire he was clearly not alone: on 3 November we are apprised of a hearing before the provost pitting Rembert on the one hand against 'Judocus Dausque, Osto Machacler and their followers' on the other, concerning 'certain words bandied about in chapter that had descended into insult'. While we do not learn the substance of this dispute it had clearly been brewing for some time. On his visitation just past (30 October) the provost had explained to the chapter that he was aware there had been 'disputes, disagreements and rancour between them, from which many particularities were arising as a result of which the liberty of the church could be imperilled'. Thus

---

[63] Requirens dominos ut sibi citationem in scriptis ad conveniendum prefatum decanum in causa coram eis / prelibatus decanus dicto decreto pretenso se opponens propter certas causas tempore et loco declarandas. Nichilominus super decreto dicte citationis fuit positum in medium an domini declarent dictam citationem vel non[.] Super quo domini unanimiter pro bono pacis et concordie ante decretum dicte citationis per moderamen(?) advisamenti quo ad iurisdictionem capituli eligere ex parte capituli unum probum virum iurisperitum / et ex parte prefati domini decani alium / et ipsi domino si non possint concordari poterint eligere tertium quiquidem tres appunctuabunt secundum quod eis videbitur expediens pro ut de iure a quo opportunamento seu laudo poterit quilibet a gravamine appellare / Et durante dicta submissione causam iam inceptam coram domino abbate de Claromaresco contra particulares personas supersedebit de? etc. inter particulares canonices volentes agere contra eundem dominum decanum[.] (II. G. 356, f. 2v, 22 October 1497)

admonished to work towards peace, the opposing parties agreed to 'put away from them all their mutual dissension, insult and rancour, and made promises never at any time to pursue the said injuries, as if they had never been uttered or happened; and these things having been done and said in the chapter in the presence of the aforesaid provost, he granted and gave a general absolution'.[64]

More of this history surfaces in records of an altercation the previous year between Dausque and the dean in the context of which the latter's rather grandiose self-image emerges in sharp profile. The origins of the dispute, concerning disagreement over the placement of a body in the choir (presumably at a funeral service), are less important here than what they reveal of the characters of the two protagonists. Hothead that he undoubtedly was, Dausque had clearly escalated the tenor of the dispute, in culmination essentially accusing Rembert of using his position to force his opinion.[65] For his part Rembert, his sense of status affronted, ordered Dausque out of chapter before petitioning for satisfaction over (what he perceived to be) his colleague's irreverence in chapter. With both parties out of the room their confrères sagely concurred that the dean might instead be offered a friendly admonition to seek concord, Dausque's words, as they ventured, not having been intended to give offence. Not about to pour oil on troubled waters, Rembert instead urged his colleagues to ponder on this until the next chapter meeting, saying that if they were not prepared by then to give him satisfaction he would seek justice for his perceived injuries elsewhere.[66]

---

[64] Lite et controversia mota et adhuc speranda inter dominos decanum ex una / et Ju[docus] Dausque Ostone Machecler et suis adherentes coram domino preposito partibus ex altera / occasione certorum verborum prolatorum in capitolo in iniuriam deductorum. Nichilominus prefatus prepositus in sua ultima visitacione quod fuit penultima mensis octobris in capitolo exposuit qualiter intellexerat quod rixe dissentiones et rancores erant inter eos ex quibus multe particularitates oriebantur[.] Exquo ecclesie libertas periclitari posset. Necnon nisi tempore pacis bene colitur auctor pacis volens quantum in eo est inducere inter confratres suos presertim pacem et unionem monuit omnes et singules ad eandem pacem factandam[.] Quibus hiis expositis dominus decanus Ju[docus] et Osto ac sibi adherentes post dictas monitiones volentes frui ipsius consilio et monitionibus parere omnem distractionem iniuriam et rancorem sibi invicem remiserunt / promiseruntque nunquam ullo tempore dictas iniurias persequere / et tamquam non dictas aut evantas fuisse / Sic factis et dictis in capitolo in presencia prefati domini prepositi absolutionem generalem tribuit et dedit. (II. G. 356, f. 3r)

[65] ... domine ego percipio quod facietis michi peius quod poteritis galice fettes [faictes] du pis que porres ... (II. G. 355, f. 119v; 19 August 1496)

[66] ... domini concluserunt quod prefato domino decano fieret monicio caritativa / ad inducendum eundem ad concordiam et pacem et non haberet egre dicta verba[.] Ad hoc prefatus decanus dixit quod domini pensarent ad hoc usque ad proximum capitulum alias si

Sure enough, three days later an unmoved Rembert demands of the chapter that 'justice be done to him for the injurious words uttered by Jodocus Dausque to the dean in chapter'. He gives the canons ten days to arrange that he receive his desired apology, leaving the threat hanging that 'he did not intend to hold back from prosecution of his right'.[67] In a measure of the weight wielded by the dean, by 2 August we see a complete volte-face on the part of the chapter, who now not only take Rembert's part but assert that they share his sense of effrontery at the 'injurious words' that were 'less than reverently uttered to the said dean and the lords'. In a final slap in the face to Dausque they even put the words of an apology into his mouth, proposing that 'he may say to the lord dean "My Lord, insofar as I have offended you and my lords by speaking thus irreverently I beseech you to forgive me."'[68]

Far from occupying a position of *primus inter pares* it is clear that the deanship – at least as understood by Rembert – permitted the exercise over other chapter members of considerable disciplinary rigour or indeed whim. A corollory of this is to give us a measure of the temerity of figures such as Dausque and (still more so) Derviller in standing up to his authority or, alternatively, of the degree of excess perceived by Rembert's colleagues in his behaviour towards them.

One further recorded case of friction with Rembert's colleagues concerns – on the face of it surprisingly given his own career – the choirboys. On 20 March 1500 we find him objecting to the current level of provision for the boys, apparently – again – in the face of the chapter's objections:

Nicolaus the dean said before the lords that provision should be made for boys of the choir in such a way that the church should not suffer loss or damage, and in the case that the lords should wish to give them [the boys] as they were accustomed to, from now on he opposed this and spoke out against one who appealed [against

---

domini non facerent sibi iusticiam protestatus fuit prosequi dictam iniuriam ubi opus fuerit et expediens videbitur. (II. G. 355, f. 119v)

67 … petiit iustitiam sibi fieri de verbis iniuriis per Judocum Dausque domino decano prolatis in capitulo … si domini non faciant sibi iusticiam non intendit propterea a persecutione iuris recedere sed tempore et loco prosequi ~~at~~ infra x dies si minime(?) fecerunt sibi rationem appellare. (II. G. 355, f. 119v)

68 Eadem die super lite et controversaria monere speranda inter dominum decanum et Ju[docum] Dausque super certis iniuriosis verbis minus quam reverenter prolatis dictum decanum et dominos offendendo causa et pro bono pacis et concordie domini sommarie et de plane ordinaverunt quod propter irreverentiam per dictum Dausque dicet domino decano domine inquantum vos et dominos meos offendi sic irreverenter loquendi supplico michi parcere. (II. G. 355, f. 119v)

him]; but he demanded of the lords that they should make [a new] provision before Pentecost, otherwise he would press his [own] appeal [against the status quo].[69]

Perhaps, as for a period in the 1450s when half the upkeep costs of the boys (as we saw in Chapter 2) were levied on their families, the church was going through a lean period calling for unwonted belt-tightening; or perhaps the dean was simply clamping down on what he viewed as excessive expenditure.

Notwithstanding an overall impression of high-handed (not to say thin-skinned) approaches to colleagues, a softer side is briefly exposed in Rembert's dealings in March 1497 with the vicar Ludovicus Caucheteur. Caucheteur, having been fined by the bursar for absence or poor service, 'flung many insulting words at him, treating him without respect. After which the lord dean in view of his imperfect behaviour gave him a warning in gentle words; but he carried on pouring out insulting words etc.'[70] Rembert's uncharacteristic generosity of spirit may be accounted to the fact that the insults were aimed at someone other than himself; but at any rate this episode perhaps reveals something of the diplomatic proclivities that had served him so well in the papal curia.

After Death

Whatever Rembert's success rate in his disputes with colleagues, there was one battle that even he was in no position to win. On 11 January 1504 'his last day closed around eleven o'clock before midnight'.[71] His death, like that of all the church's canons, triggered a well-oiled succession of posthumous activity. Pierre de Saint-Amand, bailiff of the dean and chapter, along with his assistant Baudran des Grousilliers, kept watch through the night in Rembert's house over his effects, waiting for daybreak to assemble the

---

[69] Nicholaus decanus dixit coram dominis quod fiat / provisio de pueris chori taliter quod ecclesia non habeat detrimentum neque dampnum et ut casu quo domini velint eis dare ut consueverunt ex nunc se opposuit et protestatus est de appellan[ti] sed requisivit dominis ut quod provideant infra penthecosten alias prosequetur suam appellationem. (II. G. 356, f. 19v)

[70] Eadem die Dominus Ludovicus Caucheteur vicarius quia bursarius eum marancaverat propter suos desertus eidem plura verba iniuriosa protulit ipsum irreverenter habens / ex quo dominus decanus videns suam imperfectionem verbis dulcibus annuerit ipsum persistens verba etc iniuriosa pertulit / et de dictis in ordinatis verbis petiit reparari. (II. G.355, f. 123v; 3 March 1497)

[71] Die undecima mensis Januarii Dominus et Magister Nicolaus Rembert decanus et canonicus huius ecclesie diem suum clausit extremum circa undecimam horam ante mediam noctem. (II. G. 356, f. 73r; 11 January 1504)

deputies – canons Philippus de Mussen and Jacobus Broude – entrusted
with locking and sealing his possessions and drawing up an inventory,
crucial acts when, in a time before modern banking, money and valuables
were typically kept in an individual's dwelling. This took place in the
presence also of the deputies, the bailiff and his assistant then remaining
on guard at the house. The executors being charged with fulfilling the will
of the deceased according to his wishes, the will itself was read out 'in a
loud voice' to a gathering, in chapter, of Rembert's sisters and extended
family, alongside his executors and fellow canons.[72] As was conventional,
his burial took place the same day: 'the exequies of the said deceased having
been respectfully sung, his body was borne to his burial in the nave of the
church, by the tomb or sepulchre of the blessed Omer, and beneath the
lamp there suspended, as he had ordained in his will'.[73]

Rembert's will and executors' account is – as we shall see in the
Epilogue – one of many to have survived from this period; but his is
certainly one of the most extensive and complex. Running to no fewer
than eighty-six folios, it outlines in great detail his posthumous wishes and
the tying up of his complex fiscal affairs – financial and legal matters
arising from his benefices, the gifting of possessions and money to religious
establishments, family, colleagues and the poor, devotions and foundations
for the benefit of his soul, goods to be sold – as well as his executors'
expenses in carrying them out. The executors to whom this daunting task
fell were his old partner in crime Robert de Monte (who himself however
died shortly after assuming the role) and fellow canons Marcq le Tueur and
Jehan Berlin, along with Guillaume le Clerq, bourgeois of the town.

Rembert had clearly disposed of some of his benefices by the time of his
death: besides naming him as a papal protonotary, his only position
specified besides that of dean of St Omer is his commendatory priorate
of Rumilly-le-Comte, the most proximate of the benefices listed at his
appointment as dean and one in which he clearly maintained a close
interest. As may be expected, Rembert's origins figure prominently in his
will, where along with expected and familiar saints to whom he commends
his soul – the Virgin, St Michael, Sts Peter and Paul, his name saint
Nicholas and his patron St Omer – he includes St Bertoul,[74] patron of

---

[72] II. G. 356, f. 73v, 12 January 1504.

[73] … exequiis eiusdem defuncti honorifice decantatis eius corpus traditum extitit sepulture in navi
ecclesie iuxta tumbam sive sepulcrum Beati Audomari et sub lampade ididem pendente veluti in
suo ordinarat testamento. (II. G. 356, f. 73r)

[74] Known also as Bertulphe, the spelling used for the parish church today.

the parish church of Doudeauville where he was baptised. He leaves rental money from a property he owns to found two weekly Masses to be performed in the chapel of Our Lady and St Nicholas in the same church, founded by his parents for his and their souls, plus four other Masses annually, each paid for by an endowed sum and two capons, and a monthly obit commemoration.[75] If the curate and aldermen of the church do not consent to these devotions he will give the rental money to the cathedral of Thérouanne, 'where I was a canon and where presently Guillemin Eullard my nephew is a canon'.[76] We learn that, like most clerics, he was a member of a confraternity, in his case that of St John the Evangelist, of which he was sexton.[77] Various other confraternities, along with churches, figure among the many devotional establishments on which Rembert bestows posthumous donations.

The considerable expenses for his various funerary rites, along with the eating and drinking and distributions to the poor that went with them, are all detailed in his executors' account.[78] The payments for black cloth to dress members of the poor for the funeral attest to the intercessory value perceived to reside, perhaps especially at the point of death, in the prayers of the poor. Among the many clerics, servants and others paid to attend are a single specified 'choriste', six vicars 'who sang the responses on the said day of the service after the Mass', and of course the usual six choirboys. As so often for clerics of Rembert's station, there are various series of thirty Masses ('trentals'), and even a cluster of sixty Masses on the day of his funeral. Besides the funeral in his mother church he also specified a service plus nine Masses to be performed on the same day in the parish church of St Aldegonde, to which one of his prebends had been attached, and a further service plus thirty Masses at his home church in Doudeauville.

But his largest expenses are for the foundations of two signal daily devotions. First, he left funds for three choirboys to perform 'before the high altar each day at High Mass in the presence of God their *O salutaris hostia* or *O sacrum convivium*, which may be performed before or as soon as possible after the Pater Noster, and before the Agnus Dei if my lords do not wish to permit it here'.[79] The timing specified for this adoration of the

---

[75] II. G. 484, ff. 2v, 3r, 72r.   [76] F. 3v.   [77] F. 1v.   [78] Ff. 17r–22r.

[79] 'Item donne mil livres pour dire devant le grand autel chacun jour de lan a la grand messe. aupres dieu leur O Salutaris Hostia ou O Sacrum Convivium qui soit dit devant ou tantost apres le Pater Noster devant Agnus Dei et ou cas que messeigneurs ne le voeullent permettre ici donne lesdits mil livres' (f. 4v). The listing, among the 'ornemens des enfans de coeur', in the church inventory of 1557 of 'Une casule de velours rouge figuré, de quoy on chante *O Salutaris Hostia*' seems likely to refer to this foundation, and the detailing of a small receptacle clearly suggests

sacrament was surely dictated by the expectation that the elevation itself would be marked by the singing of the Benedictus, which – given the date of his foundation and the fact that it was for High Mass – would likely on at least some occasions have been in polyphony. Certainly there would be no reason, other than the priority of an existing custom, for the singing of such texts anywhere other than at the elevation itself: Rembert, anxious to gain maximum possible benefit for his soul, clearly wished to place his musical devotion as near to the moment of grace as circumstances allowed.[80]

The sum earmarked for this observance – one thousand livres d'Artois, more than one-eighth of his enormous estate at death – is staggering, especially considering that it equals the fund assigned for the evidently much grander daily performance of the *Salve regina* by – as we learn from the next entry in the account – 'the singers and choirboys'.[81] In fact, as the payments for its performance – entered annually in the fabric accounts – reveal, the performing forces for the *Salve* were no fewer than five male voices and (presumably the full complement of six) choirboys, plus an organist.

If the foundation of the elevation verse at High Mass located Rembert's proxy presence as close as possible to the moment of the communal sacrament of the church he had so long served, his foundation of the *Salve* was a more directly personal statement. This was to be the centre-piece devotion in the chapel of the Conception of Our Lady, founded by Rembert himself, next to the chapel of St Claude (later of the Holy Sepulchre) founded by his predecessor Simon Godeffroy, in the sixth bay of the church's south aisle. The executors' account makes it clear that the

---

that the boys were singing from something notated, whether this comprised polyphony or simply a chant for extemporisation (see Louis Deschamps de Pas: 'Inventaire des ornements, reliquaires, etc., de l'église collégiale de Saint-Omer en 1557', *Bulletin archéologique du Comité des travaux historiques et scientifiques* 1 (1886), 96).

[80] This point is underscored by a similar foundation discussed by Barbara Haggh: in his testament of 1486, Philippe Siron, first chaplain of the dukes of Burgundy from 1465 to 1482, endowed funds for the singing by the canons of *O salutaris hostia* at the elevation of High Mass at St Goedele, Brussels, on unspecified major feast days. See her 'Music, Liturgy and Ceremony in Brussels, 1350–1500', 2 vols., unpublished PhD dissertation, University of Illinois at Urbana–Champaign (1988), vol. 1, 174.

[81] 'Item je donne autres mil livres pour faire chanter le Salve Regina chaqun jour de lan en le chapelle de Notre Dame de le Conception et de St Nicolay aupres de le chapelle Sire Simon Godefroy pour moy pour luy et pour tous mes amis que je prie estre faicte aupres de la chapelle de mon predecesseur doien pour laquelle faire edifier je laisse et donne viii c. lb.' (f. 4v). See also ff. 74v–75r, where details are given concerning the sources of the two thousand livres in rent and cloth of gold.

chapel was built after Rembert's death ('ediffie de nouveau ... depuis le trespas dudit feu'), its foundation stone being laid on 1 April 1504.[82] Its donor surely wishing to outdo the efforts of his predecessor, the masonry alone for this impressively apportioned space, bearing his arms in the vault, cost his estate 666 livres, with significant additional expenditure on its glass and furnishings. Work clearly progressed briskly, the glass being set in the windows on Christmas Eve and the door hung on the Eve of Easter, the workers in each case receiving pots of wine for their trouble.

The chapel survives, and while some of its appurtenances mentioned in the executors' account – the 'cuivre' (likely latten) candlesticks with doves, the painted altar, the wooden stand for the missal for when one says Mass, and all the fabric furnishings, vestments and altar equipment – have clearly vanished, much of its original ornamentation remains.[83] Most notable are the imposing limestone figures (albeit much restored), complementing the chapel's dedication, of the Virgin and Child flanked by her parents Joachim and Anne. To the right of the entrance is a stone slab inscribed with Rembert's most important foundations (Figure 6.1):[84]

The venerable and prudent person Monseigneur Master Nicolas Rembert, in his time dean and canon of this church and archdeacon of Hainaut in the church of Cambrai, had this chapel built in honour of God and the Conception of the Virgin Mary, in which he founded [the practice] that each day of the year the anthem and motet *Salve regina* be sung by the master and choirboys together with four vicars of the said church and the organist, with a verse *O salutaris hostia*, which is to be sung each day by three choirboys with two lighted torches at the time of the elevation of the holy sacrament at the High Mass. For which foundations he gave to the said church the sum of two thousand livres d'Artois[.] Likewise he gave the candle-holders that are above the choir stalls,[85] with the gates of the two sides of the choir of the said church, and founded the light which is lit there through fifteen feasts of the year at first vespers, lauds and High Mass, as can be fully apparent through letters concerning this, given and acceded to by messieurs the dean and chapter of this church, for the foundation of which illumination he gave to the fabric of this church the *dime* of Recq and four

---

[82] II. G. 484, ff. 64v–69r.

[83] See the description, and central image of the Virgin and Child, in Gil and Nys, *Saint-Omer gothique*, 253–4.

[84] The script is transcribed in Henri Loriquet, *Epigraphie du département du Pas-de-Calais*, V, 1er et 2e fasc. (*Ville de Saint-Omer*) (Arras, 1892), 14–16.

[85] Loriquet surmises that this may be a reference to the 'colonnes derrière les chaires des prêtre, diacre et sous-diacre' which, according to Deneufville, were donated by Rembert (*Épigraphie*, 16).

Figure 6.1 Tablet detailing foundations of Nicolas Rembert, chapel of the Conception of Our Lady

hundred livres d'Artois + Who died the 11th day of January in the year 1503 [1504 new style]. Pray to God for his soul.[86]

Rembert's *Salve* must have rivalled in lavishness even the Saturday *Salve* at Notre-Dame sur le marchiet. Payments for its performance are entered annually in the fabric accounts starting in 1504/5, in which year the entry notes that it is to be sung 'in the chapel newly built and founded by the said executors to the honour of God and the Conception of the Virgin Mary'.

---

[86] Venerable et discrete personne Monseigneur Maistre Nicolas Rembert en son temps doyen et chanonne de ceste eglise et archidiacre de Haynau en leglise de Cambray a fait edifier ceste chapelle en lhonneur de Dieu et de la Conception de la Vierge Marie en laquelle a fonde chacun jour de lan lanthene Salve Regina et motet estre chante par le maistre et enfans de coeur avoeuc quatre vicaires de ladicte eglise et organiste ensemble avoeucque ung vers +O salutaris hostia+ qui se chante chacun jour par trois enfans de coeur et deux torches alumees a lheure de lelevation du saint sacrement de la grant messe . pour lesquelles fondations a donne a ladicte eglise le somme de deux mil livres dArthois[.] Parieillement a donne les chandelliers estans deseure les formes avoeuc les huys des deux costes du coeur de ladite eglise et fonde le luminaire qui si alume par quinze festes en lan auls premieres vespres laudes et grand messe. Comme du tout poeult apparoir par lettres sur che donnees et passees par messieurs doyen et capitle de ceste eglise pour le fondacion du quel luminaire a donne a la fabrique de ceste dicte eglise la disme de Recq Et quatre cens livers [sic] dArthois + lequel trespassa le onsieme jour de Janvier + l'an Mil. cincq cens et trois + pries dieu pour son ame

As master of the boys, the leader of the performance is Jean Thorion, familiar to us from Chapter 3, whose role in the *Salve* is attested in the accounts for most subsequent years up to 1518, as part of a group of voices that remains remarkably consistent from year to year. The presence of an organist suggests that, as widely documented elsewhere, the *Salve* itself was probably performed at least some of the time alternatim, with organ and voices alternating on successive verses.[87] The performances, involving the cream of the church's musicians, must indeed have been impressive affairs, and Rembert was surely motivated to rival the daily *Salves* widely held in wealthy cathedrals, collegiate churches and chapels elsewhere such as that, beginning in 1483, at St Donatian, Bruges. One can reasonably assume that, as in St Donatian and indeed as in Eton College chapel during the same period, public attendance, with concomitant prayer for the soul of the founder, would have been expected.[88]

The same fabric accounts detail regular payments also for the performance at High Mass by the three boys (presumably singing in chant or counterpoint *super librum*) of the verse *O salutaris hostia*. While Rembert's will is notably coy concerning association of this performance with the moment of the elevation, the fabric accounts, like the plaque in his chapel, hang on no such ceremony, referring directly to the 'verse *O salutaris hostia* which is to be sung each day of the year perpetually at the time of the elevation of the sacrament'.[89] The fact that this foundation, enlisting the special invocatory power of the voices of innocents, cost Rembert the same sum as his much more heavily staffed *Salve* surely says something significant about the high relative cost of private incursions into celebration of the public Mass at the high altar.

Not content with an evanescent, albeit perpetually recurring, presence at the High Mass, Rembert also introduced his proxy presence into the choir in a grandly physical way via, as the dedication plaque notes, candle-holders above the choir stalls and gates at either side of the choir (presumably affording access from the ambulatory). The candle-holders would have been put to particular use for his soul via his light foundation, funded by a tithe on one of his properties and four hundred livres.

[87] See Haggh, 'Music, Liturgy and Ceremony', vol. 1, 397–8.

[88] See ibid., 401–3 for a chronological list of the foundations of weekly and daily *Salve* services at major churches in the Low Countries. On St Donatian see also Strohm, *Music in Late Medieval Bruges*, 39, 86.

[89] 1508/9, f. 13v: . . . le fondation du vers O salutaris hostia quy se doibt chanter chacun jour de lan perpetuellement alheure de lelevation du sacrement de la grand messe par iii enffans de coeur . . .

The nature of this foundation is intriguing: his candles were to burn (on the altar, around the choir and above the choir stalls) on the fifteen feasts of the year – All Saints, Christmas, Epiphany, Easter, Ascension, Pentecost, Sts Peter and Paul, the Dedication of the Church, the Deposition of St Omer and the six Marian feasts – likely corresponding to the major doubles at which the dean (while living) was typically in attendance, and articulating the continuing presence he would have hoped for in the minds and prayers of his community.[90]

Among the physical accoutrements of his demise, perhaps the greatest care was reserved for his funerary plaque. Sadly for posterity this was situated not in his chapel, where it would likely have survived, but – as noted above – before the tomb of the church's patron saint. Clearly, local work was insufficient for Rembert's lofty aspirations: the plaque, made of 'cuivre' (most likely latten), was worked in Bruges, whither his representative Guillaume le Clercq twice travelled to arrange its manufacture. Like all goods involved in commerce with Bruges, it was delivered by boat to the Haut Pont, whence it was transported by wagon to the church, where it was inscribed. The stone tomb having been set in place, the plaque was affixed, its words doubtless reminding all who passed by of its testator's status and invoking them, before the physical remains of St Omer himself, to pray for its donor's soul.[91]

Some of the later entries in Rembert's executors' account recall his long associations with the Eternal City. Donations were left in his will to Santa Maria di Loreto, and to the Roman 'confraternities of Our Lady "des banquiers", of St Sebastian in the church of S Lorenzo in Damaso, and of S Niccolo in Damaso'.[92] The reverse side of Rembert's wealth was a flood of (at least posthumous) charitable giving: his executors' account testifies to his widespread gifts to churches, hospitals and the poor, including subventions for poor students (various family members among them) away at university in Louvain and Paris. Among these was his nephew Guillaume Eullard, 'poor student of law studying at Paris', for whom he also bought a half-hours of the Use of Thérouanne.[93] The members of his large extended family all benefited from his posthumous largesse, their gifts in money and objects all carefully detailed by his executors.

Finally on 2 June 1507, more than three years after his death, Rembert's executors' account, having been inspected by its auditors and read out in

---

[90] Fabric account for 1504/5, f. 26; see also II. G. 484, ff. 4v, 15r, 74r.
[91] For details on its purchase, transportation and installation see II. G. 484, ff. 69v–70v.
[92] F. 71v.   [93] II. G. 484, ff. 30r, 31v.

chapter as was the convention, was signed off. Rembert's life had touched many and his influence had both deepened and extended the reach of the collégiale to a possibly unprecedented degree. Scarcely a musical backwater before his arrival, it had become during his time a centre of impressive talent and activity: figures including Johannes Thorion added lustre to the music-making of his church and, subsequently, private chapel, and his period as dean had begun with a flurry of copying of Masses and vespers music by no less a figure than Jean Mouton.[94] Indeed the close synchron-isation in the latter case seems unlikely to have been coincidental: while Rembert was sworn in as dean in his absence on 1 January 1494, he assumed the position in person on 9 July, some six and a half weeks before Mouton was paid for the first of his series of copying commissions. The conclusion is difficult to escape that the appointment as dean of this former singer of St Peter's, Rome, was directly linked to this, the most intensive phase of polyphonic music-copying during our period of interest. Given, moreover, his connections with and recent arrival from Rome, it is tempting to speculate that at least some of the music that Mouton copied arrived with Rembert from the Eternal City itself. Of foundational import-ance for the church's musical establishment, though, was the 'bulle conservatoire', enabled and facilitated by Rembert through his intimate connections in and knowledge of the workings of the papal curia. With its establishment, musical provision for the church in general, and the choir-boys in particular, was placed on newly solid foundations.[95]

St Omer and the Court of Burgundy: Enguerrand Le Quien

If connections in Rome drove the wheels of ecclesiastical prosperity, much of their momentum came from the secular overlords whose wealth and influence they sustained. No magnate understood this better than Philip the Good, whose long tenure as Duke of Burgundy (1419–67) saw vast expansion both in extent and type of ducally controlled benefices. While, as we have seen, a huge range of ecclesiastical sinecures was at the duke's direct collation, he kept a permanent procurator in Rome to extend his reach also across those in the gift of the pope. One occupant of this role was Pierre Bogart, Dean of St Donatian, Bruges, and also a (periodically

---

[94] All discussed above at pp. 132–4.   [95] See pp. 32–8.

resident) canon of St Omer in the 1480s.[96] For members of the Burgundian chapel, collegiate chapters constituted the richest beneficial seam,[97] and it is to this connection that we now turn.

In fact we have already met one important beneficiary of this liaison: Rembert's predecessor as dean, Simon Godeffroy, had from 1471 or 1472 to 1474 occupied the position of chapelain des maîtres d'hôtel to Charles the Bold, having previously held the same role in the chapel of Charles as Count of Charolais.[98] But our primary attention here will be focused on two members of both the Burgundian chapel and the chapter of St Omer: Enguerrand Le Quien, sommelier for the duke by 1479 and until 1484, and canon of St Omer from 1480 until his death in 1487; and Toussains de le Ruelle, chaplain of the ducal court chapel at some point up to 1419 and again from *c.*1431 to 1451, and canon of St Omer from 1425 until his death in 1470.

Le Quien's name first surfaces at the cathedral of Amiens, his home diocese, where in 1470 he assumed a canonry following appointment to an expectative six years earlier.[99] On 12 July 1471 he was in Abbeville involved in an enquiry into salaries due to clergy in the town of Rue on the Somme. In 1480, as a canon of Notre-Dame and clerk of the oratory of princes, Arras, he was granted, along with the provost of Notre-Dame, agreement for the return of confiscated possessions of the church by Maximilian I and Mary of Burgundy. He is also listed in rolls of 1480–1 as possessor of canonries at the collegiate churches of St Waudru, Mons, and St Liévin, Zierikzee. He first appears in the Burgundian accounts in 1479 and is still present on 2 April 1482, when he is listed among those receiving mourning clothes for the funeral of Mary of Burgundy, but departed at some point between March and July 1484.

---

[96] See Vaughan, *Philip the Good*, 205 and 217. Bogart had been received as a canon at St Omer, via his procurator, on 22 November 1473, having some two years earlier been named to an expectative benefice (the next one to become available) by Pope Sixtus IV, of whom he was a familiar (II. G. 354, ff. 170v–1v). He clearly aimed to maximise his financial returns in both Bruges and Saint-Omer: on 11 September 1480 we find him asking the chapter of St Omer for income for residency, even though he is enjoying the same privilege from St Donatian (II. G. 355, f. 3v). In other years though, via his procurator, our friend the cantor Johannes de Hemont, he presents to St Omer his testimony for residence only in Bruges.

[97] See Fiala, 'Le mécénat', 170.   [98] Ibid., 216 and annexe I.

[99] For Le Quien's career outside St Omer see David Fiala 'Le mécénat', 181, 187, 189, 190; and Fiala, *Prosopographie des Chantres de la Renaissance* (Tours: CESR/Ricercar; http://ricercar.cesr .univ-tours.fr/3-programmes/PCR/). For his Amiens benefice see Pierre Desportes and Hélène Millet, *Fasti Ecclesie Gallicanae*, I: Diocèse d'Amiens (Turnhout: Brepols, 1996) 132.

At St Omer his story begins on 11 July 1480 when, named as a 'canon of Arras', he appears in chapter with direct letters of collation from Maximilian (as Duke of Austria and Burgundy), provided by his papal legate for this region, Lucas Roni, Bishop of Sebenico.[100] Here Le Quien is named as a household servant and cleric to Maximilian, upon whom Lucas, in consideration of his merits, wishes to bestow a favour of patronage.[101] Just over a year later, at the main chapter meeting on 10 September 1481, he is admitted to another year's residence, but as we learn from the next entry, all has not been plain sailing: he has been challenged for his canonry by Johannes Hangion and has submitted letters in his support drawn up by the dean of Thérouanne, on the strength of which the lords have admitted him to his residency. Needless to say, Hangion appeals, leaving an infuriated Le Quien threatening to take his case to law and the apostolic see and to sue for compensation for expenses incurred. By 13 November, however, Le Quien is able to report that Hangion has renounced his claim in Le Quien's favour. The lords pronounce themselves content to admit the latter to his residency provided that Hangion does not mount an appeal and that Le Quien will provide them with evidence of his opponent's desertion or renouncement of the post before the following Easter. Until then they commit not to profit from the benefice. Clearly pushing his luck slightly (Easter falling on 16 April that year), Hangion eventually fulfils his side of the agreement, getting his instrument of renunciation (dated 26 April) to the chapter the following 27 June.[102]

It may well be – assuming they ever had a choice in the face of such powerful advocacy – that the chapter came to wish they had made a stand for Hangion: as the Burgundian timetable above attests, Le Quien's first few years of residence at St Omer were at best notional. In November 1481 he was given – his residency notwithstanding, which was not infringed as a result – a three-month waiver of his statutory residence in order to

---

[100] Sebenico, at that time part of the Republic of Venice, is now Šibenik in Croatia. For this letter of collation see II. G. 355, f. 2v, 11 July 1480. Besides being papal legate to Maximilian, Lucas Roni was a papal nuncio and orator of the apostolic see, and commissary with the power of legate. Cf .Adolf Bachmann (ed.), *Urkundliche Nachträge zur österreichich-deutschen Geschichte im Zeitalter Kaiser Friedrich III*, 1892, repr. 2017 (Vienna: F. Tempsky, 1892), 391, where he is described in 1477 by Pope Sixtus IV as 'referendarius, nuncius et orator noster ad dominia et alia loca dilecto filio nobili viro Carolo duci Burgundie'.

[101] Nos tibi qui etc. illustrissimi principis Domini Maximiliani Austrie et Burgundie Ducis familiaris domesticus et sui oratorii clericus existis premissorum meritorum tuorum intuitu specialem graciam facere volens … (II. G. 355, f. 2v)

[102] II. G. 355, ff. 22r, 22v, 24v–25, 31r.

continue his service with the duke of Burgundy.[103] In the event this was the thin end of the wedge: come the following February and the end of this notional stint, the chapter found itself perusing ducal letters requesting further extension of Le Quien's absence. The lords couch their agreement to this as being conditional on Le Quien's coming before Easter to prove – in person – that Hangion has renounced his claim, but the reality is surely that they had very little choice in the matter.[104]

Only ten days shy of Easter Day the chapter was forced to permit Le Quien yet another month's absence. Then on 27 June, the very same day the chapter took receipt of Hangion's letter of renunciation of his claim to Le Quien's canonry, they also received further petitions from the duke for his servant's continued service. By this point, their patience clearly wearing thin, the lords note that

since however the same Master Ingerandus has not made an appearance regarding the said renunciation within the period then allotted him and as he had promised, and it was agreed that he had not then been compliant with that date, he has not been able in any way to be admitted to residency, as a result of which they have not been able to comply with the same letters given the statutes and oath of this church.[105]

The reality, however, was that whatever request the ruling magnate made of a church in his realm, the chapter had little alternative but to comply, even when, as in this instance, that meant not only granting benefices to his favourites but also allowing them the emoluments of residence while they continued to serve at court. By the middle of the following year the chapter had given up fighting: on 4 August 1483 they granted Le Quien 'special grace' for another six months' service at the ducal court with his residency

---

[103] Die xxviᵃ mensis Novembris predicti domini concesserunt eidem Magistro Ingerando graciam trium mensium se absentandi insistendo servicio illustrissimi domini ducis et suis negociis non obstante sua residentia quo eo nichilominus infracta non fit. (II. G. 355, f. 25r)

[104] Ipso die ad contemplationem litterarum illustrissimi domini ducis domini continuarunt graciam factam Magistro Ingerando le Kien de sua stageria usque ad pascham proximam infra quod tempus si non fecerit apparere de renunciatione vel desertione appellationis Domini Johannis Hangion gracia huiusmodi nichilominus nulla sit. prout exprimitur supra in secundo folio posteriori. (II. G. 355, f. 27r)

[105] Ipso die presentate fuerunt certe littere illustrissimi domini ducis deprecatorie ut domini continuere vellent eidem Magistro Ingerando gratiam alias sibi ad aliquot menses factam quo ad suam residentiam[.] Quia tamen ipse Magister Ingerandus non fecit apparere de dicta renunciatione infra tempus sibi tunc prefixum et ut promiserat et constat ipsum tunc non fuisse pacificum nullo modo poterat admitti ad residentiam quare eisdem litteris obtemperare commode non potuerunt stantibus statutis et iuramento huius ecclesie. (II. G. 355, f. 31r)

income intact, stating that he will be allowed more time if he again petitions after that.[106]

In fact, though, the problem of Le Quien's status as an absentee landlord was soon to be resolved on the ground: as noted above, at some point in mid-1484 he left the Burgundian court chapel, and already in January 1484 he had been looking for accommodation at St Omer. Told by his fellow canons that, in accordance with the statutes, he could have a house to himself once one became available, he did not in the event have to wait long: on 6 February he agreed to pay thirty-two livres d'Artois, in addition to covering all necessary repairs, for the house in the cloister of canon Philippus de Mailly, and two weeks later he picked up the keys to his new home.

If Le Quien felt any compunction concerning the extent of his demands on St Omer it was certainly not evident in his pursuit of benefices. Around this same time he was working to effect an exchange ('permutation') of his own canonry in Amiens with a benefice associated with the parish church of St Denis in Saint-Omer claimed by no less a figure than the provost of Amiens, Adrianus de Henencourt. In other words he was attempting, like Rembert around the same time, to avail himself of the fruits of two canonries under the aegis of the collégiale. The snag was that Henencourt's canonry had long been the subject of competing claims at the papal curia and had been assumed by another candidate, Matheus de Bosco. As a (not wholly disinterested) procurator for Henencourt's case, Le Quien, along with de Bosco, agreed to allow the cantor Johannes de Hemont to judge the case, and to abide by his judgement. Perhaps unsurprisingly given the power stacked against de Bosco, Hemont ruled in favour of Henencourt, and de Bosco dutifully rescinded his claim, deferring to the provost to put it in the hands of the pope or of whomever had the right of its collation. This arbitration concluding one side of the deal, Le Quien petitioned the Bishop of Thérouanne to be granted the canonry and prebend, as his side of the planned permutation. The chapter, however, resisted, claiming (perhaps tendentiously) that it had not been established either that the other interested parties were dead, or that the case of the Amiens canonry had been

---

[106] Die quarta mensis Augusti. domini fecerunt graciam specialem Magistro Ingerando Le Quien suo confratri quod servire possit illustrissimo Domino Maximiliano Duci Austrie. in cuius suo servicio insistendo per medium annum a die sui recessus. sua incepta residencia infracta non sit perdendo tamen. Et si maiori gracia indigeat post elapso medio anno veniat aut scribat et domini se obtulerunt eundem generoso favore prosequi ob ipsius illustrissimi domini ducis contemplatione. (II. G. 355, f. 43v)

conclusively decided in the Roman curia. Not so easily disuaded from his ambition, Le Quien decided on recourse to law.[107]

The following April (1484) he brought his case back to the chapter. Henencourt having assumed his canonry, Le Quien now insisted that the permutation be allowed to go ahead. Following discussion by the lords, among whom Le Quien had clearly made no friends, the dean furnished him with the chapter's response. The dean states that he understands that Le Quien believes himself to be within his rights, following the litigation concerning the canonry, to proceed with the permutation with Henencourt. He notes, however, that during the period of litigation the emoluments due from a canonry revert, by ancient custom, back to the church (in other words not, as we might guess to have been their assumption, to Henencourt or Le Quien). With this manifest disincentive to settle the case clearly stated, the dean reiterates the earlier position of the chapter that it has not been clearly demonstrated to whom the rights of the prebend are due. In closing, however, he notes that if clear evidence can be advanced in Le Quien's favour, the chapter will release it to him.[108] Whatever the power and influence ranged against it, the chapter was not afraid to push

---

[107] Die nona mensis Jullii Magister Ingerandus Le Quien exposuit se iamdudum concepisse permutatione inter ipsum de canonicatu et prebende ecclesie Beati Nicholai in claustro Ambianensis seu de iure quod in illis pendit ad alteram portionem parrochialis [sic] ecclesie Sancti Dyonisii de hoc oppido quam obtinet reverendus pater Dominus Magister Adrianus de Henencourt prepositus Ambianensis super qua lis et causa diutius pependit in Romana curia inter ipsum dominum prepositum ex una et Jo Bauchere et Nicholaum Mansyon ac quosdam alios sua communiter et divisim interessentes penden[tem] quibus Bauchere et Mansyon de medio sublatis Matheus de Bosco se fecit subrogari in eorum iure et in possessionem induci. Antequam vero fuerit causa commissa. et ad aliquos actus processum in ea ipse Magister Ingerandus tamquam procurator et eo nomine dicti reverendi patris domini prepositi et Matheus de Bosco concorditer elegerunt venerabilem virum Magistrum Johannem de Hemont cantorem huius ecclesie in arbitrum seu iudicem in cuius arbitrium dictum et sententiam se submiserunt ut servatis vel non servatis terminis unico contextu sine strepitu et figura iudicii preferat prout ipse tulit sententiam pro ipso domino preposito. et ad maiorem cautelam ne ipse Matheus de Bosco provocare posset ab eadem renunciavit ibidem omni liti et cause et cedere promisit iuri suo pro eodem domino preposito in manibus sanctissimi domini nostri pape aut cuiuscumque potestatem habentis quantus opus sit atque huiusmodi dicto arbitrio et sentente acquievit prout in instrumento desuper confecto plenius continetur quapropter ad finem dicte permutationis ad effectum deducende et perficiende ipse Magister Ingerandus petiit sibi dari et concedi presentationem eiusdem parochialis ecclesie seu portionis ad dominum episcopum Morinensem. Domini tamen responderunt eidem quod non constabat eis de morte dictorum Bauchere et Mansion possessorum nec de extinctione litis in Romana curia quare presentationem suam dare renuerunt[.] Super quo refutatione ipse Magister Ingerandus petiit sibi a me fieri iustitiam et instrumentum. (9 July 1483, II. G. 355, f. 43r)

[108] The response is entered in II. G. 355, f. 52v.

back, when opportunity arose, at those seeking untrammelled access to its wealth.

For his part, though, their opponent was not about to give up either. That August the church's lawyer Petrus de Sancto Amando announced in chapter that Le Quien, on the strength only of letters from the regular patron of the benefice and without the proper licence from either the chapter or provost, had seized possession of his desired canonry, directly in the face of the church's statutes. A hearing was set for fifteen days later, with Le Quien, presumably (since he was resident) himself present in chapter, objecting that he was not prepared to attend such a hearing about a matter in which the chapter themselves had such a patently vested interest.[109]

Following this locking of horns, however, accounts of the following chapter meetings, as so often in such cases, are largely silent on the conflict. The only further detail from Le Quien's lifetime comes in the form of a record, on 9 January 1486, to the effect that 'Walrandus Caron is continued in his control of the "other" portion of St Denis for the price of forty livres d'Artois every other year; upon which master Enguerand Quien, saying that the said portion and its administration belonged by right to him, asserted that he would pursue his right.'[110] It may be that the chapter was assessing its share of income from the benefice, it being under litigation, at a reduced rate, since upon assuming the position by right Le Caron was expected to pay off a sum of money felt by the chapter to be its due.[111] This was clearly a cause of some strife between Le Caron and the chapter, to which, as noted earlier, revenues accrued during such a period of dispute

---

[109] Hac die octava mensis Augusti / Petrus de Sancto Amando tamquam sindicus huius ecclesie ac dominorum decani et capituli eiusdem exposuit dictis dominis qualiter ad suam pervenit noticiam quod Magister Engerandus concanonicus dicte ecclesie virtute littere collationis ordinarie non habentem licentiam presentavit [recte: presentationis?] ab ipsis dominis aut ab ipso reverendo patre domino preposito dicte ecclesie quibus de iure spectare dignoscitur huiusmodi presentatio / cepit possessionem alterius portionis parochialis ecclesie Sancti Dionisii quod de directo statutis et libertatibus huius ecclesie derogare videtur / Qua de re ipse procurator instanter requisivit dictis dominis ut diem assignent de hinc ad quindenam Magistro Engerando prefato super certis articulis responsuro quam diem ipsam domini assignarunt dicto Engerando qui protinus expresse protestatus est se non debere coram ipsis dominis respondere cum se se partes gerant et materia ac causa litis eosdem de directo concernat. (II. G. 355, f. 54v)

[110] ... Magister Walrandus Caron continuatus est in regimine alterius portionis Sancti Dionisii pro precio alternis annis videlicet xl libri arthesii / super quo Magister En[guerandus Le] Quien dicens sibi dictam portionem et eius administrationem de iure spectare / protestatus est suum ius prosequi. (II. G. 355, f. 63r)

[111] The relevant entry in the chapter acts, dated 30 June 1491, is on II. G. 355, f. 84v.

would normally have reverted. One thing this snippet clearly reveals, though, is that by early 1486, some two and a half years since first asserting his claim, Le Quien's status with regard to the St Denis prebend was still languishing in legal deadlock.

While ambiguities remain, a story such as this is most valuable in the present context for the nitty-gritty of its details on the relationship between one of the most opulent court chapels of the day and the ostensibly unrelated churches on whose fat its members fed. In fact for its litigant at least, a resolution never came, but it may be that by this point he was in any case engaged in a more existential battle. On 21 February 1485, Le Quien, 'suffering from a severe fever that had long vexed him, petitioned the lords for licence to return to his place of birth to allow him to recover his health'. Permission for his departure, with his emoluments intact, was granted, and by 18 May he was back, expressing his thanks for the grace bestowed on him.[112] Whether or not this affliction was a harbinger of worse things to come, however, it seems unlikely to have been conceived as such in the mind of Le Quien himself: on 8 January, 1487 he died apparently intestate, ushering in posthumous proceedings of far greater duration than any in which he had been embroiled in life.

The main items were easily disposed of: the single canonry mentioned – clearly implying that the coveted canonry of St Denis had eluded Le Quien to the end – went, via the direct collation of the provost, Johannes de Burgundia, to the distinguished scholar and cleric Franciscus de Busleyden (Frans van Busleyden).[113] Following a feeding frenzy over the disputed canonry of St Denis involving two further competing candidates in

---

[112] ... Magister Engerandus le Quien acri infirmatus febre que longo tempore eundem vexaverat petiit dominis licenciam remeandi natale solum causa sanitatis recuperande / cui ipsi domini benitate annuerunt nichil perdendo/

... reversus est ad propria Magister Engerandus le Quien regracians dominis de licentia sui recessus quam ab eis obtinuit nichil perdendo. (II. G. 355, ff. 59r, 60v)

[113] II. G. 355, f. 68v. Named here as a doctor of laws, de Busleyden was a figure of considerable status and distinction: matriculating into the University of Louvain in 1482, he had studied also at Paris, Cologne and Perugia, held prebends at Anderlecht, Brussels and Cambrai, plus the provostships of St Lambert in Liège and St Donatian, Bruges, and the deanship of the church of Onze Lieve-Vrouw in Antwerp. He was also a tutor of the young Philip the Fair of Burgundy and bishop of Cordoba. In 1499 he was named archbishop of Besançon, and just before he died in 1502 had been about to be raised to the purple by Pope Alexander VI (see Astrik L. Gabriel, 'Intellectual Relations between the University of Louvain and the University of Paris in the 15th Century', in Jozef Isewijn and Jacques Paquet (eds.), *The Universities in the Late Middle Ages*, Mediaevalia Lovaniensia I/VI (Leuven: Leuven University Press, 1978), 98–9; Paul De Win, 'Frans van Busleyden († 1502). Prelaat en diplomaat, leermeester, vertrouweling en topadviseur van Filips de Schone', Handelingen van de Koninklijke kring voor oudheidkunde, letteren en kunst van Mechelen 113 (2009), 55–103.

addition to Le Quien, it had been assumed by Walrandus Le Caron, who in August 1490 fought off a challenge for it at the papal curia – judged by none other than Nicolas Rembert – from a certain Johannes Le Caron, probably his own nephew.[114] The ensuing months saw Le Caron vacillating between conducting the benefice's pastoral requirements himself and, pleading illness and infirmity, offloading them onto a vicar. An entry from the last day of June 1491 informs us that 'as of now many years past, his "portion" [of St Denis] was collated on him "iure ordinario", the same portion being in litigation between Master Ingerando Le Quien, his predecessor, and other co-litigants [i.e. other individually interested parties], that is Johannes Vigreux and then Ro[bertus] Doizencourt'.[115] In other words, Le Caron had been able to fend off multiple competing claims and still be appointed ('iure ordinario') by the regular patron of the benefice.

Early in 1488 the report of the sale of Le Quien's goods was presented in chapter.[116] The disbursement of his finances was clearly rather more of a challenge, however: the reading-out of the completed account in chapter, a point of conclusion normally reached in a matter of months, did not occur until 6 May 1497, almost ten years after his demise. The root of the problem seems at least partly to have been debts left outstanding by Le Quien. On 8 July 1495, some eight and a half years after his debtor's death, Reginaldus Turpin, a canon of St Géry, Cambrai, appointed as procurators four canons of St Omer (including Nicolas Rembert) 'to appear before justice and the bailiff of the lords of the chapter . . . for the hearing of an ordination of the deputies concerning a certain sum of money owed to him by the late Ingerranus Le Quien . . . amounting to the sum of 120 livres'.[117] The assembling of another deputation almost two years later suggests that Turpin had not been Le Quien's only creditor: on 28 April 1497, four of Le

---

[114] 6 August, 1490, II. G. 355, f. 78v.

[115] . . . dicens et exponens qualiter iam pluribus annis effluxis dicta sua portio sibi collata iure ordinario fuit. ipsa porcione in litigio existente inter Magistrum Ingerando Le Quien suam predecessorem / et alios secum collitigantes videlicet Johannem Vigreux deinde Ro[bertus] Doizencourt . . . (30 July, 1491, II. G 355, f. 84v)

[116] II. G. 355, f. 71v.

[117] Eadem die [8 July, 1495] Magister Reginaldus Turpin canonicus Sancti Gaugerii Cameracensis constituit procuratores N[icholaum] Rembert, Georgium de Ricamiez et Ro[bertum] de Monte, Eugenium Labitte, etc. ad comparendum coram iusticia et ballivo laicali dominorum de capitolo et ibidem audiendum ordinacionem deputatorum super certa pecunie somma sibi per quondam Magistrum Ingerannum Le Quien debita ex mutuo ascendente ad sommam centum viginti librarum currentium patet per instrumentum publicum constare prout et apparere omnia que alia cura huiusmodi negocium incumbentia faciendum permittendum acceptandum recipiendum et compromittendum promisit etc iuravit etc[.] Acta fuerunt hac in capitulo . . . (II. G. 355, f. 110v)

Quien's former canonic colleagues were instructed to take possession of all the acts of inventory and executors' sales of both Le Quien and Theobald aux Cauches (presumably another debtor), 'that all things may be set out for deliberation, and to make an end to the whole business to the goal that all those in debt may be satisfied'. Finally, just over a week later on 6 May, 'the lords deputed [three of their number] to meet with [the former dean] Simon Godeffroy to draw up a sum and account and reckoning of the goods of the late Master Ingerannus Le Quien and to bring the registers and the account into chapter, that every man may have his reckoning and due payment'.[118]

Toussains de Le Ruelle

If, as one might imagine, the passing of Enguerrand Le Quien may have occasioned little lamentation from his confrères, the stock built up by Toussains de Le Ruelle, a predecessor at both the Burgundian court chapel and St Omer, seems likely to have been of a very different order. While the chapter acts are less replete with detail concerning Toussains (a consequence, perhaps, of a less fractious tenure), what we do have suggests a collegial and generous member of his chosen community. Moreover, we are exceptionally blessed in Toussains's case in the (complementary) nature of the most important materials that have survived: the account of his executors and, most signally – still in the church though not in its original location – his life-size funerary slab.

St Omer is the single most exceptional church in northern France in terms of the number of its surviving late medieval memorials, most of them to canons of the fifteenth century.[119] Of our musical dramatis personae, however, the only survivors are those to Vincent Breion, the vicar and

---

[118] ... domini ordinaverunt Dominis Ostoni Machecler, Jo[hanni] de Le Carouwe, Eug[enio] Labitte et Ro[berto] Poilly quod recuperent omnia acta inventaria et vendiciones executionum bonorum quondam Ingeranni Le Quien et Theobaldi aux Cauches / et de omnibus per consilium apponant finem ita quod de cetero omnes debitores contententur.
... domini deputaverunt Dominos Ostonem Machecler G[eorgium] de Ricamiez et Eug[enium] Labitte ad conveniendum cum Domino Simone Godeffroy et faciendum compotum et rationem de bonis quondam Magistri Ingeranni Le Quien ac registra et compota deportare in capitolo ut fiat unicuique ratio et iusticia. (II. G. 355, f. 125r)

[119] See Douglas Brine, 'Commemorating the Canons of Saint-Omer', ch. 3 in Brine, *Pious Memories: The Wall-Mounted Memorial in the Burgundian Netherlands*, Studies in Netherlandish Art and Cultural History (Boston, MA/Leiden: Brill, 2015), 90–127; and Gil and Nys, *Saint-Omer gothique*, 229–46.

music copyist mentioned in Chapter 3, and this one, featuring the single figure of the standing canon at prayer in black stone, his face picked out from the surrounding field in white marble (Figure 6.2). The inscription, incised around the slab's edge, presents a detailed and impressive roster of its dedicatee's ecclesiastical career:

Here lies Sire Toussains de Le Ruelle, once, while living, canon of this church of St Omer and of several other places, who was in his time chaplain in the chapels of Popes Martin [V] and Eugenius [IV], of Isabel Queen of France, of Messeigneurs the Dukes of Burgundy John [the Fearless] and Philip [the Good], who died in the year 1470, the 19th day of September. Pray for his soul.[120]

Named in pontifical documents as a clerk from the diocese of Noyon, Toussains first surfaces in 1410 at the Sainte-Chapelle in Paris as 'first of the choirboys of the chapel of the palace of the king', receiving a sum of ten écus d'or 'to mount their Feast of the [Holy] Innocents'.[121] On 26 December 1416 he is named as a sommelier in the chapel of the queen of France, Isabel of Bavaria, delivering, on her behalf, as (the record says) she was accustomed to do each year, a grant of £4 10s. to the boys of the Sainte-Chapelle, again for their revels on the Feast of Holy Innocents.[122] Following service (undocumented except on his tombstone) to Duke John the Fearless of Burgundy, he is listed as a singer in the papal chapel of Martin V in 1420 but seems to have departed in 1431, the first year of the pontificate of Eugenius IV. Intervening periods of absence included a documented trip to the north in 1426, as 'maître des enfants de la chapelle du pape', to recruit choirboys, resulting in a return to Rome with two boys from Cambrai. It seems likely that he joined the Burgundian chapel shortly

---

[120] 'Chy gist Sire Toussains de Le Ruelle Jadis en son vivant chanonne // de ceste eglise de Saint Aumer et de plusieurs aultres lieus le quel fust en son tamps chapplain es chapelles des papes Martin et // Eugene, de Ysabel royne de Franche de Messeigneurs les // dus de Bourgoigne Jehan et Phelippe [sic] qui trespassa lan mil CCCC & LXX le XIX jour de septembre pries pour son ame.' For a summary of Toussains's career including many of the details presented here see David Fiala, 'In memoriam', in Camilla Cavichi, Marie-Alexis Colin and Philippe Vendrix (eds.), *La musique en Picardie du XIVe au XVIIe siècle* (Turnhout: Brepols, 2012), 21.

[121] 'premier des enfans de la chapelle du palais du roy'; 'pour faire leur feste des Innocens'. See Michel Brenet, *Les musiciens de la Sainte-Chapelle du Palais* (Paris: Picard, 1910; repr. Geneva: Minkoff, 1973), 27.

[122] A Toussains de la Ruelle, sommelier de la chapelle de la Royne, qu'il a paié et baillé du sien aux enfans d'aube de la saincte chapelle du Palaiz, que la dicte dame leur avoit, et a de coustume donné chacun an, pour fere leur feste le jour des Innocens, par commendement de Bietrix du Ry, etc. IIII l. x s. (See Antoine Le Roux de Lincy, *Les femmes célèbres de l'ancienne France: mémoires historiques sur la vie publique et privée des femmes françaises, depuis le cinquième siècle jusqu'au dix-huitième*, vol. 1 (Paris: Leroi, 1848), 642.)

Figure 6.2 Funerary slab for Toussains de Le Ruelle © Carl Peterolff

after its reconstitution under Philip the Good in 1430; at any rate he is already present in 1436, the date of the first surviving documentation, and appears on the chapel's rolls for every year thereafter up to and including 1451.[123] A record naming him 'abbé de joieuse folie' in 1437 suggests that he had not, in adulthood, lost the enjoyment of revels he had first cultivated

---

[123] On Toussains's Burgundian career see Jeanne Marix, *Histoire de la musique et des musiciens de la cour de Bourgogne sous le règne de Philippe le Bon* (Strasbourg: Heitz, 1939; repr. Geneva: Minkoff, 1972), 150, 154, 197, 242–51.

as a choirboy. We know from a payment in 1439 for authorisation to exchange four of his benefices that Toussains held benefices besides those at his (presumably) home cathedral of Noyon (from 1422) and St Omer (from 1425), but their locations, save that of one to be revealed below, are not currently known.[124]

Toussains's appointment on 7 September 1425 to a canonry at St Omer began an association with the collégiale that was to last almost half a century.[125] An entry in the fabric account for 1424/5 records his payment of £16 6s. 8d. 'pour le reception de sa prebende', and while at this point he still had some twenty-five years' more service remaining under Philip the Good, he was in the interim at least sporadically present in Saint-Omer. The fabric account of 1435/6 records payment by him, along with thirteen other canons, of an 'extraordinary tax' of ten livres.[126] Like many of his station, Toussains fostered the careers of family members and other familiars: in 1449/50 he paid five sous for the chapel key for the conferral on his nephew Nicolas de Le Ruelle of the chaplaincy of St John the Baptist. In 1448/9 a chaplaincy was conferred on his servant ('varlet'), and similarly in 1451/2 he paid the charge for the presentation to a chapel of one of his servants.[127] It is clear also that he maintained links with former colleagues at the Burgundian court chapel since, both before and after he took up residence, he acted as procurator in submitting testimonials of absence at court from Nicaise Dupuis, the duke's premier chapelain for twenty-five years until his death in 1465 and an (absentee) canon of St Omer.[128]

But his was a far from merely self-interested philanthropy. In 1444/5 we encounter the first in a long line of examples of Toussains's generosity: in that year he lent the fabric, for an unspecified purpose, a sum of no less

---

[124] See ibid., 197.

[125] On the date of his appointment see R. Op de Beeck and É. van Caster, 'Les dalles funéraires gravés à effigies, conservées dans la Cathédrale Notre-Dame de Saint-Omer', *Bulletin trimestriel de la Société académique des antiquaires de la Morinie*, 20/379 (1964), 193–210.

[126] F. 3v.

[127] Primes de Sire Nicole de Le Ruelle pour le capelle Saint Jehan Baptiste a lui conferee viii sc; Item pour le droit dune clef v s sont xiii s; Item de Messire Toussains de Le Ruelle pour une capelle conferee a son nepveu et ceste le clef pour tant seullement v sc (1449/50, ff. 3r, 4r); Item dun des serviteurs Sire Toussains de Le Ruelle pour une capelle o [sic] clau v s (1451/2, f. 5v). In the event, his nephew did not long outlive him: on 22 August 1473 his chaplaincy of St John the Baptist passed, following his decease, to Mattheus Advisse (II. G. 354, f. 167r).

[128] Testimonials for Dupuis were submitted by Toussains on 13 December 1450 and 31 August 1453 (II. G. 352, ff. 119r and 122v). Other canons did Dupuis the same service in years prior to this.

than 240 livres.[129] By 1451/2 the debt was still on the collégiale's books,[130] but in the 1460s he started to receive reimbursements, with successive sums returned in 1460/1, 1463/4, 1465/6 and in the three subsequent years. The year 1451/2 – the time of Toussains's departure from the Burgundian chapel and presumably of the commencement of more regular residence in Saint-Omer – also marks evidence of his involvement in improvements to the church fabric. In that year we learn of his contributions for the repainting of 'images', for which the fabric is now paying for fabric coverings;[131] and in the same year he assigned no less than £200 (each of forty Flemish groats) 'coming from a gift to the fabric by the late Master Gotteran' towards what were evidently extremely lavish vestments coming in at a total of 520 écus d'or.[132]

But the best and most direct insights by far into the life and motivations of Toussains de Le Ruelle come, as might be expected, from his executors' account.[133] Generous, in life, in support of his church, Toussains showed largesse in death, to churches, convents, hospitals and the poor – as was standard among his confrères – but also to colleagues, relatives, servants and other members of his wide circle. Among the sums of money and material items lent by Toussains in his life, the most striking from a musical viewpoint is the loan, mentioned in Chapter 2, of two 'books of music' to Robert Fabri that now, following their owner's death, were bequeathed to him.[134] Toussains's death was clearly a windfall for the many members of his extended family, including two canons of St Quentin who were granted sums of money, and Mariette Le Vaillant and her daughter Jehannette de Le Ruelle, who received a substantial inventoried

---

[129] Item receu de le main Maistre Gautran le somme de quarante livres de gros lesquels Sire Toussains a preste a le fabrique montent ii c. xl livres (f. 2v)

[130] Et la dicte fabricque doibt a Sire Toussain de Le Ruelle pour enprunts fait a luy et dont est faicte recepte par le compte dicelle de lan rendu par Sire Loys Prerlamps et dont le dit Sire Toussains a oblicacion de le dicte eglise le somme de iii c frans de xxxII. Gros le franc val[.] ii c xl lb. (1451/2, f. 16r)

[131] Item a le dite dame Maus pour avoit livre vii aunes et demie de toille pour faire une couverture a couvrir les ymages que a fait repaindre Messire Toussains o [sic] pris de xxii laune sont xiii s ix d (1451/2, f. 14r)

[132] 'A Jehan le Roux marchant demourant a Arras pour lachat de iii chappes une cassure tunicle dalmatique avec les paremens estolle favons aubes et a mis chavis ensemble ung drap deparement a une boiste de corporal de velours bleu serre de fleurs de lis dor / la somme de v^c xx escus dor. Sur lesquels Sire Toussains de la Ruelle paia ii^c lb de xl g[ros] l[ivre] venant de don fait ale [sic] fabricque par feu Maistre Gotteran' (1451/2, f. 16r). It may be that vestments were a particular interest of Toussains: the fabric account for 1467/8 includes a payment 'Pour les distribucions des vicaires et escotois [sic] a cause dune messe de St Esprit donne par messires a Sire Toussains quant il presenta une cappe de noir velours xvi s x d ob' (f. 31r).

[133] One of a number gathered under the call number II. G. 476.   [134] II. G. 476, f. 13r.

list of household goods, from kitchenware to furniture, bed linen and firewood.[135]

As usual in connection with such survivals, particular insights into Toussains's life and proclivities emerge from the sale of his effects. Most surprising to us, perhaps, for a man of the cloth is the presence at the head of the list of two swords, three crossbow bolts, a coat of chain mail ('haultbrejon'), arm and leg armour, and various items of horse paraphernalia: saddles, bridles and harnesses (including an 'harnas de guerre'); a reminder surely that membership in the chapel of the dukes of Burgundy entailed readiness for combat not just of a spiritual nature. It is unfortunate that few of the various entries for the sale of books give any specifics, though intriguingly the one specified item – besides the expected breviary and psalters – is '.1. livre de art de musicque', sold to one Guillaume Martin. A writing desk ('escriptoire') is a perhaps not unexpected accoutrement of a senior cleric, though more suggestive of personal interests is an astrolabe, bought by Canon Jacques de Houchin, with whom we shall become more familiar in the Epilogue.[136]

But concerning actual events, the detail of the account, as would be expected from its nature, is concentrated in the period after Toussains's decease. The first step when that point was reached was to inform interested parties of his death and impending obsequies. A messenger was dispatched on a ten-day journey to inform relatives and friends in Noyon (as one might expect) but also in St Quentin (seat of two relatives who were canons), Vermandois, Péronne, Roye and 'elsewhere'. Toussains's body was sewn into a shroud and a 'tin chalice' ordered, presumably – as was customary – to be buried with him. The six pall-bearers and five poor people paid to carry the cross and torches would have headed the burial procession, the day after Toussains's death, that also comprised thirteen of his fellow canons, twenty-seven vicars, twelve escotiers, four curates, thirty-three installed priests and sixteen non-priests, and eight choirboys (two in addition to the usual six). The day of the (later) funeral service saw a much greater gathering including – besides family, friends, secular representatives of the city and other associates – twenty-two canons, five curates, twenty-six priests, eleven ordained escotiers, two vicars and one escotier who were not ordained, sixty-one 'installed' priests, no fewer than nine choirboys, and the canon, deacon, subdeacon and 'choriste' who celebrated the Mass. Eight poor people who carried the torches, along with the tomb

---

[135] II. G. 476, ff. 22v, 24r.   [136] Ff. 4r, 9v.

itself, were provided with escutcheons painted with the deceased's coat of arms by the painter David Sautil (variously Saulty or de Sauti).[137] It seems likely that, as specified in other such cases, these were to be affixed to the torches themselves.[138]

Like all his fellow canons, Toussains founded Masses, requiems and obits (services for posthumous repose performed on the anniversary of death) to be celebrated for the benefit of his soul. What is noteworthy in his case, though, is their staggering number, running easily into the thousands. Central to these celebrations were the daily Masses for which he had long paid in his lifetime, to be performed at the altar of St Blaise, a second foundation by Toussains himself in the chapel of St Thomas of Canterbury. Here, some six years before his death, he had received permission to be buried, and his Masses were timed – significantly – to coincide with the elevation at High Mass at the main altar.[139] In other words, like Rembert after him and like many others here and elsewhere, Toussains sought association with the communal moment of the church's High Mass and hence with his community's collective entreaty to the redeemer made present on the altar. A number of individual entries in the executors' account concern Masses running into hundreds: while in some cases the numbers specified – 80, 269 and 200 – are a mystery, the many endowments for 'annuels' – a daily Mass to be performed for a year starting on the day after his obsequies, that is beginning on 10 October – clearly each involve a succession of 365 celebrations, each concluded by an obit.

In some cases the choice of celebrants is likely revealing of special links: for example the cluster of fourteen priests assigned to perform two annuals in the chapel of St Blaise includes Eustache Maistresse, master of the boys in the early 1460s and a former singer at St Donatian, Bruges, and Robert Fabri, posthumous recipient of Toussains's music books and, as noted in Chapter 2, a possible relative. Striking besides their number is the range and profile of locations covered by performance of Toussains's Masses. In addition to the spread of devotions across churches, friaries and convents in his home town, others are clearly revealing of more individual

---

[137] Ff. 15r–16v. On Sautil's known activities generally see Gil and Nys, *Saint-Omer gothique*, 354–5.

[138] See Dominique Vantouroux, 'Les funérailles des chanoines de Saint-Omer (1426–1598)', *Revue du Nord* 65/257 (April–June 1983), 363.

[139] Hac die in crastino Beati Luce [17 September] anno lxiiii[to] domini mei accordarunt Domino Toussano de Ruella quod possit inhumari in capella Beati Blasii in quo dietim fundavit unam missam celebrandam hora elevationis sanctissimi sacramenti de magne misse. (II. G. 353, f. 62r)

connections. Since we know that Toussains was the holder of some currently unknown benefices and that he had, since 1422, occupied a canonry
at the cathedral of Noyon, his foundation of annual obit services both there
and at St Gertrude, Nivelles, and St Pol may suggest that he also possessed
benefices at the latter two churches. His executors' account adds concrete
knowledge of a benefice held by him at the cathedral of Chalon-sur-Saône,
whose possession had obliged him annually to supply a measure ('bichet')
of corn.[140] His provision for forty-eight Masses in the church at Lillers may
suggest a similar connection.

Finally, Toussains's executors' account provides valuable details concerning the fashioning of his (now lost) epitaph and complementary
funerary slab, which survives (Figure 6.2).[141] Preparation for the fashioning
of the epitaph included the commissioning of a painted preparatory design,
in this case by the same painter who was paid for painting the black
lettering of the finished item. This, following standard procedure, would
have been a wall-mounted item with a fixed surround fitted with closing
shutters.[142] The painter David Saulty who, as already noted, painted the
escutcheons for the obsequies, was paid also for painting the epitaph and,
although no mention is made of polychromy on the shutters, it seems
highly likely that, as in analogous cases, these were likewise adorned.

While the name of the engraver of the slab itself is not provided, this has
all the appearance, as Gil and Nys note, of Tournai work of the highest
standard.[143] The account does include payment to 'Jehan Martin engraver,
for having engraved the date of death of the said deceased on the tomb and

---

[140] Item a leglise cathedral de St Vinchent de Chalon sur la Sonne moyennant quils tendront ledit
feu quitte de fonder ung bischoit de ble perpetuellement a quoy ils dient que ledit feu estoit et
est tenu de fonder en leur dicte eglise pour lame de ses predicesseurs [sic] quant il fu receu
chanonne. (f. 24v; for the other Mass foundations see ff. 20v)

[141] See Gil and Nys, *Saint-Omer gothique*, 232–3, 255, 256, 349, 355 and 373, and Brine, *Pious
Memories*, 102, 106.

[142] 'Item a David Saulty paintre pour avoir paint lepitaphe dudit feu et le ymaige de notre seigneur
ou cloistre comme appert par quittance xviii l; Item a Pierre Micquiel huchier pour avoir fait
deux foeulles a fremer [sic] ledit epitaphe comme appert par quittance xxx s; Item a Jacques
Cocquempot fevre pour avoir fait iiii. Gon[d]s et iiii wanteles [ganteles] a pendre les foeulles
dudit epitaphe et aultres ouvraiges a lostel dudit feu comme appert par quittance xvii s vi d'
(f. 16v). On the activities of David [de] Saulty see Gil and Nys, *Saint-Omer gothique*, 354–5.
'Item a Baudechon du Molin paintre pour le faichon des patrons du epitaphe dudit feu et les
escriptures dicellui par lui fais en noir et du sauveur mis ou cloistre comme appert par
quittance xxiiii s' (f. 20v). On the activities of Bauduin du Molin see Gil and Nys, *Saint-Omer
gothique*, 348–50.

[143] See Gil and Nys, *Saint-Omer gothique*, 373.

in his epitaph'.[144] The practice of adding the date of decease to an otherwise finished memorial (as is clearly visible, for example, on the tomb slab of Du Fay) was, for obvious reasons, standard practice. As is still apparent, the quality and dimensions of the subsequently added letters on Toussains's slab differ markedly from those already finished, suggesting that the clearly more elegant lettering of the remainder of the inscription was the work of other hands, presumably in the workshop that produced this sophisticated item as a whole.[145]

Whatever resemblance the image of Toussains still visible to us today may have had to the living canon, however, the blank, hieratic stare that returns our gaze from his funerary slab would leave little abiding sense of the man in the absence of the tissue of life witnessed by his executors' account. Whatever the worldly deeds and professional machinations of the high-achieving canons of the day, traceable through fabric accounts, chapter acts and other institutional documents, it is chiefly through these absorbing survivals that we can approach, however distantly, their more fundamentally human essence. It is in search of something of this essence, hopefully mitigating in some small way impressions of a world that can sometimes seem all too alien, that we will now turn for a final perspective on the workings of this long-vanished society.

---

[144] Item a Jehan Martin entretailleur pour avoir grave le jour dudit trespas dudit feu tant sur le tombe comme en son epitafle comme appert par quittance xxxii s (f. 16v)

[145] On Jehan Martin see Gil and Nys, *Saint-Omer gothique*, 372–4. My thanks to Douglas Brine for his insights on the production of Toussains's epitaph and funerary slab.

Epilogue

A Cloistered Art: Connoisseurship and Private Music-Making

An executors' account of a medieval church canon is a window onto a distant life. Through its pages we are drawn into an existence long since ended, and shaped by circumstances very different from our own. Such an account is, in the first place, a snapshot of a life at the moment of its end: its existence, the reason behind its painstaking copying and the fulfilment of its obligations, is activated by death. As the examples of Rembert and Toussains have already revealed, its threefold purposes are in themselves prosaic: to list the deceased's effects and arrange for their disposal according to the terms of the will (a copy of which will typically be included in the document), to effect the settlement of expenses incurred before death, and to make provision for events, predetermined by the deceased while living, to unfold in its wake.[1]

Yet through the pages of such a document, occasioned by a single moment, we quickly see time's arrow moving away from that moment in two directions: into the future, yes, as the train of events following death unfolds before us; but also into the past, as we learn of the possessions and physical spaces that have shaped the life that has just ended. These are precious documents indeed: through them we gain a depth of access to a medieval life that is denied us for most of those who have died within living memory.

Events involving a life that are witnessed by such a document are inevitably concentrated towards its end, an occurrence that is timeless enough. But the way that end is met, the setting of its stage, its dramatis personae and props, say things about medieval life that are radically different from what an account of a modern death might reveal of life in the twenty-first century. The anguished progress towards life's end is its most recognisable aspect, a vivid reminder of our own mortality: illness

---

[1] The holdings of such documents in the Bibliothèque at Saint-Omer – rich sources concerning life as a canon of St Omer – are housed in bundles with the call numbers (for our period of interest) II. G. 473–85. Three volumes (Justice échevinale de Saint-Omer MSS 15B1–3) in the Archives Départementales du Pas-de-Calais at Dainville (Arras) record the wills of many further members of the clergy of the collégiale, including Jean Thorion (see Chapter 3).

and ultimate demise, if accompanied by barber-surgeons and bleeding rather than by the laboratory conditions of modern hospitals, follow a route whose inexorability is familiar enough. Yet the presence – as so often in the final stages – of a priest to say the hours of a passing soul too weak to say them himself, reminds us of the paramount concern of the dying medieval person: to make a death that is beautiful in the eyes of God and thereby to ensure favourable consideration at the celestial court for the soul suffering in purgatory. The last payments, detailed in the accounts, to clerics for performing devotions for the deceased while alive remind us of the importance of gaining favour with patron saints during life, a concern of the greatest urgency since this, it was hoped, would encourage their support at death and for however long thereafter purgatory may endure. In addition to the celebration of Masses, such devotions would typically entail the deathbed reading of psalms, vigils and other sacred tracts.

Like key moments in all other temporal cycles, the administering to the dying supplicant of extreme unction is marked by bell-ringing, informing fellow citizens of the imminent passing of one of their number.[2] Following last rites and death, likewise marked by the sounding of a bell, the post-mortem juggernaut moves swiftly into action. The body is sewn into a shroud – always by women, most often the soeurs noires de St Augustin, otherwise known as the 'soeurs de Lombardie' – and laid in a coffin draped in black, frequently emblazoned with the newly painted or embroidered arms of the deceased. Ahead of burial a vigil is kept over the coffin, with torches burning and the room draped in black. The funeral, usually succeeding death as quickly as possible, is revealed in often painstaking detail through the payments for its materials and participants: a quantity of black cloth to dress the poor (or sometimes boys, servants or escotiers) who carried the cross and torches in the funeral procession, a specified number of torches and wax for a specified number of candles,[3] all of a specified weight, with details concerning where and when they were to be placed or carried, at the vigil and at the burial service itself. Alms to the poor are specified (usually bread but sometimes also money), while payments are detailed to everyone involved in the service, as in the case of Toussains de Le Ruelle already discussed: to six canons who carried the coffin, and all others who – in strictly hierarchical order – processed after it: canons,

---

[2] For this and other details presented here see Dominique Vantouroux, 'Les funérailles des chanoines de Saint-Omer (1426–1598)', *Revue du Nord* 65/257 (April–June 1983), 361–8.

[3] The torches comprised a baton with a candle affixed, with a pendant cloth covering the holder's hand (see ibid., 363).

vicars and other priests, escotiers, choirboys and chapter officers, followed by representatives of the religious orders, members of the laity, again proceeding according to rank, and finally relatives and friends. The burial service itself embraces three Masses: the intercessional Masses dedicated to the Holy Spirit and the Virgin, and finally a requiem Mass for the soul's repose.[4]

There then follows, after a decent enough interval to allow for the informing and gathering of relatives and associates, the – typically much grander – 'service', with proportionally larger attendance and corresponding monetary payments, and related distribution of alms, all with the aim of stimulating prayers for the soul of the departed. The mortal remains now entombed, a substituting catafalque becomes the focus of lamentation, surrounded, as if it were the deceased, by candles and torchbearers distinguished, as at the burial service, by escutcheons. Finally, the ceremonial over, a dinner is held in the now vacated house, its wine and food provided at the expense of the deceased, presumably – much like the wakes of today – both in memory of a life now past and in expression of the solidarity in that memory of those left behind.

Most important from the point of view of the deceased, though, were the prayers and services, chiefly Masses, performed for the departed soul. These would commence directly, with Masses specified in other locations to synchronise with the burial service, but with many more, in accordance with the deceased's wishes, following in the days, months and years to come. Death typically triggered a spate of Masses, their scope limited only by the dead person's wealth and proclivities: Masses in the church where he worked, but also, spreading like ripples out from that church, in outlying churches, priories and monasteries with which he held benefices or maintained other relations while living. Concentrated often in very large number in the immediate aftermath of death, further Masses would be instituted on a daily, weekly or annual basis, paid for typically by lands and rents for lands owned by the deceased and earmarked for that purpose in the will. These devotions were, in the end, those of most crucial importance to the deceased, perpetually pleading his case in heaven through a period in purgatory which could, in theory, last for millennia.

Setting up a train of events designed to extend forward in perpetuity, such provisions are counterbalanced in an executors' account by a view back into life. Besides revealing the last stages in the progress to death, the

---

[4] See ibid., 363.

account may, as in Toussains's case, provide details of the fashioning and painting of the grave slab and – of signal importance since it was usually sited before or as close as possible to the altar of a patron saint – the position of the grave itself. Drawing us back into the fullness of life is the inventory of the deceased's effects. One of the first tasks of the executors would be to 'visit', or 'examine', the house of the dead person. This involved not only the drawing up of the inventory of its contents, but also the arrangement of any necessary renovation in preparation for the new tenant. Whoever this was would typically be keen to occupy the house as quickly as possible: the house of a canon, usually in the cloister of the church to which he was attached, could, particularly if it was a desirable one, be hotly contested by would-be new tenants, and the medieval equivalent of 'gazumping' was far from uncommon. The inventory and arrangements complete, valuable possessions would be boxed up and sealed, and a guard, or guards, placed on the house until such time as its contents could be disposed of according to the terms of the will.

The inventory itself offers a fascinating and privileged insight into the objects which mark out the space occupied by a medieval life. Through it we can follow the executors as they pass from room to room, cupboard to cupboard and counter to counter, listing not only each object, but also its precise position in the house. Such is the specificity of a well-prepared executors' account that it could easily enable the drawing up of a detailed map (or indeed a three-dimensional computer model) of the house and its contents. The listing, in these days before widespread banking, of jewellery and gold and silver coins, often in an astonishing range of denominations, reveals why guards would have been so vital: a canon, particularly one occupying a range of benefices, could amass substantial wealth in the course of his lifetime. Passing from hall to kitchen to bedchamber to attic and so on, pots, pans, basins, robes, hats and sheets reveal themselves, often in huge numbers: a well-to-do canon would typically maintain a considerable household with servants and facilities well up to entertaining visiting dignitaries. Here and there the rooms are host to a (frequently specified) 'ymage': a small panel painting or statue (often specified as made from alabaster or white stone) of the Virgin and Child, a favoured saint, or perhaps even of the duke, king or emperor.

But for us today the most instructive possessions listed are surely the dead person's books. Here is our most revealing access to the worldview of an educated medieval cleric, the intellectual space which he inhabited. A number of titles appear regularly: the *Consolation of Philosophy* by Boethius, the *Golden Legend* by Jacobus de Voragine, the *Livre de bonnes meurs* ('Book of Good Manners') by Jacques Legrand, and the *Pèlerinage de l'âme* by Guillaume de Digulleville, along with sundry liturgical books and – particularly in the cases of those many canons who possessed degrees in canon law – copies of the *Decretals* of Gratian. Most of these items appear, for example, in the executors' account of Guillaume Du Fay, who died in 1474: possessing thirty-four books at death, Du Fay was a more than average bibliophile among senior canons at the time.[5] Yet his collection pales when compared to that of a St Omer canon who died just over six years later.

At his death on 8 January 1481 (new style), Jacques de Houchin possessed some 376 volumes.[6] This was a truly staggering quantity of books to be owned by a private individual at this time. At least equally astonishing, though, is their range: while the largest section of their inventory – preserved today as part of Houchin's executors' account – is devoted to 'theology' (including scriptural commentary and patristics) (131 volumes), they also embrace canon and civil law (29 volumes), medicine, surgery and astrology (17 volumes), music (15 volumes, and the chief focus of interest here) and – perhaps most notably – classical and humanistic Latin texts, mostly contained in the 155-strong pair of sections headed 'books of poets and poems, and grammar and rhetoric', and 'other books of rhetoric and letters and poems'. The smattering of classical titles in other sections of the list tips the weight of emphasis still further in the same direction. Sundry other books of various kinds are scattered through the inventory, and a small additional group is listed in a sub-inventory made a couple of months after the drawing up of the main list.

While nothing specific is known about Houchin's background and education, it seems clear from his consistent styling as 'magister' that he had a master's degree, perhaps in arts or, on the evidence of the large number of legal tracts in his possession, in canon law. He emerges as a man of considerable standing in the church chapter acts, though clearly not of sufficient weight to avoid the refusal of his application for a benefice he sought in April 1474, but which, he was told, was reserved for

---

[5] Listed in Craig Wright, 'Dufay at Cambrai: Discoveries and Revisions', *Journal of the American Musicological Society* 28 (1975), 215–17.

[6] See Houchin's executors' account, preserved today among the collection II. G. 473. The inventory of Houchin's books has been published twice. See Oscar Bled, 'Une Bibliothèque de chanoine au XVe siècle', in *Bulletin de la Société des antiquaires de la Morinie* 7 (1882–6), 265–84 (easily available via the Bibliothèque Nationale's *Gallica* web resource), and Gil and Nys, *Saint-Omer gothique*, 427–37, which also gives the inventory of the following sale.

protonotaries.[7] His bibliophilic knowledge is frequently called on, most obviously to check the inventory of the church library, a task undertaken annually. But he also surfaces occasionally as one of the individuals appointed to inventory and sell the effects of another canon, as in the case of Thierry de Vitry in late 1478.[8] His most illustrious calling of this nature occurred in December 1479, little more than a year before his own death, when he was one of two canons engaged to price and arrange the sale of books and other effects belonging to the recently deceased Provost of St Omer, Simon de Luxembourg.[9] Luxembourg, whose executors' account also survives, clearly also possessed a library of some substance including, significantly, a number of classical Latin texts. Houchin himself bought volumes by Boccaccio and Isidore, among other materials, from the sale. Not content with simply buying books, Houchin also commissioned their copying: an item in the will records a payment to a certain Jacques Pontaigne 'for service rendered to the said deceased for a period of two years in writing several books and other [services] at his request'.[10] The will also demands the return to Pierre Godin, Houchin's chaplain and one of his three executors, of 'a book named the "pastorale" of Gregory [presumably the *Liber regulae pastoralis* of St Gregory the Great], written in the hand of the said Godin' ('ung livre nomme pastorale Gregorii escript de le main dudit Godin' (f. 41v)).

The ultimate expression of Houchin's self-image as a bibliophile is his request to position his grave in the cloister next to the chapel of St Jerome. Translator of the Bible into Latin and viewed as the Christian proto-scholar, Jerome was commonly invoked as a patron of scholars. Thus to seek Jerome's advocacy for his soul after death was a natural posture for Houchin, an advocacy that he sought to promote further by paying for a Mass to be celebrated every day in the chapel for a year after his funeral. If the size and scope of Houchin's library is an accurate reflection of his learning, we can surely expect that his plea to his ancient confrère was heard more clearly than most.

Beyond the sheer scale of Houchin's library, though, what mark it out as particularly striking for a private northern European collection are its holdings in classical and humanistic texts. Rare against any contemporary yardstick, its contents are entirely without peer among the collections of his

---

[7] II. G. 354, f. 175r.   [8] II. G. 354, f. 223r.   [9] II. G. 354, ff. 238v, 240v.

[10] ... pour service quil a fait audit feu par lespasse de deux ans en escripvrant [sic] pluisseurs livres et aultrement a sa requeste. (f. 47r)

fellow canons of St Omer.[11] In making this latter point, it should be acknowledged that the scarcity of classical literature in the north during this period has been overstated, or at least oversimplified, especially as regards circles linked in one way or another to the ruling House of Burgundy.[12] For sure, acquisition of classical tracts seems more typically to have fed into prevailing pedagogical traditions of grammar, rhetoric and Christian morality than of the contemplation per se of belles-lettres; indeed, as noted above, the headings of the pertinent sections of Houchin's book inventory emphasise grammar and rhetoric, with no allusion to manner of writing. Traditional proclivities would have been sufficient to feed appetites for a large proportion of the items represented in Houchin's library: acquisition of Cicero requires no special pleading for an educated and sermonising cleric seeking the highest models of Latinity in general and rhetoric in particular; and the susceptibility of the same author's writings to Christian moral interpretation further sustained their propagation. Similar preconditions drove consumption of Terence, Seneca and especially Ovid, for Christian moral reinterpretation the classical author par excellence; likewise moral reinterpretation served more than adequately to justify interest in Petrarch and Boccaccio.[13]

It would seem unlikely, in any case, that well-connected, university-educated clerics, many of whom had spent time in Rome, would be entirely unfamiliar with classical and indeed humanistic authors. All the same, Houchin's library seems to have had few peers among private collections, in depth as well as breadth. Valuable points of comparison are offered by Albert Derolez's series of (to date) seven volumes addressing *The Medieval Booklists of the Southern Low Countries*.[14] This collection offers the great

---

[11] On the exceptional nature of Houchin's collection see Geneviève Hasenohr, 'L'essor des bibliothèques privées aux XIVᵉ aux XV ᵉ siècles', in André Vernet (ed.), *Histoire des bibliothèques françaises. Les bibliothèques médiévales du VIᵉ à 1530* (Paris: Promodis- Éditions du Cercle de la Librairie, 1989), 224, 232–3. Gil and Nys note that the closest collection in terms of number, that of François de Melun, extends to 116 volumes (though, unfortunately, few of these are specified), while the average number of volumes recorded in the executors' accounts of St-Omer canons from 1455 to 1533 runs to twenty-three (*Saint-Omer gothique*, 130, 140).

[12] On ownership of classical texts by individuals with Burgundian connections see Céline Van Hoorebeeck, 'La réception de l'humanisme dans les Pays-Bas bourguignons (XVᵉ–début XVIᵉ siècle). L'apport des bibliothèques privées', in István Monok (ed.), *Matthias Corvin, les bibliothèques princières et la genèse de l'état moderne* (Budapest: Országos Széchényi Könyvtár, 2009), 93–120.

[13] See ibid., 103.

[14] Albert Derolez (ed.), Benjamin Victor (associate ed.), *Corpus catalogorum Belgii: The Medieval Booklists of the Southern Low Countries* (Brussels: Paleis der Academien, 1997–).

advantage of surveying book holdings across a broad area, and hence an opportunity to gauge the likely level of rarity of Houchin's collection.

In terms of sheer volume this survey yields little among privately owned collections to compare with Houchin's library. Its closest comparator is the 316-strong collection of Simon de Slusa, a clearly more senior cleric than Houchin who held canonries in Bruges, Liège, Mons, Ghent, Utrecht and St Romuald, Mechlelen, of which latter he was provost in 1478, besides acting, from 1461 onwards, as personal physician to the dukes of Burgundy. Donated to the University of Cologne on his death in 1499, Slusa's holdings, like Houchin's, included volumes of Aristotle, Cicero, Iuvenal, Terence, Pliny, Valerius Maximus and Petrarch, along with numerous theological, legal and medical tracts and familiar fare such as Boethius' *Consolation of Philosophy* and works by Thomas Aquinas, Albertus Magnus, Gerson and so on.[15]

Of similar heft, though with a predomimantly theological profile, was the 312-volume collection of the monk of St Bavo, Ghent, Michael van der Stoct, known from an inventory of around 1395–1400.[16] A distinctly more classical orientation is revealed by the 1483 catalogue of the 130-volume library of the Ghent lawyer Philip Wielant, which embraced numerous works by Virgil, Quintilian, Sallust, Terence, Iuvenal, Pliny, Valerius Maximus and Ovid, along with more recent classicists including Poggio Bracciolini, Aeneas Silvius Piccolomini (Pius II), Boccaccio and Petrarch.[17] Revealing of similar proclivities is the 127-strong collection, inventoried by his executors in 1482, of John Bayart, canon of the chapter of Our Lady in Kortrijk (Courtrai). Here again we encounter works by Cicero, Terence, Valerius Maximus, Ovid, Petrarch, Aeneas Silvius Piccolomini and Poggio Bracciolini, along with more expected volumes of decretals, Augustine, Ambrose and Jerome.[18]

But to judge by the inventoried lists of its canons, the most impressive nexus of private bibliophilia among canons is that concentrated at the Brussels collegiate church of St Thomas and St Gudule. Outstanding here is the collection of the canon lawyer Nicholas Clopper. Having been an *abbreviator* at the papal curia, Clopper was from 1441 counsellor to Dukes Philip the Good and Charles the Bold, and shortly thereafter maintained, from his earlier roster of benefices, only the canonries of St Gudule, St Paul, Liège, and Our Lady of Antwerp. His eclectic library of 287 volumes, inventoried by his executors in 1472, embraced works by Aristotle, Cicero,

---

[15] Ibid. III (1999), 220–30.   [16] Ibid. III, 53–71.   [17] Ibid. III, 120–5.
[18] Ibid. I (1997), 138–45.

Seneca, Seutonius, Scipio Africanus, Ovid, Aeneas Silvius Piccolomini and
John Wyclif, along with familiar items such as the *Legenda Aurea* and
works by Lactantius, Augustine, Jerome, Bonaventure, Durandus, Hugh of
St Victor, Albertus Magnus, Peter of Blois, Isidore, Gerson, and so on. The
(comparatively) more middling late-fifteenth-century collections of
Michael van Houcke, Walter Lonijs, Thomas van Liere, Martin Steenberch,
William van der Borch, Martin Tossyen and Michael Lobe (with holdings
of between 31 and 125 volumes) similarly featured classical authors including Cicero, Terence, Seneca, Valerius Maximus, Quintilian, Plutarch,
Sallust and Ovid, humanists including Petrarch, Poggio Bracciolini and
Leonardo Bruni as well as the expected range of liturgical volumes, theological and legal tracts, etc.[19]

The holdings by these bibliophiles – as by Jacques de Houchin – of
Cicero, Terence, Ovid, Seneca, Petrarch and Boccaccio would all have
responded to clear needs of an education in the liberal arts; and while such
figures as Virgil, Sallust and (in Houchin's case) Aulus Gellius are less
widespread, they were clearly far from unknown in the north, as is also the
case regarding writings by such humanists as Poggio Bracciolini, Leonardo
Bruni, Lorenzo Valla, Maffeo Vegio and Pietro Paolo Vergerio.

For much of Houchin's inventory, among the classics as elsewhere, the
surprise concerns less the nature of the volumes (though some are indeed
rarities) than their extent and range. While some titles are too generic to
allow identification, familiar patterns nonetheless emerge. The church
fathers are handsomely represented, with a strong showing by Augustine,
Gregory and Jerome, backed up by John Chrysostom, Cassiodorus,
Lactantius, Origen and so on. The numerous volumes of sermons include
the expected anthologies of Bernard of Clairvaux, while other later medieval tracts reveal a penchant for the writings of Lotario di Segni (Innocent
III) and representation of a wide range of further authors including Peter of
Blois, Bonaventure, Nicholas of Lyra and Hugh of St Victor. Items by
Aeneas Silvius Piccolomini (Pius II) include a copy of his lavishly wishful
Epistle to the Sultan Mahomet II, urging him, following the 1453 fall of
Constantinople, to renounce Islam and follow Christ. Late antique authors
are most obviously and numerously represented by Boethius, while tracts
on the movements of the planets and astrology, the decretals and

---

[19] For the collections of the canons of St Thomas and St Gudule see ibid. IV (2001), 60–140. For
summaries of the libraries of Brussels clerics see also Barbara Haggh, 'Music, Liturgy, and
Ceremony in Brussels, 1350–1500', unpublished PhD dissertation, University of Illinois at
Urbana–Champaign (1988), vol. 2, 935–47.

commentary thereon, plus a smattering of liturgical books and numerous miscellaneous items further bulk out the collection. An almost exclusive Latinity is interrupted, in a section labelled 'books in French on diverse matters', by only six vernacular volumes including the *Roman de la rose* and a French translation of Ovid's *Ars amatoria*.

Our principal concern here, though, is with a different facet of Houchin's library that marks it out as unique: its collection of books of music. These items, most of them listed at the end of the inventory, comprise no fewer than seventeen volumes. To put this in perspective, this is almost twice the number of music books owned by Du Fay at his death. Unlike the books of Du Fay, but sadly like most inventoried music books at this time, though, few of Houchin's music books receive more than a generic description. There are two exceptions, itemised separately from the main list of music books. One of these, intriguingly, is headed 'Ung livre de canchons commenchant pour danser lamourisque', its headline item presumably having been a song designed to accompany the 'moresca', a popular dance, sometimes dubbed in French the 'danse des bouffons', involving participants dressed as 'moors', or muslims, often in combat with Christians.[20] The second, perhaps less unexpected among the collection of a canon, is listed as 'ung aultre commenchant ad cenam'. Clearly opening with a setting of the vespers hymn 'Ad cenam agni providi', this seems likely to have been a volume of hymns or a more general collection of vespers polyphony.

The remainder, comprising the last section of the book inventory proper and headed 'Livres de musicque', is as follows:

Five small books of chansons and a large quire
Three of medium size
Three large books of Masses and motets / and a quire
Two medium [books] of Masses[21]

Since in the case of Houchin we are blessed in having not only the inventory of his books but also the ledger of their sale we are able to discover the identities of the individuals who bought these and the other items in his library, and the sums they realised.[22] Many of the forty

---

[20] Alan Brown and Donna G. Cardamone, 'Moresca', *Grove Music Online*, www .oxfordmusiconline.com/grovemusic/view/10.1093/gmo/9781561592630.001.0001/ omo-9781561592630-e-0000019125 (2001), accessed 10 September 2018.

[21] Chincq livres de canchons petis et ung grant coyer; Trois moyens; Trois grans livres de messes et de mottes / et ung quoyer; deux moyens a messes

[22] For a detailed account of the process of the inventorying of Houchin's books, drawn from the executors' account, see Lotte Hellinga, 'Book Auctions in the Fifteenth Century', ch. 1 in *Incunabula in Transit: People and Trade* (Leiden and Boston, MA: Brill, 2018), 12–17.

named purchasers at the sale, which lasted the five whole days from 17 to 21 September, were fellow members of the collégiale, but it is clear that the sale also drew in members of the laity and interested parties from much further afield. The executors' account records payments for announcements of the sale, including one specified at the abbey of St Bertin. Those closest to the sale and to Houchin himself were among the successful bidders: Canon Hughes de Monchy, one of the two canons who spent nine days drawing up the inventory, left the sale with six volumes; while the account's scribe, Rembert's tormentor Johannes Derviller, clearly as susceptible to classical scholarship as to irascibility, bought no fewer than twenty-two items including a volume of *Bucolicum* by both Virgil and Sallust, the pseudo-Aristotle *Rhetorica ad Alexandrum*, a *Commentum* of Aulus Persius Flaccus (presumably the *Satires*), a volume of Seneca called *Metricus*, a printed copy of the *Facetiae* by Poggio Bracciolini, a volume of Latin *Epistles* by Antonius Panormita (1394–1471), the *Achilleid* by Statius, the 'Invectiva Tullii in Verrem', presumably a copy of Cicero's invectives against Gaius Verres, and – intriguingly – a volume of 'sermons on Virgil'. The cantor Johannes de Hemont, familiar to us from Chapter 2 especially for his role in the institution of the 'bulle conservatoire', bought nine books including what was clearly a lavish copy of Boethius's *Consolation of Philosophy*, described in the inventory as 'perpulcer' and 'with the gloss of' none other than Arnoul Gréban (encountered in Chapter 3), for which he was prepared to part with £4 10s. 3d.; while the tenorist Grigorius Bourgois bought three volumes including a *Liber Beatii Gregorii*, likely a volume of writings by his patron saint.

There is some concentration of interest in classical and humanist texts among the higher clerics active at the sale – the provost of St Omer (Simon de Luxembourg), the provost of Arques and the dean of Dole – a tendency to be expected given their likely access to higher and broader education, and one also in tune with the concentration, as noted above, of larger private libraries in the hands of wealthy senior clerics. But Derviller is far from the only ordinary canon with a clear penchant for classical scholarship: the purchasing patterns of others, including Eugène Labite and Walleran Caron, reveal similar proclivities. Certainly the more expensive volumes tended to be bought by the more eminent clerics, with the pick of the collection, a 'bele bible', being sold for £18 to the dean of Dole and the next most expensive, the glossed *Consolation of Philosophy*, going to the cantor Hemont. Star turns notwithstanding, though, the majority of Houchin's books comprised manuscripts on paper, with few entries mentioning illumination; in other words, as Gil and Nys have emphasised, books designed for study rather than for show.[23]

It is clear from the prices realised and the identities of their purchasers that the music books were likewise utilitarian items not aimed at lavish consumers: the only holder even of a canonry to figure among their buyers was Mahieu Pol, who picked up the cheapest deal among the music sales, paying a paltry 7d. for 'deux aultres' 'livres as canchons'. Of the ten music books that found buyers, four were bought by Mahieu Daustin, one of the four perpetual vicars at the high altar and chaplain of the altar of St Jerome in the cloister (the site of Houchin's grave). Daustin's purchases include the only specified sale of one of the five books of Masses listed in the inventory, though it is not impossible that the books 'de cant' and 'as canchons' that were sold included others among the Mass anthologies. The prices raised were fairly modest: the highest was 4s., for 'ung aultre' 'livre as canchons' bought by Martin Lavenne, the then current master of the boys and scribe (as noted in Chapter 2) of responses in six books used for processions, clearly by the six choirboys. Most of the others realised between 3s. 3d. and 3s. 9d., while 12d. was sufficient for Lavenne to secure 'aucuns coyers', presumably the two listed in the inventory. Single volumes were purchased by the chapter's bailiff, Pierre de Saint-Amand, and by a certain Huchon Cocquet.

Any possible suggestion that these are just further aspects of what was clearly a voracious bibliophilic appetite is quickly dispelled by other items in Houchin's inventory: he clearly possessed a number of musical instruments. Thus we find that on the 'high counter' in the attic were two harps and 'ung ju de fluctes de vj pieces' (presumably a chest of instruments tuned in different ranges); two 'sonnettes de cymballes' were found in a coffer 'en la sale', while among his effects sold were a 'clavici[m]bolum' and 'ung bon monocorde'.[24] Houchin's directly musical penchant was clearly complemented by a theoretical interest: his book inventory includes a 'Tractatus musicalis' and a similarly unspecified 'Tractatus brevis musice',[25] neither of which excited sufficient interest to find a buyer. But there seems little question that, whatever his bibliophilic and theoretical interests in music, Houchin must also have been a performer.

The presence of instruments raises intriguing questions, albeit in the end of course mostly unanswerable, concerning performance practice. Especially provocative in this regard is the presence of keyboard instruments:

[23] *Saint-Omer gothique*, 131, 134.   [24] Ff. 11v, 8v and 28v respectively.
[25] Ff. 17v and 18v respectively.

the 'clavicimbolum' was presumably an early harpsichord, while the word 'monochord' at this date most likely refers to a clavichord comprised of equal-length strings tuned in unison, its varied pitches produced by tangents striking the strings at different points.[26] Houchin's possession of keyboard instruments chimes also with what would appear to have been a marked interest in the organ. As noted in Chapter 4, much of the cost of the new organ constructed by the noted Ypres organ-builder Victor Langhedul in the early 1480s was borne by 'money remaining from the testament of master Jacobus de Houchin'.[27] Since there is nothing in Houchin's inventory to suggest his ownership of keyboard music per se, it seems reasonable to assume that these instruments were used in conjunction with music written in parts, and they must hence surely have been played at least some of the time in conjunction with singers. Polyphonic lines could further have been accommodated by the case of six flutes and pair of harps, while one might perhaps imagine a role for the cymbals in the realisation of the 'mourisque'.

While the flutes and cymbals evidently did not garner interest at the sale, both of the harps and the two keyboard instruments did attract buyers. An outlay of 25s. found 'une herpe petite' a home with the vicar Jehan Dergny, along with Pierre Godin and Hugo de Monchy one of Houchin's three executors and probably a former choirboy, the man who in 1490 was to be dramatically freed from prison in Calais where he was being held (perhaps as a hostage) by the king of England.[28] Jehan Derviller acquired the other, larger harp for just 3s., its knockdown price perhaps suggesting that it was in a state of decrepitude. The two keyboards, whose sales apparently for much smaller sums than realised by the small harp suggest that they were probably of quite modest dimensions, both found purchasers. The 'clavicimbolum' went for 14s. to the priest, scribe (of music as well as text) and bookbinder Thomas de Boucoud,[29] purchaser at Houchin's sale also of the Epistle to Mahomet II. Active already by 1448/9, Boucoud must by this

---

[26] See Edwin M. Ripin, Howard Schott, John Koster, Denzil Wraight, Beryl Kenyon de Pascual, G. Grant O'Brien, Alfons Huber, William R. Dowd, Charles Mould, Lance Whitehead and Martin Elste, 'Harpsichord', *Grove Music Online*, 2001, www.oxfordmusiconline.com/ grovemusic/view/10.1093/gmo/9781561592630.001.0001/omo-9781561592630-e-0000012420, accessed 10 September 2018 ; and Edwin M. Ripin, John Barnes, Alfons Huber, Beryl Kenyon de Pascual and Barry Kernfeld, 'Clavichord', *Grove Music Online*, 2001, www.oxfordmusiconline .com/grovemusic/view/10.1093/gmo/9781561592630.001.0001/omo-9781561592630-e-0000005909, accessed 10 September 2018.

[27] See above, 147, 149. [28] For details of Dergny's career see above, 78, 85, 89.

[29] For complete details of Boucoud's book-related work see Gil and Nys, *Saint-Omer gothique*, 378–9.

time have been quite old, and indeed his absence from the records after this point may suggest that he did not have long to enjoy his purchase. The 'monocorde' found a new home, appropriately enough, with the organist, vicar and likely former choirboy Alleannie Gerin.[30]

The primary question regarding Houchin the musician, though, is where and with whom did he perform? A partial answer must surely comprise those who bought his music books and instruments, their interest likely piqued by using the same items in the company of their owner in his lifetime. But the broader answer must derive from the location of his lodgings. Occupying a house in the church cloister, Houchin was in close proximity, most obviously, to the house occupied by the choirboys and their master, the latter a role occupied around the time of Houchin's demise by Martin Lavenne, purchaser of some of his music books. Likely involvement of choirboys in such impromptu musical gatherings would relate, furthermore, to the documented familiarity of choirboys with secular songs in other locations.[31] Other houses inhabited by canons, some of them known singers, lay adjacent to Houchin's, while the dwellings of vicars responsible for performing sung Masses in the church must also have been in the vicinity. His life circumscribed in this way by the limited geography of his living and working space, it is not difficult to imagine that music played a major role in Houchin's entertainment and social interchange.

---

[30] On Gerin's career see Chapters 2 and 4. The fact that, on 11 November 1493, his vicariate at the altar of St Laurence passed to 'Philippo du Hec quondam uno de sex pueris chori' strongly suggests that Gerin was also a former choirboy. By the same token, Gerin's own first vicariate, secured on 6 July 1477 (as recorded in II. G. 354, f. 210r) following the death of its prior incumbent Egidius Gherarts, hints at an analogous, earlier, succession of former choirboys. Records from Houchin's sale are as follows: f. 27r: Sire Jehan Dergny une herpe petite xxvs; Maistre Jehan Derviler une aultre plus grande iii s; f. 28v: Monsieur de Boucout .I. clavicibolum xiiii s; Sire Alle[annie] Gerin monsieur des sos ung bon monocorde vi lb vii d [this sum must surely be a mistake for vi s vii d].

[31] Craig Wright notes, for example, that the boys of the Sainte-Chapelle in Paris sang 'beaux virelais, chançons et autres bergeretes moult melodieusement' to greet the 1467 arrival in Paris of Queen Charlotte. A proscription of *c.*1350 against the same boys singing 'mottez, balades et teles choses' in secular settings, and similar rulings in a 1435 ordinance of Notre-Dame of Paris and in Gerson's 1411 *Doctrina* for governing the conduct of the boys at the same institution clearly imply the existence of precisely such practices to protest against (*Music and Ceremony at Notre Dame of Paris, 500–1550* (Cambridge: Cambridge University Press, 1989), 192–4). Singing of secular songs by vicars and choirboys on such occasions as the Feast of St Nicholas, either outdoors or in canons' houses, as noted by Wright in the case of Cambrai, must also have been widespread (see Craig Wright, 'Performance Practices at the Cathedral of Cambrai, 1475–1550', *Musical Quarterly* 64/3 (1978), 322).

Sans pareille though the scope of his collection clearly was, however, it is clear even from the surviving executors' accounts from this period in the church's history that he was not unique among canons of St Omer in possessing books of polyphonic music, or indeed of instruments capable of involvement in its performance. Among the books of Jean Dessinges, a canon who died in 1473, was a '1 livre en parchemin notte contenant diverses antesnes', a term which could refer to any sacred polyphony, for either Mass or office.[32] The possessions of Jean Coquillan, a very wealthy canon who died in 1455 and whose elaborate epitaph also survives, included 'certain bundles of harp strings' ('Item certains fardeles de cordes de harpe' (II. G. 473, f. 22r)). The most intriguing such case, however, is the one already encountered in the executors' account of Toussains de Le Ruelle. The sale of Toussains's effects, detailed in the account, clearly attracted considerable interest, not least from Houchin himself, who purchased a number of items, including, as noted already, an astrolabe, for which he was willing to part with the modest sum of 19d.; and the 8s. paid for '.1. livre de art de musicque' (likely a volume of music theory) by Guillaume Martin, a master of the boys in the 1470s,[33] suggests a substantial volume. But the most pertinent item from the present perspective concerns the gift made to Robert Fabri, discussed in Chapter 2, of two music books that the testator had lent him while alive. What we apparently see here, then, is an expression of musical patronage involving a distinguished canon and singer lending books of music to a young vicar with a burgeoning clerical and musical career.

Fragmentary and tantalising though it is, what begins to emerge here is a culture of what we might describe as musical connoisseurship, sustained by a coterie of musical aficionados sharing their musical interests through theory, study and above all performance, within the close confines of the cloister of a major ecclesiastical institution. Such a coterie would have had many potential members, not least including singers in the ranks of the church's clergy, many of them, as has been amply attested, known also from periods of service in some of the great choral institutions of western Europe.

---

[32] As a point of comparison, Du Fay's executors' account includes an 'Item pour i livre en grant volume en parchemin contenant les messes de St Anthoine de Pade aveuc pluiseurs aultres anthiennes en noire note' (see Wright, 'Dufay at Cambrai', 228).

[33] Martin is presented as master of the boys by the cantor Antoine de Tramecourt on 4 March 1471 (II. G. 454, f. 145r).

The major question which remains, though, is how might such extra-curricular musical activity have related to the music that was taking place in the great church in whose service these men were united and to whose wealth they owed their homes and incomes? The answer, at least as far as services in the choir of the church is concerned, is likely to be very little. As noted in Chapter 3, the books in the church choir during Houchin's lifetime included only one book of polyphony, a 'grant livre en pappier et sept coyers de du [sic] grant volume nottez en deschant contenant plusieurs messes' which the accounts record was bought in the fiscal year 1462/3. It may be that masters of the boys and other singers enlisted the ritual use of further music books owned privately by themselves or others; but at least prima facie it would appear possible that a single book of Masses was sufficient to serve the regular polyphonic needs of the main choir for more than thirty years.

This was clearly a situation that prevailed by choice, a conclusion for which Houchin's will provides indirect testimony. A codicil to the will, dated only two days before its author died, details his wishes with regard to the disposal of his books. Among the terms outlined he states: 'I wish that several of the most suitable be placed in the choir of the church of Monseigneur St Aumer, on one side or the other.'[34] An item towards the end of the account details the response of his executors to this request: among the ten books selected were a *Golden Legend*, the homilies of St Gregory, a large volume of all the letters of St Jerome, the letters of St Augustine to St Jerome and Rabanus Maurus' *De natura rerum*.[35] Not one of the six books of Masses and motets figures on the list; neither does the volume containing vespers polyphony, a repertory presumably unavailable in the main choir until Jean Mouton was paid for producing a complete volume some fifteen years later.

Of course it is entirely possible that some of the Masses founded by individuals in the fifteenth century involved music books assigned to be used in the chapels where the Masses were to be celebrated.[36] Such was the

---

[34] Et voeul que aucuns des plus conveniens soient mis au coeur de leglise de Monseigneur St Aumer / a ung leiz et a laultre / (f. 5v)

[35] Two of these items survive today in the Bibliothèque at Saint-Omer: 'Omnes epistole Hieronimi in uno grosso volumine impresso', a volume of St Jerome's letters, printed by Peter Schoeffer, Mainz, 1470; and 'Gregorius I, *Moralia in Job*', in an edition printed in Basel by Berthold Ruppel, c.1472–4. Both bear traces on the bottom edge of the upper cover of the attachment of chains. See Hellinga, *Incunabula in Transit*, 14.

[36] It must be acknowledged that the two surviving contemporary inventories of movable artefacts in the side chapels (dating respectively from the 1480s and 1527) detail no books other than missals (one or more per chapel). But given that some of these chapels (including that founded

situation provided for by Du Fay's donation of two music books, including the Mass for St Anthony of Padua, to the chapel of St Stephen in Cambrai Cathedral where he was buried and where he established annual Masses for St Anthony to be celebrated with his polyphony.[37] And at least two of the confraternities – their documentation now sparse – attached to the church of St Omer were of sufficient means to have fostered polyphonic Masses had they so desired. Even in circumstances such as these, polyphony that took place within the church, for public or private observance, is likely in many cases to have been improvised on the book. Generally, though, such putative use of polyphony in the Mass would only serve to reinforce the perspective of the performance of polyphonic Masses in churches in the later fifteenth century as to a considerable extent the province of private or corporate observance in side chapels.

Even allowing for these possibilities, the conclusion seems unavoidable that much of the performance of written polyphony taking place in and around the church of St Omer in the later fifteenth century was in private gatherings. Houchin's house, now, like the rest of the cloister, sadly gone, must have been the setting for many musical soirées – presumably following compline – with voices and instruments, and possibly attendant study. In such circumstances, with sacred polyphony extricated from its context of religious ritual, the performance and study of music may indeed have been indissoluble. In Houchin, surely, we have the kind of musical individual who would have been an ideal reader for the treatises of Tinctoris: highly educated and of humanist persuasion, he may also, we might surmise, have been capable, like the theorist himself, of consulting and studying his chosen pieces of music after the manner of literature, and indeed, based on his unnamed books of music theory, cultivating an understanding of their workings.

If this picture appears plausible, it is surely rendered more so by the coterie of individuals – book producers, fellow bibliophiles and musicians – that seems to have clustered around him, and still more so by the profile of the larger community of which they were all part. If the testimony of his chaplain Pierre Godin is any guide, Houchin must have been a man

by Rembert) are known to have fostered elaborate ritual with music, one must infer that there were other kinds of proprietorial relationship between ritual and/or musical books and the uses to which they were put (II. G. 2676 and 2678; entries itemising books and artefacts in Gil and Nys, *Saint-Omer gothique*, 412–13).

[37] See Wright, 'Dufay at Cambrai', 218.

Figure 7.1 Funerary epitaph for Pierre Godin, Musée de l'Hôtel Sandelin

capable of inspiring considerable loyalty.[38] While his funerary slab, whose fashioning and painting is described in his executors' account, has disappeared along with the cloister that housed it, a poignant sense of access to it is provided by the surviving grave slab of Godin, whose cleanly incised lines can be observed today in Saint-Omer's Musée Sandelin (Figure 7.1). The clear and affecting image engraved – with attendant dialogue – into its surface depicts the moment, from Matthew 14: 31–2, when Godin's patron saint Peter, seeing Christ walking on the water, cries out 'Domine salvum me fac' ('O Lord, save me'), whereupon Christ, on saving the drowning Peter as he tries to follow suit, admonishes him 'Modica fidei, quare dubitasti?' ('O ye of little faith, why did you doubt me?') Directly mirroring this expression of devotion by his heavenly alter ego, the script etched out below the image of the kneeling Godin (being presented, for unknown

---

[38] Besides the book copied in Godin's own hand, Houchin left his chaplain numerous bequests in his will, including various items of clothing and 'ung breviaire et le journet a lusage de Rome lesquels ont este baillies a Sire Pierre Godin pour dire ses heures.' (f. 8r)

reasons, by St Andrew) informs us 'Here before the feet of the deceased master Jacques de Houchin ... lies his chaplain Sire Pierre Godin ...'[39]

The slab, unusually, records the date and even time of Godin's birth, at 11.00 p.m. on 6 May 1428, probably suggesting that, like his master (at least to judge from his library's contents), he cultivated an interest in astrology.[40] While the part of the slab that would have carried his date of death has flaked away, an entry in the chapter acts of 2 August 1493 informs us of an escoterie becoming available through his demise. The same record provides valuable further detail in informing us that 'he was for a long time one of the six choirboys'.[41] Besides his background as a singer and – as already noted – a copyist, Godin seems, like his master, to have been something of a bibliophile, or at least a keen reader: on 26 September 1487 the chapter lent 'a certain book on parchment containing epistles of St Gregory the Pope belonging to this church to Lord Petrus Godin, who promised to return it at the request of the lords'.[42] Sure enough the following 10 May, 'Lord Petrus Godin returned a book of parchment covered with boards which he had from the lords on loan'.[43]

Godin, clearly Houchin's amanuensis, links together, in connection to his master, skill in music and book-copying, plus a more general affinity for books. Notwithstanding his singular devotion, though, he was in these respects surely at the time one of numerous members of the same circle with similar skills and proclivities. If we consider just those who bought

---

[39] Crisply preserved for the most part, parts of the script of the slab have been chipped away, leaving a complete (readable) text as follows: 'Chi devant as pies de defunct Maistre Jacques de houchin en son vivant canoine de cest eg[lise] / gist son cappelain sire pierre godin presbtre et escotier natif de bouvcgnies [bouvignies] empres Orchies le [ ] nes le mardi vi jour de may a xi heures de nuyt lan mcccc. et xxvii Et trespassa le iii^e daust [ ]' The record of a chapter meeting of 9 September 1483 preserves Godin's successful petitioning for this siting of his grave: 'Ipso die domini liberaliter accordarunt Domino Petro Godin scoterio quod dum continget ipsum ab hac luce decedere habeat suum sepulturam iuxta ephitaphium [sic] Magistri Jacobi de Houchin canonici prope capellam Beati Jheromini in claustris. pro qua sepultura sponte obtulit se relicturum fabrice ecclesie unam libram grossorum.' Loriquet notes the record, in the fabric account of 1492/3, of the sale to Godin of the stone for his epitaph, along with mortar to affix it: 'Item, le xx de febvrier, pour une pierre de Brabant vendue à S^re Pierre Godin pour faire son épitafle, et ung petit de mortier pour l'assir ix s.' (Henri Loriquet, *Épigraphie du département du Pas-de-Calais*, fascicule III *bis* (Laval: Impr. Barnéoud, 1932).

[40] My thanks to Robert Nosow for this observation.

[41] Full text and further detail appears in Chapter 2.

[42] Eadem die concesserunt domini certum librum in pergameno continens epistolas Beati Gregorii Pape huic eccl[es]ie pertinentem Domino Petro Godin quem ad voluntatem dominorum restituere promisit. (II. G. 355, f. 71v)

[43] Restituit Dominus Petrus Godin librum de pergameno asseribus coopertum quem habuit a dominis in mutuum. (II. G. 355, f. 72r)

music and instruments at Houchin's sale, such a musical community would embrace the organist and likely former choirboy Alleannie Gerin, another probable former choirboy in the person of Jehan Dergny, the copyist (of both script and music) Thomas Boucoud and master of the boys Martin Lavenne, along with the scribe Derviller. Adding also the purchaser of the 'livre de art de musicque' would draw in also another master of the boys, Guillaume Martin; and if, as seems reasonable, we assume musical literacy on the part of the other purchasers of music books, we could add Mahieu Pol, Mahieu Daustin, Pierre de Saint-Amand and Huchon Cocquet to the list of possible participants in gatherings for private music-making.

But the potential circle is both much wider and inclusive, during Houchin's period as a canon, of musicians of truly international stature: men such as Toussains de Le Ruelle; Toussains's eventual successor, the former papal singer Guillaume Decault (who bought a number of items of linen at Houchin's sale); Eustache Maistresse, master of the boys in the 1460s and former singer at St Donatian, Bruges; and the tenorist Grigoire Bourgois. A constant turnover of vicars, and of choirboys led by a succession of skilled, if occasionally abusive, succentors, meant that a regular supply of voices, high and low, was always to hand. It seems unlikely, moreover, that such gatherings would have been limited to the circle of Jacques de Houchin: those who bought his music and instruments must have foreseen opportunities to use them, and the chance survival of documentation in Houchin's case surely suggests that others – before and after him – fostered private musical activities that remain unknown and unrecoverable. Tantalising in its elusiveness, such a scenario remains hugely evocative for those of us today still absorbed by a repertory that so clearly engaged its users at Saint-Omer half a millennium ago. Its traces in our heads as we near the end of the walk that, in the Prologue, led us up through the town to the former collégiale and peer – as I have many times done – towards our right as we pass along the Rue des Tribunaux, we might imagine the sounds that must once have drifted over from the direction of the cloister, and even, perhaps, hear their distant echo.

Documents Pertaining to the Suppression
of Benefices for the Upkeep of the Master
and Choirboys (See Chapter 1)

1 Memorandum Documenting the Renunciation of the Prebend of the Cantor, Chapter Act of 5 August 1490, II. G. 355, f. 78v

Johannes de Hemont consents to the suppression of his canonry and
associated prebend, the fruits of which are to be repurposed for the upkeep
and instruction of the master and choirboys. The relevant information is
provided to Nicolas Rembert, who is pursuing matters at the Roman curia,
in order for him to obtain papal permission for the suppression. The
master and the boys are to be appointed by the dean and chapter, or just
by the chapter if the dean is absent. Provision is made that the arrangement
be not detrimental to Hemont's income or privileges, and that he will
continue to be recompensed in the same way as formerly. He will receive
his emoluments at Easter and All Saints provided he is present, or via a
procurator if not. In a postscript Hemont is granted the right to sell (the
rent of) the house in which he was living or of residing in it for the rest of
his life – even having retired from his cantorship – and assigned ongoing
privileges as hitherto. For his part he is held ultimately to redeem the full
amount of the rent in order that the funds be used for the foundation of his
annual obit (marking the anniversaries of his death).

Venerabilis vir Dominus ac Magister Johannes de Hemond cantor et canonicus prebendatus ecclesie collegiate Sancti Audomari, in capitulo more solito
capitulariter dominis decano et canonicis congregatis certis de causis ad hoc
animum suum moventibus sponte consenciit extinctioni supressioni et
unioni suorum canonicatus et prebende et quod fructus redditibus [*recte*
redditus] et proventus iura obventiones et emolumenta quecumque dictorum
canonicatus et prebende convertantur ad sustentationem unius magistri
scholarum cantus seu musice et sex puerorum chori qui ab eodem magistro
cantus in musica et cantu debite instruentur et eidem ecclesie deservient in
divinis secundum formam et tenorem informationis que sequitur.

Informatio pro parte dominorum decani et capituli ecclesie collegiate Sancti Audomari de Sancto Audomaro ad Magistrum Nicolaum Reimbert, dicte ecclesie canonicum super hoc sequente ipsius ecclesie per ipsum in Romana curia prosequentem negotium.

Et primo obtinebit ipse Reimbert a sanctissimo domino nostro papa suppressionem et extinctionem etc. canonicatus et prebende dicte eccl[esi]e Sancti Audomari de Sancto Audomaro Morinensis diocesis Romane ecclesie immediate subiecte quorum fructus redditus et proventus secundum communem extimationem valorem annuum .l.^{ta} [quinquaginta] ducatus in portatis non excedunt quos ad presens pacifice possidet Magister Johannes de Hemont ipsius ecclesie cantor et canonicus et quod fructus, redditus et proventus iura obventiones et emolumenta quecumque dictorum canonicatus et prebende sic suppressorum pro sustentatione unius magistri scolarum cantus seu musice cuius presentatio ad ipsius ecclesie pro tempore cantorem et successores suos dicte ecclesie cantores. Admissio vero ad dominos decanum et capitulum vel capitulum decano absente iuxta ipsius ecclesie statuta et ut consuetum est spectabunt et pertinebunt ac sex puerorum chori qui ab eodem magistro cantus in musica et cantu debite instruentur et eidem ecclesie deservient in divinis et alias pro divini cultus augmentationem ad eorumdem dominorum decanum et capituli vel capituli decano absente. Ad quos ipsius ecclesie servicii divini dispositio tam per statuta dicte ecclesie quam ex antiqua et hactenus observata consuetudine spectare dignoscitur dispositionem et discretionem convertendi et prout eis videbitur expedire disponendam de reverendo patre Domino Johannes de Burgundia sancte sedis apostolice prothonotarii et eiusdem ecclesie pro tempore prepositi ad quem canonicatum et prebenda dicte ecclesie cum pro tempore vacationis collatio provisio et omnimoda dispositio pleno iure spectare dignoscitur ipsorum dominorum decani et capituli ac ipsius Magistri Johannis de Hemont ad presens dictorum canonicatus et prebende pacifici possessoris expresso consensu pariter et assensu perpetuo fabrice prefate ecclesie unanimiter et irrevocabiliter applicentur.

Item ne ex huiusmodi suppressione et extinctione etc. prefatus Magister Johannes de Hemont nimium dispendium patiatur eidem denarii ex dictis canonicatu et prebenda sic suppressis pro tempore provenientes seu valor eorumdem oneribus ecclesie deductis de benignitate sancte sedis apostolice sibi prout aliis canonicis in eadem ecclesia pro tempore residentibus super fructibus mense capitularis dicte ecclesie in omnibus et per omnia dicta suppressione non obstante perinde ac si in eadem ecclesia presens esset et personaliter canonicus resideret per dictos dominos decanum et capitulum vel eorum receptorem in festivitatibus Resurrectionis Domini Nostri Jhesu

Christi pro una et Omnium Sanctorum pro alia medietatibus annis singulis in oppido Sancti Audomari eidem Magistro Johanni de Hemont vel eius de gremio capituli per eum ad hec specialiter constituto seu constituenti procuratori quamdiu vixerit realiter et cum effectu solvendi reserventur constituantur et assignentur prout hec et alia per litteras apostolicas inde super confectis latius constabit et apparebit.

Modo et forma prescriptis prefatus Magister Johannes de Hemont in manibus eiusdem Magistri Nicolai Rembert et mei notarii constituit procuratores in Romana curia ad resignandum et consentiendum unioni suppressioni et extinctioni dictorum canonicatus et prebende adveniente expresso consensu reverendi patris Domini Johannis de Burgundia eiusdem ecclesie pro tempore prepositi etc.

Hiis dictis et passatis dictus Magister Johannes de Hemont in capitulo dominis decano et canonicis congregatis supplicavit ut cum sibi libuerit libere possit vendere precio seu preciis domum quam inhabitat et quod su vicaria canonicatus et prebenda annexa seu pro tempore vicarius remaneat in suis privilegiis libertatibus franchisiis et honoribus et profectibus. Cuiquidem requisitioni libere annuentes eidem concesserunt facultatem et potestatem domum suam vendendi quotienscumque sibi placuerit vel eam vita comite inhabitandi etc. cantoria sua dimissa et etc. quod vicarius pro tempore existenti in omnibus suis privilegiis libertatibus honoribus emolumentis et franchisiis de cetero intertenebunt sicuti preteritis temporibus consuetum est de antiqua et approbata consuetudine proviso tamen quod idem agister Johannes cantor tenebitur redimere ad plenum redditus sue domus quam personaliter inhabitat et quod denarii ad obitum suum fundandum convertantur etc.

2   Bull of Sixtus IV (1476), from an Eighteenth-Century Copy in II. G. 393

Papal bull approving the suppression of the minor prebend currently held by Mattheus Advisse plus the one of the twenty-eight *sine cura* vicariates serving his prebend and in his gift, and that their income be used, to ease the financial burden on the fabric, for the upkeep of the choirboys. The bull also allows for further suppressions of vicarariates associated with the church's prebends in future should that prove useful.

Sixtus episcopus servus servorum Dei ad perpetuam rei memoriam in supreme apostolice dignitatis specula meritis licet insufficientibus divina disponente clementia constituti circa ecclesiarum quarumlibet presertim insignium collegiatarum statum feliciter et prospere dirigendum assiduis studiis laboramur, et illa que ecclesiarum earundem decorem et venustatem ac in ipsis divini cultus augmentum prospiciunt quantum nobis ex alto permittitur sedula diligentia procuramus.

Sane pro parte dilectorum filiorum Simonis de Luxemburgo legum doctoris prepositi nec non decani et capituli ecclesie Sancti Audomari de Sancto Audomaro Romane ecclesie immediate subiecte Morinensis diocesis nobis nuper exhibita petitio continebat quod si custodia eiusdem ecclesie Sancti Audomari que prepositure ipsius ecclesie quam dictus Simon obtinet canonice annexa seu illius membrum existit et illam pro tempore obtinenti ratione ipsius custodie luminarum in ipsa ecclesia Sancti Audomari prestatio campanarum pulsatio et reliquiarum ipsius ecclesie custodia nonnulla que alia onera in dicta ecclesia Sancti Audomari incumbunt a prefata prepositura penitus separaretur et segregaretur ipsaque custodia ac una ex prebendis parvis nuncupatis quam dilictus filius Matheus Advisse in dicta ecclesia Sancti Audomari ad presens obtinet cui et illam pro tempore obtinenti presentatio persone idonee ad parochialem ecclesiam de Fletrenes(?) dicte diocesis dum pro tempore vacat de antiqua et approbata hactenus que pacifice observata consuetudine pertinet nec non una in viginti octo perpetuis sine cura vicariis in eadem ecclesia institutis quamprimum parvam prebendam huiusmodi predicti Mathei ac unam in eisdem vicariis per illum ad presens obtentis cessu vel decessu aut alias simul vel successive vacare contigerit supprimerentur et extinguerentur illarumque fructus redditus et proventus et emolumenta q[uecum]que fabrice dicte ecclesie Sancti Audomari pro sustentatione sex puerorum in dicta ecclesia Sancti Audomari instituendorum et in illius choro in divinis continue deserviturorum ac onerum eiusdem supportatione perpetuo applicarentur et appropriarentur necnon statueretur et ordinaretur quod de cetero reliquas vicarias huiusmodi pro tempore obtinentes que ab antiquo super fructibus redditibus et proventibus prebendarum dicte ecclesie Sancti Audomari fundata sunt et quarum collatio et provisio ad decanum et capitulum predictos de simili consuetudine pertinent ad nutum eorundem decani et capituli ponerentur et amoverentur ac presentatio persone idonee ad dictam parochialem ecclesiam dum pro tempore vacaret ad prepositum dicte ecclesie Sancti Audomari pro tempore existentem pertineret profecto ex hoc cultus divinus in ipsa ecclesia Sancti Audomari cum maiori reverentia et devotione celebraretur et non modicum susciperet incrementum idque in decorem et venustatem ipsius ecclesie cederet ac decanus et capitulum prefati onera custodia fabrice et vicariis prefatis pro tempore incumbentia facilius supportarent ac illis exinde non modica utilitas resultaret.

Quare pro parte tam Simonis prepositi quam decani et capituli predictorum asserentium quod custodie quinquaginta et parve prebende viginti quatuor ac singularum vicariarum predictarum decem librarum turonensium parvorum fructus redditus et proventus secundum communem extimationem valorem annuum non excedunt, nobis fuit humiliter supplicatum ut custodiam predictam a prefata prepositura separare et segregare illamque ac parvam prebendam predictam nec non unam ex eisdem viginti octo vicariis supprimere et extinguere illarumque fructus redditus et proventus et emolumenta quecumque fabrice dicte ecclesie Sancti Audomari predictorum sex puerorum sustentatione ac aliarum onerum eiusdem fabrice supportatione perpetuo applicare et appropriare nec non quod ad reliquias vicarias huiusmodi vicarii ad nutum decani et capituli predictorum de cetero ponantur et amoveantur et non in titulum perpetuorum beneficiorum conferantur ipsaque parochialis ecclesia ad presentationem eiusdem prepositi pro tempore existentis pertineat statuere et ordinare ac alias in premissis opportune providere de benignitate apostolica dignaremur.

Nos igitur qui ecclesiarum quarumlibet venustatem et decorem ac in illis divini cultus incrementum sinceris desideriis affectamus huiusmodi supplicationibus inclinati custodiam predictam a dicta prepositura ipsius Simonis ad hoc per dilectum filium Rolandum de Bours presbiterum Tornacensis diocesis procuratorem Simoni ad hoc ab eo specialiter constitutum expresso accedente consensu auctoritate apostolica tenore presentium separamus et segregamus illamque ac parvam prebendam quam dictus Matheus obtinet ut prefertur nec non unam ex eisdem viginti octo vicariis qua[m]primum prebendam et vicariam huiusmodi per cessum vel decessum seu quavis alia dimissione dicti Mathei et unam ex eisdem vicariis ad presens obtinentis simul vel successive vacare contigerit ut prefertur ex nunc supprimimus et extinguimus illarumque sic suppressarum fructus redditus et proventus dicte fabrice pro eorundem sex puerorum sustentatione et manutencione ac aliorum onerum ipsius fabrice supportatione perpetuo applicamus et appropriamus et nichilominus eisdem auctoritate et tenore statuimus et ordinamus quod de cetero perpetuis futuris temporibus de singulis reliquisque vicariis huiusmodi quotiens pro tempore cedentibus vel recedentibus illarum nunc et pro tempore possessoribus seu illas alias quomodolibet dimittentibus vacare contigerit personis idoneis etiam quecumque quotiens[cum]que et qualiacumque beneficia ecclesiastica obtinentibus et expectantibus qui ad nutum decani et capituli predictorum quotiens illis placuerit ab illis amoveri possint et valeant non autem in titulum perpetuorum beneficiorum provideantur parochialis quoque ecclesia supradicta quoties illam de cetero vacare contigerit ad presentationem eiusdem prepositi pro tempore existentis pertineat decernentes ex nunc quascumque provisiones quas de reliquis vicariis huiusmodi aliter quam ut prefertur fieri nec non omnia et singula que secus super hiis quavis auctoritate scienter vel ignoranter attemptari contigerit irrita et inania nulliusque valoris vel momenti existere non obstantibus constitutionibus et ordinationibus apostolicis ac statutis et consuetudinibus dicte ecclesie Sancti Audomari iuramento confirmatione apostolica vel quavis firmitate alia roboratis ceterisque contrariis quibuscumque[.] Nulli ergo omnino hominum liceat hanc paginam nostre separationis statuti ordinationis et constitutionis infringere vel ei ausu temerario contraire[.] Siquis autem hoc attemptare presumpserit indignationem omnipotentis Dei et Beatorum Petri et Pauli apostolorum eius se noverit incursurum[.]

Datum Rome apud Sanctum Petrum anno Incarnationis Dominice millesimo quadringentesimo septuagesimo sexto septimo Idus Decembris pontificatus nostri anno sexto.

3   Bull of Innocent VIII (1490), II. G. 53, f. 148r–v. Copy also in Chapter Acts, II. G. 355, f. 89r.

Bull authorising the suppression of the canonry and prebend of the cantor, its income to be diverted to the upkeep of the master and choirboys.

Innocentius episcopus servus servorum Dei ad perpetuam rei memoriam. commissum nobis desuper apostolice servitutis officium nos inducit ut illorum votis annuamus per que in singulis ecclesiis presertim Romane ecclesie immediate subiectis divinus cultus suscipiat incrementum dudum siquidem omnes canonicatus et prebendas ceteraque beneficia ecclesiastica apud sedem apostolicam tunc vacantia et inantea vacatura collocationi et dispositioni nostre reservamimus decernentes ex tunc irritum et inane si secus super hiis a quoquam quavis auctoritate scienter vel ignoranter contigerit attemptari. Cum itaque postmodum canonicatus et prebenda ecclesie Sancti Audomari de Sancto Audomaro Morinensis diocesis eidem Romane ecclesie immediate subiecte per liberam resignationem dilecti filii Johannis de Hemont nuper ipsius ecclesie canonici de illis quos tunc obtinebat per dilectum filium Robertum Fabri canonicum ecclesie Sancti Petri Ariensis predicte diocesis procuratorem suum ad hoc ab eo specialiter constitutum in manibus nostris sponte factam et per nos admissam apud sedem eandem vacaverint et vacent ad presens nullusque de illis preter nos hac vice disponere potuerit sive possit reservatione et decreto obsistentibus supradictis et sicut exhibita nobis nuper pro parte dilectorum filiorum Magistri Johannis de Burgundia notarii nostri prepositi ac decani et capituli dicte ecclesie Sancti Audomari petitio continebat si canonicatus et prebenda predicti sic resignati in dicta ecclesia supprimerentur et extinguerentur et illorum fructus redditus et proventus fabrice dicte ecclesie Sancti Audomari pro sustentatione unius in musica periti sive magistri ac sex puerorum chori qui in eadem ecclesia diurnis et nocturnis horis interessent applicarentur et appropriarentur profecto ex hoc divinus cultus plurimum in dicta ecclesia augeretur pro parte Johannis prepositi decani et capituli predictorum asserentium quod ecclesia predicta inter alias ecclesias dicte diocesis insignis existit quodque canonicatuum et prebendarum eiusdem ecclesie dum pro tempore vacant collatio et provisio ac omnimoda dispositio ad prepositum dicte ecclesie pro tempore existentem de antiqua et approbata hactenusque pacifice observata consuetudine cessantibus reservationibus apostolicis pertinent nobis fuit humiliter supplicatum ut canonicatum et prebendam predictos sic resignatos in eadem ecclesia Sancti Audomari supprimere et extinguere ac illorum fructus redditus et proventus dicte fabrice perpetuo applicare et appropriare aliasque in promissis oportune providere de benignitate apostolica dignaremur. Nos igitur Johannem repositum ac decanum et capitulum predictos et eorum singulos ac huiusmodi capituli singulares personas a quibuscumque excommunicationis suspensionis et interdicti aliisque ecclesiasticis sententiis censuris et penis a iure vel ab hominem quavis occasione vel causa latis si quibus quomodolibet innodati existant ad effectum presentum dumtaxat consequendum harum serie absolventes et absolutos fore censentes huiusmodi [end of 53, f. 148] supplicationibus inclinati canonicatum et prebendam predictos sic resignatos in eadem ecclesia Sancti Audomari auctoritate apostolica tenore presentium perpetuo supprimamus et extinguimus et eorum fructus redditus et proventus qui quinquaginta librarum turonensis parvorum secundum communem extimationem valorem annuum ut Johannes prepositus ac decanus et capitulum prefati etiam asserunt non excedunt predicte fabrice eadem auctoritate perpetuo applicamus et appropriamus ac quod ex huiusmodi fructibus redditibus et proventibus unus in musica sive cantu peritus sive magister ad ipsorum decani et capituli [nutum] amovibilis et cuius presentatio ad cantorem admissio vero ad decanum et capitulum seu in ipsius decani absentia ad solum capitulum eiusdem ecclesie pertineant necnon sex pueri qui diurnis et nocturnis horis in eadem ecclesia intersint ac ab eodem magistro in cantu sive musica instruantur in predicta ecclesia ordinentur et deputentur eadem auctoritate apostolica tenore presentium statuimus et ordinamus non obstantibus constitutionibus et ordinationibus apostolicis ac dicte ecclesie Sancti Audomari iuramento confirmatione apostolica vel quavis firmitate alia roboratis statutis et consuetudinibus ceterisque contrariis quibuscumque [.] Nulli ergo omnino hominum liceat hanc paginam nostre absolutionis suppressionis extinctionis applicationis appropriationis statuti et ordinationis infringere vel ei ausu temerario contraire[.] Si quis autem hoc attemptare presumpserit indignationem omnipotentis Dei ac Beatorum Petri et Pauli apostolorum eius se noverit incursurum[.] Datum Rome apud Sanctum Petrum Anno Incarnationis Dominice millesimo quadragentesimo nonagesimo pridie Nonis Novembris pontificatus nostri anno septimo.

4   Bull of Julius II (1506), II. G. 53, ff. 10r–11r

Bull authorising the suppression of the vicariate formerly associated with the prebend of the cantor (Johannes de Hemont) for the benefit of the master of the choirboys, on condition that he attend the offices pertaining to the said vicariate.

Bulla unionis eiusdem vicarie ad usum magistri cantus
Julius episcopus servus servorum Dei ad perpetuam rei memoriam. Ex iniuncto nobis desuper apostolice servitatis officio ad ea libenter intendimus per que singulis ecclesiis presertim collegiatis insignibus divino cultu ornatus et decor accrescat et illarum ministris de congrue subventionis auxilio valeat provideri dudum siquidem omnia officia ceteraque beneficia ecclesiastica apud sedem apostolicam tunc vacantia et inantea vacatura collationi et dispositioni nostre reservavimus decernentes ex tunc irritum et inane si secus super hiis a quoquam quavis auctoritate scienter vel ignoranter contingeret attemptari. Cum itaque postmodum quedam vicaria in ecclesia sancti Audomari de Sancto Audomaro Romane ecclesie immediate subiecte Morinensis diocesis per liberam resignationem dilecti filii Jacobi Boidart nuper in dicta ecclesia vicarii de illa quam tunc obtinebat per dilectum filium Magistrum Johannem Theobaldi scriptorem et familiarem nostrum procuratorem suum ad hoc ab eo specialiter constitutum in manibus nostris sponte factam et per nos admissam vacaverit et vacet ad presens nullusque de illa preter nos hac vice disponere potuerit sive possit reservatione et decreto obsistentibus supradictis et sicut exhibita nobis nuper pro parte dilectorum filiorum decani et capituli dicte ecclesie Sancti Audomari peticio continebat si statueretur et ordinaretur quod de cetero perpetuis futuris temporibus dicta vicaria que olim canonicatu et prebende eiusdem ecclesie Sancti

Audomari quos quondam Johannes de Hemont tunc eiusdem ecclesie Sancti
Audomari canonicus obtinebat iuxta morem dicte ecclesie associata erat et
que postquam dudum felicis recordationis Innocentio Pape viii predecessori
nostro pro parte tunc prepositi ac decani et capituli predictorum exposito
quod si dicti canonicatus et prebenda supprimerentur et extinguerentur ac
illorum fructus redditus et proventus fabrice eiusdem ecclesie sancti Audomari pro sustentatione unius in musica periti sive magistri et sex puerorum
qui in eadem ecclesiam Sancti Audomari diurnis et nocturnis horis interessent applicarentur et appropriarentur ex hoc divinus cultus in dicta ecclesia plurimum augeretur idem predecessor eorundem tunc prepositi decani et
capituli supplicationibus inclinatus dictos canonicatum et prebendam tunc
per liberam resignationem dicti Johannis de Hemont de illis quos tunc ut
prefertur obtinebat in manibus eiusdem predecessoris sponte factam et per
eundem predecessorem admissam vacantes et antea dispositioni apostolice
reservatos auctoritate apostolica perpetuo suppresserat et extinxerat ac
illorum fructus redditus et proventus fabrice predicte eadem auctoritate
perpetuo applicaverat et appropriaverat ac quod ex huiusmodi fructibus
redditibus et proventibus unus in musica sive cantu peritus seu magister
ad ipsorum decani et capituli nutum amovibilis et cuius presentatio ad
cantorem admissio vero ad decanum et capitulum seu in ipsius decani
absentia ad solos capitulum eiusdem ecclesie Sancti Audomari pertineret
necnon sex pueri qui diurnis et nocturnis horis in eadem ecclesiam interessent ac ab eodem magistro in cantu seu musica instruerentur in predicta
ecclesia Sancti Audomari ordinarentur et deputarentur dicta auctoritate
statuerat et [10v] ordinaverat prout in eiusdem predecessoris litteris plenius
continetur preter naturam aliarum vicariarum in dicta ecclesia Sancti Audomari quarum singule singulis prebendis eiusdem ecclesie Sancti Audomari
iuxta morem predictum associate sunt quodammodo manu remansit per
pro tempore existentem ipsius ecclesie sancti Audomari in musica sive cantu
huiusmodi exerceret dumtaxat teneretur ac gubernaretur ac quod ipse
magister sive peritus ultra et preter id quod sibi ex fructibus redditibus et
proventibus dictorum canonicatus et prebende suppressorum proveniet pro
uberiori sua sustentatione fructus redditus et proventus dicte vicarie qui in
solis distributionibus quotidianis interessendo divinis officiis sive horis
canonicis diurnis et nocturnis in dicta ecclesia percipiuntur cum ea integritate perciperet cum qua ceteri dicte ecclesie Sancti Audomari vicarii alias
vicarias predictas in eadem ecclesiam obtinentes percipere consueverunt
haberet et perciperet profecto ex hoc divino cultu in eadem ecclesiam Sancti
Audomari decor accrescet et decanus ac capitulum prefati facilius invenirent
qui huiusmodi magisterii cantus et dictorum sex puerorum alendorum et
instruendorum onus et curam susciperet et eo etiam in musica peritiores

evaderent quo se scirent pro instructione et alimentatione predictis ac pro multis aliis per eos supportandis oneribus ampliorem et sufficientem provisionem habituros pro parte eorundem decani et capituli asserentium canonicatus et prebende quinquaginta ac vicarie predictorum octo ducatorum auri de camera fructus redditus et proventus secundum communem extimationem valorem annuum non excedere ac eiusdem vicarie dum pro tempore vacat collationem et provisionem ac omnimodam dispositionem ad prefatos decanum et capitulum de antiqua et approbata hactenusque pacifice observata consuetudine cessantibus apostolicis reservationibus pertinere nobis fuit humiliter supplicatum ut premissa statuere et ordinare aliasque descripte oportune providere de benignitate apostolica dignaremur[.] Nos igitur prefatos decanum et capitulum ac eiusdem capituli singulares personas a quibusvis excommunicationis suspensionis et interdicti aliisque ecclesiasticis sentenciis censuris et penis a iure vel ab homine quavis occasione vel causa latis si quibus quomodo libet innodati existant ad effectum presentium dumtaxat consequendum harum serie absolventes et absolutos fore censentes huiusmodi supplicationibus inclinati prefata auctoritate apostolica tenore presentium statuimus et ordinamus quod de cetero perpetuis futuris temporibus dicta vicaria que simplex perpetuum in dicta ecclesia sancti Audomari existit officium et ad quam non consuevit quis per electionem assumi per pro tempore existentem ipsius ecclesie Sancti Audomari in musica sive cantu magister sive peritus quamdiu magisterii officium in musica sive cantu huiusmodi exercuerit dumtaxat teneatur et gubernetur quodque ipse magister sive peritus ultra et preter ad quod sibi ex fructibus redditibus et proventibus canonicatus et prebende suppressorum huiusmodi proveniet pro sua uberiori sustentationes etiam distributiones [11r] quotidianas et alia emolumenta ac iura dicte vicarie interessendo tamen divinis officiis et horis predictis in eadem ecclesiam Sancti Audomari et magisterio huiusmodi durante cum ea integritate percipiat et habeat cum qua ceteri eiusdem ecclesie vicarii alias vicarias predictas in eadem ecclesia Sancti Audomari pro tempore obtinentes distributiones ipsas percipere et habere consueverunt non obstantibus constitutionibus et ordinationibus apostolicis ac dicte ecclesie iuramento confirmatione apostolica vel quavis firmitate alia roboratis statutis et consuetudinibus ceterisque contrariis quibuscumque[.] Nulli ergo omnino hominum liceat hanc paginam nostre absolutionis statuti et ordinationis infringere vel ei ausu temerario contraire[.] Si quis autem hoc attemptare presumpserit indignationem omnipotentis Dei ac Beatorum Petri et Pauli apostolorum eius se noverit incursurum[.] Datum Rome apud Sanctum Petrum anno Incarnationis Dominice millesimo quinquentesimo sexto quarto Kalendas Maii pontificatus nostri anno tertio[.]

Bibliography

Ammirato, Scipione, *Ritratti d'huomini illustri di Casa Medici,* in *Opuscoli del signor Scipione Ammirato,* vol. 3 (Florence: Amadore Massi and Lorenzo Landi, 1642).

Anheim, Etienne and David Fiala, 'Les maîtrises capitulaires et l'art du contrepoint du XIVᵉ au XVIᵉ siècle', *Analyse Musicale* 69 (2012), 13–20.

Arnold, John H. and Caroline Goodson, 'Resounding Community: The History and Meaning of Medieval Church Bells', *Viator* 43 (2012), 99–130.

Ashdowne, R. K., D. R. Howlett and R. E. Latham (eds.), *Dictionary of Medieval Latin from British Sources* (Oxford: British Academy, 2018), online version: http://clt.brepolis.net/dmlbs/Default.aspx).

Auda, Antoine, *La musique et les musiciens de l'ancien pays de Liège* (Brussels and Liège: Librairie Saint-Georges, 1930).

Bachmann, Adolf (ed.), *Urkundliche Nachträge zur österreichich-deutschen Geschichte im Zeitalter Kaiser Friedrich III,* 1892, repr. 2017 (Vienna: F. Tempsky, 1892).

Baumann, Dorothea, 'Acoustics in Gothic Cathedrals: Theory and Practical Experience in the Middle Ages', in Marcel Pérès (ed.), *Les orgues gothiques: Actes du colloque de Royaumont, 1995* (Paris: Créaphis, 2000), 37–48.

'Musical Acoustics in the Middle Ages' (trans. Barbara Haggh), *Early Music* 18/2 (May 1990), 199–210.

Becker, Otto Frederick, 'The Maîtrise in Northern France and Burgundy during the Fifteenth Century'. Unpublished PhD dissertation, George Peabody College for Teachers, Nashville, TN (1967).

Berlière, Ursmer, *Inventaire analytique des Diversa Cameralia des Archives Vaticanes (1389–1500) au point de vue des anciens diocèses de Cambrai, Liège, Thérouanne et Tournai* (Rome, Namur, Paris: Institut historique Belge; Delvaux; Champion, 1906).

Bernstein, Jane, *Music Printing in Renaissance Venice: The Scotto Press (1539–1572)* (New York and Oxford: Oxford University Press, 1998).

Blanchet, Jules-Adrien and Adolphe Dieudonné, *Manuel de numismatique française, vol. 3: Médailles, jetons, méreaux,* volume 3 (*Le méreau en France*) (Paris: Auguste Picard, 1930).

Blavignac, Jean-Daniel, *La Cloche: Études sur son histoire et sur ses rapports avec la société aux différents âges* (Geneva: Grosset and Trembley, 1877), 33–54.

Blazy, Guy (ed.), *Trésors des églises de l'arrondissment de Saint-Omer,* catalogue d'exposition sous la direction de Saint-Omer, Musée de l'Hôtel Sandelin, 26 septembre–13 décembre 1992 (Saint-Omer: Musée de l'Hôtel Sandelin, 1992).

Bled, Oscar, 'La Bancloque de Saint-Omer', *Bulletin de la Société des antiquaires de la Morinie* 7 (1882–6), 149–76.

'Une Bibliothèque de chanoine au XVe siècle', *Bulletin de la Société des antiquaires de la Morinie* 7 (1882–6), 265–84.

'Notice sur la cloche de l'église de Saint-Denis à Saint-Omer', *Bulletin de la Société des antiquaires de la Morinie* 7 (1882–6), 114–29.

'La fête des innocents dans l'église de Saint-Omer', *Bulletin de la Société des antiquaires de la Morinie* 8 (1887–91), 57–67.

'La Vieille Chapelle du Grand Marché à Saint-Omer, 1270–1785', *Bulletin de la Société des antiquaires de la Morinie* 12 (1907–12), 767–802.

Bled, Oscar and Daniel Haigneré, *Les Chartes de Saint-Bertin, d'après le grand cartulaire de Dom Charles-Joseph Dewitte,* 4 vols., vol. 4 (Saint-Omer: Société des antiquaires de la Morinie, 1899).

Bourdon, Adolphe and Armand Collette, *Histoire de la maîtrise de Rouen* (Rouen: Espérance Cagniard, 1892; repr. Geneva: Minkoff, 1972).

Brenet, Michel, *Les musiciens de la Sainte-Chapelle du Palais* (Paris: Picard, 1910; repr. Geneva: Minkoff, 1973).

Brine, Douglas, *Pious Memories: The Wall-Mounted Memorial in the Burgundian Netherlands* (Leiden and Boston, MA: Brill, 2015).

Brouette, Émile, Les 'Libri Annatarum' pour les pontificats d'Eugène IV à Alexandre VI. IV. Pontificats d'Innocent VIII et d'Alexandre VI (1484–1503). *Analecta Vaticano-Belgica, Documents relatifs aux anciens diocèses de Cambrai, Liège, Thérouanne et Tournai. Première série,* vol. XXIV (Brussels: Institut historique belge de Rome, 1963).

Brown, Alan and Donna G. Cardamone, 'Moresca', *Grove Music Online,* 2001, www.oxfordmusiconline.com/grovemusic/view/10.1093/gmo/9781561592630.001.0001/omo-9781561592630-e-0000019125, accessed 10 September 2018.

Burchard, Johannes (ed. L. Thuasne), *Johannis Burchardi: Diarium sive rerum urbanarum commentarii* (Paris: Ernest Leroux, 1883–5).

Cardamone, Donna G., and Alan Brown, 'Moresca', *Grove Music Online,* 2001, www.oxfordmusiconline.com/grovemusic/view/10.1093/gmo/9781561592630.001.0001/omo-9781561592630-e-0000019125, accessed 10 September 2018.

Caster, É. van, and R. Op de Beeck, 'Les dalles funéraires gravés à effigies, conservées dans la Cathédrale Notre-Dame de Saint-Omer', *Bulletin trimestriel de la Société académique des antiquaires de la Morinie* 20/379 (1964), 193–210.

Cattermole, Paul, *The Bells,* in Ian Atherton et al. (eds.), *Norwich Cathedral: Church, City and Diocese 1096–1996* (London: Hambledon Press, 1996), 494–504.

Cavicchi, Camilla, Marie-Alexis Colin and Philippe Vendrix (eds.), *La musique en Picardie du XIVe au XVIIe siècle* (Turnhout: Brepols, 2012).

Clerval, Jules Alexandre, *L'Ancienne Maîtrise de Notre-Dame de Chartres* (Chartres: R. Selleret, 1899).

Collette, Armand, and Adolphe Bourdon, *Histoire de la maîtrise de Rouen* (Rouen: Espérance Cagniard, 1892; repr. Geneva: Minkoff, 1972).

Coolen, Georges, 'Un antiphonaire de la Collégiale de Saint-Omer', *Bulletin trimestriel de la Société des antiquaires de la Morinie* 19/363 (1960), 324–30.

'Le Grand Dieu de Thérouanne', *Bulletin trimestriel de la Société des antiquaires de la Morinie* 19/372 (September 1962), 636–7.

'Les jubés de la collégiale de Saint-Omer', *Bulletin trimestriel de la Société des antiquaires de la Morinie* 21/403 (1970), 321–34.

D'Accone, Frank, 'The Singers of San Giovanni in Florence during the Fifteenth Century', *Journal of the American Musicological Society* 14 (1961), 307–58.

Dalton, John Neale, *The Collegiate Church of Ottery St Mary, Being the Ordinatio et statuta ecclesie sancte Marie de Otery Exon. Diocesis, A.D. 1338, 1339* (Cambridge: Cambridge University Press, 1917).

Degrutère, Marcel, 'De l'orgue ... des instruments et des hommes', in Camilla Cavicchi, Marie-Alexis Colin and Philippe Vendrix (eds.), *La musique en Picardie du XIVe au XVIIe siècle* (Turnhout: Brepols, 2012), 275–87.

Demouy, Patrick, 'Les *pueri chori* de Notre-Dame de Reims: Contribution à l'histoire des clergeons au Moyen Age', in *Actes des congrès de la Société des historiens médiévistes de l'enseignement supérieur public. 22e congrès, Amiens, 1991: Clercs séculiers au Moyen Age*, 135–49. www.persee.fr/web/revues/home/prescript/article/shmes_1261-9078_1993_act_22_1_1596, accessed 10 June 2019.

Derolez, Albert (ed.), Benjamin Victor (associate ed.), *Corpus catalogorum Belgii: The Medieval Booklists of the Southern Low Countries*, 7 vols. to date (Brussels: Paleis der Academien, 1997–).

Derville, Alain, 'Le marché du vin à Saint-Omer: ses fluctuations au XVe siècle', *Revue belge de philologie et d'histoire* 40/2 (1962), 348–70.

'Les draperies flamandes et artésiennes vers 1250–1350', *Revue du Nord* 54/215 (1972), 353–70.

'Le nombre d'habitants des villes de l'Artois et de la Flandre Wallonne (1300–1450)', *Revue du Nord* 65/257 (1983), 277–99.

'Le grenier des Pays-Bas médiévaux', *Revue du Nord* 69/ 273 (1987), 267–80.

Saint-Omer: Des origines au début du 14e siècle (Lille: Presses universitaires de Lille, 1995).

'Les chanoines de Saint-Omer aux XIVe et XVe siècles', in Nicolette Delanne-Logié and Yves-Marie Hilaire (eds.), *La cathédrale de Saint-Omer: 800 ans de mémoire vive* (Paris: CNRS, 2000), 87–94.

(ed.), *Histoire de Saint-Omer* (Lille: Presses Universitaire de Lille, 1981).

Deschamps de Pas, Louis, 'Essai sur l'art des constructions à Saint-Omer, à la fin du 15e et au commencement du 16e siècle', *Memoires des antiquaires de la Morinie* 9 (1851), 161–251.

'Inventaire des ornemens, reliquaires, etc., de l'église collégiale de Saint-Omer en 1557', *Bulletin archéologique du Comité des travaux historiques et scientifiques* 1 (1886), 78–98.

'Les cérémonies religieuses dans la collégiale de Saint-Omer au XIIIe siècle: Examen d'un rituel manuscrit de cette église', *Mémoires de la Société des antiquaires de la Morinie* 20 (1886–7), 99–213.

'L'église Notre-Dame de Saint-Omer, d'après les comptes de fabrique et les registres capitulaires', *Mémoires de la Société des antiquaires de la Morinie*, vols. 22 and 23 (Saint-Omer: H. d'Homont, 1892–3), 3–126.

Deschrevel, Anton, 'Het orgel in de St-Maartenskerk te Kortrijk', *Koninklijke Geschieden Oudheidkundige Kring van Kortrijk* 33 (1963–4), 229–62.

Desportes, Pierre and Hélène Millet, *Fasti Ecclesie Gallicanae*, I: Diocèse d'Amiens (Turnhout: Brepols, 1996).

Dieudonné, Adolphe, and Jules-Adrien Blanchet, *Manuel de numismatique française*, vol. 3: *Médailles, jetons, méreaux*, volume 3 (*Le méreau en France*) (Paris: Auguste Picard, 1930).

Dohrn-van Rossum, Gerhard (transl. Thomas Dunlap), *History of the Hour: Clocks and Modern Temporal Orders* (translation of *Die Geschichte der Stunde: Uhren und modernen Zeitordnungen* (Munich and Vienna: Carl Hanser, 1992)) (Chicago, IL, and London: University of Chicago Press, 1996).

Dricot Michel and Janine Grassin, *La maîtrise de la cathédrale de Reims, des origines à nos jours* (Reims: Cathédrale de Reims, 1996).

Droz, Eugénie, 'Notes sur Me Jean Cornuel, dit Verjus, petit vicaire de Cambrai', *Revue de musicologie* 7/ 20 (1926), 173–189.

du Cange, Charles du Fresne, *Glossarium mediae et infimae latinitatis* (Niort: l. Favre, 1883–7).

Ducrocq, Monique, *La Cathédrale de Saint-Omer: Son symbolisme, ses grands dignitaires* (Saint-Omer: Association Cathédrale de Saint-Omer, 1997).

Dufourcq, Norbert, 'Les orgues de Notre-Dame de Saint-Omer', *Bulletin trimestriel de la Société académique des antiquaires de la Morinie* 17 (1948), 214–18.

Durand, Georges, *La musique de la cathédrale d'Amiens avant la Révolution* (Amiens: Yvert et Tellier, 1922).

Durand of Mende, William, trans., Timothy M. Thibodeau, *The Rationale divinorum officiorum of William Durand of Mende: A New Translation of the Prologue and Book 1* (New York: Columbia University Press, 2007).

Fallows, David, *Dufay* (rev. ed., London and Melbourne: Dent, 1987).

Fassler, Margot, 'The Feast of Fools and *Danielis ludus*: A Popular Tradition in a Medieval Cathedral Play', in Thomas Forrest Kelly (ed.), *Plainsong in the Age of Polyphony* (Cambridge: Cambridge University Press, 1992), 65–99.

Félix, Jean-Pierre, 'L'orgue gothique dans les Pays-Bas méridionaux', in Marcel Pérès (ed.), *Les orgues gothiques: actes du colloque de Royaumont, 1995* (Paris: Créaphis, 2000), 69–106.

Fiala, David, 'Le mécénat musical des ducs de Bourgogne et des princes de la Maison de Habsbourg. 1467–1506. Étude documentaire et prosopographique'. Unpublished PhD dissertation, Centre d'études supérieures de la Renaissance, Université de Tours (2002).

'La collégiale royale de Saint-Quentin et la musique', in Camilla Cavicchi, Marie-Alexis Colin and Philippe Vendrix (eds.), *La musique en Picardie du XIVe au XVIIe siècle* (Turnhout: Brepols, 2012), 189–227.

'In memoriam', in Camilla Cavicchi, Marie-Alexis Colin and Philippe Vendrix (eds.), *La musique en Picardie du XIVe au XVIIe siècle* (Turnhout: Brepols, 2012), 21.

Prosopographie des chantres de la Renaissance (Tours: CESR/Ricercar; http://ricercar.cesr.univ-tours.fr/3-programmes/PCR/).

and Etienne Anheim, 'Les maîtrises capitulaires et l'art du contrepoint du XIVe au XVIe siècle', *Analyse Musicale* 69 (2012), 13–20.

Fidom, Hans, 'Placement of Large Medieval Organs in Churches in the Netherlands: Reflections on a Large Medieval Organ to Be Built in the City of Groningen, The Netherlands', in Marcel Pérès (ed.), *Les orgues gothiques: actes du colloque de Royaumont, 1995* (Paris: Créaphis, 2000), 107–23.

Forest, Jean Marie H., *L'école cathédrale de Lyon* (Lyon: Briday, 1885).

Fournier, Edouard, 'Les bréviaires imprimés de Saint-Omer et d'Aire-sur-la-Lys', *Bulletin de la Société des antiquaires de la Morinie* XII (1908), 303–14.

Fowler, Joseph Thomas (ed.), *The Rites of Durham, Being a Description or Brief Declaration of all the Ancient Monuments, Rites, & Customs Belonging or Being within the Monastical Church of Durham before the Suppression*, Publications of the Surtees Society, 107 (Durham, Edinburgh and London, 1903).

Gabriel, Astrik L., 'Intellectual Relations between the University of Louvain and the University of Paris in the 15th Century', in Jozef Isewijn and Jacques Paquet (eds.), *The Universities in the Late Middle Ages*, Mediaevalia Lovaniensia I/VI (Leuven: Leuven University Press, 1978).

Gambassi, Osvaldo, *'Pueri Cantatores' nelle Cattedrali d'Italia tra medioevo e età moderno* (Florence: Olschki, 1997).

Gil, Marc, and Jean-François Goudesenne, (eds.), *L'antiphonaire de la Paix de Princes chrétiens: Calligraphié à Saint-Omer par Sire Michel Reymbault, enluminé à Lille par Soeur Françoise de Heuchin ca 1550–1561 (*facsimile edition of a St Omer manuscript antiphonal of c.1550–1561*)*. Publications of Medieval Music Manuscripts, 30 (Ottawa: Institute of Medieval Music, 2003).

Gil, Marc and Ludovic Nys, *Saint-Omer gothique* (Valenciennes: Presses Universitaires de Valenciennes, 2004).

Göllner, Theodor, *Formen früher Mehrstimmigkeit deutschen Handschriften des späten Mittelalters* (Tutzing: Hans Schneider, 1961).

Goodson, Caroline, and John H. Arnold, 'Resounding Community: The History and Meaning of Medieval Church Bells', *Viator* 43 (2012), 99–130.

Gori, Valente, 'La musica alla SS. Annunziata di Firenze dall'origine alla fondazione della cappella musicale', *Academia Musicale Valdarnese, Bollettino d'informazione semestriale, Badia di Soffena* (Castelfranco di Sopra), [1981], no. 1, 9–22; no. 2, 4–23.

Goudesenne, Jean-François and Marc Gil (eds.), *L'antiphonaire de la Paix de Princes chrétiens: Calligraphié à Saint-Omer par Sire Michel Reymbault, enluminé à Lille par Soeur Françoise de Heuchin ca 1550–1561* (facsimile edition of a St Omer manuscript antiphonal of *c.*1550–1561). Publications of Medieval Music Manuscripts, 30 (Ottawa: Institute of Medieval Music, 2003).

Grassin, Janine and Michel Dricot, *La maîtrise de la cathédrale de Reims, des origines à nos jours* (Reims: Cathédrale de Reims, 1996).

Gros, Gérard, *Ave Vierge Marie: Étude sur les prières mariales en vers français (XIIe–XVe siècles)* (Lyon: Presses Universitaires de Lyon, 2004).

Haberl, Franz Xaver, 'Die römische "schola cantorum" und die päpstlichen Kapellsänger bis zur Mitte des 16. Jahrhunderts', *Vierteljahrsschrift für Musikwissenschaft* 3 (1887), 189–296.

Bausteine für Musikgeschichte I: Wilhelm Du Fay; II: Katalog der Musikwerke welche sich im Archiv der päpstlichen Kapelle im Vatikan zu Rom vorfinden; III: Die römische "schola cantorum" und die päpstlichen Kapellsänger bis zur Mitte des 16. Jahrhunderts (Leipzig: Druck und Verlag von Breitkopf und Härtel, 1885–8; repr. Hildesheim and New York: Georg Olms, 1971).

Haggh, Barbara, 'Foundations or Institutions? On Bringing the Middle Ages into the History of Medieval Music', *Acta Musicologica* 68 (1986), 87–128.

'Music, Liturgy and Ceremony in Brussels, 1350–1500'. 2 vols. Unpublished PhD dissertation, University of Illinois at Urbana–Champaign (1988).

Haigneré, Daniel, and Oscar Bled, *Les Chartes de Saint-Bertin, d'après le grand cartulaire de Dom Charles-Joseph Dewitte*, 4 vols., vol. 4 (Saint-Omer: Société des antiquaires de la Morinie, 1899).

Haine, Malou and Nicolas Meeùs, *Instruments de musique anciens à Bruxelles et en Wallonie: 17e–20e siècles* (Brussels: Centre culturel de la Communauté française Wallonie-Bruxelles, 1986).

Harris, Max, *Sacred Folly: A New History of the Feast of Fools* (Ithaca, NY: Cornell University Press, 2011).

Hasenohr, Geneviève, 'L'essor des bibliothèques privées aux XIVe aux XV e siècles', in André Vernet (ed.), *Histoire des bibliothèques françaises. Les bibliothèques médiévales du VIe à 1530* (Paris: Promodis-Éditions du Cercle de la Librairie, 1989), 215–63.

Heck, Christian, Hervé Boëdec, Delphine Adams and Astrid Bollut, *Collections du Nord-Pas-de-Calais: La peinture de Flandre et de France du Nord au XVe et au début du xvie siècle*, 2 vols. (Brussels: Centre d'étude de la peinture du quinzième siècle dans les Pays-Bas méridionaux et la Principauté de Liège, 2005).

Hédin, Bernard, *Les Orgues du Pas-de-Calais* (Lille: Domaine Musiques Région Nord-Pas-de-Calais, 1996).

Hellinga, Lotte, *Incunabula in Transit: People and Trade* (Leiden and Boston, MA: Brill, 2018).

Higginbottom, Edward, 'Organ Music and the Liturgy', in Nicholas Thistlethwaite and Geoffrey Webber (eds.), *The Cambridge Companion to the Organ* (Cambridge: Cambridge University Press, 1998), 130–47.

Higgins, Paula, 'Parisian Nobles, a Scottish Princess, and the Woman's Voice in Late Medieval Song', *Early Music History* 10 (1991), 145–200.

Hiley, David, *Western Plainchant: A Handbook* (Oxford: Clarendon Press, 1993).

Hoorebeeck, Céline Van, 'La réception de l'humanisme dans les Pays-Bas bourguignons (XVe–début XVIe siècle). L'apport des bibliothèques privées', in István Monok (ed.), *Matthias Corvin, les bibliothèques princières et la genèse de l'état moderne* (Budapest: Országos Széchényi Könyvtár, 2009), 93–120.

Hughes, Andrew, 'British Rhymed Offices: A Catalogue and Commentary', in Susan Rankin and David Hiley (eds.), *Music in the Medieval English Liturgy: Plainsong & Medieval Music Society Centennial Essays* (Oxford: Oxford University Press, 1993), 239–84.

Late Medieval Liturgical Offices: Resources for Electronic Research, Subsidia Medievalia 23–24. 2 vols. (*Texts* and *Sources and Chants*) (Toronto: Pontifical Institute of Mediaeval Studies, 1994–5).

Huitson, Toby, *Stairway to Heaven: The Functions of Medieval Upper Spaces* (Oxford and Philadelphia, PA: Oxbow Books, 2014).

Jiménez, Juan Ruiz, 'From *Mozos de Coro* towards *Seises*: Boys in the Musical Life of Seville Cathedral in the Fifteenth and Sixteenth Centuries', in Susan Boynton and Eric Rice (eds.), *Young Singers, 650–1700* (Woodbridge: Boydell, 2008), 86–103.

Jiroušková, Lenka, *Der heilige Wikingkönig Olav Haraldsson und sein hagiographisches Dossier*, 2 vols. (Leiden: Brill, 2014).

Jungmann, Joseph, *The Mass of the Roman Rite: Its Origins and Development* (translation, by Francis A. Brunner, of *Missarum Solemnia*), 2 vols. (Westminster, MD: Christian Classics, 1986).

Kirkman, Andrew, 'The Seeds of Medieval Music: Choirboys and Musical Training in a Late-Medieval Maîtrise', in Susan Boynton and Eric Rice (eds.), *Young Singers, 650–1700* (Woodbridge: Boydell, 2008), 104–22.

The Cultural Life of the Early Polyphonic Mass (Cambridge: Cambridge University Press, 2010).

'Johannes Sohier dit Fede and St Omer: A Story of Pragmatic Sanctions', in Fabrice Fitch and Jacobijn Kiel (eds.), *Essays on Music and Musicians in Honour of David Fallows: Bon jour, bon an, et bonne estraine* (Woodbridge: Boydell and Brewer, 2011), 68–79.

'Organs and Instrumental Performance at the Collegiate Church of Saint-Omer, Northern France, in the Later Middle Ages', in Timothy J. McGee and Stewart Carter (eds.), *Instruments, Ensembles, and Repertory, 1300–1600: Essays in Honour of Keith Polk* (Turnhout: Brepols, 2013), 101–9.

Körndle, Franz, '"Usus" und "Abusus organorum" im 15. und 16. Jahrhundert', *Acta Organologica* 27 (2001), 223–40.

Laplane, Henri de, *Les abbés de Saint-Bertin*, vol. 2: 1450–1791 (Saint-Omer: Fleury-Lemaire, 1855).

Le Goff, Jacques (transl. Christophe Campos), 'Church Time and Merchant Time in the Middle Ages', *Social Science Information* 9/4 (August 1970) (translation of 'Temps de l'Église et temps du marchand', *Annales* 15/3 (May–June 1960), 417–33), 151–67.

(transl. Arthur Goldhammer) *Time, Work and Culture in the Middle Ages* (Chicago, IL, and London: Chicago University Press, 1980) (translation of *Pour un autre Moyen Age: Temps, travail et culture en Occident* [Paris: Gallimard, 1977]).

Legrand, Albert, 'Réjouissances des écoliers de Notre-Dame de St-Omer, le jour de St-Nicolas, leur glorieux patron (6 décembre 1417)', *Mémoires de la Société des antiquaires de la Morinie* 7 (1844–6), 161–202.

Le Maner, Martine, 'De lordre ancien à l'ordre nouveau', in Alain Derville (ed.), *Histoire de Saint-Omer* (Lille: Presses Universitaires de Lille, 1981), 158–64.

Le Roux de Lincy, Antoine, *Les femmes célèbres de l'ancienne France: mémoires historiques sur la vie publique et privée des femmes françaises, depuis le cinquième siècle jusqu'au dix-huitième*, vol. 1 (Paris: Leroi, 1848).

Longnon, August, *Pouillés de la province de Reims*, vol. 6, part 2 (Paris: Klincksieck, 1907).

Loriquet, Henri, *Épigraphie du département du Pas-de-Calais*, Tome V, 1er et 2e fasc. (*Ville de Saint-Omer*) (Arras: Laroche, 1892).

Épigraphie du département du Pas-de-Calais, fascicule III *bis* (Laval: Impr. Barnéoud, 1932).

Lütteken, Laurenz, 'Maîtrise', in *Die Musik in Geschichte und Gegenwart* (Kassel: Bärenreiter, 2002), 2, *Sachteil 5*, cols. 1597–1602.

Marix, Jeanne, *Histoire de la musique et des musiciens de la cour de Bourgogne sous le règne de Philippe le Bon (1420–1467)* (Strasbourg: Heitz, 1939; repr. Geneva: Minkoff, 1972).

Marshall, Kimberly, 'The Creation of Late Medieval Organ Music', in Marcel Pérès (ed.), *Les orgues gothiques: actes du colloque de Royaumont, 1995* (Paris: Créaphis, 2000), 125–42.

Marsy, Le Comte (Arthur) de, 'Jean Crignon, facteur d'orgues à Mons, et les petites orgues de l'église Notre-Dame de Saint-Omer', *Annales du cercle archéologique de Mons* 27 (1896–7), 63–7.

Martineau, Jonathan, *Time, Capitalism and Alienation: A Socio-historical Inquiry into the Making of Modern Time* (Leiden and Boston, MA: Brill, 2015).

Maurey, Yossy, *Medieval Music, Legend, and the Cult of St. Martin* (Cambridge: Cambridge University Press, 2014).

Meeùs, Nicholas, and Malou Haine, *Instruments de musique anciens à Bruxelles et en Wallonie: 17e–20e siècles* (Brussels: Centre culturel de la Communauté française Wallonie-Bruxelles, 1986).

Merkley, Paul A. and Lora L. M. Merkley, *Music and Patronage in the Sforza Court* (Turnhout: Brepols, 1999).

Millet, Hélène, and Pierre Desportes, *Fasti Ecclesie Gallicanae, I: Diocèse d'Amiens* (Turnhout: Brepols, 1996).

Monmerqué, Louis-Jean-Nicolas Desrochais and Francisque Michel (eds.), *Théâtre français au moyen âge* (Paris: Firmin Didot, 1842).

Monro, John H., 'Economic Depression and the Arts in the Fifteenth-Century Low Countries', *Renaissance and Reformation* 7/4 (1983), 235–50.

Nicholas, David, *Medieval Flanders* (London and New York: Longman, 1992).

Noble, Jeremy, 'New Light on Josquin's Benefices', in Edward E. Lowinsky and Bonnie J. Blackburn (eds.), *Proceedings of the International Josquin Festival-Conference* (London: Oxford University Press, 1976), 76–102.

Nys, Ludovic, and Marc Gil, *Saint-Omer gothique* (Valenciennes: Presses Universitaires de Valenciennes, 2004).

Op de Beeck, R. and É. van Caster, 'Les dalles funéraires gravés à effigies, conservées dans la Cathédrale Notre-Dame de Saint-Omer', *Bulletin trimestriel de la Société académique des antiquaires de la Morinie* 20/379 (1964), 193–210.

Opigez, Emmanuelle, 'Le deesis de Thérouanne et sa place dans la sculpture française du XIIIe siècle dans le nord de la France', *Bulletin de la Société des antiquaires de la Morinie* 25/465 (March 2005), 135–56.

Owen, Barbara, *The Registration of Baroque Organ Music* (Bloomington and Indianapolis: Indiana University Press, 1997).

Owen, Barbara and Peter Williams, 'Organ, IV: the classical and medieval organ 6: The church organ, 1100–1450', *Grove Music Online*, 2001, www .oxfordmusiconline.com/grovemusic/view/10.1093/gmo/9781561592630 .001.0001/omo-9781561592630-e-0000044010, accessed 11 September 2016.

'Organ V, 1, and 2: Developments, 1450–1500', *Grove Music Online*, 2001, www .oxfordmusiconline.com/grovemusic/view/10.1093/gmo/9781561592630 .001.0001/omo-9781561592630-e-0000044010, accessed 11 September 2016.

Pars hyemalis [-estivalis] breviarii ecclesie collegiate sancti Audomari (Paris, per Didier Maheu [et] Jacques Ferrebouc, 1518).

Perkins, Leeman L., 'Musical Patronage at the Royal Court of France under Charles VII and Louis XI (1422–83)', *Journal of the American Musicological Society* 37 (1984), 507–66.

Petillon, Claude, 'Les élites politiques de Saint-Omer dans la première moitié du XVᵉ siècle d'après l'enquête de 1446', *Revue du Nord* 91 (1999), 83–116.

Picker, Martin, 'The Habsburg Courts in the Netherlands and Austria, 1477–1530', in Iain Fenlon (ed.) *The Renaissance: From the 1470s to the End of the 16th Century* (Basingstoke and London: Macmillan, 1989), 216–42.

Pirro, André, 'Jean Cornuel, vicaire à Cambrai', *Revue de musicologie* 7/20 (1926), 190–203.

'Leo X and Music', *Musical Quarterly* 21 (1935), 1–16.

Planchart, Alejandro Enrique, *Guillaume Du Fay*, 2 vols. (Cambridge: Cambridge University Press, 2017).

Polk, Keith, *German Instrumental Music of the Late Middle Ages: Players, Patrons and Performance Practice* (Cambridge: Cambridge University Press, 1992).

Pounds, Norman J. G., 'Population and Settlement in the Low Countries and Northern France in the Later Middle Ages', *Revue belge de philologie et d'histoire* 49/2 (1971), 369–442.

Pounds, Norman J. G. and Charles C. Roome, 'Population Density in Fifteenth Century France and the Low Countries, *Annals of the Association of American Geographers* 61/1 (1971), 116–30.

Quenson, François, *Notre-Dame de St-Omer* (Douai: Wagrez, 1830).

Quitin, José, 'Les maîtres de chant de la cathédrale Saint-Lambert à Liège aux XVᵉ et XVIᵉ siècles', *Revue Belge de Musicologie* 8 (1954), 5–18.

Reynolds, Christopher, *Papal Patronage and the Music of St. Peter's, 1380–1513* (Berkeley and Los Angeles, University of California Press, 1995).

Rigollot, Marcel Jerôme, *Monnaies inconnues des évêques des innocens, des fous, et de quelques autres associations singulières du même temps* (Paris: Merlin, 1837).

Ripin, Edwin M., Howard Schott, John Koster, Denzil Wraight, Beryl Kenyon de Pascual, G. Grant O'Brien, Alfons Huber, William R. Dowd, Charles Mould, Lance Whitehead and Martin Elste, 'Harpsichord', *Grove Music Online*, 2001, www.oxfordmusiconline.com/grovemusic/view/10.1093/gmo/9781561592630.001.0001/omo-9781561592630-e-0000012420, accessed 10 September 2018. ',

Ripin, Edwin M., John Barnes, Alfons Huber, Beryl Kenyon de Pascual, and Barry Kernfeld, 'Clavichord', *Grove Music Online*, 2001, www.oxfordmusiconline.com/grovemusic/view/10.1093/gmo/9781561592630.001.0001/omo-9781561592630-e-0000005909, accessed 10 September 2018.

Robertson, Anne Walters, 'Remembering the Annunciation in Medieval Polyphony', *Speculum* 70 (1995), 275–304.

'The Savior, the Woman, and the Head of the Dragon in the Caput Masses and Motet', *Journal of the American Musicological Society* 59 (2006), 537–630.

Rombouts, Luc, *Singing Bronze: A History of Carillon Music* (Leuven: Lipsius Leuven, 2014) (transl. of *Zingend Brons. 500 jaar beiaardmuziek in de Lage Landen en de Nieuwe Wereld* (Leuven: Davidsfond, 2010).

Roome, Charles C., and Norman J. G. Pounds, 'Population Density in Fifteenth Century France and the Low Countries', *Annals of the Association of American Geographers* 61/1 (1971), 116–30.

Roose, Patrick, 'Langhedul', in Malou Haine and Nicolas Meeùs (eds.), *Dictionnaire des facteurs d'instruments de musique en Wallonie et à Bruxelles du 9ᵉ siècle à nos jours* (Brussels: Mardaga, 1986), 242–3.

Sarum Customary Online, part of The Experience of Worship in Late Medieval Cathedral and Parish Church, www.sarumcustomary.org.uk/, accessed 21 June 2019.

Schott, Howard John Koster, Denzil Wraight, Beryl Kenyon de Pascual, G. Grant O'Brien, Alfons Huber, William R. Dowd, Charles Mould, Lance Whitehead, and Martin Elste. 'Harpsichord', *Grove Music Online*, 2001, www.oxfordmusiconline.com/grovemusic/view/10.1093/gmo/9781561592630.001.0001/omo-9781561592630-e-0000019120, accessed 10 September 2018.

Small, Carola, 'Artois in the Thirteenth Century: A Region Discovering Its Identity?', *Historical Reflections* 19 (1993), 189–207.

Smith, Darwin, 'Greban, Arnoul', in Ludwig Finscher (ed.), *Die Musik in Geschichte und Gegenwart* (Kassel: Bärenreiter, 2002), 7, cols. 1542–5.

'*Memoriale' de maestro Antonio Alabanti prieur de la Santissima Annunziata de Florence (1477–1485), Édition, introduction, index et glossaire*, 2 vols. and facsimile, Habilitation à diriger des recherches (HDR), Université de Paris I, 2010.

'Le budget de maître Antonio Alabanti, prieur de la Santissima Annunziata de Florence (1477–1485)', in Olivier Mattéoni (ed.), *Classer, dire, compter. Discipline du chiffre et fabrique d'une norme comptable à la fin du Moyen Âge* (Paris: Comité pour l'histoire économique et financière de la France, 2015), 217–47.

'La réforme musicale à la Santissima Annunziata de Florence (1478–1485) et la politique religieuse de Lorenzo de'Medici', *Drammaturgia* 14 (2017), 7–52.

Sortor, Marci, 'Saint-Omer and Its Textile Trades in the Late Middle Ages: A Contribution to the Proto-industrialization Debate', *American Historical Review* 98 (1993), 1475–99.

'The Ieperleet Affair, the Struggle for Market Position in Late-Medieval Flanders', *Speculum* 734 (1998), 1068–1100.

Spufford, Peter, *Monetary Problems and Policies in the Burgundian Netherlands, 1433–1496* (Leiden: Brill, 1970).

Staats, Sarah, with the collaboration of Caroline Heid, Donatella Nebbiai and Patricia Stirnemann, *Le catalogue médiéval de l'abbaye cistercienne de Clairmarais et les manuscrits conservés* (Paris: CNRS Editions, 2016).

Starr, Pamela, 'Music and Music Patronage at the Papal Court, 1447–1464'.
    Unpublished PhD dissertation, Yale University (1987).
    'Rome as the Centre of the Universe: Papal Grace and Music Patronage', *Early Music History* 11 (1992), 223–62.
Straeten, Edmond Vander, *La musique aux Pays-Bas avant le XIXe siècle*.
    Documents inédits et annotés, 8 vols. (Brussels: C. Muquardt, etc., 1867–88; republished in 4 vols., New York: Dover, 1969).
Strohm, Reinhard, *Music in Late Medieval Bruges* (2nd, rev. ed., Oxford: Clarendon Press, 1990).
Symes, Carol, *A Common Stage: Theater and Public Life in Medieval Arras* (Ithaca, NY, and London: Cornell University Press, 2007).
Thibodeau, Timothy M. (trans.), *The Rationale divinorum officiorum of William Durand of Mende: A New Translation of the Prologue and Book 1* (New York: Columbia University Press, 2007).
Thiébaut, Jacques, 'L'art monumentale', in Alain Derville (ed.), *Histoire de Saint-Omer* (Lille: Presses Universitaires de Lille, 1981), 233–52.
Thompson, Glenda G., 'Music in the Court Records of Mary of Hungary', *Tijdschrift van de Vereniging voor Nederlandse Muziekgeschiedenis* 34/2 (1984), 132–73.
Towne, Gary, 'Music and Liturgy in Sixteenth-Century Italy: The Bergamo Organ Book and Its Liturgical Implications', *Journal of Musicology* 6 (1988), 471–509.
Vantouroux, Dominique, 'Les funérailles des chanoines de Saint-Omer (1426–1598)', *Revue du Nord* 65/257 (April–June 1983), 361–8.
Vaughan, Richard, *Philip the Good: The Apogee of Burgundy* (London and Harlow: Longmans, 1970).
    Charles the Bold: The Last Valois Duke of Burgundy (repr. Woodbridge: Boydell, 2002 [first published London: Longman, 1973]).
Viriville, A. Vallet de, 'Essai sur les archives historiques du chapitre de l'église cathédrale de Notre-Dame à St-Omer: Catalogue des archives de Notre-Dame: première série- Liaisses', *Mémoires de la Société des antiquaires de la Morinie* 6 (1841–3), I–LXXXVII.
Wallet, Emmanuel, *Description de l'ancienne cathédrale de Saint-Omer (Pas-de-Calais, ci-devant Artois), autrefois Notre-Dame de Sithiu, et Morinie, maintenant paroisse Notre-Dame* (Saint-Omer/Douai: Baclé/author, 1839).
Walsh, Richard J., *Charles the Bold and Italy (1467–1477): Politics and Personnel* (Liverpool: Liverpool University Press, 2005).
Wegman, Rob C., *Born for the Muses: The Life and Masses of Jacob Obrecht* (Oxford: Oxford University Press, 1994).
    'From Maker to Composer: Improvisation and Musical Authorship in the Low Countries, 1450–1500', *Journal of the American Musicological Society* 49 (1996), 409–97.

Wessely, Othmar, 'Bruck, Arnold von', *Grove Music Online*, 2001, www
.oxfordmusiconline.com/grovemusic/view/10.1093/gmo/9781561592630
.001.0001/omo-9781561592630-e-0000004124, accessed 5 December 2015.

Williams, Peter, *The European Organ, 1450–1850* (London: Batsford, 1966).

Williams, Peter and Barbara Owen, 'Organ, IV: the classical and medieval organ 6:
The church organ, 1100–1450', *Grove Music Online*, 2001, www
.oxfordmusiconline.com/grovemusic/view/10.1093/gmo/9781561592630
.001.0001/omo-9781561592630-e-0000044010, accessed 11 September 2016.

'Organ V, 1, and 2: Developments, 1450–1500', *Grove Music Online*, 2001, www
.oxfordmusiconline.com/grovemusic/view/10.1093/gmo/9781561592630
.001.0001/omo-9781561592630e-0000044010, accessed 11 September 2016.

Win, Paul De, 'Frans van Busleyden († 1502). Prelaat en diplomaat, leermeester,
vertrouweling en topadviseur van Filips de Schone', *Handelingen van de
Koninklijke kring voor oudheidkunde, letteren en kunst van Mechelen* 113
(2009), 55–103.

Wright, Craig, 'Dufay at Cambrai: Discoveries and Revisions', *Journal of the
American Musicological Society* 28 (1975), 175–229.

'Musiciens à la cathédrale de Cambrai, 1475–1550', *Revue de musicologie* 62/2
(1976), 204–28.

'Performance Practices at the Cathedral of Cambrai, 1475–1550', *Musical
Quarterly* 64/3 (1978), 275–328.

Music and Ceremony at Notre Dame of Paris, 500–1550 (Cambridge: Cambridge
University Press, 1989).

Wye, Benjamin van, 'Ritual Use of the Organ in France', *Journal of the American
Musicological Society* 33 (1980), 287–325.

Young, Karl, The Drama of the Medieval Church, 2 vols. (Oxford: Clarendon
Press, 1933).

Zanovello, Giovanni, '"In the Church and in the Chapel": Music and Devotional
Spaces in the Florentine Church of Santissima Annunziata', *Journal of the
American Musicological Society* 67 (2014), 379–428.

Index

For EU product safety concerns, contact us at Calle de José Abascal, 56–1°, 28003 Madrid, Spain or eugpsr@cambridge.org.

www.ingramcontent.com/pod-product-compliance
Ingram Content Group UK Ltd.
Pitfield, Milton Keynes, MK11 3LW, UK
UKHW051008240426
470322UK00018B/561